The Theory and Practice of
Critical Thinking

Raymond S. Ruble, Ph.D.

The Theory and Practice of Critical Thinking
Copyright © 2006 by Raymond S. Ruble, Ph.D.

ISBN: 1-892056-46-1
Library of Congress Control Number: 2006926798

Printed in the United States of America

Pictured on the cover: one of many species of closed brain corals common to tropical oceans

TABLE OF CONTENTS

Preface to the Teacher and the Student

Critical thinking is a relatively new subject area on the pre-college scene. While critical thinking has always been part of the meat and potatoes of philosophy since its inception among the ancient Greeks, philosophy itself is only starting to make headway at the high school level. As a result of this, there have been no texts aimed at the high school audience. This book attempts to fill that void. Traditionally education has had little or nothing to say about *how* to think; it has concentrated instead on teaching *what* to think. But there is a great deal more to successful thinking than mere memorization and mastery of content. Accordingly, it is not my intent to convince you to go "my way or the highway" on any of the examples presented in the text. Instead, critical thinking skills should be seen as intellectual tools which can and should be applied in a number of valid and interesting ways to the job at hand.

There are too many important concepts and principles contained in this book to be covered in the course of a single semester. Accordingly, any critical thinking class will only be able to cover some of the material contained in this book, and this book in turn does not cover all of the range of issues which are important to critical thinking. But this text is still a big chunk of material to study. As a budding critical thinker you have the responsibility to do your best to master as much of the material presented here as possible. I will do what I can to help you, but ultimately it is up to you.

To assist you in your learning I have included in each chapter a slew of assignments requiring the application of the skills presented throughout that chapter. Obviously it will be impossible for you to cover more than a small fraction of these assignments in the course of a semester; there are too many assignments and too little time to cover them adequately. But that is fine. You should find some of the examples familiar; some others are zany, and I have included them because they are zany—there is no conflict between the weird and the educational. However some of the examples will contain information that is unfamiliar to you. When this happens, you have two choices: you can take the time and effort to find out more about the material before you analyze it, or you can ignore the unknown example and go on to ones with which you are already familiar. While it is often an excellent idea and quite helpful to research the unfamiliar examples, it simply may be too time consuming. When this is the case feel free to move on to more familiar examples, because my goal is to give you experience with successful analyses rather than to frustrate you with unsuccessful ones you haven't got time to research appropriately. Of course, you could always choose the third option of botching the analysis of examples with which you are completely unfamiliar, but let's leave that to politicians.

A good critical thinker should be able to do the sorts of tasks presented by the various assignments, even if s/he cannot do each and every specific one with the same level of ability. Practice, practice, practice—the formula for success in any area stands firmly on hard work. To assist you in this practice, I include my own analysis of selected examples as well as updated examples on my web page at www.appstate.edu/~rublers. You are invited to log on to this site or e-mail me at rublers@appstate.edu with questions. This is my version of "answers to odd-numbered exercises are in the back of the book." In the back of this book you will find a glossary with a multitude of concepts and their definitions.

Speaking of concepts, each chapter of the text contains a list of concepts discussed within that chapter. The goal of this text is to get you to achieve a level of fluency with these concepts that you can apply readily and correctly to most any example you encounter. But because there are so many concepts to master and so little time to do this in a standard semester, I have also included a shorter list of foundational concepts for each chapter. If time limits the amount that can be spent on this material, at least try to master the list of foundational concepts. Whatever else you do, read carefully and master the Introduction and Chapter One; the concepts and principles contained in these two sections are basic for the whole rest of the subject matter. After that, the material can be presented in any order, whatever works well for you.

Finally, **keep this book**. Keep reading and studying the material in it. You cannot master these concepts and principles without a great deal more effort than the course in which you are reading it can hope to supply. You have spent years studying math, science and English; critical thinking is just as important to master and just as applicable to the rest of your life as are English, science and math. Like these other subjects, critical thinking will change the way you see the world.

"To be rational is so glorious a thing that two-legged creatures generally content themselves with the title."

—John Locke[i]

Introduction

Some Thoughts on Thinking and Critical Thinking

I. WHAT IS THINKING?

Ancient Greeks such as Aristotle defined humans as rational animals. A more complete definition of mankind contends that humans as a species are animals who possess the capacity of being rational, along with the mental faculties of emotion, willpower, and self-consciousness. Philosophers since the time of the ancient Greeks have tried to analyze and understand the nature of thinking and why our rational faculties are often in conflict with our emotions and/or our willpower. In the last several hundred years these topics also have attracted a considerable amount of attention from anthropologists, sociologists, psychologists, and very recently, from those working in the new discipline of artificial intelligence, which concerns itself with the capacities of computers.

Whether you are a beginner or an expert in a given subject matter, **ordinary thinking** is anchored to a set of concepts. Concepts give you ideas that enable you to think and act in a subject area. Persons unfamiliar with a given subject matter are ignorant of the ideas that guide the activities of those who are familiar with it. This is why new subject areas can look so difficult and strange when one is exposed to

them for the first time. **Education** means making the unfamiliar familiar. Education begins with **indoctrination**, the instilling of a doctrine or a subject matter into a student. To become familiar with the unfamiliar, you must learn the doctrine's concepts, rules, and paradigms that define it. **Concepts** express the ideas contained within the subject area. **Rules** tell how to combine the concepts inherent within the subject correctly. **Paradigms** are examples of materials and procedures that are so important to the proper understanding of a given subject matter that they structure and define the discipline. Paradigms are definitive examples: Einstein is the paradigm genius, Michael Jordan is the paradigm basketball player. Indoctrination is a matter of learning what the concepts, rules, and paradigms are in that area, how to apply them, and why they are important.[ii]

Generally it is not difficult to determine whether you have learned a given subject matter. Learning can be demonstrated by a variety of testing procedures. The purpose of testing is to determine whether you have succeeded in making the unfamiliar familiar. Testing ordinary thinking occurs on three levels of understanding: memorization and restatement of basic concepts, rules and paradigms; correct application of concepts, rules and paradigms; and explaining these concepts, rules and paradigms to someone else not already familiar with them. Students who only satisfy the first condition have at most an elementary grasp of the subject matter in question. In order to be said to have a thorough knowledge of the subject matter, students must be able to perform at all three levels, and that usually takes a great deal of experience and practice.

The three levels of understanding are involved in the **apprenticeship model of learning**. At the first level you are asked to duplicate what you have been taught. This is the realm of specific facts, such as the fact that the World Trade Center was destroyed on September 11, 2001, or $2 + 2 = 4$. There is no substitute for knowing the basic concepts, rules and paradigms of a given discipline. However, there are two special problems about learning associated with this level. The first is drudgery; sometimes learning facts is downright boring. The second problem is more complicated; there are always too many things to learn. Time is short and energy finite, but the material to be learned is potentially infinite. Of the infinite list of material, what should be the focus? What can be put off until later? Different teachers, courses, and schools are notorious for answering these questions differently, yet they must be answered in a manner that best utilizes the student's time.

On the second level of understanding, you are required to apply your knowledge of a subject matter to issues and examples not directly presented to you in grasping material on the first level. You are asked to expand on what you have been taught. For example, in school you may be asked to write an essay on a book you have been reading or to work on some applications of mathematical formulas you have just learned. You should be able to do this if you have grasped the meaning and importance of the concepts, rules and paradigms taught at the first level. Rules apply not just to stock situations, but to the many novel situations that are always a part of life's experiences.

The third level of understanding requires you to teach others what you have already learned. The idea involved here is that you don't really know a subject well until you have taught someone else part of that subject. This requires a different variety of intellectual aptitudes than either the first or second level. It is legitimate to ask whether you really know a subject if you are not able to teach anyone else something about it. If we really are to learn, we cannot be simply students, but must be teachers as well.

These three levels of understanding make up the apprenticeship model of learning. To apprentice under someone is to study or work under a person who is already a master of a given subject matter. The apprentice starts out by learning the basics and gradually proceeds to the second level by being asked to work on novel projects under the eye of the master. Finally, after a suitable amount of experience, the apprentice becomes the master, able to pass his or her knowledge of a subject on to others. But even recognized masters go back for retraining under others in the form of special workshops and seminars wherein new first level material may be examined, new second level procedures may be practiced, and new paradigms may be learned and discussed. Gaining understanding, i.e. utilizing rationality properly, is a life-long process.

Ordinary thinking provides the material which critical thinking probes and discusses. **Critical thinking** transcends the limitations of ordinary thinking in that it is an analysis of the strengths and limitations of the concepts, rules and paradigms that are found in any given subject matter or that are common to all subjects. Arguments from analogy, for instance, are found in all subject areas. Learning the value and limitation of analogical reasoning is one of the exercises of critical thinking. Philosophers call critical thinking a **meta-discipline** because the application of critical thinking to the assumptions contained within the specific subject areas of ordinary thinking. Critical thinking is a core component of philosophy.

Philosophy, translated literally from its Greek roots *philo* (love) and *sophia* (wisdom), is the love of wisdom[iii]. Wisdom is a value-laden concept that can be broken down into two categories (the names of which are taken from Greek): *sophia* (theoretical wisdom) and *phronesis* (practical wisdom). *Sophia* concerns the study of important abstract principles necessary for the understanding of the nature of the universe and how humans ought to relate to it. What, for example, is justice, such that everyone ought to get his or her just deserts? *Phronesis* is the study of good judgments by which humans make good choices and live good lives. What constitutes a just decision in a specific situation, as, for example, when our car has just been hit in the parking lot? Critical thinking is a vital component of both *sophia* and *phronesis.*[iv]

II. ASSUMPTIONS

All thinking takes place within a subject area. You cannot think without thinking about some thing. Thinking about a specific subject is an assumption of thinking. **Assumptions** are presuppositions that make possible the thoughts and activities we construct based upon their presumed truth. Extending this building metaphor, assumptions are the foundations upon which thoughts are erected.[v] I must assume, for example, that the rules of grammar according to which I write this book do not change from the beginning of the book to the end. The rules of grammar do not evolve, though the contents of my book might. Many of these assumptions apply only to a specific, limited subject area (e.g., three strikes and you're out), but some of them cover many areas (e.g., play the game by the rules). There may even be assumptions that must be held to be true in order for anyone to hold any opinion about anything whatsoever. One of the major goals of philosophy is the examination of this last statement. Are there any ideas that everyone must assume in order to have beliefs about anything at all?[vi]

Regardless of how this last question is answered, it is trivially true (though some find this to be the height of wisdom) that there are many different assumptions that may be used to anchor any given opinion on a topic. Differences of opinions about things are common in human interactions; sometimes the difference stems from the application of different assumptions regarding a given topic. This is unsurprising. After all, if two people are standing in different places, they are likely to have different visual perceptions of the same object, and the situation is mirrored with different assumptions regarding the same topic.

One way of recognizing how different assumptions affect different beliefs about things is to label some assumptions **facts** and others **opinions**. Facts are usually understood to be those matters about which everyone agrees, or which are undeniably true, or about which an already established method (looking, measuring, etc.) could determine easily whether they are true. It is a fact that $2 + 2 = 4$, that the earth revolves around the sun, and the Boston Red Sox won the World Series in 2004. Opinions are the opposite of facts, that is, they are issues about which there is no agreement, or which are not obviously true (or even true at all), or about which there is no ready method with which to determine easily their truth. Terrorists should be ruthlessly hunted down and exterminated; red is prettier than blue; and soccer is harder to play than basketball are all examples of opinion. *Facts are assumptions that we know or can prove; opinions are assumptions we only can believe.* Facts must be true, but opinions may well be false. This line of reasoning also assumes that for any given belief it is rather straightforward and easy to distinguish whether that belief is based on fact or (mere) opinion.

However, things are more complicated than this. The commonly held fact/opinion dichotomy makes some important distinctions, chiefly between knowing and believing, between having an agreed upon methodology for deciding an issue and not having one, and between what is undeniably true and what is not. It is naïve to suggest, however, that these distinctions can be applied easily to any and all issues, quickly determining which of them are facts and which are opinions. Issues are usually more complicated than this traditional approach admits. In many cases, both sides of the dichotomy can be applied legitimately to a given issue or by looking at the same issue from different perspectives. It is also the case that this way of distinguishing between facts and opinions has an ambivalent position regarding the nature of opinions. On the one hand, the position that all opinions are equally valid is a particularly nasty form of the **relativity theory of truth**, which claims that truth and knowledge are relative to and dependant upon the judgment of an individual or culture. On the other hand, some opinions are flat out right (or wrong) based on the evidence that supports or contradicts them.[vii] In addition to this, the labels "fact" and "opinion" also serve as **conversation stoppers**—devices to get those we disagree with to stop bugging us either because what we think we know we believe to be undeniably true. "That's just your opinion," or "It's a fact—how can you not see that?" are examples of how we disarm and trivialize possible objections to our own positions. Because of these sorts of potential defects, it is wise to be careful when labeling issues as either facts or opinions.

One of the major failings of our educational system is the inattention paid to the role assumptions play in thinking. This means that as the products of the system, students are unlikely to have given this key topic any thought whatsoever. Instead, students blithely go through life in happy ignorance of the assumptions that form the foundation of their knowledge of themselves and the world around them. But the ignorant pay a price; not to be aware of the assumptions you bring to experience is to be unconsciously dominated by these assumptions. To reduce issues to simple facts or mere opinions is to be ruled by this dichotomy. To be dominated by unknown assumptions is to be a victim unaware of your own victimization.[viii] Assumptions that dominate and victimize the person who uses them are called **prejudices**. Indoctrination has a decisive down side: teachers often hear their students say, "But that's what I've always been taught," or, "I've never heard of that," when discussing an issue in class, as if these conversation stoppers say all that is needed to be said about the topic in question. These conversation stoppers are so prevalent they can be labeled the **"that's what I've always been taught"** and the **"I've never heard of that"** fallacies. A fallacy is not just an incorrect way of thinking, it is also a method of prematurely aborting the thought process itself.

It is important to remember that the process of indoctrination is not bad in itself; students do have to learn certain basic things in order for culture to continue to thrive. Indoctrination becomes objectionable only when students thereby are rendered incapable of suspending assumptions when they become counterproductive to critical thinking. Indoctrination only becomes a fallacy when it stifles thinking. The root error underlying both of the aforementioned fallacies is the assumption that if you have been taught something, what you have been taught is the truth, the whole truth and nothing but the truth, and that what you have not been taught cannot be correct at all. This is the absolute death of critical thinking, forming a mind-set that makes it literally inconceivable that you could be wrong about a specific issue and giving rise to the conversation stoppers mentioned above. In contrast, critical thinking is the root of many a **conversation starter**.

There are three aspects of assumptions that need to be distinguished carefully. The first one, already mentioned above, is that people generally fail to recognize the existence of their assumptions. This tendency is particularly acute when we are dealing with topics with which we have a strong emotional commitment. What happens all too often in these cases is the subjugation of reason to slavery by the passions. The impassioned defense of our beliefs can cause reason to go right out the window, and deep commitment to an idea does not make that idea true, or even sane. Mental hospitals are filled with people who are committed passionately to their completely unfounded beliefs.

The second problem with assumptions is that unexamined assumptions easily lead to the dogmatic affirmation of ideas that may in fact by questionable. **Dogmatism** is the belief in a doctrine as true beyond question. This is one of the most common forms of errors in reasoning. Because the truth of any opinion rests upon some set of assumptions or other, dogmatism easily commits the mistake of **begging the question**, that is, of answering a question regarding some position dogmatically held by affirming the truth of the position questioned, regardless of its objective validity. Dogmatism is manifested both as an intellectual position on a given topic and as an attitude towards reasoning that is analogous to physical blindness. When you believe dogmatically in the truth of some opinion, you may be intellectually blind to the many questions that can (and should) be asked regarding the doctrine in question. When you express your opinions about an issue in a dogmatic fashion, you act as if you are physically blind to alternative ways of viewing the same topic. Anyone can be a dogmatist or act dogmatically about any issue. Good reasons for believing things about a given topic will withstand critical examination. Merely having reasons that cause you to maintain a position is not the same as having *good* reasons for maintaining that your position is correct. *Critical thinking is the search for good reasons for our beliefs*, and strength of conviction is not typically a good reason.

The third problem with assumptions is the temptation to develop a relativity theory of truth as a simple-minded reaction to dogmatism. Students who dislike a range of dogmatically asserted opinions frequently think that it is the height of wisdom to go to the opposite extreme and (dogmatically) maintain either

that nothing whatsoever can be known to be true or that anything that is known to be true is nonetheless true only for the individual who professes it. Both of these reactions are forms of **skepticism**. A skeptic is a person who doubts that (1) s/he knows (or can know) a certain thing, or (2) some other particular person or group knows (or can know) a certain thing, or (3) a certain thing can really be known by anyone at all. In the extreme form, a skeptic can become a cynic[ix], who is a person who belittles someone else's beliefs about something by declaring that the other person's beliefs are really self-serving rationalizations designed to disguise the real (in the cynic's opinion) self-interested reasons for holding the doctrine in question.

Skepticism and cynicism have their proper uses, however. A cynical reply to a position might be a useful way of unmasking lying and hypocrisy. A skeptical reply may be a useful way of unearthing hidden assumptions. In a culture in which everything seems to be for sale if the price is right, in which apparently honest people are found frequently with their hands in the cookie jar, and in which even the most profound and honest often are mistaken in their convictions, it may be very wise to listen to what the skeptic or cynic has to say. But cynicism and skepticism can be carried too far; it is true neither that everything is up for grabs, nor that everyone is out simply to line their own pockets. If skepticism or cynicism is an appropriate response to some affirmed doctrine, it should be a carefully reasoned response, not merely some form of a snappy put-down.

Analyze the following examples by applying the concepts presented above.

A. "It was the best of times; it was the worst of times." Charles Dickens, *Tale of Two Cities*

B. "I must confess that General Robert E. Lee's face did not look as bright as tho' he were certain of success. But yet it is impossible for us to be any otherwise than victorious."

John Dooley, 1st Virginia regiment, on July 3, 1863, shortly before his unit was involved in Pickett's ill-fated assault against Union positions on Cemetery Ridge during the battle of Gettysburg.

C. Defining sexual harassment has become more important to many companies because of the rising number of cases going to court and the large monetary awards from state juries, says an official with a company that conducts business seminars. "Sexual harassment is not just sex," said Margie Lilly, director of human resources for Piedmont Associated Industries. "It's any kind of behavior that discriminates against a sex. Unwarranted or unwanted behavior is the best clue as to what sexual harassment is or isn't. It's frustrating for many companies and hard to pin down. It can be something as simple as talking to a woman in a demeaning manner."   —News item

D. "I am not a crook."

   —President Richard Nixon, in response to allegations that he was involved in Watergate

E. "If it doesn't fit, you must acquit."

   —O.J. Simpson's lawyer, Johnnie Cochran, speaking to the jury while holding up a blood-stained glove

F. "It's duck season!"   —Bugs Bunny
  "It's rabbit season!"   —Daffy Duck

III. EPISTEMOLOGY

Complications such as those presented above concerning dogmatism and relativism are discussed by philosophers under the heading of **epistemology**. The term epistemology is derived from two Greek words, "*episteme*" and "*logos*," and is translated in English as theory (or study) of knowledge. This division of philosophy is concerned with the issues of what we know and how we know it. The answers that philosophers have given to these questions historically have served as the basis for the development of special disciplines based on various knowledge claims divided according to the objects investigated. Today these disciplines are called the sciences; physics, biology, history, psychology and such have all sprung from the tree of philosophy.

Epistemology is concerned with the question, "How is any specific thing known?" But this question can be understood in two different senses: "How did we discover/find out about that?" and "How is that known to be true/false?" The first sense deals with questions about the source—where did you see/read/hear it? Who told you? Answering these questions is not of particular concern to philosophers, because usually no questions are raised for philosophy about the discovery process—I saw it on TV; I read it in my history book, etc. The second sense deals with how we should go about verifying whether something is really true or not. This is a question of prime philosophical importance. Sometimes we think we know things that others disagree with or are unsure of. If I claimed to know now that the Pittsburgh Pirates will win the next World Series, would you believe me? Should you believe me? What if I claim to know that I will survive my own death or that the universe was created in 4004 BCE? The question is not simply whether these claims are true or false, but how beliefs about them could be confirmed or verified by anyone. This is the essence of epistemology: What would or could count as good reasons for saying that we know these sorts of things or that we know anything at all?

People usually have reasons for believing what they believe, but the reasons we have may or may not be good reasons. **Reasons** motivate and explain our behavior. **Good reasons** motivate and explain our behavior for the right reasons. Not all reasons are good reasons. There are an infinite number of bad reasons for thinking we know something. It is not the job of the philosopher to attempt to catalogue all of these reasons; for that we have the separate sciences. To make matters even more complicated, a careful distinction must be made between the question of whether what we believe is true or false and whether or not we believe it for good reasons. These are two distinct issues. You may believe that something is true or false. You may have poor reasons or good reasons for your belief. There are four possible combinations here:

1. Your belief is true, and you believe it for good reasons.
2. Your belief is true, and you believe it for poor reasons.
3. Your belief is false, and you believe it for good reasons.
4. Your belief is false, and you believe it for poor reasons.

We tend to confuse the first possibility with the second, and the third with the fourth. Often we are only interested in whether our beliefs are true or false. Philosophers want us to be a bit more subtle. As the second class shows, there is such a thing as being right for the wrong reasons, and the third class shows that there is such a thing as being wrong for the right reasons. The field of epistemology takes the issue beyond the question of whether someone's beliefs are true or false to the question of whether they are based on good reasons or poor ones.

There is a school of thought in epistemology called empiricism. Like all schools of thought in epistemology, empiricism is a doc-trine attempting to evaluate the question of what counts as a good reason for believing something. **Empiricism** claims that all knowledge about the world is somehow obtained through experience (chiefly sense experience) and is verified solely through experience. Thus the empiricist claims that the verification of knowledge claims about the world relies intimately upon the use of sense perception and observation. For the remainder of this book I am going to assume that the empiricist's analysis of knowledge is basically correct.[x]

How could the empiricist analyze the following knowledge claims?

A. Claims about what is going on in Iraq right now.

B. Claims about what happened in history.

C. Claims about what will happen in the future.

D. Claims about the theory of evolution.

E. Claims about ESP.

F. Claims about the truths of mathematics.

G. Claims about scientific laws of nature, e.g. gravity.

H. Claims about the mental states of humans and animals.

CONCEPTS

You should be able to define the following concepts, explain to others not familiar with them what each means, invent your own examples correctly illustrating these concepts, and apply them correctly to novel applications.

- Apprenticeship model of learning
- Assumptions
- Begging the question
- Concepts
- Conversation starter
- Conversation stopper
- Critical thinking
- Cynicism
- Dogmatism
- Education

- Empiricism
- Epistemology
- Fact
- Fallacy
- Good reasons
- Indoctrination
- "I've never heard of that" fallacy
- Meta-discipline
- Opinion
- Ordinary thinking

- Paradigm
- Philosophy
- Phronesis
- Prejudice
- Reasons
- Relativity theory of truth
- Rules
- Skepticism
- Sophia
- "That's what I've always been taught" fallacy

NOTES

i. John Locke, 1632-1704, was an English philosopher and the author of the first major work in epistemology to be written in the English language, *An Essay Concerning Human Understanding*, first published in 1690. The quote is taken from a letter written by Locke to Anthony Collins, 24 January, 1704.

ii. For a discussion of the important role paradigms play in the development of science, see Thomas Kuhn, *The Structure of Scientific Revolutions*, 2nd edition, (Chicago: The University of Chicago Press, 1970). What Kuhn has to say about the role paradigms play in thinking in the sciences can be generalized for other disciplines as well.

iii. According to Plato the term "philosophy" was coined by Pythagoras, the same man who was so fond of right triangles. See Plato's *Symposium* for more on this.

iv. Aristotle explicitly distinguishes between phronesis and sophia, though he believes phronesis is anchored in sophia. See his *Nicomachean Ethics* for more on these and other specific categories of wisdom.

v. The use of a building metaphor to describe knowledge is very popular among philosophers, particularly during the 17th and 18th centuries. See Renee Descartes's *Meditations*, 1639; John Locke's *An Essay Concerning Human Understanding*, 1690; David Hume's *A Treatise on Human Nature*, 1739; and Immanuel Kant's *Critique of Pure Reason*, 1781.

vi. Unsurprisingly, in the twenty-six hundred years of Western philosophy various philosophers have taken radically different positions regarding this issue. Participants in the ongoing discussion range from philosophers like Plato and Kant, who affirm the absolute validity of some idea or other as absolutely necessary assumptions for any thinking process, to philosophers like Nietzsche and Quine, who argue that there are no universally valid assumptions necessary to any thinking process.

vii. The problem of epistemic relativism was discussed by Plato in his book the *Theaetetus*, wherein are found the first known arguments against relativism. These arguments are discussed still by philosophers. See, for example, A. C. Grayling, *The Refutation of Skepticism* (Peru, IL: Open Court, 1985).

viii. This was recognized long ago by Socrates (469-399 BCE), who stated that an unexamined life is not worth living. For more about Socrates' recognition and critique of the power assumptions play in our thinking process, see Plato's *Apology*.

ix. The original cynics were followers of Socrates who created their own school of thought after Socrates' execution by the Athenian government in 399 BCE. Led by Antisthenes and Diogenes, they derived their name from the Greek *kyneos*, "like a dog," for their habit of barking at their opponents' arguments.

x. Empiricism is given its classic formulation by David Hume in his *Treatise of Human Nature*, first published in 1739. Empiricists are not without their critics, who are called **rationalists**. In general, any rationalist believes that there is at least some knowledge about the world that can be obtained independently of sense experience. Many philosophers have been rationalists. In addition to the discussion by Plato cited in note 5, empiricism is analyzed and critiqued by Immanuel Kant in his *Critique of Pure Reason*, 1781. The adequacy of empiricism is subject still to extended debate by philosophers.

CHAPTER ONE

Perception and Knowledge

INTRODUCTION

Watching TV, driving a car, cooking dinner, talking to friends—each of these many activities which make up our daily lives has one thing in common: the focusing of our attention on our surroundings. Our very ability to live in the world demands that we pay attention to our environment through the information received via our senses. **Perception** is our window to the world, and the information received through our senses is a necessary ingredient in the construction of what is called perceptual or observational knowledge. Philosophers have long recognized that experience is anchored to perception in some fashion or other.[i] Because all of us normally take the evidence of our senses as unquestionably true, you might well wonder what all the philosophical fuss is about. There is a school of thought called **naïve realism**. This position holds that the things we perceive really do exist just like we perceive them to be, and that the process of perception accurately transmits knowledge of these things to the mind of the perceiver. Therefore, viewers with the same sensory equipment looking from the same location at the same object will necessarily see the same thing. Our senses somehow

simply read off knowledge about the world just like a stockbroker reading a ticker tape. There is a saying for this: "Seeing is believing."

But a moment's reflection shows that this isn't always true. Sometimes you can see something and not believe it, as when the magician saws the lady in half. You know that the lady hasn't really been cut in half, but it surely looks like she has! What is going on here? If naïve realism is true, how can you perceive something and not believe it? Or consider this example: Once I was driving in my car and thought I saw a bald eagle. Bald eagles are not known to live where I live. Did I really see one? It depends on whether what I caught a glimpse of was really an eagle or not. I saw it, but I'm not sure just what it was that I saw. Clearly to settle this issue I needed to gather more information, but that wasn't possible because I had to watch the road. I know what a bald eagle looks like, but I don't know whether I really saw one in that situation. Cases like this are not uncommon.

This gets us to the heart of the problem. Though we normally take the evidence of our senses as unquestionably true, "taking something to be true" is an activity. It is a performance on our part. Naïve realism goes wrong in suggesting that perception is passive in charac-

1

ter. It suggests that once you look at an object, the object somehow forces itself upon your attention; you just need to open your eyes and look. But successful perception requires more than merely opening your eyes and looking; it requires that the perceiver's mind actively make a judgment about what it is the mind perceives. Is that an eagle, or just a big bird? The observer must make a decision about that, and sometimes a quick one too, in order to see what is out there.

I. OBSERVATION

Let us look more closely at observational knowledge. Imagine that you are driving in the car with me when I see the bird, but you don't see it. We would ordinarily explain this situation by saying that you didn't see the bird and I did. Perhaps you simply failed to see anything because you weren't looking at anything. But let us assume now that you *were* looking and you saw a goose. This is a common enough occurrence and it can be used to explain how perception works.[ii] How is it that you saw a goose while I saw what I took to be an eagle?

The first component of perception is the **evidence** provided to the senses. Obviously if there is no evidence presented to our senses we are not going to perceive anything. The evidence provided to our senses that allows us to perceive anything at all is called **data**, and when data are gathered only through the senses, they are known as **sense data**. Sense data are a necessary component of perception, but the mere collection of sense data is not yet perception. Sense data are like a box of puzzle pieces; while unassembled the pieces are only potentially a picture. In order to produce the perception *of something* (the image that is the assembled puzzle), the mind must utilize a series of judgments about the data the senses have collected. The mind must actively do something with the collected data. There are four judgment factors that are simultaneously involved in even the simplest of perceptions. For purposes of explanation, I will discuss each of them independently.

The first factor is **seeing as**. I saw the bird as an eagle; you saw it as a goose. *There is no seeing at all without seeing the data of perception as some specific sort of thing.* Most of the time we see the same thing as the same thing; that is, there is usually a common and unquestioned sharing of perception. This is one of the things that make communication possible. We live in an environment that overwhelmingly is experienced in a common fashion. We see things much as others see them. We see the goose as a goose, the eagle as an eagle. Sometimes, though, different people see the same object as different specific things; one person sees a goose, and another person sees an eagle when looking at the same bird. The other judgment factors that enable us to have perceptions can explain nicely why we sometimes see different things when we look at the same object.

The second factor of perception is **seeing-that**. To see that the bird in the air is an eagle is to see more than what is present immediately to the senses. The data immediately available to our senses is too limited. There are also things that must be true of the perceived object if it is seen as an eagle. Since perception is a form of knowledge, it is appropriate to say that if you see this thing as an eagle you also see (know) that if you try to pet it you will be injured. Eagles aren't pets; they have sharp talons and beaks, which you know even if the specific bird you are now seeing is too far away to allow you to see its talons and beak directly (i.e., via the senses). But if the bird were actually a goose, then things wouldn't be quite so dangerous. There would be no talons, for example. We live in a world of present perceptions, but all of these perceptions themselves have a past and a future, and they are perceptions of things that also have pasts and futures. The bird, be it an eagle or a goose, existed before it was seen and doesn't cease to exist after it has left our line of sight, and it has attributes currently invisible to us as well. *Seeing-that gives our present perceptions their other temporal and spatial dimensions and allows us to extend our perceptual knowledge claims to what lies beyond the immediate range of our senses.*

Seeing-that depends on the intellectual faculty of **imagination**. Our imagination allows us to fill in the holes in our perceptual data. Perceptual data often are incomplete. If you see the bird as an eagle, then there is virtually no end to the other things you "see" instantly. While you actually may see only the front of the eagle, you also see that if you were looking at it from a different direction you would see its back, and so forth. You see that it must have flown to where it is now; birds can't just walk up into the sky. The list goes on and on, and it is not arbitrary. You do not see that this eagle will make a neat hang glider, for example, and you do not see that triangles only have three sides, because it is a bird, not a flying geometrical figure. Though the imagination can construct an unlimited amount of fictitious pictures of the world, it must be limited by theory and evidence if it is to construct a picture correctly from incomplete data.

What sorts of data are missing from each of the following examples? Discuss how the imagination might "fill in the blanks."

A. Traffic is backed up for miles on the interstate.

B. "That dog must be friendly. See, he's wagging his tail."

C. "Okay, young lady. You were out past your curfew; you must have been up to no good."

D. "We had a saying that 'Those who can't do, teach, and those who can't teach, teach gym.' Of course, those who couldn't do anything were assigned to our school."
　　　　　　　　　　—Woody Allen, *Annie Hall*

E. "Dad, did they have the wheel when you were my age?"　　　—Max Ruble at nine

Why is it that you immediately see that certain things are appropriate to say about the object once it is seen as a bird, while other things are not appropriate? Because you know what birds are, you understand the theory "bird"; that is, you understand what it takes to be a bird. All of our perceptions are thus **theory-laden**. To perceive the bird as a bird (and be correct) or as a hang glider (and be incorrect) is only possible for those who already possess the concepts of birds and hang gliders. Being theory-laden is the third judgment factor that accounts for perception. It is the theory "bird" that allows your imagination to generate the list of perceptions about the past and future of what you're seeing now. Theories are like instruction sheets for the imagination; they tell you how to go about assembling things, in this case perceptual things. In our example they tell you how to distinguish between an eagle and a goose, a bird and a hang glider. But they also tell you much more. Because the theory "bird" tells you that birds don't walk on air, you see that this bird could not have walked into the air where you see it. It may surprise you to learn that *most perceptual knowledge is almost always dependent upon conceptual knowledge*, but it is. If you don't know anything about eagles (you've neither seen nor heard of them before), you will not be able to see this eagle as an eagle. Either you will see this as some other thing perceptually similar to the concept of which you are already familiar (such as "kite"), or you will not see the eagle at all. You might at most see it in general terms, such as a flying object. To get you to see it as an eagle, I'll have to explain to you about eagles. For a good illustration of the role theory plays in perception, look inside a TV, a stereo, or a car engine next time you get the chance. What do you see? If you are like most of us, all you see is a bunch of wires and whatnot, and that's because we do not understand the concepts of the components which make up these fantastically complex objects.

To say that our perceptions are theory-laden is to say more than that our perception of a bird depends upon the prior understanding of the idea "bird." The understanding of the concept of a bird is also inevitably bound up with the understanding of a great many different ideas, such as animal, flying, feathers, and so forth. Obviously any individual's understanding of the notion "bird" may vary somewhat from the understanding of someone else. The avian expert surely knows much more about birds than the layperson. But this also means that while both the expert and the layperson may be looking at the same bird at the same time, in a sense these two individuals are not seeing the same thing. Since perception is based upon conception, a difference in our conceptual framework necessarily means a difference in our perceptions. While the data that these two observers receive through their senses may be fundamentally similar, their experiences of the bird are *not* similar. The expert, for example, may perceive no danger from the eagle (think of Australian Steve Irwin's exclamation, "Ain't she a beauty!") while the layperson sees the eagle as dangerous. This whole business can get very complicated quickly owing to the different levels of knowledge possessed by different observers. In general, it may be stated that *different observers will perceive the same object differently despite possessing the same sense data when their perceptions of the data are determined by different theories or by different understandings of the same theory.*

Because our own perceptions of the data are usually taken by us as unquestionably true (and therefore unquestionably shared by all other persons), we frequently are surprised when someone fails to share our perception of the data. When disagreements occur, the only rational way to untangle them is to resort to a presentation and defense of the theory being utilized to generate any particular perception of the data. The application of different theories to the same data causes both different *seeing as-es* and different *seeing-that's*. The eagle is seen as dangerous by one, as harmless by another. The one sees that it should be avoided, the other not. Thus all disagreements involving perceptual objects either may be (1) dissolved by agreeing upon one common theory or viewpoint under which the particular perceived object is to be understood, or (2) recognized, at least, should it become impossible to reach a conceptual agreement upon a theory or viewpoint in terms of which the perceived object is to be understood.

The fourth judgmental component of perception is **mind-set**. Each of us brings a collection of mental baggage with us as we encounter our perceptions. This mental baggage, or mind-set, encourages us to see things in certain ways, involving as it does psychologically conditioned patterns of expectations and responses. Frequently we are not even conscious of the factors that condition us to expect certain perceptions and to respond to them in a certain manner, but we are conditioned nonetheless. *The rule is that expectations tend to get fulfilled and call for conditioned responses.* Not surprisingly, cognitive openness and cognitive closure are deeply influenced by mind-set. Whether you will see this object as an eagle or a goose hinges in part on what you expect to see. How you respond to this perception is dependent upon your previous conditioning. If you and I have just been talking about eagles, then I am much more likely to "see" a certain bird as an eagle in the situation discussed above. Different previous experiences, knowledge, and training give people different mind-sets about objects. Different mind-sets encourage different reactions to the same data. There is certainly nothing mysterious about this sort of situation; it is a common enough occurrence.

The mental operations of mind-set and theory-ladenness clearly are interrelated closely, and it is a good thing for us that they are so interrelated. As I remarked above, our complex world almost always gives us too much data and not enough of the right kind of data. *Ways must be found of eliminating from consideration much of the data that would otherwise overwhelm us while supplying missing data through the use of our imagination.* Herein lies the greatest virtue of possessing a mind-set. In most of our experiences our minds are already set to see and react to incoming stimuli only in a certain manner. It is therefore possible for us to concentrate on only part of what we are bombarded with and ignore the other possible data as irrelevant to our present purposes. So, for example, when you are taking a test it is possible to filter out the extraneous noises being made by your classmates or the lawn mower which has just started up. Individuals who are fully concentrating on exciting activities such as fighting battles, playing in rugged sports contests, or having a wonderful time with their friends may find afterward, much to their surprise, that they are wounded or injured, sometimes even quite seriously, and they never noticed when it actually happened. Have you ever had your leg fall asleep while you were watching a good movie? That's mind-set at work.

There are, however, drawbacks to mind-set as well. While research has shown that observational ability may be improved dramatically by firmly establishing a mind-set, an entrenched mind-set may well prevent the recognition of important data that contradicts the truth of what the mind has been set to see. If you are set to see an eagle, it may be very difficult for you not to see a goose as an eagle, regardless of the sense data being provided by the object. Mistaken perceptual modes can be difficult to eradicate. Thus we all fall prey to pig-headedness at times, a phenomenon that is usually easy to recognize in someone else, who we say is "just being stupid, prejudiced, or obstinate." Psychologically, however, we have a very difficult time in applying these labels to our own cases.

Theory and mind-set organize the data of our perceptions and supply that data with the meaning it has. Not all data in a given perceptual situation is equally important. Some data in the perceptual situation is rejected out of hand (like the lawn mower that starts up during your test), and some data is of marginal importance (like the order in which your test questions are written). However some data are absolutely vital to a proper understanding of what is being perceived in any given perceptual situation. These data are called crucial data.

Crucial data are irreplaceable data around which is built any proper understanding of what is being experienced. Omitting or misunderstanding crucial data necessarily results in an incorrect understanding of what is perceived. The theory-ladenness and mind-set of a

perceiver determine which bits of data are crucial for a given perceptual situation. When disputes arise about the meaning of any given perception, the disputants must rest their cases on claims concerning crucial data. Two questions must be resolved: "Which pieces of data are crucial?" and "Why are these data crucial?" Settling these two questions is usually sufficient to settle the dispute. If you and I disagree about that which we perceive, I can only win you over to my side of the issue by showing you which elements in the situation are crucial for my perception of it and why these elements are so crucial. If you see a bird as a goose and I see it as an eagle, I can only prove my point by showing you some part of the perceptual situation that your goose theory cannot account for. Similarly, my account can be defeated if you can point to features of the situation that my theory fails to explain. Neither of us needs to be pig-headed here; the crucial data will settle the issue.

For a good illustration of what I have been discussing, look at Figure 1 below.

FIGURE 1

This oft-reproduced picture is known as the Young woman/Old woman figure. When you first looked at this illustration, which figure did you see automatically? Most people report seeing the young woman first. Can you see both the young woman and the old woman at will? A small percentage of people has a very difficult time seeing both (obviously not at the same time), and can only see one or the other. It took me two weeks to see the old woman. At first I was driven nuts because I knew that both figures were there, I just couldn't see the image as a picture of an old woman. But after a time, bingo! Now I see the old woman too; in fact, like most people, I can see whichever figure I choose to see. The explanation of this is obvious. When I first looked at the picture, my mind had been set by the theory "young woman" and that is how I saw it. Even when I tried to apply the concept "old woman" to the picture, my imagination failed me. This failure was very frustrating; I know what "old woman" is supposed to look like, so why couldn't I see this image as an old woman when I can easily recognize old women in other cases? Remember the rule mentioned above: expectations tend to be fulfilled and usher in conditioned responses. It is sometimes difficult to change those expectations, even with the best of intentions. Or perhaps I was just being stupid; for that is probably what you would say about someone who never could see the old woman, no matter how hard s/he tried, even after you pointed out the relevant crucial data and explained why the data were crucial. In this case, not being stupid comes down to the ability to see the picture whichever way we choose, and this ability presupposes that we possess the theory "old woman" and the theory "young woman" together with the crucial data relevant to each theory. It also means that we are capable of breaking the conditioning process that predetermines us to see the picture in only one way.

What if you choose to see this image as a picture of a football? Clearly, you would be wrong. An important feature of the fourfold analysis of perceptual knowledge is the ease with which that analysis explains mistaken or wrong-headed perceptions. Certainly perceptual mistakes are common enough. Perceptual mistakes occur when we see objects as things they are not. Because our *seeing as* went wrong, our imagination applied the incorrect *seeing-that*. Maybe our view of the object was distorted by empirical conditions, or we may have incorrectly seen it as a certain thing because we applied the wrong theory to the gathered sense data. Perhaps we applied the wrong theory because we viewed the wrong data as crucial because our minds were set to see something different than what was really there (although there may be other reasons for applying incorrect theories to objects). In any event, we cannot simply choose to see data in any way we want if our aim is to arrive at perceptual knowledge. Some ways of seeing things simply are incorrect, but some other possible ways of seeing things may be correct depending upon...what?

Discuss the following claims of perceptual knowledge in accordance with the concepts presented above.

A. ANDREAS, PA. State transportation officials are trying to find out why workers repairing a stretch of Route 895 paved straight over a dead deer.

"I never saw anything like that before in my life," [said] Keith Billig, the mayor of nearby Bowmanstown, about 65 miles northwest of Philadelphia.

The state Department of Transportation is investigating, spokesperson Rich Kirkpatrick said. "It was careless on the part of those involved," he said. "It is against state policy to pave over a deer," said Walter Bortree, an engineer for the department. "If in fact the deer was in the work area, it should have been removed before the work was done," he said.   —News item

B. "I tawt I taw a pooty tat."   —Tweety Bird

C. "Is that a rat or a squirrel in our bird feeder?"

D. "I've just seen the price of new cars. Didn't they forget to put a decimal point somewhere?"

E. Pitcher: "It was a strike." Batter: "It was a ball."

F. "Gran'mama, what **big** eyes youse gots."
—Litl' Red, *Girls of the Hood*

II. EYEWITNESS TESTIMONY

On August 16, 1987, Northwest Airlines Flight 255 attempted to take off from Detroit. It didn't make it. The resulting crash and fire killed 158 of the 159 persons on board. Why did the plane crash?

> A Northwest flight crew waiting to take off at the airport reported seeing Flight 255 staying on the ground longer than usual, said John Lauder, an NTSB investigator.... Lauder said the flight crew reported seeing no fire before the crash....
>
> But Herman Voss, 43, a Wayne County equipment operator, was insistent Wednesday that he saw a fire. "I saw it [the jetliner] taking off from the ground and it was barely up in the air," he said. "There were flames shooting out of the rear end, then it bent left and headed back down again and it disappeared on me. Then there was a great big explosion. The plane was on fire. *I saw it with my own two eyes.*"
> —News item

Herman Voss insists that he saw that the plane (a McDonald Douglas MD80) was on fire in the rear (where the engines are located) before it crashed; yet a Northwest Airlines flight crew insists there was no fire prior to the crash. What are we to make from this? Quite a bit.[iii]

Eyewitness testimony presents an important source of information for us in attempting to reach an understanding about events that take place outside of our own experience. Each of us only perceives a small part of what transpires in the world, and our lives would be much poorer if we were unable to utilize the information presented to us by others. In law courts, eyewitness testimony has traditionally been considered the backbone upon which the presentation of evidence rests. Yet psychologists and philosophers have long recognized that the appeal to eyewitness testimony is not without its problems. Eyewitness testimony is a tool for the collection of knowledge that has strengths and limitations just like any other tool.

The strengths of eyewitness testimony are obvious. As the empiricist notes, knowledge depends upon experience. Our own knowledge depends upon our own experience, but we know that our own experiences are limited, and therefore we are apt to consider the experiences of others as supplying equally valid information to us. Who better to supply this additional information than those who have first hand knowledge of what we were not around to see for ourselves? As Herman Voss said, "I saw it with my own two eyes." Since we were not there to see the airplane crash, why not accept the word of one who was? And that is just what we normally do. Thus, the acceptance of the reports of others greatly enlarges our own storehouses of information—so far, so good. The acceptance of the accuracy and truthfulness of the eyewitness reports of others generally provides us with reasons for believing things with which we have no direct experience.

But do the reports of others always provide us with good reasons for accepting what is being presented to us? Clearly not; eyewitness can be mistaken. Even omitting intentional lies told by those who wish to deceive us, observation reports are still certainly far from infallible. In fact, there are certain general types of errors which mistaken eyewitness testimony is prone to make. Among these types of error are the following:

1. Those caused by the empirical conditions under which the observations are made.

2. Those associated with the theories under which the observer's perceptions are ordered.

3. Those pertinent to the psychological mindset of the observer.

4. Those centered around the attempts observers make to accurately recall what they have observed.

Consider first the category of the empirical conditions under which observations are made. It is appropriate to raise questions about the accuracy of these observations when there is doubt as to whether the observer had sufficient time to make the observation. Did events happen so fast that no one could reasonably be expected to perceive exactly just what did happen? Secondly, was the observer really in a good position to make an accurate observation? Could s/he have gotten a good look at what happened? Did s/he get a good look? Thirdly, if the observer was using some sort of instrument to aid his or her perception, such as eyeglasses or the proverbial drinking glass against the motel room wall (let alone more sophisticated equipment such as binoculars, telescopes, microscopes, and electronic listening devices), what was the condition of these instruments? Were they in proper working order and well maintained? Were they properly used? What is the limitation of their range? What are their capacities? Defective equipment or equipment used improperly cannot be expected to supply accurate data, and thus observational reports based upon data they do provide should not be accepted as accurate either.

Concerning the category of the theories under which the observer's perceptions are ordered it is appropriate to ask for a presentation of these theories. If you claim to have seen a goose and not an eagle, what, if anything, do you know about geese and eagles? What if you claimed to have seen of UFO? What do you know about them? *Persons with training in a given discipline generally make more perceptive and accurate observers of phenomena within that discipline.* Airline pilots are better observers of flying phenomena than lay persons are. Their lives and the lives of their passengers depend on this. Persons who lack the requisite knowledge of a given subject usually have their perceptions of the data in question determined by theories with which they are familiar, and their imaginations easily may run away with them. This means that the uninformed will more easily see the data as something which the data in

fact does not correctly present, or they will fail to see the real significance of the data in question, or they will fail to distinguish crucial data from data which are less important. If the data are seen as something they are not or crucial data is missed, then the inferences made from that incorrect understanding of the data are necessarily going to be mistaken.

Next, there are the psychological conditions concerning the mind-set of the person making the observation. There are many things that may go wrong here. First of all, what was the mind-set of the observer? Was the observer expecting something to happen such that even though it did not happen, s/he mistakenly perceived that it did? Perhaps the observer had a vested interest in seeing something that resulted in a perception of something happening when, in fact, it did not. If a scout master tells the troop that the first one to see an eagle on the day's nature walk will not have to do the dishes for a week, then the little tykes are more likely both to see eagles when they are there and to "see" geese and low-flying B-52s as eagles when, clearly, they are not. Mistakes like these can be made with the best of intentions and by even the most intelligent of observers. Each of us has to beware of perceiving what we wish to perceive or are conditioned to expect rather than what is really present.

The same problem occurs in groups as well as with individuals. In the example above, the whole scout troop is likely to see the low-flying B-52 as an eagle. Mass hallucinations or misperceptions are common facts of life when each of the members of the group may reasonably be expected to have the same mind-set. This situation is well illustrated by groups of individuals who report being abducted by UFOs for obscure medical experimentation. These sorts of claims are rightfully rejected out of hand because they are so farfetched. A great deal of more specific evidence is necessary to validate them, though it somehow never seems to be forthcoming because of "government cover-ups" or "advanced alien technology." Here the relevant issue becomes what the difference is between advanced alien technology, government cover-ups, and delusions in the minds of those making these sorts of claims.[iv]

Finally, there are problems associated with the attempt to accurately recall what has been observed. Relying upon the observational reports of others usually involves relying upon the memory of those other persons. But *memory is notoriously fallible because it involves the recall and reconstruction of events.* We are all familiar with cases in which we have been asked to recall some particular bit of information (on a test, for example) and have confidently answered, only to find out later that we really did not know what we felt so sure about. There are two distinct problems here.

The first problem involves questions of self-confidence. Studies by psychologists have revealed that people tend to believe the observational reports of others more readily when these reports are made with great confidence by the reporters. The empirical rule of thumb seems to be something like this: The greater the confidence in the truth of what is reported, the more likely the audience is to believe the report. But this rule of thumb is a fallacy, which I shall call the **confidence fallacy**. There is, in fact, no correlation between how confident you are about being right regarding your perceptions and how correct you really are. Surprising though it may seem, you can be confident and wrong as well as confident and right. Therefore questions about the confidence you place in your own reports are best seen as remarks about your *beliefs* regarding the accuracy of your reports, and not about their *actual* accuracy.

The second, and perhaps more surprising, problem is that a person's memory may itself change. You may honestly think you accurately remember something you observed while you are recalling your observations, and yet you may still be wrong. This is called the **false memory syndrome**. What is remembered is not determined merely by previous events, it is also determined by the intellectual operations the observer performs in the attempt to recall those previous events. The intellectual operations involved in recall are subject to post-event influences such as questioning by others (like the police) interested in reconstructing what you actually witnessed. It is very difficult for someone else to get you to recall accurately what you previously witnessed without unwittingly altering the theories under which your observations were understood while they were being experienced directly or under which they are now being reconstructed in memory.

Memory is reconstruction. The methods employed to remember an observation may do just that—reconstruct, or rearrange, what you think you so accurately remember. At times this reconstruction may even be deliberate, as when someone has good reasons for believing your original perception of events was faulty. In cases like this, the interrogator is likely to suggest different theories of reconstruction in an effort to jog or improve your memory. Sometimes this is a correct procedure because your memory really was faulty. But sometimes this is an incorrect procedure because your memory originally was not faulty. It only became faulty due to the prompting of the interrogator. The only way to determine whether your memory changes are correct or not is to resort to methods of confirmation available independently of your own memory claims, namely other empirical evidence. In cases where there is no other empirical evidence to substantiate your story, the truth about what you observed may never be discovered.

By now you should recognize that this whole business of observation is rather complicated. But that is the situation we are always in. Fortunately, most of what we perceive is pretty straightforward and works automatically. But I hope that you have seen just how complicated the seemingly simple process of observation really is, and that you can appreciate the possible complexities which we get into when attempting to evaluate observational reports.

Incidentally, what about Herman Voss's claim about the crash of Flight 255? He was very confident about what he thought he saw.

"I saw it with my own two eyes," he stated. Did he? Well, he saw something, but further investigation failed to discover any signs that the plane's engines were on fire before the crash. However it did unearth evidence to show that the plane's flaps and slats were incorrectly set during takeoff, resulting in insufficient lift to keep the plane in the air. Thus Voss's report was mistaken; he didn't really see what he was so sure he saw.[v]

Discuss the following reports as they regard memory issues.

A. What are some of your earliest memories? Do you have any good reasons to believe that they are accurate?

B. Barbara and John Sharpe had been married for 12 years when the accident happened. On May 29, 1991, Barbara's van was broadsided by a car. John rushed to the Regional Medical Center in Orangeburg, SC, where he found that Barbara's injuries were not life-threatening. He kissed her on the forehead, but he felt something was wrong. "I finally asked her did she know who I was. She said no." She had no memory of anything before the accident.

Six years later, she still does not remember anything. But on Saturday the Sharpes got married again. "John married Barbara number one on Sept. 22, 1979," Barbara Sharpe said. "So we decided to get as close to that date as we could. We did the same thing for me, Barbara number two. One of the hardest things about this situation," she added, "is the people who have passed on. I can get to know the living ones all over again. But those who have passed on are just lost to me."

Other things were different for her too. "My tastes changed after the accident. I looked in her closet and I didn't like anything in it," she said, referring to the pre-accident Barbara in the third person. "She wore a lot of colors. I like earth tones and I wear a lot of black."   —News item

C. Bro: "I could have sworn I left my car keys around here somewhere!" Sis: "Where did you leave them last?"

D. Do you remember the names of all of your first grade classmates?

CONCEPTUAL KNOWLEDGE

Perception is a form of knowledge that depends on the data of the senses and memories and the introspective awareness of our own self and our thoughts, feelings, and desires. But data and concepts are always interwoven. Data are data because concepts and theories maintain that they are data. Data uncategorized by concepts would be meaningless to us. "Less even than a dream," as Kant puts it.[vi] Perceptual knowledge, the objects of which are things perceived via the senses, is theory-laden, and theories presuppose concepts, which are themselves the objects of **conceptual knowledge**, or **understanding**. Some conceptual knowledge contains elements of perceptual knowledge, and some does not; however, almost all perceptual knowledge contains elements of conceptual knowledge. Thus, *almost all knowledge is at least partially conceptual in nature.* Take the following example of differing perceptions of "little." Molly is a foot shorter than her twin Max, but she is older by two minutes. Molly: "I'm the oldest! Max is my little brother." Max: "I'm the biggest! Molly is my little sister." Either claim could be correct, depending upon which understanding of the concept "little" you embrace.

Historically, some philosophers have distinguished two sorts of knowledge claims: the analytic and the synthetic.[vii] This distinction has since become one of the classical ways of distinguishing between two importantly different types of knowledge claims. It is necessary to differentiate the activity of judging from the content of what is asserted when the assertion is expressed as a statement. The *activity* of judging is neither true nor false. The *content* of the judgment when expressed as a statement is either true or false. This is illustrated nicely by the **correspondence theory of truth**, which states that claims are true because they correspond to the facts to which they point. The proposition "The cat is on the mat" is true only if the cat is indeed on the mat.[viii]

Analytic propositions are those which can be known to be true simply by knowing the meanings of the terms contained within them. They are characterized by the fact that if they are true, they cannot ever be false (or if they are false, they can never be true). Analytic truths are true for all possible worlds and therefore are known also as **necessary truths**. For example, in any possible reality, the whole is greater than any of its parts; parts must always be smaller than the whole they comprise. **Synthetic propositions** are those which cannot be known to be true simply by virtue of the meaning of the terms of which they are composed. Additional (usually empirical) information must be added to determine whether any synthetic proposition is true. Because it requires empirical confirmation, a synthetic proposition is such that even if it is true now, it could be false at any other time or place. For this reason, synthetic propositions are called **contingent truths**; they are not true in all possible worlds. For example, in this world and according to its specific recipe, a Big Mac has 36 grams of fat, but that total can change if the ingredients used to make it are changed.

All knowledge involving concepts can be expressed in propositions that are either analytic or synthetic. Whether a given proposition is taken to be either analytic or synthetic makes a great deal of difference for the method used in determining its truth value. Because analytic propositions are true (or false) for all possible worlds, no particular fact about the world we happen to live in (optimistically called the "real" world) is relevant in determining whether they are true or false. The truth value of an analytic proposition is determined simply by analyzing the meanings of the concepts which are contained within it. If, for example, you know what "2", "+", "=", "4", and "5" mean, then you know that it is necessarily true that $2 + 2 = 4$, and it is necessarily false that $2 + 2 = 5$. The truth value of a synthetic proposition can be ascertained only by considering the material that the proposition refers to and determining whether this material really exists in the manner claimed by the proposition. If it does, the proposition is true; if it does not, the proposition is false. You must import some information about the world to determine who the current President of the United States is, for example.

True analytic and synthetic propositions can both be said to state the facts. A **fact** is something which is the case. It is a fact that there is only one universe. But a fact could necessarily be the case (if it is expressed by an analytic statement) or only contingently be the

---

EXAMPLES OF ANALYTIC AND SYNTHETIC PROPOSITIONS

Analytic
A. A triangle has three angles.
B. A triangle has three sides.
C. Bachelors are unmarried males.
D. $2 + 2 = 4$
E. $2 + 2 = 5$
F. If A is greater than B and B is greater than C, A is greater than C.

Synthetic
A. Today is Tuesday.
B. It is raining outside.
C. George Bush is the President of the United States.
D. Ray Ruble is the President of the United States.
E. Water runs downhill.
F. Payday is Friday.

---

case (if it is expressed by a synthetic statement). Necessarily, is there only one universe, or is this only contingently true? Usually it is easy to tell the difference between statements about what is necessary and what is contingent, but not always. Sometimes disputes arise over a particular example. Consider the claim, "Humans always behave selfishly."[ix] Is this a fact? If it is, what kind of fact is it: Is it contingently the case or necessarily the case? To answer these questions consider the following question: Would it make sense to search for a valid counterexample? Suppose an opponent of this claim presented an example, would a defender of the claim be forced to admit defeat? By no means—the defender could always say that the supposed counterexample was not really valid. If this sort of situation continued with the opponent presenting counterexample after counterexample while the defender rejected each example in turn as invalid, then you would be wise to suspect that the opponent was treating the claim as a synthetic judgment while the defender was treating it as analytic. This sort of confusion must first be clarified before any headway in the discussion can be made.

Discuss whether the following examples contain necessary facts or contingent facts.

A. Politicians are all crooks.
B. The soul survives the death of the body.
C. Space has only three dimensions.
D. Anyone who disagrees with me is wrong.
E. Time travel is impossible.
F. Women are better than men.
G. Rock and roll is better than classical music.
H. If it looks like a duck and quacks like a duck, it's a duck.
I. "How can we lose when we're so sincere?"
   —Charlie Brown

In determining whether any particular statement is analytic or synthetic and true or false, it should be noted that the same fourfold analysis must be applied that was used to analyze judgments about perceptions. Even though the knowledge claims analyzed here are not primarily claims about perceptions (though some may have components that can be derived only from perception), this makes no difference to the methodology of the analysis. Knowledge is knowledge, whether it is perceptual or otherwise. To avoid any confusion, however, it is helpful to distinguish carefully between perception, which gives us perceptual knowledge, and the other forms of cognition, which provide conceptual knowledge, as discussed above.

In following the analysis of perception presented earlier in the chapter, conceptual knowledge has an element that I shall call **understanding as**. Just as there is no perception without seeing as, there is no conception without understanding something as some specific thing. There is no such thing as subject-less conception. All conceptual knowledge claims are claims of (or about) some particular subject, such as nuclear physics, the economic theory behind the latest tax law revisions, or who will win the next World Series.

Secondly, all conceptual knowledge involves **understanding-that**.[x] Here understanding-that fulfills two functions: first, understanding-that signifies that any conception can be expressed by asserting a statement that is either true or false; it also signifies that any given conceptual claim is tied to a host of other possible claims by the laws of logic and the theory in which the subject matter of the judgment is embedded. No one understands just one single thing in isolation from everything else. Even the simplest conceptual claim (e.g. "A = A" or "A + B = B + A") makes sense because it is contained in a complex theory which gives it meaning. In the example "A = A," "A" stands for any variable. "Variable" is a theory embedded term. Isolated ideas are meaningless, for ideas get their meanings from the theories that contain them.

Thirdly, *conceptions, like perceptions, are theory-laden.* In the example just above, "A = A" is shown to be theory-laden. A more complex claim, such as, "The more money you have, the more you need," only makes sense because it is embedded in a group of other ideas about the concepts, facts, and paradigms of psychology and economics. An individual claim can neither be understood nor evaluated solely by itself. You also have to determine and assess the theories in which the claim is embedded in order to determine what the claim means, whether it is true or false, and how it is tied to other conceptual claims and observational statements. Appeal to theory provides the indispensable means of determining much of what you need to know in order to assess an individual claim.

Finally, any conception is the product of a judgment. Judgments are produced by individuals or groups of individuals who necessarily operate from some mind-set or other. As is true for perceptions, conceptions are the products of minds. There is no such thing as a conception that does not exist in the mind of some person. Although for purposes of analysis it is possible to abstract the knowledge claim from any particular person who makes it, all knowledge is still someone's knowledge. Conceptual mind-set prepares us to expect only certain other ideas to be relevant to an original claim and to react in certain predictable ways to a given original claim. Mind-set, for example, conditions one person to treat the claim that humans always behave selfishly as analytic and another person to treat the same claim as synthetic. Like perceptual knowledge, conceptual knowledge (understanding) allows us to perform certain tasks without which thinking about any given thing would be unproductive, or even impossible. First, understanding allows the thinker to comprehend the topic in question. Secondly, understanding allows the thinker to distinguish between relevant material and irrelevant material for a given topic. There are always too many possible things to think about and too many possible connections to make; some means must be found to pare down the list.

Our understanding allows us to categorize and order the ideas at issue into an intelligible system. Systematic knowledge makes sense out of individual ideas by placing these ideas within the context of other ideas. Through this process, our understanding makes it possible for us to construct a correct account about the issue in question. In order to systematize our knowledge successfully, we must be able to point to certain pieces of **crucial material,** which we treat as basic for any correct understanding of the subject in question. Alternative accounts then can be evaluated or rejected because of their inability to correctly account for the crucial material. Mistaken judgments have a foothold at this point in the systematization process, as sometimes there are too many possible ways of understanding the situation. Prior to 9/11, the CIA and FBI knew of the possibility that al-Quaeda members were undergoing flight training, but they were unable to put all of the puzzle pieces together until after the al-Quaeda plan had been carried out successfully. Had they systematized their knowledge of the al-Quaeda members' activities correctly, the planned attacks could have been stopped relatively easily. Sometimes the consequences for failing to put the puzzle pieces together soon enough are very difficult to bear indeed.

In many ways this is just what critical thinking as sophia ultimately points to—giving correct theoretical explanations for crucial material. As phronesis, critical thinking aims at achieving correct actions and practices by utilizing crucial material. Which pieces of information are crucial for a good account of a given issue or for proper actions depends upon the issue in question and the application of the proper theories to that issue. This is where the apprenticeship theory of learning comes fully into play. The apprentice must come to know, within a given discipline, which pieces of information are crucial for which conceptual operations and what theory provides the proper understanding of this material. The masters under whom the neophyte apprentices are expected to know these things. After a suitable period of exposure and practice with a given subject area, the apprentice is expected to pick up the cannons of judgment appropriate to that subject area and to apply these independently of the tutelage of the master. These cannons of judgment tell the thinker how to work intelligently and make wise choices within a given subject. Understanding cannons should not be confused with learning mere facts about a subject. Beginners may come to know a little bit quite easily, but a little bit of learning is a dangerous thing. It may tempt us to assume that we know a great deal more than we really know, and it can be especially dangerous when it tempts us to make unwise choices based on our limited training. If we do not know the cannons of judgment for a given discipline, the little bit of knowledge we possess is of limited use and may easily invite misuse.

Analyze the following examples using the concepts presented above.

A. "We know that Iraq has weapons of mass destruction and will not hesitate to give them to al-Quaeda for use against us."
—President Bush in the run-up to the U.S. invasion of Iraq in March of 2003

B. Pluto's days as one of our solar system's nine major planets may be numbered. Two groups from the International Astronomical Union are thinking about reclassifying the relatively puny planet—either calling it a "minor planet" or lumping it in with an entirely new class of objects. With a diameter of only 1,440 miles, Pluto, the planet farthest from the sun, is smaller than the Earth's moon. And while other "major planets" have roughly circular orbits, Pluto carves out a sweeping ellipse that frequently takes it closer than Neptune, planet No. 8, to the sun.

"For at least 20 years, it's been obvious that Pluto doesn't fit," said University of Maryland astronomer Mike A'Hearn, who heads the Planetary Systems Science Division of the Astronomical Union. A'Hearn wants to create a new class of objects for ice balls that orbit beyond Neptune and call them Trans-Neptunian Objects. Pluto would be Trans-Neptunian Object No. 1.

Brian Marsden of the Internation Astronomical Union's Minor Planet Center said he has a better idea: reclassify Pluto as a "minor planet," of which there are thousands, then make it take a number. New Mexico astronomer Alan Hale, co-discoverer of the comet Hale-Bopp, suggested the debate is somewhat silly since there really is no clear definition of what a planet is. And besides, "a hypothetical resident of Jupiter would probably laugh at our calling Earth a 'major planet.'" —News item

C. Little boys tease little girls all the time. Should this ever issue in a lawsuit?

D. "I'll do well in college; I've always done well in school."

E. "How hard can driving a car be? I've driven go-carts before. It's the same thing." —Max

Information does not need to be confusing or difficult in order to be appropriate for perceptual and/or conceptual analysis. One common way in which we communicate with each other is by sharing our experiences. These experiences may contain little, if any, technically difficult facets or unusual components, though they may be highly different from everyday life. In any event, when we share our experiences, we must still utilize the four-fold components of perceptual and conceptual analysis presented above. The sharing of our experiences requires the presentation of crucial data because it is the data that give the experiences significance. Frequently accounts are made in response to two questions: "How did it go?" and "What was it like?" The "How did it go?" questions ask for a performance evaluation. The "What was it like?" question does not ask for a comparison, which the use of the word "like" may seem to suggest; rather, it asks for an account of the topic that the listener can understand and relate to.

For each of the following examples discuss "How did it go?" and "What was it like?"

A. Classroom exams

B. Sporting contests or formal performances

C. Proms or other important dates

D. Meeting your girlfriend's or boyfriend's parents for the first time

E. Vacations

F. Job experiences

G. Visits to the dentist or doctor

H. Your first car wreck

WHAT IS KNOWLEDGE?

All knowledge is the knowledge of something. But what is knowledge just by itself? What does it mean to have knowledge independently of any actual subject matter? This question is one of the oldest philosophical issues.[xi] Many philosophers who have discussed this issue agree that **knowledge** is understood best as **justified true belief**. To believe something is to have an opinion about a given topic—to think that something is the case. Of course, *beliefs* can be either true or false, but *there is no such thing as false knowledge*. Prior to the 2004 Presidential election, if you believed that Senator Kerry was going to win, you would have had a false belief; if you believed that President Bush was going to win, you would have had a true belief. *For any belief to qualify as knowledge, it must be true.* However, it cannot be accepted as true by the thinker for the wrong reasons. For a belief to qualify as knowledge it must be justified, which means that the thinker must believe it for the right kinds of reasons. One analysis of what constitutes the right kinds of reasons is called reliabilism. **Reliabilism** maintains that justified beliefs are justified if they are the result of generally adequate instruments or other problem solving methods. Car gas gauges, for example, reliably (though not infallibly) tell how much gas remains in a car's gas tank.

Reliable beliefs must be caused in the right way by the right process to be knowledge. What constitutes the right kinds of processes? It depends on the issue. Justification is a matter relative to the subject matter and the discipline in question. Frequently justification consists of correctly applying *conceiving-that's* to *conceptions of*, as when a student of mathematics proves Pythagoras's theorem, or the detective reconstructs the scene of the crime. These activities involve the intellectual faculties of recognizing, imagining, understanding, confirming (or doubting), and explaining the material at hand. At its core these abilities rest upon a poorly understood intellectual faculty called **intuition**. Intuition enables the mind to recognize the truth of certain basic ideas or the appropriateness of a process directly, independently of any ability to explain how this recognition occurs. It is intuitively obvious, for example, that though practice does not make perfect, you are not likely to perform well what you've not practiced.

One possible explanation of the intuitive ability which the mind possesses is that it depends upon the basic structure of the brain, which causes it to respond in specific ways to certain stimulus patterns. There are advantages and disadvantages to having a brain that is "hard-wired" in this fashion. The chief advantage of the process is that it is done automatically and easily (and therefore quickly). The chief disadvantage is that it may be done incorrectly, producing "intuitively correct" but actually false beliefs. It might seem intuitively correct to continue to pet my cat Moses, who is currently purring and rubbing himself against your arm, only to find him snarling at your throat in the next nanosecond.[xii]

To avoid problems like intuitively correct while factually incorrect judgments, some philosophers also want to add a condition to the current account of knowledge. This condition is that you must have been caused to believe something because of the reasons which would actually verify the truth of your belief or intuition before your belief can be considered knowledge. The goal of this sort of analysis is to eliminate knowledge based on lucky guesses and gossip, for example. This whole issue is still a topic of debate.[xiii] In any event, philosophers generally accept the claim that knowledge is justified true belief even if they still are not sure how to best understand the various elements of justification in some cases.

In no case, however, should you equate justification with **strength of conviction**. How strongly you believe something has nothing to do with whether that belief is true or justified, let alone factually correct. This is one of the most common mistakes made by people, especially in those cases involving so-called intuitive knowledge and in those cases in which people claim to know things on the basis of **faith**. Having faith in something or in someone means accepting the reality of that thing or the truth and value of what a person says or stands for when that reality, truth, or value presently (or permanently) exceeds the possibility of verification. Because the objects of faith go beyond the present possibility of knowledge, it is simply nonsense to call faith a form of knowledge. *Faith exists in the absence of knowledge, not as a form of knowledge.* It is perfectly possible to have a mistaken faith in something or someone, and in this sense faith resembles belief rather than knowledge. Faith (or strength of conviction) may or may not be an admirable thing, but it should be equated with conviction and *not* with truth or knowledge. To confuse conviction, especially passionately maintained conviction, with knowledge is to fall prey to another instance of the confidence fallacy as well as cognitive closure. Do not stand on your soapbox and cry, "I know in my heart!"—it adds nothing but confusion to the issue at hand. Anyone can get a soapbox, and anyone can "know" anything in his or her heart, but this is not knowledge, or understanding. Rather, it is an excuse for the faithful to avoid facing that, in fact, there is no actual knowledge regarding the issue.

There is another meaning associated with faith that does not regard it as passionate conviction, namely, that which defines faith as the commitment to the utilization of a given set of rules or an agreement to "play by the rules." This sort of faith is essential for any form of activity. Unless I have faith in my car's brakes, it would be fairly dumb to drive it. If I did not have faith in Slugger Ralph, it wouldn't seem like a good idea to use him as a pinch hitter in a clutch situation if better alternatives were available to me. In this sense of the term, faith is equivalent to belief, but because the term "faith" is used and not "belief," there is a tendency to conflate it with the sense discussed above and end up arguing (incorrectly) that all "faiths" are equally valid. Accepting such an argument would commit us to the notion that all beliefs are equally valid, which is a silly, unhelpful form of cognitive openness.

Apply the analysis of knowledge presented in this section to the following claims.

A. The sum of the exterior angles of a triangle is 360 degrees.

B. The federal budget deficit can be eliminated without raising taxes.

C. Human beings are always attempting to maximize their pleasure and minimize their pain.

D. By using peyote some North American Indian groups directly experience God.

E. Columbus was not the first European to visit North America.

F. The temperature of the Earth is slowly rising because of the greenhouse effect.

G. There is intelligent life on other planets.

H. Cheaters are only cheating themselves.

EPILOGUE

Our knowledge of the world is constructed by the knowing mind out of many factors bound together by the intellectual operations of seeing-as, seeing-that, conceiving of, and conceiving-that, all of which interweave data by means of the concepts, rules, and paradigms contained in theoretical and practical knowledge. In the succeeding chapters we will look at some of the methods and techniques that are used by the mind to construct knowledge of the material given through sensation and perception to form the fabric of the world we consciously inhabit. We shall begin by looking at the role language plays in constructing our knowledge. Then we shall look briefly at the method of deductive logic to see how it allows our minds to construct compound claims out of their logically separate components. Finally, we shall proceed to see how inductive arguments, the scientific/critical method, causal arguments, analogies and metaphors, and arguments from authority further allow us to become critically aware of the complicated business that encompasses our knowledge of reality.

CONCEPTS

You should be able to define the following concepts, explain their meanings to others not familiar with them, invent your own examples that correctly illustrate the concepts, and apply them correctly to novel applications.

- Analytic proposition
- Conceiving of (understanding as)
- Conceiving that (understanding-that)
- Conceptual knowledge
- Confidence fallacy
- Contingent truth
- Correspondence theory of truth
- Crucial data

- Crucial material
- Data
- Evidence
- Faith
- False memory syndrome
- Imagination
- Intuition
- Knowledge as justified true belief
- Memory
- Mind-set

- Naïve realism
- Necessary truth
- Perceptual knowledge
- Reliabilism
- Seeing as
- Seeing-that
- Sense data
- Strength of conviction
- Synthetic proposition
- Theory-laden
- Understanding

Foundational concepts: Crucial data, imagination, knowledge as justified true belief, mind-set, seeing as, seeing-that, theory-laden

NOTES

i. The earliest systematic discussion of the claim that knowledge is rooted in perception is found in Plato's *Theaetetus*, written sometime around 370 BCE.

ii. The account of observational knowledge I am giving in this chapter is developed from a discussion of scientific knowledge by Norwood Russell Hanson in his *Perception and Discovery* (New York: Freeman, Cooper, and Company, 1969). Hanson's position is not without its critics. See, for example, "The Theory Ladenness of Observation," by Carl Kordig in *Introductory Readings in the Philosophy of Science*, edited by Klemke, Hollinger, and Kline, (New York: Prometheus Books, 1980). For ease of discussion, I am going to confine myself to cases of visual perception, though a similar account can be given for auditory perception, tactile perception, and so forth.

iii. The issues presented in this section are more fully discussed by Stephen Norris and Ruth King in "Observation Ability: Determining and Extending Its Presence," *Informal Logic* (vol. VI, #3, 1981): 3-9. See also Wells and Loftus, *Eyewitness Testimony* (New York: Cambridge University Press, 1984) and C.A.J. Coady, *Testimony: A Philosophical Study* (Oxford: Clarendon Paperbacks, 1992). The Wells and Loftus book is an anthology of interesting articles on various aspects of eyewitness knowledge.

iv. Descartes was one of the first modern philosophers to worry about the problem of delusions. He identified their causes as "brains clouded by the unrelenting vapor of black bile." See his "First Meditation" in his *Meditations of First Philosophy* (1641) for one of the places he presents this concern.

v. For a further discussion of what happened to Flight 255, see the April 1988 issue of *Life Magazine*. Herman Voss's observations were not the only ones investigators discounted.

vi. See his *Critique of Pure Reason* (1781). There may, however, be such a thing as raw, theory-neutral data. I do not want to exclude this possibility, though I'm not aware of any good example of it.

vii. *Ibid.* This distinction was popularized by Immanuel Kant. The distinction between analytic and synthetic propositions is criticized by American philosopher Willard Van Orman Quine in an essay entitled "Two Dogmas of Empiricism," reprinted in his book, *From a Logical Point of View* (New York: Harper & Row, 1963).

viii. The correspondence theory of truth was first proposed by Plato in his *Sophist*. Its accuracy and adequacy have been subject to endless discussion since. See, for example, *Contemporary Readings in Epistemology*, edited by Michael Goodman and Robert A. Snyder, (Englewood Cliffs, NJ: Prentice Hall, 1993) for one of many anthologies on this and other related subjects in epistemology.

ix. This claim was given a famous formulation and defense by Thomas Hobbes. See his *Leviathan* (1651) and *De Homine* (1658). The claim goes under the rubric "psychological egoism."

x. Here I have chosen to ignore the distinction between knowing-that (which can always be expressed as propositional knowledge) and knowing how (which can be expressed only by performance). In this text I am concerned only with knowing-that, though the apprenticeship theory of learning indicates that there is a closer similarity between knowing-that and knowing how than is usually acknowledged because of the differences between the logic of these notions. For the classical discussion of the logic of knowing how and knowing-that, see Gilbert Ryle, *The Concept of Mind* (New York: Barnes & Noble, 1949).

xi. Though the first systematic attempt to define knowledge in itself is found in Plato's *Theaetetus*, the issue was discussed by earlier Greek philosophers, many of whose works survive only in fragments.

xii. For more about the nature of intuition and the relationship between intuition, pattern recognition, and understanding-that, see Howard Margolis, *Patterns, Thinking, and Cognition* (Chicago: The University of Chicago Press, 1987).

xiii. See Edmund Gettier, "Is Justified True Belief Knowledge?" *Analysis* (vol. XXV 1963): 121-3 for a classic critique of the claim that knowledge is justified true belief. This often reprinted article has spawned a long discussion of the issue. For a discussion of these ideas see the article "Knowledge and Belief" in vol. 4 of *The Encyclopedia of Philosophy and Empirical Knowledge*, 2nd ed., edited by Paul K. Moser (Lanham, MD: Rowman & Littlefield Publishers, 1996).

"There's glory for you!"
"I don't know what you mean by 'glory,'" Alice said.
Humpty Dumpty smiled contemptuously. "Of course you don't—till I tell you.
I mean 'there's a nice knock-down argument for you!'"
"But 'glory' doesn't mean 'a nice knock-down argument,'" Alice objected.
"When I use a word," Humpty Dumpty said, rather in a scornful tone,
"it means just what I choose it to mean—neither more nor less."
"The question is," said Alice, "whether you can
make words mean so many different things."
"The question is," said Humpty Dumpty, "which is to be master—that's all."

—Lewis Carroll, *Through the Looking Glass*[i]

CHAPTER TWO

What's in a Word?

INTRODUCTION

What's in a word? In a word: plenty. Historically, we have not given much attention to our everyday language. After all, just about everybody we know speaks our own native language, and there is little impetus to pay much attention to the words we use as long as those with whom we converse understand our point. But, frankly, very often the people with whom we communicate do not get our point, and we frequently do not get the points being made by others. Breakdowns of communication between persons are good signs that insufficient attention has been given to either the underlying thoughts giving rise to what we wish to communicate or to the chief vehicle through which we attempt to communicate, i.e., language.

Undeniably, language is the vehicle of thought. If I ask you to think about an issue, I frame my question in a language and expect you to answer that question in a language. The **Sapir-Whorf hypothesis of linguistic relativity** maintains that *all thought occurs only using language, and the words you use in thinking about any given subject determine* how *you think as well as* what *you think about the issue at hand.*[ii] This is the strong version of the hypothesis. The weak version maintains that language merely *influences* thought rather than wholly determining it.[iii] If you ever have struggled with learning a foreign language (which requires you to think consciously about what words in that language correctly express what you are thinking in your native tongue), you can testify to the truth of at least the weak version of the Sapir-Whorf hypothesis.

Whether or not the strong version of the Sapir-Whorf hypothesis turns out to be entirely true, one of the claims made by it is clearly true, namely that a large part of learning to think simply is learning how to use a given language correctly. One of the things I would do, for example, to get you to think about issues of which you are presently ignorant, is to introduce you to some technical terms, the understanding of which allows you to think about things of which you were previously oblivious. Over the centuries many different disciplines have arisen that allow those conversant with them to think about things which are literally inconceivable to those who have no knowledge of these disciplines. The ancient Greeks, for instance, could not think about space flight because they lacked the concept of space flight and all the other terms for aspects of this subject, which we now take for granted. Thus a large part of learning to think means learning the vocabulary of a given discipline.

Another condition of thought set by language is that in order to think, we first must learn sets of rules. Learning a language like English or a set of technical terms like those used in the game of basketball or the field of biology means learning a set of rules for the creation and guidance of thought and conduct in that area. If I want to teach you the game of basketball, I have to train you not simply to dribble and shoot the ball, I have to get you to understand the concepts of double-dribble, free throw, zone defense, and so forth. If you do not understand what these terms mean, you will not understand the game, even though you might be able to play it up to a point. Understanding something even as apparently simple as basketball is an exceedingly complex task.

The language you speak and the thoughts that this language allows you to think make an enormous difference both in what you think about a given subject and how you think about it. Philosophers have long recognized this.[iv] In this chapter, I will introduce you to some of the major functions of language, as well as some of the complexities that arise from the use of language.

THE FUNCTIONS OF LANGUAGE

Broadly speaking, language has three major functions: **cognition**, **expression**, and **direction**. Language is used in its cognitive sense when its main purpose is to convey information; in its expressive sense when its main purpose is to convey or express feelings and emotions; and in its directive sense when its main purpose is to convey commands, orders or instructions. It should be noted that specific uses of language rarely perform only one of these functions at a time. Commonly the same written or verbal expressions are used simultaneously to achieve several goals at once. This hardly should be surprising, but confusion and miscommunication can result easily if speakers, writers, and audiences ignore this. Indeed, it is sometimes far easier to mis-communicate than to communicate.

Language is used so frequently in its cognitive sense that there is a tendency to assume that cognition is the most important, or even the only, function of language. In cognition, language is used to make **statements**. Statements are linguistic expressions that purport to tell the audience what is in fact the case. Because statements purport to state what is in fact the case, all statements are either true or false, and *only* statements can be true or false. Questions and directions are expressed in sentences that are neither true nor false. Thus, if a particular spoken or written passage contains claims that are either true or false (regardless of whether you know which), you can be sure that the language in the passage is being used in the cognitive sense. If I tell you, "Today is Friday," I make a claim. If today is in fact Friday, my claim is true; if today is not Friday, my claim is false. Even if you are unaware of what day of the week it is, you can be certain that the claim made uses language cognitively.

At this point, it might be helpful to address briefly the question of what makes a statement true or false. The usual answer given to this question by philosophers is called the **correspondence theory of truth**.[v] According to the correspondence theory of truth, a true statement is true because it corresponds or points to some real state of affairs in the world. These states of affairs are usually called facts or reality. Thus the statement, "Today is Friday" is true when it points to the correct state of affairs in the world, namely, when the day is Friday, and false when it points to the wrong state of affairs, e.g. it is actually Thursday.[vi]

Language is used expressively when it is intended to convey to the audience the emotions being communicated by the author. If I am trying to drive a nail with a hammer and I hit my thumb instead of the nail, I am likely to give forth a whole string of colorful metaphors. It should be noted that language that is used expressively is neither true nor false. If I cheer when my favorite team scores the go-ahead touchdown late in the game, my language cannot be considered to be true or false. Emoting is not the same thing as making a statement.

Sometimes the same linguistic expression may be used to make a statement and to express emotion at the same time. If I say about Pickett's ill-fated charge during the Battle of Gettysburg that it was "a glorious waste of first-rate infantry," I am stating that the charge was a stupid military decision as well as expressing my admiration for the men who died heroically participating in it. While it may be either true or false that Pickett's heroic charge was a stupid military decision, my admiration for the men who participated in it is neither true nor false. Notice that one of the words I use to describe Pickett's Charge—heroic—has by itself both a descriptive and an emotive component.

Finally, language is used in a directive way to issue commands and orders—directions. These uses of language convey to the audience the author's attempts to control the decisions and actions of the audience. If I say to you, "Close the window," I am attempting to get you to do something specific. Like expressive language, directive language is neither true nor false. There is no such thing as a true or a false command. Directives may be wise or they may

be silly, pointed or pointless, appropriate or inappropriate, but they cannot be true or false.

Language that is directive also can be informative or expressive as well. The sign "WET PAINT" on a newly painted park bench attempts to keep you from sitting on the bench until the paint has dried, but it is also informing you that the bench has been freshly painted. If you fail to see the sign or fail to understand it, sitting on the bench is quite likely to evoke the cry, "Wet paint!" (among other phrases) from you. Frequently language that appears to be cognitive has a function that is primarily directive. If I tell you that a particular item is new and improved or a best buy, I really am trying to influence your purchases under the guise of giving you information.

There are two other common functions language has which are worth noting, **ceremonial** and **performative**. Ceremonial language is utilized on certain important occasions in which the repetition of certain words is used to perform an important ritual that traditionally has to be done in a specific manner to be considered correctly done. Weddings, funerals, church services, graduations, and occasions of state typically use a great deal of this sort of language. The performative use of language may also be found in ceremonies. Performative language seeks to bring about a state of affairs simply by the utterance of the appropriate formula. When the minister says, "I now pronounce you husband and wife," the pronouncement of the words themselves is understood as making the couple a married couple. As is true with expressive and directive uses of language, the ceremonial and performative uses do not by themselves involve statements that are either true or false. Ceremonies and performances may be moving or trivial, boring or majestic, but they cannot be true or false.

Critical thinking requires you to be aware of which functions language uses in a given situation. Language may serve a multiple number of functions, and different modes of evaluation are appropriate for each of these functions. There is always the possibility that you may become confused in a given case and fail to recognize the appropriate mode of evaluation for a given example. There is no golden rule-of-thumb that allows you to recognize which language applications occur in a given example, but it is always important to *pay careful attention to the author's intentions.*

What uses of language are contained in the following examples?

A. "Never give a sucker an even break."

—Mae West

B. After watching the latest presidential election campaign, I have become convinced more than ever of the accuracy of Plato's definition of democracy: a government of fools elected by morons.

C. With tax that will come to $39.95.

D. "On the whole, I'd rather be in Philadelphia."

—inscription on W.C. Fields' grave

E. To open, cut along the dotted line.

F. "I pledge allegiance to the flag..."

G. If you have to ask the price, you cannot afford it.

H. "I'll be back."

—Arnold Schwarzenegger, *The Terminator*

DEFINITIONS

One of the important ways to avoid the confusion and mis-communication that stems from the failure to pay appropriate attention to the various functions language may fill is to pay careful attention to the various sorts of definitions that serve to label, describe, and characterize those things defined. A **definition** is a linguistic device that attempts to establish exactly the meaning of a word or phrase or pin down the objects to which the word can point correctly. Definitions serve five primary functions: a) eliminate vagueness, b) eliminate ambiguity, c) increase vocabulary, d) explain theoretical ideas, and e) influence beliefs or attitudes. Different types of definitions are designed to emphasize each of these distinct functions. I shall discuss each of the functions

of definitions in turn and explain what kind of definition is associated with each function.

All definitions share two characteristics; every definable term has a **denotation** and a **connotation**. A term's denotation is a set made up of all the things the term correctly may be used to point or refer to. The term "university" refers or points to Harvard, Oxford, University of Chicago, and so on, but not to the local junior college or high school. A term's connotation is a set of rules used to establish the term's denotation. A university is an educational institution of the highest level, usually made up of undergraduate and graduate colleges. In order to determine whether any particular school may be referred to correctly as a university, it is necessary to understand the connotation of the word "university".

Most definitions refer to the defined concept's connotation rather than its denotation, and this is entirely proper, because you cannot tell whether a term correctly points to an object until you first know the term's connotation. This is why your teachers may not be pleased when you are asked to define a term and all you can supply is an example, even if the example is valid. That being said, there are terms that can be supplied with **ostensive definitions**, with which an author attempts to define a term by supplying a paradigm example of it for inspection. There are certainly things that are initially easier to understand through an example. The attack on the World Trade Center on September 11, 2001 is a horrifying yet accurate example of "being caught with one's pants down," so to speak.

However, it is still important to mention that there is no substitute for learning a term's or phrase's connotation in addition to whatever ostensive definitions can teach us. There are two potential pitfalls inherent in using ostensive definitions. First, it can be difficult to know for certain that the learner in fact abstracts the right lesson from the example in question. Secondly, it is frequently the case that particular things have possible applications that are difficult to classify through the use of an example, as examples may oversimplify a complex issue.

Turning now to the main uses of definitions mentioned above, let us first consider the use of definitions to eliminate vagueness. Many of the words commonly used in a living language are vague. A **vague** word is a term that may be applied properly in a range of possible applications. Because the possible application of a term may vary greatly, it is often desirable to know more precisely what part of the range is intended in a given context. Precising definitions are designed to narrow the possible applications of a vague term. A precising definition makes more specific what is otherwise too vague in its application to suit our needs accurately. If I tell you that I have fixed you up with a tall blind date, you will likely want to know just how tall this person is, 6', 6'4", 7'? What exactly does the word "tall" mean here? A precising definition supplies the answer.

When scientists write reports of experimental findings, they try to be as specific as possible in defining the meaning of the terms they use to refer to the important variables in their experiments so that those who read their accounts may check their results by replicating their experiments. In order to replicate one scientist's experiment properly, another scientist must know with a high degree of precision what the first scientist understood by the language contained in the original report. To do this, the original report will offer **operational definitions** of the key variables involved. An operational definition is a kind of precising definition in that it will nail down the specific meaning of the variables involved in an experiment, as understood by the scientist(s) conducting the experiment for the first time.

The second use of definitions is to clear up ambiguity. Many frequently used words in many languages are **ambiguous**, which means that they can have at least two entirely separate and distinct meanings. Some words in English have dozens of distinct meanings. Many words are homophones, sounding alike to the ear but having distinct meanings if they are understood as nouns or verbs. Consider (to) duck [verb] and (a) duck [noun]. Normally, the context in which the ambiguous word is spoken or written will serve to indicate to the audience which of its possible uses is intended in a specific instance, but trouble sets in when an author intends one meaning of a term and the audience understands another. Confusion of this sort easily can result in a **verbal dispute**, which occurs when each party involved is concentrating on a different meaning that the disputed word legitimately possesses.

Suppose I told you, "Meet me by the main entrance." The main entrance might be the biggest one, the one most people use, or the one that you and I usually use. There are various possible combinations here. Lack of communication can result in this type of situation easily, and it can go undetected by either party because both parties are quite sure that they understand the other. Since each side of the dispute is certain that it is using the term in question correctly, great puzzles can arise as to how the other side(s) can fail to see what the one side knows to be obviously true. When this happens, philosophers say that the thinkers have committed the fallacy of **equivocation**, the use of a word or phrase having multiple meanings, each equally possible. Ambiguity can be subtle; sometimes a thinker may use a term ambiguously in a given situation without recognizing that s/he has done so. *Removing the fallacy involves recognizing one's failure to see the ambiguity inherent in the situation, i.e., admitting that there is another possible and legitimate interpretation of the term being used.* Bringing the ambiguous meanings of the disputed term(s) to light should resolve the dispute if the dispute is only verbal (as opposed to being also ideological, for example).

Definitions also are used to increase vocabulary, and such definitions are **lexical definitions**, those found in a dictionary. This type of definition is designed to clear up cases of ambiguity or to settle vocabulary questions. Lexical definitions are so common and important that the word "definition" frequently is understood in only this particular sense. A dictionary simply lists each of the ordinary meanings of a word as it is used by a population in order of the frequency of its use. The most frequently used meaning is listed first in the dictionary and so on. For example: "Heat (heet) *n.* 1. A form of energy produced by movement of molecules, capable of transmission by conduction or convection or radiation. 2. The sensation produced by this, hotness. 3. Hot weather." Confusion about words that arise from ambiguity typically can be resolved in principle by discovering which of the lexical definitions of the word the author intends in that situation. Suppose I am standing in line at the theatre box office, and you cut in front of me at the last minute. Rather than stage a big scene, I turn to my companion and say, "Miscreants before beauty." Have I insulted you? You won't know unless you know the lexical definition of "miscreant."

At times language users misuse language. There are two common forms of linguistic mistake: **semantic mistakes** and **errors in syntax**. **Semantics** is the study of the origin and meaning of words. If you think that a miscreant is a witty fellow, you have made a semantic mistake. **Syntax** (or grammar) is the study of the proper arrangement of words. Lexical definitions are used primarily to clear up semantic mistakes, and are not of much use in correcting syntactical (or grammatical) errors, unless the syntactical error results from the misuse of the parts of speech, e.g., the substitution of a verb for a noun or an adverb for a verb. When a language user unintentionally misuses language in this fashion, it is usually sufficient to point out the misuse to the person who has erred, a habit of which English teachers are inordinately fond.

When a language user willfully misuses language, as does Humpty Dumpty in the passage at the beginning of this chapter, it may be sufficient to point out to the person who is misusing language that the misused word really does not have the meaning the author attributes to it. Treating the term as if it really has the incorrectly assigned meaning simply invites confusion (a confusion that Alice attempts to avoid).

It is almost always correct to say that a word really means what the community of language users uses it to mean rather than what any individual (such as Humpty Dumpty) wants it to mean. In this sense, a given definition of a word may be correct (actually used in that manner by the community) or incorrect (not used in that manner by the community).

The purpose of a definition that explains a theoretical idea (definition type "d" above) is to uncover the truth about reality. Human beings are far from omniscient. This troublesome circumstance would not be nearly as problematic if we were unaware of it or if (as a species) we weren't so curious to fill the gaps in the knowledge we do possess. But, alas, we recognize that we do not know many things while simultaneously desiring to know everything. The attempt to bridge the gap in our knowledge leads to, among other things, a great deal of disagreement concerning what is really the truth regarding any given issue. When disagreements about the nature of reality arise, individuals must resort to **theoretical definitions**. A theoretical definition is designed to explain the real meaning of some term within the context of what the language community takes to be its proper explanatory theory. "Heat is really molecular motion; what it feels like to us is strictly secondary." Here the term "real" refers to what is the case independently of whatever the language community happens to think about the issue in question.

To ask what is really the case about something may be a question about that thing's **essence**. The essence of something is comprised of those characteristics that each must be present to make that thing the specific kind of thing it is. For example, triangles have to have the property of having three angles; this is a part of their essence. There simply cannot be any such thing as a two-angled triangle—it is a nonsensical concept. *While a lexical definition only reports how a given community of language users in fact uses a given term, theoretical definitions attempt to uncover the ultimate nature of reality and define terms according to it.* Different explanatory theories about the ultimate nature of reality give rise to different explanations of the same phenomena and thus to different theoretical definitions of the terms used to refer to this reality.

This is not as strange as it might sound. Consider this illustration: In *Heavy Drinking: The Myth of Alcoholism as a Disease*[xi], philosopher Herbert Fingarette argues that alcoholism is not really a disease. Whether Fingarette's position on alcoholism is correct turns, in part, on how the term "disease" is defined. Fingarette's argument runs like this: science has failed to discover a single unifying cause of alcoholism. Genetic, metabolic, tolerance and withdrawal, psychological, and social hypotheses of alcoholism all are incomplete and unsatisfactory explanations of what is really not a medical issue in the first place. If science has failed after repeated attempts to discover an adequate single explanation of alcoholism, then alcoholism cannot really be a disease, because all diseases have single and unifying causes.

Notice that Fingarette's argument depends on a certain theoretical definition of "disease." According to his argument, diseases are things that have single unifying causes. Since it is certainly true that science has yet to establish that alcoholism results from a single underlying cause, he believes that he has shown that alcoholism really (or properly) should not be classified as a disease. But is it really true that all diseases have single unifying causes? While some diseases such as small pox have single causes, how plausible is it at this stage of our understanding to say that cancer, for example, has a single unifying cause? We simply do not know this yet. Fingarette's theoretical definition of "disease" therefore may be incorrect.

The final function of definitions is to influence attitudes and beliefs. Perhaps I am being too hard on Fingarette in the example just cited above. Perhaps he really is stipulating that when we use the word "disease," we ought to mean simply "an illness of an organism having a single unifying cause." If so, then Fingarette's theoretical definition is also a **per-**suasive definition and a **stipulative definition**. Remember that language has both expressive and directive functions in addition to its use as informative. It is entirely common to find the same definition simultaneously serving multiple functions. Persuasive definitions attempt to influence attitudes and beliefs, while stipulative definitions usually are used by their authors to introduce an entirely new term to the audience. Both types of definitions are used mainly to attempt to persuade the audience to adopt the speaker's viewpoint when reasoning about a particular topic.

A living language is intrinsically dynamic. Language users frequently find that no existing word adequately captures what needs to be said. When this happens, we are confronted with two choices: we either may use an old word to mean something new, or we simply may invent an entirely new word, a **neologism**. Using old words to express entirely new concepts is inherently risky, as the audience seeing or hearing these words quite naturally will identify them with their old meanings and easily become confused because of this. In order to avoid this form of confusion, authors are free to coin their own terms for new ideas, the meaning of which is then stipulated (or assigned) by the author. Neologisms, however, can also cause confusion until the frequency of their use makes them common currency in the realm.

Discuss the different types of definitions and labels in the examples below.

A. "Just as we were called colored, but were not that, and then Negro, but not that, to be called black is just as baseless. To be called African-Americans has cultural integrity." —Jesse Jackson

B. "Since 1981...70,000 executions have occurred [in Iran], with double that number now in jails as political prisoners.... Khomeini [is] one of the Hitlers of the 1980s. 'Killing is mercy,' he said in 1984, 'for it seeks to rectify the person. A person sometimes cannot be rectified unless he is cut up and heated up.... You must kill, burn and lock up those who are in opposition.'" —News item

C. "All pigs are created equal, but some are more equal than others."

    —George Orwell, *Animal Farm*

D. I need glasses to drive because I'm blind in one eye and can't see out of the other. It follows that I have a disability. Therefore, I should be able to park in a handicap parking space.

E. If you are not for us, you are against us.

F. "I fondly remember a time when real Republicans stood for fiscal responsibility."

    —Senator John McCain, R-Ariz.

G. The glass is half-empty. The glass is half-full.

H. "Children, there's a time and place for that kind of behavior. It's called college."

    —Chef, *South Park*

SETTING THE AGENDA

Language users are not interested only in presenting "facts" to their audiences, they also are interested in getting their audiences to view these facts in certain ways, or to react to them with what the language users consider to be appropriate reactions. In order to elicit the appropriate reactions from their audiences, speakers and writers often choose language that is emotionally loaded or is at least designed to get their audiences to see things from certain perspectives. One of the best ways of achieving these goals is by utilizing persuasive and stipulative definitions.

Notice how Humpty Dumpty tries to set the agenda in his discussion with Alice. Humpty Dumpty, you will remember, defines "glory" as "a nice knock-down argument." Alice replies correctly that "a nice knock-down argument" is not the (lexical) definition of "glory." What Alice says is correct, but irrelevant to Humpty Dumpty's own agenda. Humpty Dumpty really is interested in who is going to be allowed to set the linguistic agenda, the language speaking community (in the form of its rules of semantics and syntax) or the individual speaker (in this case, Humpty Dumpty himself); "The question is which is to be master...." Humpty Dumpty opts for the mastership of the speaker, but only as long as *he* is the speaker. Unfortunately for Humpty Dumpty's perspective, any number of speakers can play this game. If too many play this sort of game with language, communication inevitably will grow into a Tower of Babel.[viii]

You should be aware of how important it is to set the agenda of a discussion. **Setting the agenda** has two important functions, the first of which is establishing what you are going to talk about. Someone or something always sets the agenda in this sense when you are thinking or discussing an issue. If an agenda has not been set, there is either nothing or too much about which to talk or think. Secondly, setting the agenda attempts to establish certain value-laden positions about the items under discussion. A person who seeks to set the agenda in a discussion may well be interested mainly in attempting to persuade the listeners or readers to adopt a certain attitude or set of beliefs about the values interwoven into the discussion. If this is successful, s/he will have placed the **burden of proof** on his or her opponent to refute the values established by the agenda in question.

It is important for the critical thinker to be aware that an agenda has been set and how the settled agenda tends to channel thinking on the topic in question. Never underestimate the power of language to set the agenda. "Mere words" are incredibly powerful tools for controlling thought. One of the classic presentations of the power of language is contained in George Orwell's famous novel, *1984.* In this book, Big Brother has been depressingly successful at setting the agenda for his totalitarian society through the use of adroit persuasion techniques such as "Newspeak," which, among other things, continually rewrites the dictionary so as to remove meanings from terms. Newspeak works according to the strong version of the

Sapir-Whorf hypothesis of linguistic relativity: a language containing fewer words than contemporary English makes the development of subversive activities virtually impossible because such developments are unthinkable, and subversive thoughts are unthinkable because such thoughts cannot be conceived of without language that allows for their basic expression. Simply stated, if you can't say it, you can't think it; if you can't think it, you can't do it.

> The purpose of Newspeak was not only to provide a medium of expression for the worldview and mental habits proper to the devotees of Ingsoc [English Socialism], but to make all other modes of thought impossible. It was intended that when Newspeak had been adopted once and for all and Oldspeak forgotten, a heretical thought—that is, a thought diverging from the principles of Ingsoc—should be literally unthinkable, at least so far as thought is dependent on words. Its vocabulary was so constructed as to give exact and often very subtle expression to every meaning that a Party member could properly wish to express, while excluding all other meanings and also the possibility of arriving at them by indirect methods. This was done partly by the invention of new words, but chiefly by eliminating undesirable words and by stripping such words as remained of unorthodox meanings, and so far as possible of all secondary meanings whatever... Newspeak was designed not to extend but to diminish the range of thought, and this purpose was indirectly assisted by cutting the choice of words down to a minimum.[ix]

While we have not experienced such an extreme editing of our own language, it is quite easy to see how such control can be exerted on a much smaller scale within the context of a particular discussion. It is important always to be alert to the use of such devices by any language user.

There are other means that language users employ to set the agenda for thinking about a given topic. The use of **sexist language** is one of the most commonly used methods. Sexist language is language that either (a) identifies the sex of a person when to do so is inappropriate to the context of the discussion, (b) treats both sexes as if they are really only of one sex (almost always male), or (c) treats one sex (almost always female) as if it were inherently inferior to the other. I shall consider examples of each of these forms in turn.

Some uses of language are sexist because they identify the sex of the person(s) when to do so is inappropriate to the issue. Consider the following list of occupations: fireman, policeman, airman, mailman, cowboy, actor, fisherman, Congressman, housewife. Each of these terms identifies persons not only by the kind of work they do, but also by the sex of the person doing the work. These words not only pick out certain people, but they also implicitly suggest that members of only one sex normally or properly engage in these kinds of occupations. But the suggestion is false. Members of both sexes normally and properly engage in these kinds of occupations. The language used to refer to workers in these occupations is inherently sexist in that it literally maintains that there can be no female firemen, Congressmen, etc. and no male housewives, but this is obviously false. Some of these words can be replaced by already-existing non-sexist terms: firefighter, police officer, member of Congress, homemaker, and so forth. But English currently contains no non-sexist terms for the terms "actor," "fisherman" ("fisher-person?"), or "mailman" ("postal service employee" is too cumbersome). Further refinement of English is needed to remove the unfortunate sexist connotations from occupational designators that in fact refer to members of either sex.

The grammar of English also can be inherently sexist. The chief problem here lies in some of the pronouns used in English. Plural pronouns generally present no problems; "we," "they," "us," "our" and "your" are all plural pronouns that present no sexist connotations. But some singular pronouns most certainly do. The only non-sexist singular third-person pronoun available in English is "it," which is not proper for use when referring to a human being. If I want to refer to just one person, I have to refer to that person as "him" or "her," or "he" or "she." Proper English grammar requires the use of one of these terms in cases that really are intended to be gender-neutral pronoun references. Seemingly by default, "he" generally is made to do double duty for both "he" and "she."[x]

Further investigation shows that the problem simply gets worse. Sometimes one of a pair of terms that are used to describe opposite characteristics within a given range also can be used neutrally to describe the whole range of items in question. When this happens, linguists call the term that can be used indifferently to refer to the whole range of items or only to one end of the range a **marked term**.[xi] Consider terms like "tall" and "short" or "heavy" and "light." When we refer to height or weight generically, we normally say, "How tall is he?" or "How heavy is she?" To refer to a term as "marked" is not simply to characterize it theoretically: *Marked terms are essentially evaluative.* "Man" is just such a marked term. In English it is proper to refer to the whole human race as "mankind" or "men." Take, for example, the following statements: "All men are created equal," or "Mankind is halfway between apes and angels." "Man" in its various forms also is properly used to refer only to males, of course. Generally the terms "male" and "female" are used only to designate males or females respectively, but grammatically, females also can be referred to properly as males. For example, "It's every man for himself!" Therefore, as with all strong marked terms, labeling a woman as a man suggests that male is really the more valuable sex to be. This situation is brilliantly addressed in Simone de Beauvoir in *The Second Sex*:

> [W]hat is a woman?...A man would never get the notion of writing a book on the peculiar situation of the human male.... A man never begins by presenting himself as an individual of a certain sex; it goes with-

out saying that he is a man. [But] the terms *masculine* and *feminine* are used symmetrically only as a matter of form, as on legal papers. In actuality the relation of the two sexes is not quite like that of two electric poles, for *man* represents both the positive and the neutral, as is indicated by the common use of man to designate human beings in general; whereas woman represents only the negative, defined by limiting criteria, without reciprocity.... A man is right in being a man; it is the woman who is in the wrong. It amounts to this: just as for the ancients there was an absolute vertical with reference to which the oblique was defined, so there is an absolute human type, the masculine.[xii]

As de Beauvoir points out, sexist language is inherently value-laden. When these values are questionable, the agenda set by the value-laden language needs to be called into question. However, *language is not only laden with sexist values; it is also laden with racial or ethnic values.* **Racial** or **ethnic language** is language that either (a) identifies the race or ethnic character of a person when to do so is inappropriate within the context of the discussion, (b) treats all racial or ethnic groups as if they are all members of one racial or ethnic class (in English speaking cultures white, Northern Europeans usually are assumed to be the paradigm class), or (c) treats all racial or ethnic groups as if they were inherently inferior to the paradigm class.

Racial or ethnic value-laden language and sexist value-laden language contain morally objectionable conceptions of the people to whom they refer, and many of these conceptions are the same in both types of language. These labels are used to perpetuate inferior social roles for the groups to which they refer, and they are used to limit illicitly the potential for individual growth and status for the individuals of these groups. They are also used to justify implicitly the culturally dominant position of those who use this language. Persons who are both female and members of socially subordinate racial or ethnic groups suffer a double-whammy: they are victimized by the racial, ethnic, or sexist language of the dominant class, and they are victimized by the sexist language of members of their own racial or ethnic groups.

The use of **slang** is another common way of setting the agenda for a particular way of viewing an issue. Slang is highly informal language usually found outside of normal or conventional usage. This language is used to point at, characterize, and evaluate that to which it refers. Some neologisms first introduced as slang end up becoming part of the official language, but most slang stays outside of the cultural mainstream.

Slang originates in subdivisions of culture in order to meet the subdivisions' special needs that are not met by the language of the dominant culture. In this sense, slang resembles **jargon**, which is language identified with certain professions or trades (as in the jargon of the philosopher) designed to indicate distinctions that the dominant culture sees no need to make. Slang and jargon have the advantage of being short and (frequently) snappy, allowing its users to communicate a great deal with just a single word or phrase. Jargon, however, unlike slang, tends to be descriptive, not evaluative, in its intent.

Most uses of slang are inherently evaluative. *The function of slang is not simply to pick out and neutrally describe that to which it refers, but rather to pass judgment on the object in question.* If you call someone a "jock," you haven't said simply that this person participates in sports. Similar things can be said for "nerd" or "Goth." You also have expressed an evaluation of this person that typically is negative, though it doesn't have to be. Slang is interesting to the critical thinker primarily because of the evaluations inherent in its use. Racial, ethnic, and sexist language is full of slang and much of this slang is highly uncomplimentary. Language such as this is so value-laden that it is obvious what type of agenda it sets for "communication" between persons when it is used.

There are still other ways of injecting an agenda into a discussion through the careful selection of language. Employing **euphemisms** is one of them. Euphemisms are emotionally neutral or positive expressions that are used to characterize emotionally negative things or activities so as to make what is inherently questionable more respectable. The Godfather does not terrorize his victims into submission by threatening to dismember them, he "makes them an offer they can't refuse." The U.S. Air Force in Vietnam did not bomb innocent civilians, it "engaged in protective-reaction strikes." I "carry out unconventional warfare," but you "practice terrorism." My son "has just joined a small religious organization" where he is "re-evaluating his priorities in life," but your son "has been kidnapped by a cult" where he is "being systematically brainwashed to reject everything that is decent and good."

If language can be used to express many euphemisms, it surely can be used to express many **malphemisms** as well.[xiii] Malphemisms are emotionally negative expressions that are substituted for emotionally neutral things or activities so as to raise objections about what is not inherently objectionable. To call someone a "bleeding heart liberal" is to suggest that there is something inherently bad about being concerned for the poor. Someone who thinks that 25,000 nuclear warheads are enough for national security is "soft on defense." Anyone who supports the Palestinian uprising in the occupied territories is a "Nazi." Anyone who would attempt to balance the federal budget partially by reducing domestic spending seeks to balance the budget "on the backs of the poor."

Euphemisms and malphemisms share a common characteristic: both are rhetorical devices that seek to change the focus of discussion about a given issue into channels about which their users feel more confident. Propaganda makes frequent use of both of these devices. **Propaganda** consists of the use of language designed to persuade the audience about the truth, justness, or rightness of its subject matter. In propaganda persuasion becomes more important than objective truth, or perhaps to put this more accurately, in propaganda the suggested definitions are declared the truth about the subject in question.

Much of the language involved in propaganda is thoroughly embedded with cognitive connections and emotional associations that make it possible for speakers and writers to say a great deal more than the simple lexical definitions of the utilized vocabulary. The same can be said for the language that is ordinarily and non-controversially used to describe what is taken to be reality by the vast majority of language users within a given community. Though it may sound strange, words *mean* more to us than they *say*, strictly speaking. While this is desirable because it is convenient, it is frequently too convenient. Painting a situation with euphemistic or malphemistic language makes it possible for a language user to make his or her case quickly, but the reason why we should reject this seduction is that it begs the very question at issue: How can the situation properly be defined or characterized in the first place? Rejecting the easy temptation of euphemistic or malphemistic language puts the situation back where it belongs—on the substantive debate concerning the merits of the case. Winning an argument by smuggling your conclusion into the very way you define the issue is a cheap substitute for sustained, critical thought. Avoid it, and be on the watch when others do it.

Discuss how language is used to set the agenda in the examples below.

A. If you have to ask the price, you cannot afford it.

B. Deciding who is a "real" Indian has become one of the most divisive issues facing Native Americans today. In Connecticut, the 383 members of the Mashantucket Pequot tribe share profits from a casino that clears more than $1 million a day from slot machines alone. The tribe gets 50 calls a month from people who figure they must have Pequot blood in them. Some of them cannot even pronounce the name of the tribe.

C. 9/11 shows that Muslim extremists are all cowardly terrorists. People who would hijack an airplane and fly it into a building are simply too gutless to fight for their cause in a fitting manner.

D. "Someone else for president."
"Don't blame me, I voted for the other guy."
—from bumper stickers

E. How much wood could a woodchuck chuck if a woodchuck could chuck wood?

F. "Toasty Cereal: New and improved!"

G. An adequate income is $100 more a week than you make.

H. "You call this a book! Where are all the pictures?"

I. An early name for AIDS was GRID [Gay-Related Immune Deficiency] because it was believed that only homosexuals contracted AIDS.

J. "Go ahead, punk, make my day."
—Clint Eastwood in *Dirty Harry*

K. "Whatever is, is right."
—Alexander Pope, *An Essay on Man*

L. "It depends on what the meaning of 'is' is."
—President Clinton in response to the charge that he had a sexual relationship with his intern, Monica Lewinsky

CONCEPTS

You should be able to define the following concepts, explain their meanings to others not familiar with them, invent your own examples that correctly illustrate the concepts, and apply them correctly to novel applications.

- Ambiguity
- Burden of proof
- Ceremonial function of language
- Cognitive function of language
- Connotation
- Definition
- Denotation
- Directive function of language
- Equivocation
- Essence
- Euphemism

- Expressive function of language
- Jargon
- Lexical definition
- Malphemism
- Marked term
- Neologism
- Newspeak
- Operational definition
- Ostensive definition
- Performative function of language
- Precising definition
- Persuasive definition

- Propaganda
- Racial or ethnic language
- Sapir-Whorf hypothesis of linguistic relativity
- Semantics
- Setting the agenda
- Sexist language
- Slang
- Statement
- Stipulative definition
- Syntax
- Theoretical definition
- Vague language
- Verbal dispute

Foundational concepts: Cognitive function of language, directive function of language, essence, euphemism, malphemism, setting the agenda, theoretical definition

NOTES

i. Lewis Carroll, *Through the Looking-Glass* (New York: W.W. Norton & Company, 1971), 163. Lewis Carroll, the pen name of Charles Dodgson (1832-1898), was an ordained minister in the Anglican Church who taught mathematics at Oxford University.

ii. Plato (428-348 BCE) defines thinking as "the inward dialogue carried on by the mind with itself." See his *Sophist*, 263e. Another great philosopher, Rene Descartes (1596-1650), considered the use of language to be so fundamental to humanity that he rejected the possibility that non-human animals or machines could either speak or be taught to use a language of any kind.

> [I]f there were machines which bore a resemblance to our body and imitated our actions as far as it were morally possible to do so, we would always have [one] very certain test by which to recognize that, for all that, they were not real men.... [T]hey could never use speech or other signs as we do when placing our thoughts on record for the benefit of others. For we can easily understand a machine's being constituted so that it can utter words.... But it never happens that it arranges its speech in various ways, in order to reply appropriately to everything that may be said in its presence, as even the lowest type of man can do.... [T]here are no [humans] so depraved and stupid, without even excepting idiots, that they cannot arrange different words together, forming of them a statement by which they make known their thoughts; while, on the other hand, there is no other animal, however perfect and fortunately circumstanced it may be, which can do the same.

> From *Discourse on the Method*, translated by E. S. Haldane and G.R.T. Ross, (New York: Dover Publications), 116-117.

iii. See D.I. Slobin, *Psycholinguistics* (London: Scott, Foresman, and Company, 1974), and J.N. Hattiangodi, *How Is Language Possible?* (Peru, IL: Open Court, 1987). See also Benjamin Whorf, *Language, Thought, and Reality* (Boston: MIT Press, 1956).

iv. See Plato's *Cratylus* for an early discussion on the role language plays in thought. In the 20th century, the works of philosophers such as Bertrand Russell (1872-1970), Rudolf Carnap (1891-1970), A.J. Ayer (1910-1995), Ludwig Wittenstein (1889-1951), P.F. Strawson (1919-), Suzanne Langer (1895-), J.L. Austin (1911-1960), and Noam Chomsky (1928-) have played significant roles in this ongoing investigation.

v. This theory was discussed explicitly for the first time by Plato. See his *Sophist*, 263ff.

vi. Notice that the statement "Today is Friday" can be true when said at one time and false at another. There is a philosophical puzzle here: if a true statement corresponds to the facts, to what does a false statement correspond—non-facts? What could a non-fact be?

vii. (Berkeley: University of California Press, 1988).

viii. Humpty Dumpty's concerns about language mastery were anticipated by the English philosopher Thomas Hobbes (1588-1679), whose Leviathan (1651) assigns the role of language master to the political sovereign of the commonwealth.

ix. *1984* (New York: Harcourt, Brace, and Co., 1949), 246-7.

x. Thus, when the grammatical context normally requires the use of the word "he" in what is truly a gender-neutral situation, I have adopted "s/he" as a non-standard, but acceptable, alternative.

xi. See John Lyons, *Introduction to Theoretical Linguistics* (Cambridge: Cambridge University Press, 1971), 79. Janice Moulton's article, "The Myth of the Neutral 'Man'," reprinted in *Feminism and Philosophy* (Totowa, NJ: Littlefield, Adams & Co., 1981), 124-137, contains a useful discussion of how marked terms propagate sexism. For a good general overview of some of the many issues involved in sexist language, see *Sexist Language*, edited by Mary Vetterling-Braggin, (Totowa, NJ: Littlefield, Adams & Co., 1981).

xii. Simone de Beauvoir, *The Second Sex*, translated by H.M. Parshley, (New York: Alfred A. Knopf, Inc., 1953), xv-xvi. De Beauvoir (1908-1987), French philosopher and social critic, was one of the leading French intellects of this century. Her major work, *The Second Sex*, marks the beginning of contemporary feminist studies.

xiii. "Malphemism" is a neologism I have coined; it seems to express my point appropriately.

CHAPTER THREE
Deductive Arguments

INTRODUCTION:
THE NATURE OF ARGUMENTS

In Chapter One you were introduced to the four-fold factors that enable the mind to construct perceptions from the data given to the senses. The first two of these factors are seeing as and seeing-that. If you saw the bird in the sky as an eagle, then you knew that certain other things were true too; but how did you know which things were also true? Because perceptions are theory-laden, and you know the theory eagle. Your ability to extend your knowledge beyond the data immediately present to your senses by utilizing the knowledge embodied in theories depends upon (among other things) the application of certain rules of **logic**. Logic studies the concepts, rules, and paradigms that govern the correct use of reasoning. Knowledge of your present surroundings (seeing something as...) and knowledge of what is not immediately present to your senses (seeing that...) are both impossible without the application of reason. Therefore, let us turn our attention to a bit of logic.[i]

The study of logic is one of the oldest branches of epistemology.[ii] Logicians seek to separate the correct uses of reasoning from its incorrect uses. In making this distinction, logicians speak of **arguments**. By the term "argument" I do not mean a fight you may have with someone, but a series of claims, some of which (called **premises**) purport to provide evidence for the truth of others (called **conclusions**). A **claim** is a statement that maintains that something or other is the case. The **Law of Excluded Middle**, one of the laws of logic, mandates that *all claims are either true or false*. There are no other (or middle) possibilities between being true or being false. To say that all claims must be either true or false is to say that all claims have a **truth-value**. Claims must be either true of false, but not both at the same time. This is called the **Law of (Non)Contradiction** by logicians, and it is one of the basic laws of logic. Claims typically are contained within the sentences that make up our language—consider, for example, all of the claims made by the sentences that compose the previous paragraph. However, not all sentences contain claims. Many perfectly proper, grammatically correct sentences do not maintain that something or other is the case, but ask questions or express commands or emotions instead. The sentence "Does this bus go to Times Square?" does not make a claim. Neither do the sentences "Close the window!" or "Go team! Fight! Win!" None of these sentences state anything that is either true or false. In order to determine whether a given sentence expresses a claim, there is no substitution for the understanding of what the sentence says.

All arguments contain at least two claims, one premise and one conclusion. No argument can consist of just one claim. A claim such as "If it rains, the ball game will be called off," does not by itself present an argument, but only a hypothetical (or conditional) statement, the logic of which I will discuss below. While any argument may contain more than one premise, logicians generally agree that *an argument contains only one conclusion*. If a given set of claims contains more than one conclusion, it is said that these claims compose a **compound argument**, or a set of arguments. The number of arguments in the set consists of the number of conclusions contained in the claims. To further complicate matters, the same claim may be both a conclusion of one argument and a premise of another argument at the same time. This is another reason why these common occurrences are called compound arguments.

One of the first difficult tasks for the beginning logic student is the identification of the arguments contained in any given set of claims. You can't analyze and evaluate an argument until you can identify it. To identify an argument is to determine which of its claims are premises and which one is its conclusion. The premises purport[iii] to provide the evidence for the establishment of the truth of the conclusion. The conclusion is what the premises purport to establish. Consider the following argument:

Example I.

1. If it rains more, the game tonight will surely be called off.
2. It looks like it's going to rain again.
3. Therefore it doesn't seem very likely the game will be played tonight.[iv]

Claims 1 and 2 in this argument are the premises. Claim 3 is the conclusion. Claims 1 and 2 purport to establish the truth of claim 3.

Frequently, not all of the premises of an argument are stated explicitly. Sometimes the conclusion itself may even be missing. Cases like this, which are very common, are called **enthymemes** by logicians. *Enthymemes are theory-laden; they assume that the reader or listener can fill in the missing parts of the argument using the context in which the argument is presented or from commonly presupposed background information.* For instance, if you asked me whether tonight's game was still on I might simply say to you, "If it rains any more the game will be called off, and it looks like rain now," assuming that you can draw the requisite conclusion for yourself. Before you can evaluate an argument that is an enthymeme, you have to fill in the missing parts of the argument. This may not be very easy, especially if you don't know much about the subject matter of the argument in the first place.

To determine whether any given claim is a premise or a conclusion in an argument, you have to understand what all of the statements mean. If you don't understand the claims of the argument, you won't be able to evaluate it. In identifying particular passages as premises or conclusions it is helpful to look for certain words which frequently serve as **premise indicators** or **conclusion indicators**. Words that serve in English as common premise indicators include: because, since, as, in virtue of, in view of, and given that. Words that serve as common conclusion indicators include: therefore, thus, hence, so, consequently, it follows that, as a result, and implies. There are, of course, many examples of premises and conclusions that do not contain any of these indicator words, and sometimes the uses of these words are not intended to indicate premises or conclusions. Again, to determine which claims made in a given discourse are premises and which ones are conclusions there is no substitute for understanding the meaning of every statement presented in that discourse.

Once an argument (along with its separate parts) has been identified, it can be evaluated as either a good argument or a poor one. In a good argument, the premises provide good reasons for saying that the conclusion is true. In a poor argument, they do not. While good arguments are not labeled by a common name (other than good arguments), poor arguments usually are called **fallacies**. To say that an argument is a fallacy is not to say that its conclusion is false, though that may be the case. Rather, it is to say that its premises fail to provide adequate support for its conclusion. *Fallacies may have true conclusions, but their true conclusions are unsupported by their premises.*

There are two different kinds of arguments—deductive and inductive. The difference between deductive and inductive arguments is easy to state in principle, but not always as easy to establish in practice. An argument is **deductive** if the premises purport to establish the conclusions *with necessity.* All deductive arguments claim that the conclusion follows necessarily from the premises, so that if the premises were true (whether they actually are true or not) the conclusion would have to be true, too. **Inductive** arguments only claim that *the premises make the conclusion likely or probable*, not necessary.

To determine whether any given argument is deductive or inductive you have to understand which of the two relationships (probability or necessity) binds together the premises and the conclusion. Sometimes this is easy. Either the words of the argument or the context of their use make the answer obvious. But sometimes it is very difficult to tell whether a given example is intended to be understood as an inductive or a deductive argument. When this happens, it is best to treat the example first as deductive and then as inductive. *A good deductive argument is a different kind of argument than a good inductive argument,* and the rules used to determine whether deductive arguments are good are different rules than those used to determine whether inductive arguments are good. An argument may be a bad deductive argument but a good inductive argument at the same time. This is why it can be important for purposes of evaluation to treat a given example first as a deductive argument and then as an inductive argument. For the remainder of this chapter, I will be concerned solely with the rules used for evaluating deductive arguments. I will consider the evaluation of inductive arguments in later chapters.

SOUNDNESS AND VALIDITY₁

Validity₁ and soundness are the factors that distinguish a good deductive argument from a poor one. A good deductive argument is both valid₁ and sound. **Sound arguments**[v] are valid₁ arguments that have *only* true premises and true conclusions. Logic is generally of no use in determining the truth of the premises of an argument. In fact, logic isn't even interested in attempting to determine whether the premises of an argument are true or not. That's not the function of logic. *Logic is concerned* solely *with the relationship that ties together the premises and the conclusion.* The premises of arguments are like the flesh of living beings. Bones are what allow the flesh to hang together, and logic is the study of bones, not of flesh. This bone/flesh relationship is illustrative of the concept of validity₁ in deductive logic. To determine whether an argument is sound, you have to use logic to determine first whether the argument is valid₁, and then you will have to go outside of the confines of logic to your empirical experience of the world to determine whether the premises are true. Therefore a good argument is one that concurs both with the rules of logic and with certain facts about the world. As human beings we are all interested in determining whether an argument is good. As logicians, we are interested only in determining whether the argument is valid₁. But validity₁ is part of what makes good arguments good, so all of us need to learn a little logic.

Before I continue with this section, I emphasize some truths about validity₁. In ordinary English the word "valid" can be used interchangeably with the word "good," so that "a good argument" and "a valid argument" typically mean the same thing. Logicians wish to avoid the confusion that may result from this by confining the term "valid$_1$" only to deductive arguments. I will follow this standard practice, but I will use the subscript ($_1$) to indicate that the term "validity" in this case means the logical sense of the term, and not its ordinary sense. And finally, the word "true" cannot be used to characterize an argument. There is no such thing as a true argument. Only propositions (or claims) can be true or false. *Arguments either are valid or invalid, wonderful or crazy, sound or unsound, profound or stupid. They are never true or false.*

Though the concept of validity$_1$ is deceptively simple in theory to define, many people have a difficult time in grasping its meaning. *An argument is valid$_1$* if and only if *it is impossible for all of its premises to be true and its conclusion false at the same time.* Validity$_1$ concerns the relationship between the premises and the conclusion rather than their individual correctness. In a valid$_1$ argument the conclusion would have to be true if the premises were all true. But the premises don't have to be true for the argument to be valid$_1$—for that matter neither does the conclusion. The definition of validity$_1$ simply maintains that if the premises were true (whether they actually are or not) the conclusion would have to be true too. "Yeah," you ask, "but are the premises really true? Is the conclusion really true?" And logic answers, "I don't care whether the premises or conclusions are actually true or not. That's not the issue here." Concern with the truth of the premises or the conclusion at this stage of the argument is an illustration of failure to accept the logical task (see below). If you are worried about the truth of the premises or the conclusion, you have moved past the question of validity$_1$ to the question of soundness.

Many students persistently confuse validity$_1$ with whether the premises of an argument are true. This error is easy to commit because, as discussed above, the ordinary language use of the word "valid" simply means "good." When asked to assess the validity$_1$ of an argument, you might focus instead on the question of whether any of the claims in it are true, or whether the argument "makes sense." Psychologist Mary Henle calls this error the **failure to accept the logical task**.[vi] This error consists in substituting for the task you are assigned—which is the determination of validity$_1$—another possible task, such as the determination of the truth-value of the given claims of the argument or of claims different from those presented because you don't like or understand the actual claims. This sort of mistake is very common. Avoid it. Be sure that you actually are doing what you are supposed to be doing. If you are asked to determine an argument's validity$_1$, then determine that argument's validity$_1$.

How can you tell whether any given deductive argument is valid$_1$? This takes both an understanding of the rules of deductive logic and plenty of practice applying these rules. Real life cases are frequently much more difficult to assess than the nice, tidy examples I supply. You know that, and logicians do too, which is why they have spent thousands of years devising the simplest possible methods for determining the validity of arguments. Their results have been very good indeed. Here are some examples of valid$_1$ and invalid$_1$ arguments that apply what I have just said. Note the possible combinations of truth-values: 1) true premises and a true conclusion; 2) false premises and a true conclusion; and 3) false premises and a false conclusion, *but not* 4) true premises and a false conclusion.

Example II.

1. If you drop an atomic bomb on Hiroshima, then lots of people would be killed.

2. An atom bomb was dropped on Hiroshima.

3. Therefore lots of people were killed. [true premises, true conclusion]

Example III.

1. If I'm Santa Claus, then 2+2=4.

2. I'm Santa Claus.

3. Therefore 2+2=4. [false premises, true conclusion]

Example IV.

1. If I'm Santa Claus, then Germany won World War II.
2. I'm Santa Claus.
3. Therefore Germany won World War II. [false premises, false conclusion]

Examples II, III, and IV are all examples of valid₁ arguments. Had their premises all been true, their conclusions would have to be true too. They are all valid₁ arguments because they are all examples of the same valid₁ **argument format**. An argument format is the internal structure of the argument. In the case of examples II, III, and IV that structure is:

    1. If A, then B.
    2. A
    3. Therefore B.

Any argument with this format is automatically valid₁ because the argument format is a valid₁ format. In this case the format is called **modus ponens** by logicians. All instances of the modus ponens format are automatically valid₁ because of the format alone.

Consider the following argument:

Example V.

1. If I'm Santa Claus, then my wife is Mrs. Claus.
2. My wife isn't Mrs. Claus.
3. Therefore I'm not Santa Claus. [true premises, true conclusion]

This example is a substitution instance of another valid₁ argument format called **modus tollens** by logicians.

    1. If A, then B.
    2. Not B.
    3. Therefore not A.

This is the logical format for any modus tollens argument. Modus tollens is identical to modus ponens in that both have hypothetical claims as their first premise. They are logically different formats in that the second premise of the format modus tollens negates the consequent of the first premise (the part of the hypothetical starting with "then,"), whereas

the second premise of modus ponens affirms the antecedent of the first premise (the part of the hypothetical starting with "if").

Now consider the following examples:

Example VI.

1. If I'm Santa Claus, then 2 +2 = 4.
2. 2 +2 = 4.
3. Therefore I'm Santa Claus. [false premises, false conclusion]

Example VII.

1. If it rains any more, the game will be called off.
2. The game was called off.
3. Therefore it must have rained. [true premises, true or false conclusion]

Examples VI and VII are examples of the formal fallacy of **affirming the consequent**. They follow the format:

    1. If A, then B.
    2. B.
    3. Therefore A.

Remember that the consequent is the "then" clause of a hypothetical claim. To say that its truth entails the truth of the antecedent—the "if" clause of the hypothetical claim—is a mistake of logical form, hence it is a formal fallacy. In Example VI, I may or may not be Santa Claus, but not because 2 + 2 = 4. In Example VII, the game may have been called off for reasons other than rain (an invasion by Martians, for example).

Consider this example:

Example VIII.

1. If you win the Publisher's Clearinghouse Sweepstakes, you'll be rich.
2. You didn't win the Publisher's Clearinghouse Sweepstakes.
3. So you can't be rich. [true premises, true or false conclusion]

Example VIII is a substitution instance of another common formal fallacy, **denying the antecedent**. It has the following format:

1. If A, then B.
2. Not A.
3. Therefore not B.

To deny the antecedent is to assume mistakenly that the "if" clause provides the only possible support for the "then" clause of the claim, and if it isn't true, the consequent can't be true either. Contrary to the claims of Example VIII, Bill Gates and Donald Trump are both rich even though neither of them has won the Publisher's Clearinghouse Sweepstakes.

The formal fallacies of denying the antecedent and affirming the consequent are difficult to distinguish from the valid₁ argument formats of modus tollens and modus ponens. This is true for two reasons. (1) All four formats have the same first premise, namely "if A, then B." And (2) we see the connection "if A, then B" as the different connection "A = B," where "A = B" is understood as "B if and only if A." Thus "if A, then B" is mistakenly understood as (1) "if and only if A, then B," and (2) "if not A, then not B," and (3) "if B, than A," and (4) "if not B, then not A." But, as we have seen, claims 1, 2, 3, and 4 do not amount to the same thing. If the format "if A, then B" did mean "A = B," then all four formats would be valid₁. But "if A, then B" does not equal "A = B." Practice is required to distinguish between them.

Evaluate the validity of the following arguments.

A. 1. If it snows hard, school will be called off.
    2. It didn't snow.
    3. So school wasn't called off.

B. 1. If it snows hard, school will be called off.
    2. It snowed hard.
    3. So school was called off.

C. 1. If it snows hard, school will be called off.
    2. School was called off.
    3. So it must have snowed hard.

D. 1. If it snows hard, school will be called off.
    2. School was not called off.
    3. So it must not have snowed hard.

Here is another formal fallacy to be aware of. Consider these examples:

Example IX.

1. If you drop an atomic bomb on Hiroshima, then lots of people would be killed.
2. An atom bomb was dropped on Hiroshima.
3. Therefore the U. S. won World War II. [true premises, true conclusion]

Example X.

1. If you drop an atomic bomb on Mars, then lots of Martians would be killed.
2. An atom bomb was dropped on Mars.
3. Therefore Germany lost World War Two. [false premises, true conclusion]

Example XI.

1. If you drop an atomic bomb on Hiroshima, then lots of people would be killed.
2. An atomic bomb was dropped on Hiroshima.
3. Therefore Germany won World War II. [true premises, false conclusion]

Examples IX, X, and XI are all formal fallacies. Example IX is an invalid₁ argument because even though its premises and its conclusion are all true, its conclusion still could have been false. Though it happens in fact to be true, it doesn't *have* to be true given the premises mentioned. *It is the trademark of a valid deductive argument that its premises necessitate the truth of its conclusion*, which is not the case in this example. Examples IX, X, and XI are invalid₁ *not* because their premises or conclusions are false, but because their premises fail to provide evidence that is even relevant to establishing the truth of their conclusions. They are instances of the formal fallacy called **non sequitur** by logicians. "Non sequitur" means "it does not follow;" that is, the conclusion does not follow from the stated premises. Non sequitur arguments follow the format:

1. If A, then B.
2. A.
3. Therefore C.

This format is invalid₁ because their conclusions are not contained within their premises. As a general rule of validity₁ an argument's conclusion must appear somewhere within its premises or it is a non sequitur.

Discuss the following non sequiturs:

A. 1. Iraq starts with an "I."
    2. If we win the war against terrorism, we must be prepared to fight against countries with names that start with the letter "I."
    3. Therefore Iowa and Idaho are next.

B. 1. If we go to the movies, you'll want popcorn.
    2. If we eat too much popcorn, we'll need the giant size drink.
    3. Therefore, if we go to the movies, we'd better get candy.

II. SOME OTHER VALID₁ ARGUMENT FORMATS

Argument forms involving hypothetical claims of the sort presented above are not the only common argument forms. Some arguments link two or more hypothetical statements together to form a chain of premises. Consider Example XII:

Example XII.

1. If Osama bin Laden gets away with the attack on the World Trade Center, he will strike again.
2. If he strikes again, his next attack will be even more deadly.
3. If his next attack is more deadly, it will involve nuclear, biological or chemical weapons.
4. So if Osama gets away with the World Trade Center attack, he'll strike us with nuclear, biological, or chemical weapons next.

Example XII is an **extended hypothetical** in that it merely links together a series of hypothetical claims. In principle, there is no limit to the number of hypothetical claims that can be

linked in this manner. The rules that govern simple hypothetical argument formats are the same ones that govern the extended hypothetical argument format.

Evaluate the validity₁ of the following extended hypothetical arguments.

A. 1. If Emma is going to go to the prom with Boyd, she'll need a new dress.
    2. If she is to get a new dress in time for the prom, she needs to get to the mall before it closes.
    3. The mall closes in an hour.
    4. So she needs to get going pronto.

B. 1. If I watch another episode of *American Idol*, I'll be forced to listen to more terrible screeching.
    2. If I listen to any more screeching, I'll get another migraine.
    3. I'll do whatever it takes to avoid another migraine.
    4. So I won't watch another episode of *American Idol*.
    5. Or I'll only watch it if the TV is on mute.

C. 1. If we get another pet, it will have fleas.
    2. If we get fleas, I'll get bitten.
    3. If I get bitten, I'll scratch like crazy.
    4. If I scratch like crazy, I'll make myself bleed.
    5. The sight of my own blood makes me sick to my stomach.
    6. So if we get a new pet, I'm going to get sick to my stomach.

Here is another example of a valid argument format.

Example XIII.

1. Either we can go to the mountains or we can go to the beach for our vacation this year.
2. The beach is covered with an oil spill, so it's out.
3. Therefore we're going to the mountains for our vacation.

This argument form is called **disjunctive syllogism** by logicians because one of the premises (in Example XIII, the first premise) lists two (or more options) and the following premises rule out all but one of the options contained in the first premise. The conclusion then asserts the remaining option. With disjunctive syllogism there is no limit to the number of choices listed, but *the argument form is only deductively valid₁ if all but one of the listed choices are subsequently ruled out by the remaining premises.*[vii]

Care must be taken with this form of argument. It does not say that the last remaining option is the case if the first option is the case. That would be a formal fallacy.

Example XIV.

1. Either we can go to the mountains or we can go to the beach for our vacation this year.
2. We can go to the beach.
3. Therefore we're going to the mountains for our vacation.

Example XIV is a formally invalid₁ argument. The problem here is that the terms "either/or" are ambiguous. In one of the meanings of "either A or B," selecting option A is perfectly compatible with also selecting option B. ("You can either have apple pie or chocolate mousse for desert, or be a pig and have them both for that matter.") In the other sense of "either/or," choosing one option prevents you from choosing the other, as in the case of an SAT multiple choice question. It is only when all of the other options are *eliminated* that the remaining one is affirmed. When one option is affirmed, nothing follows about the status of the other options because of the ambiguity of "either/or."

Secondly, though a particular disjunctive syllogism argument may be valid₁, it may not be sound. If all available options are not listed in the either/or premise, the example might be a **false dilemma**, that is, an argument form that ignores other real choices. Or the other premises of the argument may fail to rule out all of the options except one. Either of these faults would make the argument invalid₁.

Finally, though a particular disjunctive syllogism may be formally invalid₁, it still may be a strong inductive argument. This depends on certain factual considerations concerning the truth of the premises of the argument. Finding out, for example, that either of two shirts on sale is still available doesn't do you much good if you can't afford either, but buying either or both may be tempting if you can afford both.

Evaluate the validity₁ of the following disjunctive syllogisms.

A. 1. For dessert tonight you can have apple pie or chocolate mousse.
   2. Wait a minute; we're out of apple pie.
   3. Therefore you can have the mousse.

B. 1. That bird up there is either an eagle or a goose.
   2. Eagles have been extinct for years.
   3. Therefore it must be a crow.

C. 1. When your car won't start it's either out of gas or the battery's shot.
   2. The headlights work, so the battery's all right.
   3. Therefore you're out of gas.

D. 1. The killer is either Ms. Plum, the Tooth Fairy, Cock Robin, or the Count.
   2. The Count's fingerprints are all over the murder weapon.
   3. Therefore, Ms. Plum must be innocent.

In summary, to assess the logic of an argument, use the following procedure: First, identify the argument. Determine which of its claims are premises and which claim is its conclusion. Secondly, determine whether the argument is deductive or inductive. Thirdly, if the argument is deductive determine its validity₁. Fourthly, if the argument is valid₁ determine whether it is sound. If a deductive argument is valid₁ and sound then you have the best possible reason to believe that its conclusion is true based upon the evidence presented by its premises.

Evaluate the following arguments.

A. 1. If you think I'm getting into that boat, you're crazy.
2. It leaks like a sieve.
3. The sky is getting dark, and it looks like its going to pour.
4. I want my mommy.

B. 1. If you keep driving like that, you're going to wreck.
2. You show no sign that you've got the intelligence to drive sanely.
3. Therefore, if I drive with you, I'm doomed too.

C. 1. Roses are red.
2. Violets are blue.
3. Ralph's face is red.
4. He's in love with you.

D. 1. Since Bush took office America has been on a ceaseless war against terrorism.
2. If terrorism triumphs, this country is doomed.
3. But we've never lost a war yet.
4. So we'll beat terrorism too.

E. 1. "Our ideas reach no farther than our experience."
2. "We have no experience of divine attributes and operations."
3. "I need not conclude my syllogism; you can draw the conclusion yourself."
—David Hume,
Dialogues Concerning Natural Religion

F. 1. All men are mortal.
2. All Greeks were men.
3. Socrates was a Greek.
4. Hence Socrates probably was mortal.

G. 1. If you play some rap music backwards, you can hear the words "Vote for girlie Democrats."
2. Everyone knows that rap music was written by the devil.
3. So Satan is a girlie Democrat.

H. 1. Either you can go to college for your undergraduate degree, you can join the military, or you can go right into the work force.
2. You're too dumb to go to college, and you're too chicken to go into the military.
3. Therefore you're headed to the work force. Practice saying, "Do you want extra fries with that, man?"

I. 1. If you go to the bank every day, soon you'll run out of your parents' money.
2. If you run out of your parents' money, you'll have to earn your own or be a failure in life.
3. You'll never earn your own money.
4. So if you go to the bank every day, you're bound to be a failure in life!

CONCEPTS

You should be able to define the following concepts, explain their meanings to others not familiar with them, invent your own examples that correctly illustrate the concepts, and apply them correctly to novel applications.

- Affirming the consequent
- Antecedent
- Argument
- Argument format
- Claim
- Compound argument
- Compound claim
- Conclusion
- Conclusion indicators
- Consequent
- Deductive argument

- Denying the antecedent
- Disjunctive syllogism
- Enthymeme
- Failure to accept the logical task
- False dilemma
- Formal fallacy
- Hypothetical statement
- Inductive argument
- Law of (non)Contradiction
- Law of Excluded Middle

- Logic
- Modus ponens
- Modus tollens
- Non sequitur
- Premise
- Premise indicator
- Simple claim
- Sound argument
- Statement
- Statement form
- Valid₁

Foundational concepts: Argument, conclusion, deductive argument, failure to accept the logical task, formal fallacy, inductive argument, logic, premise, sound argument, valid₁

NOTES

i. For a good survey of the main issues of logic see Irving Copi, *Introduction To Logic*, 11th edition, (New York: MacMillian Publishing Company, 2004). I can do no more here than briefly point out certain key ideas of logic of which no educated person should be ignorant. It is a scandal that most individuals do not study logic until they enter college. Imagine not studying math or science until you get to college!

   You will find that this chapter is much easier to follow if you pay attention carefully to the exact meanings of the definitions you are about to encounter. Most mistakes that are made by introductory logic students are the results of the failure to learn the exact meanings of the terms employed by logicians.

ii. The Greek philosopher Aristotle (384–322 B. C.) generally is credited with the development of logic. See his *Categories*, *On Interpretation*, and *Prior Analytics*.

iii. I keep on using the word "purport" because a given statement may claim (or try) to provide evidence for a conclusion but in fact fail to do so because, for example, it is simply irrelevant to establishing the truth of the conclusion. Arguments are constructed by humans, and what any given individual believes to be relevant towards establishing his or her conclusion may not in fact be so. If s/he believes that his or her claim is relevant towards establishing the conclusion and thus sticks it into the argument for that purpose as a premise, then at least the premise *purports* to establish the truth of the conclusion.

iv. I have numbered each of the claims to help make it easier to refer to them. When identifying and analyzing arguments, it is generally useful to number each separate claim. This practice will also help you to see the structure of the argument.

v. For the remainder of the chapter I will use the term "argument" with reference only to deductive arguments unless I signify otherwise.

vi. Mary Henle, "On the Relationship Between Logic and Thinking," *Psychological Review* (vol. 69, 1962): 366-378.

vii. The options deductive argument format is closely related to Mill's method of residues (see Chapter Six, Section V) and the problem solving method of trial and error (see Chapter Ten, Section I.).

CHAPTER FOUR

Inductive Arguments: Probability and Statistics

In the previous chapter, I introduced you to the concept of an argument and distinguished between deductive and inductive arguments. A deductive argument is one in which the premises purport to establish its conclusion with necessity, whereas an inductive argument's premises only purport to establish its conclusion with some degree of probability. In this chapter, we will look at some of the important ideas contained within the wide-ranging field of inductive logic. Then in Chapters Five and Six, we will put together the ideas presented in Chapters One, Three, and Four to see how they combine to produce the scientific/critical method of problem solving and to generate the causal arguments so commonly used by the scientific/critical method.

All inductive arguments—and there are many kinds—have one thing in common; they all maintain that their conclusions follow from their premises only with some degree of possibility or other, and never with absolute certainty (as is the case with deductive arguments). The most commonly used terms signifying the degree of possibility with which the conclusion of an inductive argument is said to follow from its premises are the words "probably" and "probability." Other words which are synonyms for the concept of probability are the words "likely," "apparently," "could," "could be," "may," "maybe," and so forth. While the appearance of these words in arguments is a good indication that the argument is inductive, there are plenty of common arguments which will contain no terms indicating whether their creators intend them to be understood as inductive or deductive arguments. In determining whether any given argument is really inductive or deductive there is no substitution for an understanding of what the argument says. Sometimes even the creator of an argument may not know whether the argument is intended to be understood as inductive or deductive. When this happens, the only fair thing to do is to treat the argument first as a deductive argument, applying the canons for assessing deductive arguments to it, and then as an inductive argument, applying the canons for assessing inductive arguments to it. There is nothing that prevents any particular argument from being both deductive and inductive at the same time. It all depends on how the argument is understood.

The rules for assessing inductive arguments are not the same as those used for assessing deductive arguments. While deductive rules are primarily concerned with the concept of validity₁, validity₁ is not an issue in inductive logic. In the previous chapter, we looked at a few of the common formal fallacies found in deductive logic, including denying the antecedent and affirming the consequent. Both of these fallacies produce formally invalid₁ arguments, but either of these intellectual operations may produce plausible inductive arguments. This is because inductive arguments are evaluated in terms of their **strength**. A strong inductive argument is a good argument, and a weak inductive argument is a poor one. There are many degrees of strength, and one inductive argument may be slightly, moderately, or much stronger than another. It always makes sense with any inductive argument to say that the addition of further evidence will strengthen (or weaken) the probability that the conclusion follows from the argument's premises.

Consider the following argument: "If Ralph is late, then he had an accident. Ralph isn't late. Therefore, he didn't have an accident." If this is intended as a deductive argument, it is an example of the fallacy of denying the antecedent, but if this is intended as an inductive argument, it may be pretty strong. Accidents tend to be time consuming and can delay our arrival—it all depends on the type and severity of the accident you get into. Some are more time consuming than others, though, and maybe Ralph had only a minor accident that failed to inconvenience his travel time at all. Whether or not the conclusion is true does not affect the strength of the argument here, rather, as with deductive arguments, it is the relationship between the premises and the conclusion that is important.

Finally, consider this argument: "If it rains, the baseball game will be called off. The game was called off. Therefore, it rained." Again, if this is considered to be a deductive argument, it is a fallacy (in this case the fallacy of affirming the consequent) because there are reasons for calling games off other than rain. Considered as an inductive argument, howev-

er, this may be a strong one. The most frequent reason for calling baseball games off is in fact rain. But baseball games can also be called off because the umpires went out on strike at the last minute, because the visiting team failed to show up, or because war was declared. Again we have a fallacious deductive argument that could be a good inductive argument, though the addition of further evidence would help us to evaluate it better. The addition of further evidence will always help you evaluate the strength of an inductive argument.

I. GENERALIZATIONS

One of the most common forms of inductive arguments goes under the name of **generalization**. While there are many different versions of generalizations, they all share certain common characteristics:

1. They all refer to classes of things which share at least one—and usually many—possible variable(s). Consider the class of used cars or athletic contests or test results. The class of used cars contains variables with respect to the ages of the cars, their prices, their mileage, etc.

2. They all pick out a few examples (called the **sample population**) from the main class (called the **whole population**). "I wrestled once..." "I used to drive a 1960 VW Beetle..." "The first time I took the SAT..."

3. They discover certain characteristics about these samples. "...against a person who outweighed me by 150 lbs," "...which had a top speed of 42 miles per hour," "...I scored a 1300."

4. They all then proceed to draw conclusions about the whole population based upon the evidence presented by the sample. "Never wrestle against a person who outweighs you by 150 lbs. unless you want to lose." "If you want to drive a car with pick-up, don't drive a Beetle." "I'm a genius at taking tests."

In possessing the characteristics above, *generalizations can be defined as inductive arguments*

*which move from truth claims about sample popula-
tions of a particular variable to truth claims about
whole populations for that variable.* Generalizations
are one of the most frequently encountered
forms of argument. The armed forces of this
country, for example, recently have become
concerned about the strength of the bolts
which are used to hold together parts of military equipment. It is feared that millions of
these bolts may be substandard, which in this
case means that they are likely to break easily.
Fragile bolts are not the best things out of
which to construct tanks, ships, and planes.
But how could anyone know that so many of
these bolts were fragile? Certainly all of them
could not be tested without spending a fortune. The military did what anyone would have
done in such a situation, they tested a few of
the bolts selected at random and generalized
from the results. Illustrations like this could be
produced infinitely.

But how good is this type of argument? It
depends. Remember, these are all inductive
arguments, so the evidence being presented by
the premises is only purporting to make the
conclusion likely (or highly likely). What is it in
the evidence being presented by the premises
about the sample population that makes conclusions regarding the whole population likely?
It is the assumption that the sample population
is **representative** of the whole population with
regard to the variable in question. To say that
the sample is representative of the whole population is to say that, with regard to the variable
being considered (strength, engine power,
intelligence), what is true of the sample is true
of the general population class because all
members of the class are relevantly similar with
respect to this variable. Even though he outweighs me by 150 lbs., this opponent is just like
any other opponent who outweighs me by 150
lbs. My 1960 VW engine is typical of its kind. My
1300 SAT score is typical of all of my test scores
(or at least all of my possible SAT scores). If the
assumption of relevant similarity regarding
these variables is true, the inductive argument
based upon it is a strong one.

The key to evaluating arguments like these
lies in assessing the claim of relevant similarity
regarding the specified variables. Remember,
the factors you are dealing with here are variables, which by definition range over a number
of possible values. Is the opponent that I once
wrestled really typical of the class of wrestling
opponents? Maybe so, but maybe not. To determine this sort of thing I would normally have to
have more information. Was this opponent, for
example, an experienced wrestler or weight
lifter, or perhaps on steroids? Does he answer to
the name "Hulk" and get green when he's mad,
or am I just a wimp? If further information shows
this opponent of mine to be truly typical of the
class of wrestling opponents as a whole, my conclusion is well founded. Inductive arguments
moving from claims about a few examples, or
even one example, to conclusions about a whole
population are perfectly reasonable if the properties singled out by the variable in question really are shared with sufficient similarity by the
whole population. I will call this type of inductive
generalization a **relevant similarity argument**.

While relevant similarity arguments are
common and useful forms of inductive arguments, there are several fallacies closely associated with them. The first is called a **hasty generalization**. To commit the fallacy of hasty generalization is to make a generalization when it
is not known whether the sample is sufficiently
similar to the whole population it represents,
and when the sample in fact may not be sufficiently similar to the whole population. If the
sample is unrepresentative regarding the variable in question, the argument is weak. In my
wrestling, I don't know whether my sample is
representative or not; all I have is some evidence (the small sample) about the whole. To
make the argument stronger I need more evidence about the representativeness of the sample. For obvious reasons, this fallacy is called
the fallacy of an unrepresentative sample or a
small sample, depending upon which aspect of
the problem needs to be stressed.[i]

Typically, it is assumed that there is a correlation between the size of the sample and the

representativeness of the sample—the larger the sample size, the more representative the sample is likely to be, but this assumption may not always be true. On the one hand, a sample of one unit may be large and representative enough of a given variable if all the other variables in the range are sufficiently similar to it regarding the variable in question. The problem, of course, consists in knowing whether that condition has in fact been met. On the other hand, even some large samples (of several individual units) may be unrepresentative if they are not drawn from a wide enough range of the general population. *Remember that samples are samples regarding some relevant variable or other.* Variables range through a number of possibilities (or they wouldn't be called variables), and if an insufficient sampling of this range is taken, the fallacy of either a small or unrepresentative sample is going to be committed. A defensible use of the generalization argument demands that the arguer select his or her samples from a sufficiently wide range of possibilities so that it is reasonable to assume that a sufficient number of examples are selected from all of the important possible types. This condition is called the **requirement of total evidence**.

"The requirement for total evidence" is, perhaps, an unfortunate choice of words in that it suggests that the critical thinker would almost always have to know more than s/he could reasonably be expected to know in a great many situations. Only an omniscient being could really know the total evidence in most cases. To avoid this embarrassment, the requirement for total evidence is usually interpreted as maintaining that the critical thinker must make a reasonable effort to satisfy the following conditions:

1. S/he must make every reasonable effort to assure the accuracy of the data being considered.
2. S/he must not fail through inattention or sloth to consider whether key issues are being ignored in the argument being analyzed.

3. S/he must consider whether the premises of the argument are relevant to the conclusion being advanced.

Condition (1) may be difficult or impossible to satisfy in a great many cases depending both on the evidence presented and the empirical nature of the case itself. Condition (2) touches on the main problem within your control as a critical thinker; poor thinking tends to ignore key factors in the argument under discussion, *especially data that doesn't fit the preferred conclusion.* Other important factors include those associated with the representativeness of the sample and with the population range. Care must be taken to assure that the sample fairly represents the range of the actual variable at issue and not some other possible variable associated with the question under consideration. The variables that are key for a given argument depends, of course, on the actual argument in question. Similarly, condition (3) demands that you determine whether the data and rules advanced in the premises are related in the correct manner to the conclusion being advanced. Again, whether this is true or not depends upon the issues in the given argument.

Any generalization argument which commits the fallacy of either a small or an unrepresentative sample contradicts the second condition of the requirement for total evidence. Depending on the argument advanced, the third condition may also be violated. The mistake made by the Bush administration to consider accurately the "evidence" that Iraq possessed weapons of mass destruction is a glaring foreign policy error resulting from the administration's failure to utilize the requirement for total evidence. Iraq had no weapons of mass destruction, and correct intelligence claims to that effect were ignored in favor of mistaken claims that it did.

Do not be tempted to commit another mistake commonly made when analyzing relevant similarity arguments. Just because a particular relevant similarity argument happens to be a hasty generalization, it does not follow necessarily that the argument's conclusion is false.

The conclusion of a hasty generalization argument may be quite true. The reason that this argument would be a fallacy, however, is that the actual evidence brought forth fails to provide much in the way of support for the truth of the conclusion. *To say that an inductive argument is a fallacy is to say that it fails to offer sufficient support for the truth of the argument's conclusion.* This is not to say that the conclusion of the argument is false. Inductive fallacies are simply weak inductive arguments; they need not be arguments with false conclusions. A fallacious inductive argument fails to provide anywhere near the amount of evidence it would really take to establish the truth of what it purports to establish, whereas a strong inductive argument succeeds in providing sufficient reasons for saying that what it purports to establish is indeed true. Fallacious inductive arguments provide poor reasons for belief, and strong inductive arguments provide good reasons for belief.

How good are the following generalizations? What could be done to improve them?

A. Three of my classmates in critical thinking were football players. They all did poorly. It looks like football players aren't cut out to do philosophy.

B. When I was a senior, I dated three girls in a row who were left handed. None of these dates led to another date. After getting rejected for the third time, I gave up on trying to date left handed girls. Now I'm only going to date left handed boys.

C. Russia broke the Salt II agreement and the ABM treaty, therefore Russia will violate the new Caviar Control Treaty, too.

D. With just a little bit of help from steroids, Barry Bonds holds the record for the most home runs in a season in major league baseball. Therefore Joe Weakling could hold the home run record if he had some help, too.

Another fallacy associated with relevant similarity arguments is the **law of small numbers**. In the law of small numbers a few (or even one) instances of a negative report is believed over what are already known to be many instances of positive reports. For example, if you once find that your boyfriend lied to you, you may decide never to trust him again, even though you know that he has never lied to you before. Constructing this in the form of an argument, Judy could reason like this: "Anyone who lies to me once may lie to me again. My boyfriend, Ralph, lied to me once. Once is once too many. Therefore Ralph may lie to me again. Bye, Ralph." An argument of this sort would be truly irrational because it violates the second condition of the requirement of total evidence. Remember that here you are dealing with a variable (how much anyone tells or shares with someone else) of which you already know the value in a great many cases, but because of this one negative case you choose to treat the variable as a constant: Ralph is never to be trusted again. It would, however, be rational to say that he is never to be trusted fully again, but that was already true before he lied to you, because truth telling is a variable. How much anyone tells to anyone else depends upon many fluctuating factors. No one can ever tell the truth, the whole truth, and nothing but the truth, contrary to what we swear to in courts of law.

Arguments committing the fallacy of the law of small numbers form a subset of the many forms of fallacies associated with **availability heuristic**. Availability heuristic is a set of thinking procedures which over-estimate the importance of particular pieces of data simply because these data make a psychologically strong impression on your mind due to their current availability. Because they are "staring you right in the face," so to speak, you easily can succumb to the temptation to overestimate their importance. Judy's argument presented above illustrates this phenomenon nicely. She trusted Ralph only to find out that he lied to her once. The shock of having her trust betrayed motivated her never to trust Ralph again. Judy is then guilty of ignoring the relevant consideration that Ralph has proven trustworthy many times in the past and the fact that truth telling is a variable, not a constant.

The law of small numbers is similar to the small sample fallacy. It looks like a special kind of small sample problem, but there is an important difference between the small sample fallacy and the law of small numbers. I'll use the problem of the military bolts mentioned earlier to explain this. If you were a member of the military investigating this problem, you would commit the small sample fallacy if, knowing nothing about any of the bolts in advance, you selected only a few from all of the millions, tested only these, and formed your judgment on the basis of this alone. You would commit the fallacy of the law of small numbers if you already knew that many (or most) of the bolts were good before you even started yet you still proceeded to select only a few, tested these, found some defective ones, and declared that the whole batch wasn't any good on the basis of the test evidence, ignoring the fact that you already knew that many (or most) of them were good in the first place. *The fallacy of the law of small numbers lies in the irrational rejection of known prior knowledge about the variables of some sample in favor of very limited new knowledge about only a tiny fraction of those variables.*

One way to attempt to salvage a rational argument out of an argument using the law of small numbers is to go back and reinterpret some or all of the positive examples as cleverly disguised negative examples. "OK, so I caught my boyfriend lying to me for the first time, but was that really the first time? Now that I think about it, I can see a bunch of other examples, too." This is a clever way to try to satisfy the second and third conditions of the requirement of total evidence. If your reinterpretation was accurate, you would no longer be committing the fallacy of the law of small numbers. But, commonly enough, your reinterpretation is an incorrect example of seeing as and is itself motivated by the fallacy of the law of small numbers! As I said in the introduction to this book, just because humans have the capacity to think rationally doesn't mean we always do. Sometimes our fallacious ways of thinking are dearer to us than rationality, especially when they are associated with things with which we have strong emotional involvements. If we are forced to choose between being rationally correct but emotionally uncomfortable, and irrationally incorrect but emotionally comfortable, we frequently choose to be irrational. Such is human nature, but at least acknowledge your irrationality in this type of case. Don't claim when you are committing the fallacy of the law of small numbers that you are really being reasonable.

Explain whether the following examples commit the fallacy of the law of small numbers.

A. I used to like cheesecake, but one time I ate some and got really sick. I'll never eat cheesecake again.

B. Just my luck! The first day I had my license I ran over a dog. I'll never drive again.

C. Work in a high rise office building? Nope, not me. I saw what happened on 9/11.

D. I owned a Ford once, and it was always falling apart. I'll never buy another one again.

E. I took a critical thinking class last year and I didn't understand anything. Don't take a critical thinking course or you won't understand anything either.

F. In an unusual case, doctors have reported an instance of a man who laughed so hard while he was drinking cola that he snorted the cola through his nose. Then, through a cascade of "extravagant complications," he suffered a sinus infection which led to gangrene that led to the loss of his nose, both legs, nine fingers and his penis. "Laughing while you drink cola is no laughing matter," doctors warned. The patient is currently being fitted with prosthetic devices.

—News item.

II. PROBABILITY

It is sometimes convenient to cast generalization arguments into statements of **probability**. To say that slugger Ralph is batting .300 means that three times in every ten at bats Ralph gets a hit. The odds on your chances of being hit by lightning are one in a million. Ninety per cent of the Volvos sold in America are still on the road, so if you bought a Volvo in the last ten years, it's probably still running. All of us are familiar with arguments like these. Science uses probability arguments quite frequently too, especially in disciplines like psychology, sociology, and economics. But probability arguments are poorly understood and frequently misused by lay persons and scientists alike. In this text, I am only interested in the kinds of uses and mistakes the average person is likely to make using probability reasoning. How do probability arguments work and what mistakes can be made in utilizing them?

In order to use probability reasoning, it must be the case that the subject you are considering occurs with some degree of **frequency**. Frequency means how often a particular situation occurs. Normally, very rare or isolated events cannot be handled adequately using probability arguments because there are not enough examples of these rare events to supply the necessary data. *Probability reasoning also applies only to* **variables**, which are factors which may manifest themselves in a number of possible ways. The extent to which a variable may vary is called its **range**.

There are two kinds of probability determinations, **a priori** and **a posteriori**. A priori probability reasoning presupposes that every possible value of a variable within its range is *equally likely* to occur both in the long run *and* in every given case. Another way of putting this is to say that the value of a variable which actually occurs is determined strictly by **the laws of chance**. A posteriori probability reasoning does not presuppose that all possibilities are equally likely, and the likelihood of the given possibilities is a major issue to determine in a posteriori probability judgments.

A simple illustration of this that you are probably familiar with can be found in any game that utilizes dice. The typical die is a small plastic or bone cube with one to six dots engraved successively on each of its sides. The

variable in question here is which side will land face up on any given role. The range of the variable is one through six, and each side possesses the same chance of landing face up on any given roll. This has been determined *a priori*, or *prior to experience*. Should these last conditions really be met the die is said to be **fair**. If someone rigs the game by loading the die, each face will no longer have an equal chance and the results will be **skewed**. Whether or not the dice have been loaded can be determined only *a posteriori*, or *after your experience*, by a physical examination of the dice. It cannot be determined simply by rolling the die and noting the results. Once the die has been rolled a number of times and the results have been recorded, the actual frequency of the results may be determined. The actual (or a posteriori) frequency of a given event may well differ dramatically from the a priori probability of any outcome. I shall now explain a priori and a posteriori probability in greater detail.

A. A priori probability

The first form of probability assessment I will talk about is called **mathematical**, **theoretical**, or **a priori probability**. In order to use a priori probability assessments in a given situation, it must be possible to specify independently of experience three conditions:

1. You must know the range of the variable in question.
2. You must be able to specify what constitutes a success.
3. You must know that each of the items in the range is equally likely to occur. Another way of putting this condition is to say that the actual results are due to the laws of chance alone.

If all three of these conditions can be met in a given case, then a simple equation can be used to determine the various probabilities in question prior to the actual running of the event. *The probability of any given event in question is equal to the number of possible successful results divided by the range of all the possible results.* A **successful**

result is one you are interested in obtaining. Probability assessments are expressed either as fractions, in which case the numerator represents the frequency and the denominator the range of the subject at issue, or they can be expressed as percentages, which are determined by dividing the numerator (frequency) by the denominator (range).

What are your chances of rolling a 4 on any one role of the die? Because 4 is stipulated as the successful result in this example and because there are six equally possible outcomes, you have one chance (the number 4) out of six of rolling what you want on any given roll and five chances (the numbers 1, 2, 3, 5, and 6) at failure. Your odds of success on any given role are therefore 1/6, or 16.66%, or .166. This sort of situation is called a **simple probability estimate**. In all simple probability estimates if you add together your chances of success and your chances of failure, you will always get the number 1. If your chances of winning are 100%, this is expressed by the number 1; if you have no chance of winning, this is expressed by the number 0. *Probability estimates always range between 1 and 0.*

What are your chances of rolling either a 3 or a 4 on one role of the die? This kind of situation is called a **compound probability estimate** because what need to be determined are the odds of achieving more than one success. You know that you would succeed if you rolled a 4 and that your chances of doing that on any role are 1/6. You also know that rolling the number 3 constitutes a success and that the odds of doing that on any one role are the same as that of rolling a 4, namely, 1/6. To determine the odds of rolling either a 3 or a 4 on one roll simply add the two fractions (1/6 + 1/6 = 2/6, or 1/3). In general, when there is more than one result which is defined as a success, the probability of achieving a success in any given roll is determined by adding the probability of achieving each of the successes with that roll. This is called the **rule of addition**. This rule is used whenever the word "or" appears in the statement of the problem, that is, whenever you have to calculate the probability of X or the probability of Y. Note that the rule of addition applies *only* when the word "or" describes a try or a series of tries. You have to be careful in applying this rule across tries. You could not argue correctly, for example, that because the chances of a coin landing heads are 1/2 for every flip the rule of addition entails that if you flip the coin twice it has to land heads at least once (1/2 + 1/2 = 1). While the word "twice" means that you have two tries, the results of each flip are determined independently for that try. To ignore this would be a fallacy. You might as well argue that six rolls of the die guarantees that you will roll each of the numbers 1, 2, 3, 4, 5, and 6, which, of course, is not the case at all.

What happens when the initial statement of the problem includes the word "and?" What are the odds of rolling X and then Y? What are the odds, for example, of rolling 4 twice in a row? Some people find this kind of question a little tricky, but it isn't. Remember, in this kind of situation each separate roll starts the whole process all over again. As before, you calculate the odds of rolling the first four at 1/6, and then you repeat the process and get the same figure for the second 4, namely 1/6. To determine the odds of both of these events happening successively simply multiply the fractions. This is called the **rule of multiplication**. 1/6 times 1/6 = 1/36, so your chances of getting two 4s in a row are one in thirty-six. Notice that the rule of multiplication dramatically decreases the odds in favor of a success because the multiplication of the denominator quickly exceeds the addition of the numerators used in the rule of addition.

The rules of addition and multiplication are two of the rules used in determining what are called **objective probability estimates** because probability in these cases is determined strictly by mathematical laws. Probability estimates which are not determined strictly by mathematical laws are called **subjective probability estimates**. We shall look more closely at these later.

There are two sources of confusion about these sorts of examples which can be seen easily if we look at card games. The first is mechanical; many people have a difficult time doing the arithmetic. The second source of confusion is conceptual; in addition to confusing the laws of addition and multiplication, many people confuse frequency with relative frequency. **Frequency** refers to the number of possible successes. The number of possible chances for success changes in a card game if the first card drawn is a success and the card is not reinserted. Frequency refers *only* to the numerator of the probability fraction for any given probability determination. **Relative frequency** refers to the comparison of the numerators of the numbers being compared by probability fractions. *Relative frequency and frequency are interchangeable only when the denominators (the ranges) of the probability fractions being compared remain unchanged.* Otherwise, frequency and relative frequency are entirely different things. In order to determine relative frequency, you have to determine whether the denominator has changed. If the denominator has changed, the comparison of probability fractions will produce only a relative frequency, not a frequency. In the card example used above, whether or not the first card drawn is reinserted settles the question of whether you are comparing frequencies or relative frequencies. Do not confuse the two.

What information must be gathered to make the following a priori probability estimates?

A. The odds of drawing a high card in a single try.

B. The odds of drawing a high card in either of two tries.

C. The odds of drawing a high card twice in a row.

D. The odds of winning in roulette on each spin of the wheel.

E. The odds of winning the big prize on each spin of the wheel in *Wheel of Fortune*.

B. A posteriori probability

This form of probability is also called **empirical** or **applied probability**. Remember, there are three conditions which must be met before using a priori probability: what constitutes a success, the range of the phenomena in question, and that each possibility is equally probable. Such knowledge is easily illustrated by the simple games of chance which I utilized above. Because it is generally possible to stipulate what will constitute a success beforehand I will ignore this aspect of the issue, but what happens when either the second or the third condition is not met? Indeed, they usually aren't, and so we enter the realm of a posteriori probability.

A posteriori probability judgments do not presuppose that either of the last two conditions for a priori probability judgments have been, or even can be, met beforehand for a given subject matter. Since these two conditions frequently are not met, you will often find yourself in a position where you will have to make do with an a posteriori probability judgment. Here are some examples with which you are already familiar:

A. Should you bring your umbrella to class with you today? It's a pain to haul around, especially since you frequently forget and leave it in the room after class is over, but having it sure beats getting soaked. Will it rain today? What are the chances?

B. What are the chances that the Carolina Panthers will win a Super Bowl before the Chicago Bears? The Panthers have never won the Super Bowl; the Bears won it in 1985.

C. Fifty per cent of all marriages end in divorce now in the U. S. Assuming that you want to avoid getting divorced, does this mean that your chances of doing so are only 50/50? And so forth.

It is easy to see in cases like those just cited why a priori probability judgments are of little use. There are simply too many variables present for which the range needs to be determined, and it is silly to say that each possible result is equally likely. Consider the first example. What are the chances that it will rain today? Whether it rains or not, what are the chances that you will forget your umbrella after class is over and leave it in the room? Isn't it less likely that you will forget your umbrella after class if it is raining when school lets out? How much less likely is it? Quantifying answers for all but the first of these questions seems to be silly given our current state of knowledge, and even the quantified answers given to the first question by the weather forecast don't carry a great deal of weight with most of us. So how should you deal with these common problems?

Consider the case of a fan trying to determine the odds on a particular sports contest. A lot of money frequently rides on the **betting line**, which is an attempt to predict before hand the actual results of the contest and establish how much money you will have to bet to win a certain reward. Should a team's fan consult the betting line? The betting line is a subjective, a posteriori probability assessment made by the bookie. The bookie has no way of determining a priori who is really going to win the contest. Though there is so much money at stake, like any other person, the bookie can only make an "educated guess" about the actual outcome. This guess is calculated by weighing factors like the record of the teams' previous matches against each other (some teams "own" other teams, but that is fairly rare), each team's current record (including each team's recent showings—is either of the teams on a streak?), the location of the game (there is frequently a home field advantage), expected weather (some teams play better in certain weather conditions), and the state of health of certain key players (a last minute injury to a star player can dramatically alter previous assessments of the odds). In determining the odds of a given sports event, our hypothetical bookie is using the theory of generalization I discussed in the previous section, and assuming that something like the previous track record of each of the teams involved will continue to hold true for the case in question. The formulation of these generalizations depends on the careful observation and recording of data, though a team's fan might well ignore the data in favor of loyalty. Incorrectly recorded data is very likely to skew the resulting prediction, as would a data base that is too small. How do you know whether you have correctly recorded the data and taken sufficient pains to assure that a great enough range of data has been canvassed? These are questions which have only empirical answers, which is why this type of calculation is termed an a posteriori probability argument. There are no absolute answers here. It is the hallmark of the educated person to be aware of the methods and pitfalls associated with making these sorts of decisions in a given field. Even the so-called experts can disagree about these things, and plenty of people have lost their shirts gambling on the predictions of "experts."

What information would you need to gather in order to calculate the following a posteriori probabilities?

A. The chances of beating your big high school rival in the next football, soccer, or basketball game.
B. The chances of being the next American Idol.
C. The chances that it will snow a foot next winter.
D. The chances of being hit by a tornado or hurricane next storm season.
E. The odds of winning *Survivor*.
F. The chances of getting attacked by any one of the wackos in your school.

III. SUBJECTIVE PROBABILITY ASSESSMENTS AND THE GAMBLER'S FALLACY

So far we have been looking at *objective* probability assessments, in all of which the probability estimates are determined strictly by mathematical laws or by extrapolating from previous experience. We have seen that there are two kinds of objective probability assessments—a priori and a posteriori—distinguished by the means used to determine frequency and range. Regardless of whether the frequency and the range are determined a priori or a posteriori, once they are determined, an objective probability assessment uses only mathematical laws to calculate subsequent probability estimates. Probability estimates which are not determined strictly by mathematical law or past evidence are called **subjective probability estimates**. There are many types of subjective probability estimates, and in this section I will show you only some of the more common ones.

Remember the case of the bookie trying to establish the betting line for a particular game? If the bookie decides that going through all of the motions discussed above is too much trouble, s/he might decide to establish the betting line by choosing his or her favorite team, or on the basis of how good looking each team's uniforms are, or by throwing darts at a dart board, or by any one of a number of other screwball methods. Needless to say, these would all be lousy ways of determining the odds. Ironically, these may be the only ways many people use to "figure" the odds. No bookie who tried these methods would stay in business for long. Occasionally, though, such methods seem to work. Imagine that you picked the Bears to beat the Falcons by seven points because you liked furry creatures and were allergic to feathers and seven is your lucky number. The fact that the Bears did succeed in beating the Falcons by seven may convince you that you're good at this sort of thing, but it shouldn't, because in this case you would have been right by accident. One of the most common forms of subjective probability estimates is called **the gambler's fallacy**. Suppose you are watching the imaginary dice game played with one die mentioned above and recording the scores as the die is rolled. You record the following scores: 6, 2, 3, 6, 5, 1, 1, 3, 6, 2, 3, 2, 5, 2, 6, 6, 1, 6, 3, and 5. Before the next roll you look at your records and see that while the number 6 has turned up six times in the last twenty rolls

the number 4 has failed to turn up at all. You reason from this that in the near future the number 6 is less likely to turn up and the number 4 is more likely to turn up. After all, you think, the rolls are determined by the laws of chance and the laws of chance should even things out now. If you reason in this fashion, you will commit the gambler's fallacy.

The gambler's fallacy concerns a misunderstanding of the laws of chance. In a simple game like the one above, the side on which the die lands is governed strictly by the laws of chance (that is, the game has not been rigged in any way), and objective probability dictates that on the average each number has an equal possibility of turning up; but this does not mean that in fact each number will turn up an equal amount for any particular section of the game you choose to consider. People who commit the gambler's fallacy may employ a form of anthropomorphism by subtly personifying the laws of chance in the form of Lady Luck, so to speak, whose job is to watch over these types of games and who reasons like this: "Gee, I've been asleep at the switch here. I just noticed that in the last twenty rolls I caused six 6s to turn up and no 4s. I better straighten that out right now. I'll make 4 turn up six times in the next twenty rolls and I won't allow 6 in there at all. I hope no one noticed or they'll probably report me to the Justice Department under the Patriot Act." That simply is not how the laws of chance work. If the game in question really is governed solely by the laws of chance, the odds on rolling any given number never change, no matter what has been rolled in the past. The root mistake is in the gambler's assumption that past rolls somehow affect the course of future rolls—they don't.

Real games governed strictly by the laws of chance (such as slot machines, craps, and the roulette wheel) are slightly more sophisticated but essentially similar versions of our imagined dice game. The winning number or slot is determined strictly by the laws of chance, and the game is set up so that it costs players more to play in the long run than the laws of chance dictate that the players will win. The difference is called the house percentage and it is what allows the gambling house to make a predictable (and large) amount of money over the long hall in spite of the occasional case in which some gambler actually wins big. In fact, the occasional big winner is very good for the business of the gambling house because publicizing the winner's name helps to perpetuate the belief in the gambler's fallacy itself through people's fallacious use of availability heuristic, resulting in more business—and ultimately larger profits—for the casino. Remember, the only people in a casino who are not doing any real gambling are the casino's owners and employees; they are betting on a sure thing.

Be careful here. *The gambler's fallacy only refers to games of pure chance or those parts of games governed solely by the rules of pure chance.* Lots of games also involve plenty of skill in addition to factors of chance. Take baseball, for example. If Slugger Ralph is hitting .300 during the current season, this means that Ralph gets three hits in every ten at bats on the average. But here the phrase "on the average" clearly refers to a posteriori probabilities, which are not determined simply by the pure laws of chance, but depend heavily on skill. Better hitters get more hits than poorer hitters, which is why their batting averages are higher. Batting averages are records of past performances and these performances are indications of a variety of factors such as strength, coordination, vision, and other native abilities, as well as a bit of luck.

A card game like poker or bridge presents a nice illustration of the combination of luck and skill that go into successful play. A good poker player is good only marginally because s/he is lucky. A good poker player keeps track of which cards have been dealt to whom (in so far as such information is available), how many cards have been dealt, and which cards the player needs to improve his or her hand. Then, and only then, can the poker player reasonably calculate the odds of improving his or her hand by discarding old cards and drawing new ones. Good poker players, in addition to having poker faces, know how to calculate the percentages and place their bets accordingly.[ii]

IV. RISK ASSESSMENTS

People commit more kinds of mistakes and subtle errors than either the gambler's fallacy or the others mentioned above. Consider the following:

The U.S. is preparing for the outbreak of an unusual Asian disease, which is expected to kill 600 people. Two alternative programs to combat the disease have been proposed. Assume that the exact scientific estimates of the consequences of the program are as follows: If Program A is adopted, 200 people will be saved. If Program B is adopted, there will be a 1/3 probability that 600 people will be saved, and 2/3 probability that no people will be saved.

Which of these programs would you favor?

Additional problem: Same as above. But if Program C is adopted, 400 people will die. If Program D is adopted there is 1/3 probability that nobody will die, and 2/3 probability that 600 people will die.

Which of these two programs do you favor?[iii]

If you had to choose between Programs A and B, which would you prefer? Which would you prefer if you had to choose between Programs C and D? In the illustration cited above, one group of individuals given the choice between Programs A and B overwhelmingly favored Program A (72% to 28%), while another group of individuals given the same problem and the choice between Programs C and D overwhelmingly favored Program D to C (78% to 22%). But Program A is the same program as Program C, and Program B is the same program as Program D (though in each case the programs are described differently). Yet 72% favored A, and only 22% favored C, while 78% favored D to only 28% for B. What gives here?

Choices about risks, like all other decisions, are made in some context or other. Theory-ladenness and mind-set are two of the structural factors that govern the context in which choices are framed. From the point of view of any rational theory, for these choices to be rational the same choice should be preferred regardless of how the choice is described. But people frequently ignore this fact in framing their decisions. Practical mind-set seems to dominate theoretical consistency, and certain descriptions of these programs seem to accord better with certain elements of most persons' mind-sets. The majority of the respondents in the study who were asked to choose between options A and B and favored Program A seemed to have been motivated by **risk aversion**, which is the desire to save what they already have. The majority of the respondents who were asked to choose between C and D favored D apparently because they were motivated by **risk taking**, which is the desire to obtain what they don't already have. Thus the change in the perspective of the respondents induced by different descriptions of the same case, irrational as it may seem, was a direct function of the different mind sets invoked in the respondents by the different descriptions of the choice situation.

Risk aversion and risk taking also lead to poor judgments about the actual (or objective) probability of future events. Do you always wear seat belts when you ride in an automobile? Some people always do, some do sometimes, and some never do. When seat belts were first introduced as standard equipment in vehicles in the 1960s, and more recently in the 1980s when various states started to introduce mandatory seat belt laws, many individuals resisted wearing seat belts in spite of the fact that statistics have shown repeatedly that wearing seat belts can reduce the chances of personal injury in accident situations significantly. When asked to justify the failure to wear seat belts, a common response was to engage in **biased discounting**, which is the underestimating of the actual likelihood of very bad conse-

quences. Biased discounting is a form of risk taking, though many people would not want to look at it in this way. "It can't happen to me," is the common expression for this. A related fallacy is **wishful thinking**, which is the overestimating of the actual probability of some very good consequences happening. Wishful thinking is a manifestation of risk aversion. "You may have already won $10,000,000," declares the blurb from Publisher's Clearinghouse Sweepstakes. Sure you may have, but don't spend your money too soon, because your chances of winning are about 1/500,000,000.

Humans are very poor at assessing risks objectively because irrational factors often easily override rationality. Consider the car driver who gets into a wreck while swatting at a bee that has flown into the car. Which is more potentially dangerous, the bee sting or the wreck? **Rational risk assessment** must take into account three factors:

A. the objective probability of harmful or good consequences,
B. the severity or extent of the harmful or good consequences, and
C. the reversibility of the harmful or the good effects.

These three conditions, of course, are empirically dependent on what is actually harmful or beneficial in a given situation, a question which ordinarily we are not capable of answering a priori. Generally, the more likely the potentially harmful consequences a given course of action may have, the greater the severity of that potential harm, and the more difficult it would be to reverse the damages once done, the more risky the behavior in question.

Biased discounting and wishful thinking often are buttressed by an appeal to **anecdotal evidence**, which is comprised of short and dramatic stories designed to illustrate some point. As such, they represent good illustrations of the use of availability heuristic to bolster the phenomenon of wishful thinking. The person who offers anecdotal evidence in lieu of a sustained analysis of a complex problem shows that s/he wishes that the problem were as easy to solve as the (frequently imaginary) situation depicted by the anecdote. When, however, the original situation really is as simple as that depicted by the anecdote, such a form of reasoning is an illustration of analogical argumentation, which may be quite legitimate. When it is not, it is simply a simple-minded, though perhaps entertaining, disaster for critical thinking.

Assess the following risk assessment examples from the point of view of the issues presented above.

A. I have an uncle who was driving on a foggy road in Wisconsin one night. He hit a cow and demolished his brand new Cadillac. Now he's staying away from Wisconsin.

B. Sure, working in Iraq is dangerous, but the bullet hasn't been made which will get me.

C. Sharks? What sharks? Surf's up!

D. I saw the film of that plane crash. Me fly? No thanks. I'll drive instead.

E. After getting a whole lot of grief for holding his 8 month old child three feet away from a crocodile, Steve Irwin defended his actions by saying "I just wanted to teach the littl' nipper not to be afraid of the big nipper."

F. Michael Jackson got the same grief for dangling his infant son over a second story balcony. In response to his critics he said, "Steve Irwin did it. Ain't he a beauty!"

G. "There are white lies, lies, and black lies. Then there are statistics."   —Disraeli.

V. STATISTICS

One hundred years ago most people lived with a vastly different mental world view. In many ways life really was simpler back then. Three developments changed that forever: the formulation of the scientific/critical method as a problem solving tool, the rise of the belief that it is the function of government to solve problems found to be too complex and intractable for individuals to handle alone, and the inven-

tion of the computer, an indispensable tool needed for handling the large amounts of data generated by the application of the scientific/critical method to problem solving situations. The world most of us live in now is one which is overrun with data. When this data can be quantified, as it frequently can, it appears in the form of **statistics**. Statistics are so omnipresent and essential to our existence that modern life could not exist without them.

Since you constantly are being assaulted with statistical claims, it is important that you at least have some notion of the basic ideas which go into their production and distribution, as well as some ideas about how statistical claims can be misused to give the false impression of knowledge where none, in fact, exists. In this section, I shall discuss some of the basic concepts necessary to the understanding and assessment of statistical claims. In the next section, I shall look at some of the common kinds of fallacies statistical reasoning may foster.

Statistical reasoning is one of the primary methods of producing generalizations from a limited amount of quantified data.[iv] Because there are normally far more data available than any individual can assimilate, data which is readily available is usually just a small subset of all possible data. The expanse of all possible data regarding a given variable is that variable's range. From a variable's range, a select subset of data is actually gathered, and that subset is called a **sample**. A sample is always a selection from a broader range. Why make such a selection in the first place, why not simply use the whole of the variable's range? The range of a variable is usually too vast to collect completely or it is too expensive in terms of time, equipment, money, and so forth, to pursue more than a limited selection.

There are two separate issues about sampling which need to be taken into consideration: the method by which the sample is chosen and the size of the sample. One standard method used to select the members of a class who are going to be subjected to statistical analysis is the method of **random sampling**. A random sample is one in which each member of the subject class has an equal chance of being chosen. Remember, a sample is a selection from a (much) larger class all the members of which share some common variable. By definition, variables vary over a range of values for the subject class. Suppose you were interested in ascertaining something about the weight of adult human beings. Adult human beings range from the very tiny (such as midgets, who may weigh as little as 20 pounds) to the very large (such as giants, who may "top out" around 1000 pounds). Most adult human beings, however, weigh between 100 and 250 pounds. If only individuals at the midget or the giant end of the scales were chosen in the sample, the results would be highly skewed. Here is where the size of the sample becomes important. When using inductive arguments involving statistical analysis, the larger the sample size (up to a point) the stronger the inference. Since random sampling gives each member of the subject class an equal chance of being chosen by the sample, the smaller the sample, the greater the likelihood that the individuals chosen at the extreme ends of the variable's range will skew the results of the analysis, while a larger sample provides a greater likelihood that most of the members chosen are from the middle of the range. The more X's you choose at random from the class of X, the more average X's you almost certainly will choose. After enough X's have been chosen at random, the addition of further X's becomes pointless because so many average X's will have already been chosen that the addition of a few X's on the extreme ends of the scale will fail to make a statistically significant difference to the analysis. How many X's constitute "enough" depends on the nature of the subject matter and the form of the study, though for many common studies the numbers are surprisingly low, e.g., less than 1000 subjects.

Suppose you were doing a market survey by telephone about whether people prefer Pepsi to Coke. If you called only one person and that person wasn't home, should you conclude that no one preferred Pepsi to Coke? Of course not. What if you got through only to one person and that person simply said "I hate Coke," before hanging up? Again, hardly the basis for a judgment. Now suppose that you reached 10 people and 7 preferred Pepsi, 2 preferred Coke, and 1 had no opinion. At least now you have some data to work with, but you should not have a great deal of confidence generalizing from this data. If you did, you likely would be committing a small sample fallacy. But suppose you next surveyed 10,000 people and 7,000 preferred Pepsi, 2,000 preferred Coke, and 1,000 had no preference. In this case, it is highly likely that the conclusion "People prefer Pepsi to Coke by a margin of 7 to 2" is very well supported by the existing data. Indeed, the inclusion of 10,000 subjects in such a survey is hardly necessary to arrive at a conclusion equally as well founded, provided the actual subjects chosen are selected in an unbiased manner.

You can determine various things from data like this alone. The first thing you can find out from this data is the **average** person's preference. The word "average" is ambiguous, so statisticians prefer to distinguish three different kinds of averages—mean, median, and mode. The **mean** is the arithmetic average. It is determined by adding all of the scores and dividing this total by the number of scores. Determination of the mean is the starting point of most statistical analysis. The appearances of scores on one extreme end of the range will greatly affect the mean if they are not counterbalanced by an equal number of scores on the other extreme. The **median** is the score in the middle if the scores are rank ordered from the highest to the lowest. Fifty percent of the scores will be above the median, fifty percent below. When there is an even number of scores, the median is the mean of the two middle scores. The **mode** is the score which appears most frequently. There may be two or more modes if there are a number of scores which appear equally often.

When speaking about averages, it is important to be clear about which sense of the term is intended when the term is used. Entirely different points can be made by using the same term. If you heard the claim, "The average pick-up truck on the road today in America is a Ford," you might be confused if you did not realize that the term "average" is being used here to signify mode. The mode is the number which appears most frequently, though relative to the combination of all of the other possible numbers the mode may be very tiny indeed. There may be more Ford pick-up trucks on the road today in America than any other single model, but the total of all other pick-up truck models combined far outnumber the number of Fords on the road. Similarly, you may hear, "Ford pick-ups are average-priced trucks," and be misled unless you realized that the term "average" here stands for median. If Ford pick-up trucks really were at the median of the price range (ignoring for purposes of the argument the different prices of different models of Ford trucks), then half of all other makes of pick-ups would be more expensive than Fords and half less expensive. And finally, if you heard "The average pick-up truck sold today costs $16,000" you may be misled unless you realized that here the term "average" signifies mean, so that if you took every pick-up truck sold today and added their prices together and divided the total by the number of trucks sold you would arrive at the $16,000 price tag mentioned in the example. Remember, the "average" pick-up may carry a $16,000 price tag, yet you actually may be unable to find one that really sells for $16,000.

Returning to the human weight example mentioned above, suppose you were interested in determining whether there was a correlation between a person's weight and SAT score. You first need to select a sample of persons who have taken the SAT and record their scores and their weights and then determine the mean for each of these samples. Most statistical analysis of data starts with the determination of the mean of the samples in question and proceeds by comparing these means with the means of other samples taken at random

from the range of possible data. In order to do this, you are going to have to select more sample sets of SAT scores and weights and compare them to determine their means. Sample populations which are compared do not have to be very large before successive samples collected begin to yield remarkably similar means. Sample sizes of 10 may be quite sufficient for your purposes though sample sizes of 20 could be used to be on the safe side. Sample sizes of about 100 are almost never used in cases like this. Collecting that many units per sample is almost always a waste of time.

Statisticians are primarily concerned in comparing the mean values of various sample populations. If each member of each sample set is selected at random (by chance alone), the resulting variations between the sample means of the same variable for different sample sets also occur due to chance alone, and the amount of variation between sample means for a given variable is due primarily to the size of the sample sets being compared. The larger the sample size up to a given amount (remember, you don't need to include very many items in each sample), the less likely their means are to differ in a statistically significant sense.

Determining the means of various SAT sample sets and various weight sample sets allows for the possibility of quantifying the probability that fluctuations between the sample means of the two separate variables of weight and SAT scores are due to something in addition to chance alone, presumptively some sort of causal relationship between weight and SAT score. To simplify the possibilities a bit for purposes of the discussion, the causal relationship could be that change in weight causes change in SAT scores or change in SAT scores cause change in weight. The correlated fluctuations between the two variables could be either **positive**, meaning that when one variable went up the other one did too, or **negative**, meaning that when one variable went up the other one went down. For purposes of the discussion, let's assume that you are interested only in testing the possibility that changes in weight cause changes in SAT scores. For whatever crazy reasons, you wish to test the hypothesis that heavy test takers achieve better results on the SAT than light test takers. Weight would then represent the independent variable, SAT scores the dependent variable.

Were the appropriate data to exist for this illustration (it doesn't because this is a fictitious example) it could be shown that the difference between the mean SAT scores and the mean weights for various sample sets can be determined mathematically, within a range of possible error, to be due to some sort of causal relationship between weight and SAT scores. If the data were of a certain sort, then it could be shown that the relationship between SAT scores and weight is **statistically significant**. Like the notion of validity₁ in deductive logic, statistical significance is a concept which applies to data independently of the subject matter of the data. There is nothing *conceptually* inconceivable about SAT scores being dependent upon the body weight of the person taking the test. Whether any two variables are causally related in a statistically significant way is determined simply by applying the appropriate statistical analysis to the data in question.

In this SAT/weight example, you are interested in determining whether there is a correlation between weight and SAT scores such that the operations of chance coupled with changes of weight cause changes in SAT scores. This is your hypothesis and in the literature about statistics and the scientific/critical method it is signified by the sign "H_1." H_1 is contrasted to the sign "H_0," which signifies what is called the **null hypothesis**. The null hypothesis means that there is no causal relationship between the variables specified by the hypothesis, and changes in variables are due to chance alone. *The purpose of applying a statistical analysis to the data is to rule out the null hypothesis.* If a comparison between the mean weight for a given sample of persons and the mean SAT scores for those persons is statistically significant at the .05 level, it means that in only 5 out

of 100 samples would this statistical relationship result from chance alone. Because there is always the possibility of error regarding the representativeness of the data sampling, good statistical arguments will include some reference to this factor. This is called the **margin of error**. Most researchers accept the .05 level as having established good statistical evidence that a causal relationship does indeed exist within the stated margin of error. Sometimes researchers want even greater precision than this, and they will apply an analysis which is significant at the .001 level, which means that there is only 1 chance in 1,000 that the sample data was due to chance alone.[v]

If results obtained at the .001 level are more precise than results obtained at the .05 level, why not use the .001 level every time? In addition to the practical facts that the .001 significance level requires more research subjects (which might not be available), takes more time to run, and is more expensive, there are also two types of theoretical errors statistical analyses can commit here. A **Type 1 error** is committed when the researcher wrongly accepts H_1 and rejects H_0 on the basis of the statistical analysis. The probability of committing this is equal to the significance level adopted. On these grounds alone you would be better off pursuing a .001 significance level than a .05 significance level, because at the .05 level there is always the possibility of a **false positive**. This occurs when it seems that the test results indicate a correlation or a causal relationship when none in fact exists. Unfortunately, there are also **Type 2 errors**, which are committed when you wrongly reject H_1 and accept H_0 on the basis of the statistical analysis. The higher the significance level, the greater the chance of committing a Type 2 error. Type 2 errors are also called **false negatives** because they fail to find correlations or causal relationships which do indeed exist. If the variable mentioned in H_1 proves to be overwhelming in the amount of effect it produces, there is little chance of committing a Type 2 error. On the other hand, if the variable in H_1 proves only to have a slight or moderate effect there is a great chance of missing this if a high significance level is adopted. The higher the significance level, the easier it is to miss subtle effects. Researchers know this and thus frequently compromise by adopting a .05 significance level so as not to miss subtle but important correlations.

Here's another way to see this. In criminal trials the jury must make a decision as to whether the prosecution has met its burden of proof (i.e., defeated the null hypothesis). If the jury sets its standards of proof too high (the .001 significance level), it will free guilty people (false negatives). If it sets its standards of proof too low (the .05 significance level), it will convict innocent people (false positives). There is no getting around this dilemma. It requires *phronesis* on the part of the jury members.

Discuss the problem of false positives and false negatives in the following cases.

A. Two members of your class are accused of cheating because the pattern of their answers in an objective test is "suspiciously similar."

B. Jury member #1: "I don't need to hear the evidence. She looks guilty; that's good enough for me." Jury member #2: "Funny, I think she's gorgeous; she must be innocent."

C. Mom to son: "You look puny, and you're not even interested in looking at the new *Victoria's Secret* catalogue. You must have mono."

D. Mom to daughter: "You look puny, and you're watching *A Wedding Story*. You must be in love."

E. "Whoa! Last night this woman with an ultra-sultry voice tried to get me to switch my long distance carrier over the phone. I must have a secret admirer."

Finally, you may see statistical information from our imagined study about peoples' weights and SAT scores presented in the form of a graph. The function of the graph is to provide a pictorial presentation of statistical information. Graphs are presented with two axes. The horizontal axis represents the range of the variable being considered, the vertical axis the

frequency of appearance of items in the range. The resulting picture is called a **frequency curve**. When a variable to be graphed is selected because its values are determined only by the laws of chance, the resulting picture is called a **normal distribution curve**. Its well-known bell shape is depicted in Figure 1.

Figure 1. The Normal Distribution Curve

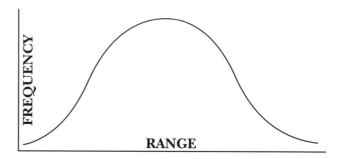

Though the normal distribution curve shown above rarely exactly matches the frequency curves formed by graphing actual empirical data, an enormous number of empirical variables approximate it so closely when graphed that features which are true for the normal distribution curve may be treated as if they are also features of actual empirical distribution curves. Weight and SAT scores are variables for which this is true. In general, any empirical variable which occurs frequently over even a small range can be accurately analyzed with a normal distribution curve.

There are two especially important features of the normal distribution curve you need to know about—**standard deviation** and **percentile equivalencies**. Standard deviation is a measure of the average degree with which items in a given range differ from the mean for that range. By convention, the mean of a given frequency range is established at 0, which is located at the exact center of the normal curve's range. In a normal distribution curve the mean, the median, and the mode are all identical, namely 0. Standard deviation is a measurement of the average amount by which items in the range differ from 0.[vi] Standard deviation is signified by the Greek letter K. For any normal distribution curve, 34% of the sample lies on the high (or right hand) side of the range (starting from 0), and 34% lies in the low (or left hand) side of the range (again starting from 0). Thus 68% of the items which are found on a normal distribution curve lie within one standard deviation (1K) of the mean. A further 14% of the items found on the curve lie within the next standard deviation on each side of the normal curve, meaning that 28% of the total sample falls within the second standard deviation and a total of 96% of all the items on the curve fall within the first two standard deviations (2K). By statistical definition, there are few scores more than two standard deviations away from the mean.

Sometimes it is more helpful to the analysis to express this information in terms of percentile equivalencies. The percentile equivalency tells what percentage of the total sample lies within each standard deviation. For purposes of the analysis the mean of the curve (0) is equivalent to 50%, -1K at the 16th percentile (34% below the mean) and +1K at the 84th percentile (34% above the mean), and so forth. To say that there are scores on a given percentile, for example 60%, is to say that 60% of all the scores are at or below that percentile. Figure 2 depicts a normal distribution curve with standard deviations and percentile equivalencies noted.[vii]

Because almost all of the scores lie within two standard deviations from the mean, it is rare to find a score that lies in the third stan-

dard deviation range. Scores in the third standard deviation are uncommon and hard to obtain. Scoring in these areas of the range should be very hard to do relative to the ease with which most average scores are made. For example, it is hard to score a 400 or a 1600 on the SAT, but relatively easy to get a 1000 because 1000 is about the mean for the test.

Scores that are at the extremes tend not to be duplicated during retests. They tend to appear closer to the mean. This is called **regression towards the mean**. This may at first seem surprising, but it shouldn't be. In his heyday, Michael Jordan might have only scored 6 points in a game, or he might have scored 60. But both of these possibilities are highly unusual, and should either occur, it is far more likely that his score in the next game will be much closer to his 28 points per game career average.

Empirical distribution curves may also be skewed. A skewed curve is one which fails to closely approximate a normal distribution curve. Curves can be skewed in three ways: randomly, positively, and negatively. A randomly skewed curve may have several peaks or no real peak at all. Random skewing indicates either a more or less even distribution of sample data (if there are no real peaks on the curve) or an insufficient amount of sample data (if there are several peaks). If there is only one peak, but it is to the left of the normal center line, you have a **positive skew**. If there is only one

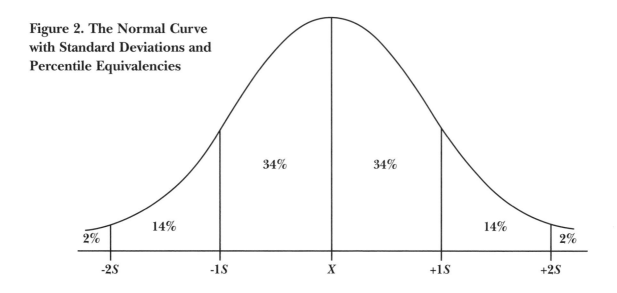

Figure 2. The Normal Curve with Standard Deviations and Percentile Equivalencies

34%   34%

14%   14%

2%   2%

-2S   -1S   X   +1S   +2S

peak, but it is to the right of the normal center line, you have a **negative skew**.

An empirical distribution curve that is skewed may indicate that something other than chance is affecting the distribution of the data. With randomly skewed distribution curves insufficient data may be the culprit, though it is difficult to rule out the effects of chance when you are working with a limited amount of data. The gambler's fallacy discussed above may be committed easily by too quickly leaping to a false conclusion from insufficient data. It is usually much easier to figure out the problem if the curve is positively or negatively skewed. Rigging what is supposed to be a game of chance results in positively or negatively skewing the resulting data. In the case of standardized tests like the SAT or end-of-grade testing, a negative data skew may indicate that the test was too easy, a positive skew that the test was too hard. In the case of weight measurement, a negative skew may indicate that the tested population has a diet which is higher in fats and carbohydrates than normal, or perhaps gets too little exercise. In any event, further study is needed to determine the reason for the skewing of the data. The working assumption here is that normally distributed data does not need further explanation, positively or negatively skewed data does.

VI. COMMON ERRORS IN STATISTICAL REASONING

There are many ways to go wrong when employing statistical arguments. Faulty statistical arguments are amazingly commonplace. By bearing in mind the discussion given in the last two sections, the critical thinker can protect himself or herself from some of these mistakes. All of these errors can be classified into two groups: a) those stemming from an inadequate collection of data and b) those stemming from the inadequate analysis of collected data. I will discuss some of the more common types of mistakes made with statistical reasoning in each of these areas.[viii]

A. Errors stemming from the inadequate collection of data

These types of common errors are also known as sampling errors. There are two basic subdivisions of this type of error, those connected with faulty attempts at random sampling and those connected with other mistakes in data collection. A random sample is one in which each item in a given set has an equal chance of being included in any particular sample. If you are selecting from a sequence of numbers on a random number table, you can tell that your sample is random a priori. How you can be assured that the sample of the empirical data you have gathered a posteriori is truly random is quite another thing. Do you remember having to line up in grade school gym class and count off by twos? This was done by the gym teacher as a method of attempting to insure a random grouping. But it sure didn't take you and your friends long to see this coming and stand at appropriate places in line to assure that you would all be included in the same group. The result was the product of a **biased sample**. Biased samples may look random to the untrained eye, but they are not. To make things even worse, samples which look obviously "loaded" may in fact really be random. Humans have an amazing ability to see data patterns where none in fact exist.

Public opinion polling is especially vulnerable to these types of problems. You are all familiar with opinion polls, which seem to spring up like crab grass in the summer around the time of national elections. Opinion polling is a risky business. There are numerous examples of opinion poll predictions which have been amazingly accurate. There are also numerous examples of opinion poll predictions which have been totally wrong. Just such a fiasco occurred during the 2000 presidential election returns in Florida when the TV networks first gave the state to Gore, than to Bush, then to no one. This fiasco aside, however, TV news has not given up conducting election surveys and making predictions on the basis of the survey's results. Exit polling is a good example of this kind of practice. In an exit poll voters who have just finished voting are questioned about their opinions. At its worst, you are likely to hear: "Good morning. This is the seven a.m. news. Voting opened in today's Presidential election at six. CNN exit polls now predict that Smedley will win the Presidency over Bleep by 52.415% to 47. 58499%, while 27% of the voters in Florida will not have the strength to punch a hole all the way through the ballot and 3% of the California voters won't vote because Gov. Schwarzenegger hurt their feelings by calling them 'girlie men.' Details at eleven."

How is it that TV stations seem to be able to predict so early and so confidently who will be the winner of a political contest? Not simply by conducting random sampling, but rather through the use of **representative sampling**. In representative sampling the potential range of the variable (in this case the voting public) is divided into its known, major voting block subdivisions, such as blue collar workers, yuppies, Blacks, women, left-handed Lithuanians, girlie men, and so forth. Each major subdivision then is treated as a separate sample and an attempt is made through exit polling to sample at random a certain percentage from each subgroup. The results of the individual subgroup surveys are then totaled and the findings announced. This type of prediction has proven to be so accurate at times that it is feared that voting patterns in the Western part of the U. S. will be disrupted by results announced from the Eastern part of the country, and the major networks have promised not to make these kinds of announcements until the appropriate polls all have closed.

Opinion polling can go badly wrong too. The *Chicago Tribune* probably made the most famous goof of all time in this regard in 1948. In a close contest the *Tribune* predicted that Thomas Dewey would beat Harry Truman and printed its next day's edition with the headlines "Dewey Wins!" Well, Dewey didn't win. Late voting on the West coast gave California and the whole election to Truman, who appeared on the next day with a big smile on his face holding up a copy of the unfortunate headline. When polling goes wrong, it frequently goes wrong because one fair sample may randomly vary from another, which is why polls should come with a margin of error attached (usually + or - 3%), or because biased samples are wittingly or unwittingly chosen. Sometimes it is possible to produce a biased sample simply by wording the questions asked in such a way as to produce the desired effect. Examples of this hardly have to be as crude as this: compare a) "Smedley is a convicted child molester whose victims included his own children. Do you think that such a slime-ball deserves to be President?" with b) "Smedley has first-hand knowledge of the meaning of suffering. He was tragically separated from his own children by a heartless bureaucracy. Don't you think that such a compassionate person is fit to be President?" You need not be a genius to figure out which description of Smedley is likely to elicit your support.

Present your own examples of opinion poll questions which would bias the results of the following surveys:

A. The age at which one should be allowed an unrestricted drivers license.

B. The re-institution of the draft.

C. The right to freely download music off the internet.

D. Whether to go to a movie featuring Julia Roberts or one featuring Hobbits, Elves and Orcs.

There are several other common sampling mistakes. The first one is the appeal of **questionable statistics**. Questionable statistics are statistical claims which you may be inclined to accept at first glance, but they prove to be dubious upon further inspection. Questionable statistics are just that—questionable. Further examination is necessary to determine whether they are in fact accurate, and indeed they may be. Arguments employing statistics seem to appeal to our intellects because they satisfy a desire for precision. Not all claims to precision, however, are equally worthy of belief. How many people, for example, have already died in America from AIDS? 250,000, 300,000, 350,000, 400,000? As of the 2005 all four of these figures have been used. What will it cost to stabilize Iraq as a democracy? $100 billion, $500 billion, $1 trillion? Again, any of these figures may easily appear in debates on this issue. When precise statistical claims are made, it is appropriate for the critical thinker to ask the questions: Who says? How does s/he know that? How can these claims be verified? You, yourself, cannot be expected to know everything, but you can know when another's claims to knowledge are worthy of suspicion.

How would you properly resolve the following claims involving questionable statistics?

A. The percent of your entering high school freshman class who will never graduate from high school.

B. The amount of weight you will put on in your first year of college. [Traditionally called the "freshman fifteen."]

C. The number of career changes you will make during your lifetime.

D. The number of times your kids will say "Are we there yet? Are we there yet? Are we there yet?" on your vacation as you are backing out of your driveway.

A fallacy closely related to questionable statistics is the **fallacy of unknowable statistics**. Unknowable statistics are not simply questionable, no one could know whether they were true or not; they are impossible to verify or falsify. If I claimed that exactly 382,571 Americans have died from AIDS as of July 1st, 2005, I would be claiming to know something only an omniscient being could know. Certainly some AIDS victims have died from this disease without anyone else knowing that AIDS was the real cause of their death. Medical record keeping simply isn't that precise.

Frustrating as it may be, there are plenty of things that are unknowable in principle or in practice because there simply is insufficient evidence available to warrant these claims. And there is unlikely ever to be enough evidence to allow it to be known, for example, that there are 47,000,000,011 stars in the Milky Way or 62.37459% of the human population who will ever live will have died before they turn 40 years of age, and so forth. As hard as this may be to accept given our desire for precision, the best we can do probably is to say that there are billions of stars in the Milky Way and lots of people die before they turn 40.

Why are the following cases of unknowable statistics?

A. The number of times you will breathe before you draw your last breath.

B. The amount of money you will make in your lifetime.

C. The amount of bills you will still owe no matter what possible answer is given to example B above.

D. The number of inane bumper stickers you will read during the next election.

E. The number of times you will hear the word "like" when teenagers are talking.

B. Errors stemming from the inadequate analysis of data collected.

Even after the data have been collected, the job of the statistician if far from over. The significance of the data must still be assessed. Bits and pieces of data themselves are meaningless until their significance can be established by putting them into the context of a theory, the structure of which enables you to make sense out of the tidbits of information presented by the raw statistics.

Analysis of statistical data seeks to discover and discuss the context in which the data is presented. Statistical arguments involve generalizations from the sample data presented to certain conclusions about the whole range of the variable. As such, statistical arguments are relevant similarity arguments, which have already been discussed above in Section I. It is important when analyzing this sort of argument to keep an eye out for possible problems with hasty generalizations involving small or unrepresentative samples or the law of small numbers.

Analysis of statistical arguments is also subject to problems of ambiguity. It is important for the critical thinker to be aware that these arguments are about sets of variables, all of which may or may not fall legitimately under one common class name. When a common class name has significantly different meanings, statistical generalizations using common names which ignore these differences fall prey to the fallacy of ambiguity. In the example used in Section V above about trucks, an argument which failed to distinguish between trucks in general and pick-up trucks in particular is subject to this sort of confusion. To avoid this kind of fallacy you must have sufficient information concerning the theories in terms of which the labels used in the argument make sense. Operational definitions need to be supplied when applicable in order to head off confusion caused by ambiguity.

Finally, there are various ways of presenting data in such a way as to invite conclusions that may be highly misleading. The first way of doing this is by lying. If I said to you "Nine out of ten doctors surveyed recommend Burpo for upset stomachs," I would be lying if I neglected to tell you either that the term "doctor" meant Ph.D., not M.D., or that I actually had to survey 100 doctors before I could find nine of them who recommended Burpo.

There are more subtle forms of misrepresentation than blatant lying. I may commit the **broad-based fallacy**, which is done by taking a rare event and making it more commonplace by moving from one group (those who really are at risk) to a much broader group (such as the general population). Tay-Sachs disease, for example, is a fatal genetic disease which affects a limited number of ethnically Jewish individuals who come from Eastern Europe. If I took the figures for the frequency of Tay-Sachs cases among the class of those who are really poten-

tial victims and generalized these figures for the entire U.S. population, I could easily produce in you a false sense of alarm when in fact you have no risk of passing this disease to your children unless you and your spouse are both from the possible target population. The root mistake here is the failure to distinguish between frequency and relative frequency.

Similarly, I might mislead you by making a small change appear large by presenting the total number of incidents of some situation as a single group, or making a large change appear small by presenting the change as a rate per unit despite the very large number of units involved. As an example of the first type of argument, consider the scare that swept the nation in the late 1970s when the phenomena of Toxic Shock Syndrome received such publicity. After several unfortunate deaths, studies traced the cause of the death of apparently healthy women to the type of tampon they had been using, many of which were marketed by Proctor and Gamble under the trade name "Rely." Several deaths were reported in February of 1978 and about a half dozen more the next month. If I argued in April of 1978 that the number of reported deaths doubled in the last month, what I said would have been true, but highly misleading, as something like 60,000,000 American women used tampons during the month of March without experiencing any problems. Even doubling the chances of a very rare event does not significantly increase your odds of being effected. But tampon sales temporarily plummeted, and Proctor and Gamble took Rely off the market. This is a classic example of the law of small numbers argument. Tampon sales quickly went back to normal when Toxic Shock Syndrome was no longer treated as newsworthy.

Similarly, if I wanted to downplay a common event, I might do so by spreading the results of some change over the units involved. When the electric company wishes to get approval for a rate increase to offset the cost of some defunct nuclear power plant, for example, it might argue that the proposed rate increase "only" added one cent to the average kilowatt-hour rate. But that "only" adds up to hundreds of millions of cents per month when you consider the number of kilowatt-hours the electric company sells to its customers per month. While a situation like this is not a form of out and out lying, it is certainly a case of presenting the desired conclusion in such a way as to maximize the chances of impressing an uninformed audience who might not be so prone to agreement if the argument was presented in a different light.

Discuss data collection problems in the following cases.

A. What your actual miles per gallon will be for your car during any given time frame.

B. That instant replay will overturn the decision made on the field in any given challenge.

C. That a male performance enhancement drug actually will enhance one's performance.

D. That an SAT study course will actually increase your SAT score.

CONCEPTS

You should be able to define the following concepts, explain their meanings to others not familiar with them, invent your own examples that correctly illustrate the concepts, and apply them correctly to novel applications.

- Anecdote
- A posteriori probability
- A priori probability
- Availability heuristic
- Average
- Betting line
- Biased discounting
- Broad-based fallacy
- Exit polling
- Fair
- False negative
- False positive
- Frequency
- Frequency curve
- Gambler's fallacy
- Generalization
- Hasty generalization
- Inductive argument
- Law of small numbers
- Laws of chance
- Margin of error

- Mean
- Median
- Mode
- Negative correlation
- Negative skew
- Normal distribution curve
- Null hypothesis H_0
- Objective probability estimate
- Percentile equivalencies
- .05 level and .001 level
- Positive correlation
- Positive skew
- Probability
- Questionable statistics
- Random sampling
- Range
- Rational risk assessment
- Regression towards the mean
- Relative frequency

- Relevant similarity argument
- Requirement of total evidence
- Risk aversion
- Risk taking
- Rule of addition
- Rule of multiplication
- Sample
- Small sample
- Standard deviation (K)
- Statistically significant
- Statistics
- Strength
- Subjective probability estimate
- Type 1 error
- Type 2 error
- Unknowable statistics
- Unrepresentative sample
- Wishful thinking

Foundational concepts: A posteriori probability, a priori probability, availability heuristics, frequency, generalization, mean, normal distribution curve, the null hypothesis H_0, probability, questionable statistics, range, rational risk assessment, requirement of total evidence, sample, standard deviation (K), statistics, unknowable statistics

NOTES

i. For more on the relationship between small samples and unrepresentative samples see Thomas Leddy, "Is There a Fallacy of Small Sample?" *Informal Logic* (vol. VIII, #1, Winter 1986): 53-56.

ii. See Joseph L. Cowan, "The Gambler's Fallacy," *Philosophy and Phenomenological Research* (vol. 30, 1969): 238-251.

iii. Taken from Amos Tversky and Daniel Kahneman, "The Framing of Decisions and the Psychology of Choice," *Science* (vol. 211, January 30, 1981): 453-458. Another work by the same authors, which discusses the same issues is "Rational Choice and the Framing of Decisions," *Journal of Business* (vol. 59, #4, part 2, 1986): 251-277.

iv. Some of the pioneering work on the use of statistics in scientific/critical analysis was done by Sir Ronald Fisher. See *Statistical Methods for Research Workers* (Darien, CT: Hafner, 1970), originally published in 1925, and *The Design of Experiments* (Edinburgh: Oliver & Boyd, 1966), originally published in 1935.

v. I am not concerned here with how this comparison actually is computed, as this type of information is beyond the scope of an introductory book such as this. In general the larger the sample size, the smaller the margin of error for that sample size. For information about how to actually design and run statistical tests on data, see Gordon Wood, *Fundamentals of Psychological Research*, 3rd edition, (Boston: Little, Brown, and Co., 1981). For an interesting critique of this whole approach, see Paul E. Meehl, "Sir Karl, Sir Ronald, and Soft Psychology," *On Scientific Thinking* edited by Ryan Tweney, Michael Doherty, and Clifford Mynatt, (New York: Columbia University Press, 1981), 252-261. Also see Michael Doherty, "Null Hypothesis Testing, Confirmation Bias, and Strong Inference," *loc cit.*, 262-267.

vi. The mathematical definition of standard deviation is the square root of the mean of the squares of the deviations from the mean. This figure is determined for any sample by (1) determining the mean of all the scores, (2) determining by how much each square differs from the mean, (3) squaring each of the numbers found in step 2, (4) adding each of the numbers found in step 3, (5) determining the mean of the figure arrived at in step 4, and (6) determining the square root of the number found in step 5. Here is where the use of a computer can come in very handy.

vii. Taken from Gilbert Sax, *Principles of Educational and Psychological Measurement and Evaluation*, 2nd edition, (Belmont, CA: Wadsworth Publishing Company, 1980), 237.

viii. See Robert Hooke, *How To Tell the Liars from the Statisticians* (New York: Marcel Decker, Inc., 1983), for an elementary account of some common errors in statistical reasoning, and Howard Kahane, *Logic and Contemporary Rhetoric*, 9th edition, (Belmont, CA: Wadsworth Publishing Co., 2002), especially Chapter 4, page 97ff for a presentation of a multitude of examples of shoddy arguments involving statistics and Joel Best, *More Damned Lies and Statistics: How Numbers Confuse Public Issues* (Berkeley: University of California Press, 2005), for a presentation on the misuse of statistical evidence in public policy debates. Kahane's book is especially fun for those who like to "philosophize with a sledgehammer," as Nietzsche puts it.

"Don't play that slow country music. I drink more, and think sore, and sing right along." So goes a ditty penned by a researcher who spent 10 years studying the effects of country and western songs on people at a bar in Missoula, Mont. The researcher, James Schaefer of the University of Minnesota, concludes that wailing, lonesome, self-pitying music tends to make people drink faster. No doubt about it. Country and western can be a prescription for trouble among people with little self-control. One reason is the lyrics: sad songs about lost love, personal freedom, truck driving and the solace of drinking. The songs and lyrics of Hank Williams, Jimmy Rogers, Jerry Lee Lewis, Johnny Cash, Merle Haggard, Jerry Jeff Walker, Willie Nelson and Waylon Jennings were particularly powerful drinking inducements.

—News item

CHAPTER FIVE

The Scientific/Critical Method

INTRODUCTION

In Chapter One, you were introduced to the field of perception and the role observation plays in the formation of knowledge. In Chapter Three, you were presented with a brief discussion of deductive arguments, followed in Chapter Four by an examination of inductive arguments. In this chapter, I will put together some of the ideas presented in these three chapters to show you how the scientific/critical method works both in theory and in practice. The scientific/critical method is the most efficient problem solving technique devised by humans. Unquestionably, the world as you know it could not exist except as the product of this problem solving methodology. While the modern world is far from perfect, the complexities of contemporary life call for an understanding of the methodology which has done so much to produce these complexities.

As soon as I mention the word "**science**" I can see some of you shudder. Unfortunately, not only is the general level of education about science in this country at a woeful level, there is also a tendency to assume that it is unimportant to know much about the sciences anyway. A common cultural attitude towards science seems to be "Thanks, but no thanks." Scientific knowledge generally is held to be arid, obscure, and only for the intellectually overweight. The fruit of scientific understanding, technology, is treated by many people in the same manner in which so-called primitive people attempted to manipulate their surroundings, namely, by **magic**. Magic attempts to force the compliance of some part of the environment by the mere usage of the right words or formula, which is as about as effective as getting my kids to behave merely by talking to them. Similarly, we modern humans attempt to force our environment to comply with our wishes by seeking to push the right button. And when pressing the right button doesn't work, we call the repairman, the modern equivalent of the witch doctor (or Dr. Phil).

The smug attitude with which we attempt to manipulate the forces of our environment is intellectual chauvinism at its worst. It is also stupid and self-defeating, and, worst of all, in some ways it is political suicide. Our democratic form of government presupposes that the electorate has opinions that are based on good reasons and firm understanding. Asking a bunch of scientific illiterates to vote intelligently on issues such as cloning, global warming, or the political issues involved with AIDS control is like asking children to perform brain surgery on themselves and then act surprised when the results turn out to be a disaster.

"But there's so much to learn," you might say. It is certainly true that there is much to learn. In fact, there is far too much for any given individual to learn in science. Scientists themselves are well aware of this fact. This is why most scientific knowledge is found in the community of scientists, each individual of which possesses general knowledge of his or her field and specialized knowledge of only pieces of that field. As an enlightened member of a democratic community, you rightfully should be expected to possess some of the same broad background information as a scientific specialist. While everyone cannot be expected to know a lot about any or all of the branches of science, the average layperson should know enough to fill in the gaps in his or her knowledge with specialized information when important public policy decisions, such as those dealing with global warming, need to be made or when personal issues, such as how to protect one's self from possible contamination by chemical weapons, arise.

Perhaps you think that science is just plain hard, but there are two ways of getting around this. First, as a culture we need more individuals like Carl Sagan, Stephen J. Gould, and Steven Hawking. These individuals, brilliant scientists in their own right, are adept at explaining the basics of their disciplines in a popular fashion. A good science writer can make what is technically complex fascinating to read by presenting the basics of a subject in a simple straightforward manner. Popularizing science, however, is tricky; there is always the danger that the writer may oversimplify and distort the subject matter in the attempt to explain its basics to an audience of neophytes. Bearing this in mind, it is a useful idea to seek out and utilize well written popular accounts of technical subjects—should such material be available—as a way of getting a foothold on material you might otherwise find uninteresting. Popular accounts, however, are like *Cliff Notes* in that it is intellectual suicide to rely too heavily on them for your knowledge of a given discipline.

Secondly, there is a basic philosophical problem at work in the lament that learning science is too difficult. As Aristotle recognized long ago,[i] young people are primarily motivated by pleasure. To say that a given subject matter is difficult implies more than it is hard to learn, it is also to say that the study of it produces little or no immediate pleasure. Your favorite subjects in school are not simply those in which you do well, but those you enjoy studying to begin with, which is then made manifest in your good performance. Conversely, the subjects you dislike most are probably those in which you excel the least, due to the fact that you don't enjoy the study of them. Some people, alas, don't enjoy studying anything and therefore don't tend to do well in school. It is a good sign that you are an adult if you are able to study what you do not enjoy now under the assumption that the enjoyment of some related benefit will come later. This is called *delayed gratification.* Adults, generally, are expected to be good at delaying gratification while children are not held to the same standard. Therefore, as Mary Poppins recognized, the trick is to turn the work of a child into a game for that child.

How that can be done without trivializing the work is another, and perhaps more difficult, question to answer.

Some people find science difficult because they treat it as merely an endless collection of facts, rather like a jigsaw puzzle with an infinite number of pieces. While it is certainly true that science consists of an endless collection of facts, to treat it like an endless jigsaw puzzle can be a mistake, unless, of course, you are fanatically into jigsaw puzzles. Most of us take no pleasure in endless tasks because we fail to see any kind of payoff in them. Science promises three forms of payoffs—**explanation**, **prediction**, and **control**. *The primary purpose of science is the explanation of the phenomena to which our attention has been directed.* Successful explanation leads to successful prediction; if you know why something happens, you are also in a position to tell when this thing is likely to occur next and under what conditions it is likely to occur. Knowing the likely conditions for its occurrence is certainly helpful in attempting to control its occurrence. You must first understand, for example, what AIDS is and how it works before you can predict who is likely to get it and under what conditions it is likely to be spread. And when you know these last two things you are in a much better position to control its course.

Even if science is an infinite jigsaw puzzle, it can be broken down into non-infinite components. I wish to suggest to you, however, that a better way to conceive of **scientific/critical methodology** is not simply as a gigantic jigsaw puzzle, but as a methodology for constructing finite jigsaw puzzles out of the gigantic puzzle we call the universe. Science is primarily the way of putting the puzzle together and only secondarily the actual puzzle itself. This method of putting the puzzle together is known as the scientific method or the method of hypothesis testing, and in this text I will call it the scientific/critical method. It is the most effective problem solving technique ever invented.[ii]

Science is best understood as a collection of problem solving strategies, and not simply as the factual material produced by these strategies. These strategies can be applied independently of the subject matter involved, so you do not necessarily have to know a great many facts about any specific science to apply the scientific method. It is a mistake to assume that this problem solving methodology applies only to those which traditionally have been labeled the "hard sciences"—chemistry, physics, biology, and so forth. This methodology can be applied successfully to a far wider range of problems, including those of the so-called "soft sciences," like psychology, sociology, and anthropology, as well as issues you are likely to encounter in everyday life. The scientific/critical method is a four-fold process involving (a) defining the problem, (b) formulating a hypothesis to solve the problem, (c) testing the hypothesis, and (d) evaluating the results of the test. I will discuss each of these aspects of the scientific method separately.

I. DEFINING THE PROBLEM

A problem is a gap. This gap involves three aspects: where you are at present, where you want to be or ought to be, and the space between these positions. Where you are at present is the **starting point** of the problem, the **solution** to the problem is where you want to be or ought to be and the distance between these two points is called the **problem space**. Gaps may be either in your understanding or in your ability to accomplish some task or in both your understanding and in your abilities. I will speak of the first type of gap as an **understanding gap** and the second type of gap as a **performance gap**. In order for a performance gap to be recognized, it first must be understood as such, so performance gap problems always presuppose some prior understanding of the problem.

The first stage of the scientific/critical method is the characterization of the three aspects of the problem. Normally, problems cannot be solved until they first are seen in general as problems ("The first step to recovery is admitting you have a problem...") and then as specific types of problems in particular. Just as it is true for observational knowledge, there can be no knowledge of a problem without seeing the problem as some type of problem or other. Problems that are seen as problems in which the starting point, the solution, and the gap in between can be formulated clearly or specified, I will call **well-defined problems**. However, well-defined problems are not the only kind of problems out there. Sometimes thinkers are unsure how to best formulate (or even understand) the starting point of some issue, or they might not be able to define a solution, even in principle (let alone whether the "solution" is a good solution). Sometimes they might not have any idea how to solve the problem or why a so-called solution makes sense as a possible means of bridging the gap between the starting and finishing points. If anything of this sort is true of the problem in question, I will call that problem an **ill-defined problem**.

Ill-defined problems are the ugly ducklings of the problem solving world. Unfortunately, like the proverbial ugly duckling, they don't get a great deal of respect or attention, and many people would just as soon pretend that they don't exist at all. Ill-defined problems are not ill-defined simply because they are complicated or hard; well-defined problems can be complicated and hard too. But a complicated, well-defined problem can be solved by breaking it down into the simpler problems which compose it. Ill-defined problems are far more ill-mannered. Ill-defined problems get no respect because they are messy and difficult (or impossible) to get a grip on. They're a pain; that people don't like them is no surprise—they give us migraines.

Before an ill-defined problem can be solved, it must be treated pragmatically as a well-defined problem. Problems may be ill-defined because they really consist of multiple, complicated messes. Consider world hunger, for example. It sounds straightforward; to solve world hunger, simply feed people. Brilliant! But before the problem of world hunger really can be solved, it must first be recognized that there are really many interrelated problems involved in what is characterized simply as just "world hunger." What does it mean to be hungry? Who is chronically hungry and how often are they hungry? What does their normal diet consist of? How can their normal diet be augmented? What new types of food would suffice to take the place of the diet of the chronically hungry? Where is this new food to be obtained? How is it to be distributed? Who is to pay for all of this? What types of social/political/ideological factors condition the lifestyles of those affected by hunger? No one can solve the problem of "world hunger" simply by itself. But maybe someone can solve some of these component problems by treating them as if they were well-defined problems in the first place.

Problems may be ill-defined because either their starting points or their solutions are not clearly understood. It is always possible to characterize the starting point and the solution of a given problem in a number of ways. How the starting points and solutions are defined will make a great deal of difference concerning the legitimacy or appropriateness of any particular attempt to bridge the problem space. Debates frequently arise concerning the best or correct way to characterize the starting points and solutions for a given problem. In my world hunger illustration, one person could see this as basically a problem of limiting the number of hungry mouths to feed. This might entail a solution which emphasizes birth control as a desired means to the solution. Another person could characterize the problem as basically an issue of the correct distribution of current food resources. This might entail a solution which emphasizes efficiency of transportation methods as a desired means to the solution. Yet a third person might characterize the problem as an ideological one created by a given population's unwillingness to adopt potential sources of protein available to it. The list goes on. Alternative ways of understanding the problem usually recommend very different means of achieving the desired solution.

To make things even more complicated, it is sometimes the case that the very understanding of the problem itself will undergo modifications. In the course of attempting to produce a given solution by utilizing a means of bridging the problem space that first seemed eminently reasonable (given the initial way in which the problem was characterized), a problem solver may discover that failure to produce the required solution forces the reformulation of the way in which the problem itself is conceived. A proponent of a particular solution to the world hunger example who sees the issue as a matter of the efficient distribution of existing resources may discover that the political or ideological climate of various nations or states effectively prevents his or her attempts of achieving the desired results, and thus s/he may be led to reformulate his or her understanding of the problem as political rather than economic in nature. *The ability to reformulate your very understanding of a complex problem is a characteristic (of several) that distinguishes you as a critical thinker from a person who dogmatically insists that a particular problem has to be characterized in only one certain way.*

Are the following problems well-defined or ill-defined? If the problem is ill-defined, is it ill defined because it is a complex problem, because its initial state is poorly understood, or because its final state is poorly understood? Finally, if the problem is ill-defined, does your definition of the problem undergo modification as you attempt to make it a well-defined problem?

A. You meet someone in one of your classes to whom you are instantly attracted. You would like very much to get to know this person better, but you are shy. How can you meet this person without ruining your chances of getting to know him or her because of your shyness?

B. You have got to get to school in the morning but your car won't start. What do you do now?

C. You are a detective and your job is to determine who stole your friend's car.

D. You are not doing well on your critical thinking tests. How can you do better?

E. You want to go to Florida over Spring break, but you have no ride, no money, and your parents say no way. Now what?

F. Your teacher is a jerk. How can you do well in this person's class?

Once a well-defined problem is understood as a certain type of problem, it is also the case that it is understood that certain things are true about the starting point, solution, and problem space of that problem. As is the case with observational knowledge, scientific/critical knowledge[iii] is not simply a single still picture of a present state of affairs, but always has the awareness of some of the many factors which make sense out of the limited data presented by any single mental conception of a particular issue. In other words, *the understanding of a particular problem as a given state of affairs is theory-laden. The understanding of a given problem is also the product of a certain mind-set.* Theory-ladenness and mind-set determine the formulation of hypotheses designed to solve the problem in question.

II. FORMULATING HYPOTHESES

Once a given issue has been distilled into a well-defined problem, the attempt can be made to generate one or a number of **hypotheses** designed to bridge the gap between the initial state and the solution. A hypothesis is an idea which is assumed to be true for the purpose of solving the problem. Hypotheses are **heuristic devices**. A heuristic is a practical rule of thumb which shows some promise as a means for the accomplishment of some desired goal, in this case the problem you are working on. To generate a hypothesis is to come up with an idea which may or may not prove to be true, but at least is not already known to be false. The purpose of the next stage of the scientific/critical method will then be to test the hypothesis to see whether it is actually true, but before hypotheses can be tested, they must be formulated.

What is the best way to formulate a reasonable hypothesis concerning any given problem? Alas, there are no algorithms for the development of hypotheses. An **algorithm** is a problem solving technique which is guaranteed to work if it is applied correctly, but there are no sure-fire techniques for assuring that the hypotheses you dream up to solve a particular problem will even be reasonable, let alone true. A reasonable hypothesis is one that has some chance at success and is worth the time and effort needed to test it, *but a hypothesis can be reasonable and still be false.* Testing is designed to determine whether or not a reasonable hypothesis is true. After a particular hypothesis has been discovered and successfully tested, it may be the case that the hypothesis now seems obvious. Researchers kick themselves for failing to see the "obvious" but obviousness usually only appears in hindsight. Foresight is the ability to see the "obvious" in advance. "Obviousness" is a function not simply of theoretical understanding, but also of mind-set; if your mind is set not to see something, you probably won't see it. Only *after* you have come to see it (for whatever reason) does it becomes obvious, which is why obviousness is so closely associated with hindsight and not with foresight.

The most important place to look for a hypothesis to solve a particular problem is the theory in which your very understanding of the problem is embedded. To see your problem as a problem in the first place, you must assume the truth of a whole complex of related material. You cannot recognize world hunger as a problem, for example, unless you also recognize that people need food to eat, that certain things like dirt and sand cannot be digested, that food must be grown or hunted and cannot be produced by waving a magic wand, and so forth. You might think that all of this is mere common sense, and it is, if "common sense" stands for the knowledge of the theories which so much of our everyday life takes for granted.

In general, the more you know about the subject matter in which your problem is embedded, the easier it is to make the mental connections necessary for the production of reasonable hypotheses concerning problems in that subject area. Prior knowledge breeds possible hypotheses like guppies produce babies.

Sometimes, hypotheses come from the strangest places. The history of science contains many examples of scientists who have discovered important hypotheses when they were not immediately engaged in thinking about the problem with which they were directly concerned. This phenomenon is known as **serendipity**, the ability to combine (often by accident) what is seemingly unrelated. The folktale that Isaac Newton "discovered" gravity when he was hit on the head by an apple while reclining under a tree is an untrue, but interesting, illustration of this phenomenon. In reality, August Kekulé discovered the nature of the carbon atom one summer day in 1854 when he dozed off while riding a bus in London. As he slept, he dreamed that he saw atoms holding hands and dancing in a chain. A few years later another dream, this one about snakes, led him to further refine his hypothesis. There are some famous near misses, too. Oxford physicist Frederick Smith narrowly missed his chance for fame and fortune by discovering X rays when he noticed that photographic plates stored near a cathode-ray tube were likely to get fogged up. Failing to put 2 and 2 together, Smith had his assistant move the storage place of the plates and left it at that. It was left up to Wilhelm Roentgen to notice the same phenomenon and correctly add the equation. To this day, units of atomic radiation are measured in Roentgens, not in Smiths.[iv] Sorry about that, Fred; that's mind set for you.

III. TESTING HYPOTHESES

It is usually easy to discover or invent a variety of hypotheses concerning any given topic. The real problem lies in sifting through all of the possible candidates to determine which one of them is worth the further time and effort involved in testing. Testing is time-consuming and expensive, so some means must be found to sift among the possibilities and to rule certain possible hypotheses out immediately. This is known as the problem of **test worthiness**. The test worthiness of a hypothesis is determined by the following six conditions: relevance, verifiability, falsifiability, compatibility, predictiveness, and simplicity. Testing a hypothesis is only worthwhile if it looks a priori (that is, before actually running the test) like it will satisfy all six of these conditions. Failure to satisfy any of the six conditions is generally a good reason for rejecting the proposed hypothesis out of hand. I shall discuss each of these conditions in turn.

A. Relevance

A test worthy hypothesis (H_1) is relevant to the problem you are trying to solve. While this hardly may seem surprising, it is surprising how often even this seemingly simple condition is violated. *To say that H_1 is relevant to a problem is to say that some fact you are trying to explain is logically deducible from the background theories and laws that you understand to govern the subject area at issue* in combination *with the proposed hypothesis, i.e., that is not deducible merely from the background theories and laws alone.* A good hypothesis adds to the explanation of the problem something which cannot be determined without the hypothesis. Another way of saying the same thing is that a good hypothesis expands the material which the existing theory can explain. If the existing theory can already explain the phenomena in question without the use of the proposed hypothesis, or if the proposed hypothesis and the existing theory do not entail the phenomena to be explained, the new hypothesis is irrelevant to a proper understanding of the issue.

Suppose you are a detective seeking to identify the murderer of a person who was stabbed from behind. It would be useful for you to determine whether the killer was right or left handed, and this usually can be deter-mined by considering the path the knife traced through the victim's body. Now suppose the medical examiner maintains that the autopsy shows that the victim was stabbed by a right-handed person wearing a yellow shirt, though no fibers of yellow cloth were found on the victim or at the scene of the crime. Unless there is some evidence (such as yellow fibers found on the victim) which could be explained *only* by the hypothesis that the killer wore a yellow shirt, the yellow shirt aspect of the hypothesis must be dropped as it explains nothing that cannot just as well be explained without it. The part of the hypothesis about the killer being right handed, however, is needed to explain the actual path the knife cut through the victim's body, and so that part of the hypothesis is relevant to the phenomena in question.

The model of scientific explanation I am advancing here is called the **deductive nomological model**.[v] The term "nomological" refers to the **laws** and **theories** which form the backbone of any given discipline. To say that any statement is a law (or a law of nature) is to say that it is an empirical proposition which refers universally and necessarily (or statistically) to all of the members of some class of phenomena. Because empirical laws refer to all possible members of a given subject class, and not only to the actual members of the class which happen to exist here and now, empirical laws properly have a hypothetical form, that is, they all can be put properly into if...then statements. To say, for example, that the law of gravity is true is to say that *if* anything is a material object, *then* it is attracted to each and every other material object in proportion to their masses and inversely proportional to the square of the distance between them. Because the laws of nature refer to whole classes of objects and because some classes are subsets of larger classes, there are various levels of natural laws. To use a biological illustration, some possible law about how the bodies of mammals function would be a subset of a law about how living bodies function because the class of mammals is a subset of the class of living bod-

THE THEORY AND PRACTICE OF CRITICAL THINKING

ies. Science seeks to discover both the laws governing the actions of various classes of things and the proper relationship between these laws. If there were no laws of nature, science could not exist.

To discover these laws scientists also utilize theories. The word "theory" has two common uses which should not be confused. In the first use the word "**theory₁**" is simply a synonym for hypothesis, as when I say, "That's just your theory," meaning, "that's just your idea and it could be wrong." This is not the meaning of the word "theory" intended here. When scientists use the word "**theory₂**" they mean a research program designed to solve a range of problems of the sort under consideration. Finally, scientists also use the term theory to mean **theory₃**, which refers to a whole system of ideas devised to explain a large range of phenomena. Evolutionary theory₃ and atomic theory₃ are two examples of this; evolutionary theory₃ is not "just a theory₁," a mistake made frequently by those who write letters to the editors of newspapers.

A good theory₃ must include three elements: statements presenting the definitions of the key terms contained in the theory, statements explaining the relationship between these key terms, and statements relating these key terms to actual or possible phenomena the theory is designed to explain. Theories₂ serve as platforms for research, but a good theory₃ will go beyond theory₂. It will always explain more facts then were used to devise the theory₂; that is, *a good theory₃ can be extended indefinitely to cover many different facts which weren't even known when the theory₂ was first developed.*

Usually, theories₃ contain terms referring to entities which have not been directly observed yet. These unobserved entities are called **theoretical entities**. Theoretical entities are assumed to exist when it is necessary to postulate them to explain phenomena which otherwise would have no possible explanation. For a long time atoms could not be observed, but it was necessary to postulate their existence to account for an enormous range of actual

and observed phenomena. The parts of atoms such as electrons, protons, and neutrons still cannot be directly observed, but there are many reasons for saying that they must exist.

Finally, the deductive nomological model presupposes that certain **background conditions** are indeed true. Background conditions refer to all of the circumstances which you must get right to assure the accuracy and reliability of your experiment. These conditions will include a research design sufficient to provide a real test of the hypothesis in question and not simply a sham, for example, the conditions covering the adequacy of the equipment used in the experiment. Do they work? Were they turned on? Are they capable of measuring what you want measured? Were they used correctly? And so forth. Background conditions also include the accuracy of calculations involved in the experiment and accurate reporting of the results of the experiment. To say, then, that a good hypothesis (theory₁) is relevant to what you are trying to explain is to say that, when coupled with theories₂ and theories₃, laws pertaining to the subject matter at issue, and background conditions, the hypothesis allows for the deduction of certain observed consequences (or a priori predictions about these observed consequences) which cannot be obtained merely from the theories₂ and laws and background conditions alone.

It should be noted that the construction of a valid deductive argument with premises including laws, theories₂, background conditions and the hypothesis in question (H_1), then serves as a strong *inductive* argument for showing the probable truth of H_1. It does not show deductively (that is, necessarily) that H_1 must be true, because other hypotheses (H_2, H_3, etc.) might satisfy the same conditions too, perhaps even better then the H_1 being tested. *Hypothesis testing does not provide the same kind of logical certainty found in deductive arguments.* This is one reason why scientific ideas, laws, theories₂, and explanations are always subject to revision or replacement by better ones.

B. Verifiability[vi]

Verifiability is an important notion in hypothesis testing. Indeed, it's probably one of the first things to come to mind when you think about testing your hypothesis. To say that a hypothesis H_1 is verifiable is to say that it provides predictions about future observations which turn out to be true when experiments designed to test the hypothesis are run. It seems intuitively obvious that a good hypothesis ought to make successful predictions about the course of events, but there is more to it than that. To say that a hypothesis is verified is *not* to say that it has been proven, if to prove something means to establish it beyond all shadow of doubt. To insist on that condition would be to eliminate science altogether, as any scientific claim is always subject to revision pending further evidence (though all scientific claims are not equally easy to revise). The evidence which would call for the revision of a hypothesis is typically much simpler than the evidence required for the revision of theories$_2$ or laws. Vulnerability to revision is one of the defining characteristics of science; therefore, to say that a given hypothesis is verified can only mean that the results of the successful experiment tend to confirm or support its truth. Good hypotheses tend to have their truths confirmed in repeated instances.

It is important here to distinguish between verification in practice and verification in principle. When you think of verification, you are probably thinking of verification in practice, meaning that the experiment has actually been devised and successfully completed. However there are lots of cases in which a given hypothesis can be devised but not tested successfully owing to conditions which have nothing to do with the truth value of the hypothesis. There are plenty of practical limitations to hypothesis testing. Testing takes time, usually costs money (sometimes a great deal of money), frequently requires equipment, and so forth. If you haven't got the time, the equipment, or the money to run an experiment you cannot verify your hypothesis in practice, though it still may be easily verifiable in principle. To say that it is verifiable in principle is to say that if you did have the time, equipment, and money to run the experiment you could have generated a test which would have been relevant towards determining the truth of your hypothesis.

To further complicate matters, it sometimes is difficult to devise a practical test for a given hypothesis which would verify the truth of *only that hypothesis*. It is always possible to think up a number of hypotheses to explain a given situation, and extreme care must be taken in devising a test appropriate for only one among the indefinitely large number of possible hypotheses which could conceivably explain what you are seeking to explain. It may, in fact, be impossible to think up such a unique test. Should this be the case, your hypothesis would not be verifiable in principle, at least as of yet. When this unfortunate state of affairs occurs, you cannot know whether or not your hypothesis is verifiable in practice; your hypothesis could be true, but you are not going to be able to determine this.

Not all tests designed to verify hypotheses are created equal. Some tests are more important or significant than others, and when this happens, philosophers (and scientists) call these tests **crucial experiments**. An experiment is a crucial experiment if it is believed by the scientific community to be so significant for establishing the truth of some controversial issue that the community, in fact, is willing to count the results of the test as definitive. When Albert Einstein, for example, postulated his theory of relativity in the beginning of the twentieth century, most physicists were skeptical. In this case, skepticism was based, among other things, on one of the aspects of Einstein's theory which claimed that light waves were subject to the influence of gravity. This seemed absurd to the scientists at the time. How could gravity attract light? How could this even be tested? This stumped everyone for a time until it was suggested that the hypothesis entailed the claim that light waves from distant stars passing near the vicinity of the sun ought to be refracted by the gravity of the sun. Fine, but the light rays emitted by the sun totally obscure the light waves coming from the distant stars, and it's hard to turn the sun off. But sometimes the sun is "turned off" by the actions of the moon during a solar eclipse. If the position of certain known stars could be determined at night in the absence of the sun (which is certainly easy enough), and then measured against the apparent position of these same stars as their light waves passed close to the sun during a total solar eclipse, a comparison of these positions which showed an apparent shift in the position of the stars would tend to confirm Einstein's audacious theory. But total solar eclipses don't happen every day, so everyone had to sit on their hands until one showed up, which was not for several years. Finally on May 29, 1919, a total solar eclipse was set to occur, but only for West Africa and Brazil, far from existing telescopes. Observers trekked out to set up their equipment in distant lands while Einstein and others waited in Europe on pins and needles for their reports, because it was agreed that the results of this experiment would go a long way towards establishing Einstein's theory of relativity as credible. Word finally was telegraphed back to the capitals of Europe; "They moved!" Einstein's predictions were confirmed and, "over night," the acceptance of his theory swept through the scientific community.[vii]

C. Falsifiability[viii]

It is easy to see that falsification is the flip side of verification. If a good hypothesis needs to be subject to the canons of verification, then it needs equally well to be subject to the canons of falsification. As is the case with verifiability, it is important to distinguish between falsification in principle and falsification in practice. In practice, the same limitations of equipment, time, and money governing verification govern falsification. I will say no more about this aspect of the matter; instead, I wish to call your attention to the important function falsification plays in the practice of the scientific/critical method. This role is so vital to science that real science cannot exist without it. After a moment's reflection, it may strike you as strange; why should a scientist seek to prove that his or her own hypothesis is really false? If the scientist thought that it might be false, why would s/he bother to mess with it in the first place?

Hypotheses are devised to explain some phenomenon or other. Any given hypothesis may be either true or false, and the problem is to determine which; tests are designed to perform this function. It is usually the case that the same test will serve either to verify a given hypothesis (if the test results turn out to be positive) or falsify the hypothesis (if the test results turn out negative). Paradoxical as it may sound, a falsified hypothesis can be just as useful in the advancement of knowledge as a verified one, because the falsification of a hypothesis tells you what you have good reason *not* to believe, just as the verification of the hypothesis tells you what you have good reasons to believe.

A good scientific hypothesis is highly falsifiable but not falsified. A hypothesis is a tentative solution to a problem, an educated guess. Any hypothetical solution to a problem maintains that whatever it proposes is the correct solution to a specific problem, and any other conceivable solution is incorrect. Any hypothesis states that whatever it proposes is true and all other possibilities are false. A good illustration of this is found in the children's game *Clue*. If you say that the murder was committed in the library by Mr. Plum with a gun, then you are also at the same time denying that the murder was committed in any other room by any other character using any other weapon. Your hypothesis is highly falsifiable; if the murder was committed by any other character or in any other room or with the use of any other weapon, you would be wrong. But if the murder really was committed by Mr. Plum in the library using a gun, then your theory, though easily falsifiable, is not in fact falsified. Good hypotheses are risky in that lots of things could, in principle, falsify them; the riskier the hypothesis, the better it is.

It takes courage to subject your hypothesis to the risk of testing; no one likes to be proven wrong, and egos are frequently on the line. It is only natural to try and minimize the consequences of an experiment that apparently refutes your pet theory. Suppose that you were Einstein in the famous experiment cited above. What would you have said if the message from Africa stated that there was no apparent change in the position of the background stars? "Gee, guys, back to the old drawing board. Just call me Mr. Mudstein from now on." Given what was at stake, probably not. An apparently convenient way out of this mess would be simply to deny that the negative results really refute your pet theory. This kind of move, which in fact is often made by thinkers because it is so tempting, would be a philosophical mistake. Denying that any and all negative results of experiments designed to test your hypothesis are really negative (or could ever be negative) no matter how the experiment is changed or modified to test your pet theory is the essence of irrationality.

One common way to persist in the irrational affirmation of a questionable theory is through the introduction of *ad hoc* **hypotheses**. An *ad hoc* hypothesis is one which is advanced by the thinker solely for the purposes of explaining away inconveniently negative evidence. An *ad hoc* hypothesis has no other reason for its existence, and it has nothing else going for it; there is no positive evidence for its truth other than the apparent help it gives the thinker in saving his or her pet theory. If the crucial experiment designed to test Einstein's theory of relativity had had negative results, Einstein could have attempted to save his idea from extinction by arguing that the scientists who made the disconfirming observations lied about them because they had it in for him because he was Jewish, and so forth. Lacking independent confirmation, this kind of claim is simply silly. *Ad hoc* hypotheses are to be avoided at all costs, but hypotheses don't come

with labels on them (*ad hoc*: wash in warm water; tumble dry), so they may not be as easy to recognize as you think.

One wrinkle in the falsification process involves the special difficulties inherent in the attempt to prove a negative. **Proving a negative** establishes the non-existence of something. Such a feat can be quite a bit trickier than establishing something's existence. When a search for data fails to find any, it does not follow that there are no data; the search may have been insufficient, and a wider search may discover data, or it may not, and there is usually no a priori, infallible way of determining whether a search has been exhaustive. Data searches are matters which combine both sophia and phronesis. To assume that a search has been exhaustive may be an illustration of a fallacious **argument from ignorance**, which occurs when one argues that the absence of known evidence is a sufficient condition for establishing the truth of a negative claim about the existence of the object in question ("I've never seen Santa Claus, so he must not exist."). Again, the ignorance of relevant evidence may be a more accurate assessment of the incompetence of the investigator than the falsity of what is at issue. Questions may easily be begged here.

Another closely related means of irrationally affirming the truth of a questionable hypothesis in spite of all apparent evidence to the contrary is to practice **confirmation bias**. Though experimentation is designed to determine whether a hypothesis is true or false, there are a host of reasons why a thinker would be happy to embrace the results of a given test of his or her pet theory if the results were positive and yet extremely reluctant to embrace the results of the same test should the result turn out to be negative. Jobs, status in the scientific community, prestige, and other important factors may ride on the successful results of the hypothesis testing. Confirmation bias stems from the thinker's mind-set. It consists in the desire to look only for the evidence which will verify a pet theory and in willfully neglecting to seek evidence which will falsify it. Should such unsought negative evidence none-the-less turn up, confirmation bias encourages the investigator to simply ignore it, or what is even worse, to treat it as funny evidence which really supports the theory! This becomes a sort of "Heads I win and tails you lose," situation. Persons who don't have the same stake in the truth of the questionable theory are usually in a better position to see this kind of intellectual shoddiness as having taken place than are those who fall prey to it. It is usually easier to see the errors others commit than to see yourself as having committed the same mistake. To avoid this, scientific communities insist on blind peer reviews by disinterested observers of materials submitted for publication.

Minimizing the possibility of being victimized by fallacies like confirmation bias is one of the important reasons why falsification is such an important criterion for good hypothesis testing. Instead of simply asking "What would prove my theory correct," ask yourself with honesty what would disprove your theory. As awkward, hard, humiliating, and frustrating as it may be to admit that you are wrong, if you refuse to count any possible result as disconfirming your theory you are not maintaining your theory on a rational basis, but as some kind of a priori dogma. Rationality is inherently a risky business where the ego is concerned.

D. Compatibility

A good hypothesis must be compatible with previously affirmed knowledge. Whatever truth is, all the things which are true are by necessity consistent with each other. The testing of a given hypothesis, therefore, can safely assume that what is already known to be true within a given subject area will remain true. These other truths make up the background of theories and laws used in constructing and testing any particular hypothesis. In this manner, hypotheses are like parts of puzzles. Once you have fit some of them together, new ones must go into places in a manner that doesn't require the previously established ones to be thrown

out. If a given hypothesis is obviously incompatible with what is already known in a given field, it is almost certain to be summarily rejected, and it should be. As previously stated, it is always possible to devise multiple hypotheses to explain phenomena. Not all can be tested, so some method or other must be utilized in cutting down the number of explanatory candidates, and compatibility is used to help pare the list. In this fashion science is highly conservative; it prefers to stick with what it already has.

There is still a problem here. In any established scientific discipline there are always plenty of **anomalies**. An anomaly is some phenomenon which the existing explanatory schema seemingly cannot explain. Humans are a long way from being omniscient, so there will always be things we do not or cannot know; it is the function of rationality to fill in the gaps in our knowledge as much as possible. By anomalies, I don't mean simple gaps in knowledge—real anomalies are meaner than that. Some phenomenon is anomalous in a given system if even repeated attempts to explain it in terms of the theories$_2$ and laws of the discipline fail to do so. The darn thing shouldn't be there, but there it is! Usually only one of two things can be done with an anomaly—you either can work on it some more until it is solved or ignore it for now and hope that someday someone will eventually explain it. This is the scientist at work as a conservative.

Sometimes, thinkers get fed up with trying to solve a problem using the old system and are equally unwilling to wait for someone else to eventually bail them out. When this happens, thinkers look around for some really new and different ways to explain these anomalous phenomena. And this means that thinkers are sometimes willing to temporarily suspend the criterion of compatibility with the old system. The operative assumption now is that the old system is never going to solve these anomalies because in some important way or other, the old system is simply wrong; this is how revolutionaries are born. The history of the development of science is filled with the names of some of these great revolutionaries, people like Copernicus, Galileo, Darwin, and Einstein, to mention some with whom you are probably already familiar.

True revolutions are rare, but important, developments in the history of knowledge. A revolution changes the basic theories and laws used in common hypothesis formulation and testing. In doing this, the revolutionary system even changes the meanings of the basic terms employed by the old system. The concept of matter, for example, means one thing to Newtonian physics and quite another thing in relativity theory. Old guard thinkers and revolutionaries are quite literally speaking different languages and talking about different things even when they are apparently referring to the same phenomena. Unsurprisingly, this can lead to a great deal of confusion for the thinkers involved in the struggle as well as for the student of the discipline.

But even the most radical of revolutionary thinkers are usually also deeply conservative. Revolutionaries seek to explain the anomalous phenomena that the old system apparently cannot properly explain. There are always plenty of things that the old system has already explained, and the revolutionary needs to be able to explain these things too; the baby need not be thrown out with the bath water. So compatibility counts for the revolutionary too, and it counts deeply. The revolutionary sees the new system as a better way of serving the concept of compatibility than can be done through the use of the old system of thought.[ix]

E. Predictiveness

Hypotheses are generated for testing not simply because they allow you to understand a given situation, but also because they are thought to have certain important consequences if they are true. The consequences they are believed to have if they are true are the things that they predict. Predictions are those claims which follow logically from the conjunction of the theories$_2$ and laws of the

discipline and the given hypothesis in question. If the predictions of a hypothesis turn out to be false, it counts as a reason to reject the validity of the hypothesis. This condition has already been discussed under the aspect of verification and falsification.

There is another angle to this. Hypotheses also can be evaluated in terms of the number of true predictions they produce. In general, the more predictions a given hypothesis produces, the better the hypothesis, and the more true predictions a given hypothesis produces, the stronger the hypothesis. Sheer number of predictions is important because it gives the thinker many opportunities for verification and falsification; a large number of true predictions can justifiably increase the thinker's confidence in the truth of the hypothesis because it becomes increasingly improbable that these predictions were right by accident. A hypothesis which produces few predictions is deficient because it gives the thinker little to work with and it might contain only lucky guesses. A large number of true predictions will reduce the likelihood of the hypothesis being right by mere chance as opposed to really being true.

F. Simplicity

A good hypothesis is a simple hypothesis. To say that a hypothesis is simple is to say that it proposes no more than is needed to explain the phenomena in question. This rule is frequently called **Ockham's razor** after the fourteenth century monk who first formulated it: "Plurality is not to be assumed without necessity."[x] A simple hypothesis that explains all of the evidence is preferable to a more complicated hypothesis that assumes the truth of things unwarranted by existing evidence. In the example I used above about the person who was stabbed to death, the simplest explanation warranted by the facts was that the murderer was right-handed. To affirm that the murderer was right-handed *and* wore a yellow shirt exceeds the available evidence and does not present a good hypothesis until such time as further evidence can support the contention that the murderer wore a yellow shirt.

In summary, a good hypothesis is relevant to the problem it is designed to solve, it makes predictions which are both verifiable and falsifiable in principle and in practice, it is compatible with existing knowledge, it makes possible many predictions about the future course of events, and it is the simplest hypothesis compatible with all the known evidence. It should be noted that these six conditions of good hypotheses testing are all ideals. In practice, it is quite common for the thinker to emphasize only one or a few of them in designing a particular experiment. Sometimes one thinker will come up with either significantly different hypotheses or different ways of testing the same hypothesis because s/he is concentrating on different criteria from those of a colleague who is working on the same problem. The choice of which criteria to emphasize in any given case is a manifestation of the individual thinker's critical judgment and knowledge of the discipline, but the thinker should be able to explain why any particular criterion is to be emphasized in that given case over any of the others. The emphasis of different criteria in hypothesis selection and testing need not cause any confusion as long as it is recognized that these different criteria are mutually complementary.

Using the principles of the scientific/critical method of hypothesis testing, how would you devise and test hypotheses to determine the truth about the following issues?

A. There are still American POWs being held captive in Iraq.

B. Too much TV watching is turning American children into mental midgets.

C. If you over-inflate the tires on your car you will get better gas mileage.

D. Your great-grandmother was Anastasia, the long lost Crown Princess of Russia.

E. Your father is a CIA spy.

F. You have a mental block when it comes to doing math.

G. Most Nobel Prize winners in the Twentieth Century are firstborn children.

H. 9/11 was the result of a governmental conspiracy.

IV. EVALUATING THE RESULTS

After experiments are run, the work of the scientist or critical thinker is far from over; the results of the experiment still have to be evaluated. To evaluate anything is to assess that thing's value. Because values are the source of evaluation and evaluation is a necessary component of the scientific/critical thinking enterprise, scientific/critical thinking is not an automatic, value-free way of thinking. There are three types of closely interrelated values inherent in the scientific/critical thinking methodology: intellectual, pragmatic, and social. I shall discuss each of these in turn.

A. Intellectual

The goal of the intellect is to understand the truth. One of the intellectual values furthered by the pursuit of the scientific/critical method is pure knowledge and its contemplation. Human beings are animals possessed by curiosity, and knowing the truth is thought to be one of the most important goals of life. Good thinking, as practiced by the formulation and successful testing of true hypotheses about the world, is a highly effective means of reaching the goal of abstract understanding and thus of satisfying human curiosity. Curiosity is usually satisfied by the production of **explanations**. The term "explanation" has various senses:

1. In one sense of the term, something is explained when it (or its occurrence) no longer is felt as surprising. Explanation seeks to transform the surprising into the ordinary. In a closely related fashion, explanations also transform what is unfamiliar (and therefore perhaps surprising) into what is familiar or already known to us.

2. Regarding classes of events involving things like human or animal activities or actions,

explanations take the form of reasons or motives; they purport to offer the reasons why, for example, someone did something or refrained from doing anything in a certain situation.

3. A sense of explanation which frequently overlaps with the one just mentioned involves the reference to purpose. Someone has a purpose for doing what s/he did if s/he had some sort of goal in mind. The goal of the activity presents the activity's purpose, and knowledge of that goal will explain the point (and thus the nature) of that person's activity. Objects may have purposes too, in that they may be designed to perform certain functions. The purpose of the hand brake on a car is to provide additional braking power when the car's engine and transmission aren't doing the braking.

4. Another sense of explanation involves the inclusion of that which is to be explained into a class of events. When the item to be explained is itself already a class, explaining it consists in showing that the original class is a subset of a greater class. The reason, for example, that this Tabby has fur is because Tabby is a cat and cats have fur. The reason cats have fur is that cats are mammals and mammals have fur.

This last kind of explanation raises the problem of a **regress argument**. In an adequate explanation, the premises of the argument should not contain any questionable claims which are in turn just as much in need of an explanation as the conclusion of the argument. In the example above, if Tabby has fur because Tabby is a cat and cats have fur, why is it that cats have fur? Cats are mammals and mammals have fur. Well then, why do all mammals have fur? And so forth. An adequate explanation cannot simply repeat in its premises the subject of the conclusion being explained; there must be some way of appropriately stopping the regress from premise to premise.

Science seeks to offer the kind of explanation presented in (4) above while, at the same time, avoiding the regress problem. But this raises the problem of where to stop the regress of explanatory premises. Science seeks to explain the nature of an individual event or state of affairs by including it in a known class of events, each member of which possesses characteristics essentially similar to that which is to be explained, and it seeks to explain classes of events by subsuming them to other classes. Ultimately, the most far-reaching classes of events in terms of which everything else is explained would contain **laws of nature**. A law of nature makes a claim about a uniformity of events. These uniformities are either absolute (All X's are Y's) or statistical (A certain percentage of X's are Y's). In science nothing is explained without some ultimate reference to law.[xi] While science also seeks to render the unfamiliar familiar, to make the surprising unsurprising, and to give the reason or purpose behind certain sorts of actions, all of these senses of explanation ultimately rest on the concept of law. If there were no laws of nature, there could be no science.

Good hypothesis formulation and testing are at the heart of science. Here the critical thinker seeks to determine whether the results of the experiment s/he was running confirm or refute the proposed explanation suggested by the hypothesis. Just as importantly, were the means used to formulate and test the hypothesis in accordance with good scientific/critical methodology as laid out above? In reasoning it is not enough to be correct, you must be correct for the right reasons. To be correct for the right reasons is to show that the phenomenon in question is covered by the relevant laws of nature. Contemplation of the results of a successful experiment coupled with the knowledge that the correct means were used to produce these results is one of the highest rewards of the scientific/critical method.

B. Pragmatic

The pragmatic values of thinking are probably those which first spring to your mind when you think about the value of reason. The pragmatic value of reason lies in the answers it gives to our practical everyday concerns. There are so many of these, and you are already so familiar with them, it would be pointless even to begin to list them. They all have in common the fact that the scientific/critical mode of thinking is generally the most efficient means for satisfying these concerns when they can be satisfied, though perhaps nothing can satisfy them because not all problems necessarily can be solved.

One of the most visible manifestations of this type of value is the abundant technology which so structures our world that life literally would be unrecognizable without it. While there are certainly many other ways of thinking that are not obviously scientific and critical, none of these other methods of thought produce much in the line of technological artifacts, and even when they do, it is because they are also harnessed to the scientific/critical mode of thought. Technology is mechanized problem solving, that is, problem solving which is practiced in a normal, mechanical basis. Technology presupposes that certain types of problems will occur consistently and repeatedly and therefore can best be approached by the repeated application of the same solution technique. Transportation, for example, is an ongoing problem, and it is solved by inventing convenient types of vehicles (e.g., cars, boats, or planes) which can repeatedly perform the same function. While this problem solving technique for transportation sometimes breaks down, it does in fact work amazingly well most of the time. When it breaks down or becomes outdated, the solution is usually seen in terms of more and/or better technology.

The idea that there is a technological solution to recurring problems has been around so long that it is one of the defining characteristics of human beings. Humans are animals that make things for pragmatic purposes. Individual persons and whole cultures are evaluated in terms of their level of technological sophistication. Those which employ unsophisticated forms of technology are called "primitive" and "backwards," terms which are seldom meant as compliments. There are certainly advantages to being technologically unsophisticated. Think of all the instruction sheets you wouldn't have to worry about understanding! But few of us would voluntarily exchange our modern life for a primitive one.

From the pragmatic perspective, good hypotheses are those which enable us not only to solve our own personal problems, but to advance the state of technology so as to make possible the mechanization of problem solving procedures.

C. Social

So far, I have more or less left out one large area in terms of which the scientific/critical method and its offspring, intellectual contemplation and technology, are frequently evaluated, and that area is the broader area of the impact critical thinking has had on society. Undeniably critical thinking has transformed society even in your relatively short lifetime. If an individual who died in 1900 was resurrected today in any but the most isolated places in the world s/he would have a difficult time believing s/he was still on the planet Earth. The intellectual and technical developments in the last century have been truly profound, but these changes have also been expensive, not simply in terms of dollars and cents, but more importantly in terms of the intellectual and social systems destroyed or significantly changed. The scientific/critical method has wrought a revolution in the way we look at our selves and our world; whole societies and ideologies have fallen to this revolution, for better or worse.

While major technological change is inevitable, whether the changes caused by the development in technology are desirable is quite another question. As I said, technological development is not without its price. There are those who worry about the possible effects technological development may have on individuals, communities, whole societies, or even the Earth itself.[xii] The development of nuclear energy presents a good example of this quandary. Even the makers of the first atomic bombs had severe doubts about the wisdom of what they were doing.[xiii]

Although I want to suggest to you that one of the hallmarks of good thinking is that it makes possible new technological developments, there are those who are deeply distrustful of some possible future (or even present) technological developments (consider the current debate over cloning humans, for example). It has become fashionable to speak of "forbidden knowledge," that is, knowledge of how to do things which would be very dangerous or even downright evil to know or do. The argument against the development of certain technology is that it is simply folly to trust fallible humans with this sort of power. As Francis Bacon remarked, "Knowledge is power." Is power always good? Of course not. Anticipating Bacon, Teiresias remarks in Sophocles' *Oedipus Tyrannus*, "Wise words; but O, when wisdom brings no profit, to be wise is to suffer."[xiv] Like many other philosophical debates, this one refuses to go away. It calls our attention to the problematic nature of the development of human knowledge.

What positive or negative values can be associated with the following examples of technological development?

A. Cloning humans or animals.

B. Genetically altering food crops.

C. Curing cancer or other major diseases.

D. Creating artificial intelligence.

E. Colonizing the moon, Mars, or other places in our solar system.

V. EXPERIMENTATION INVOLVING HUMAN SUBJECTS

There are some special problems which occur whenever the scientific/critical method is utilized in experiments involving human beings. These problems include both intellectual and moral entanglements. I shall discuss each in turn.

Experiments involving human subjects are performed frequently. Medicine, psychology, education, and economics are three disciplines heavily involved with testing theories about the nature of human beings and the effects various aspects of our environment have on us and our behavior. Consumer products testing and marketing, urban planning, and sports and other performing arts are just some of the areas in which these theories are implemented. All of these activities place special demands on the experimental method adopted to insure the accuracy and validity of experimental results.

Experimenting with humans differs in many ways from experimenting with inanimate objects like electrons, Frisbees, and rocket engines. Human beings have the capacity to become aware of the fact that they are research subjects and to react to this fact in ways which might undermine the **validity**$_2$ of the experiment. To say that a particular experiment or test is valid$_2$ is to say that it in fact measures what it is supposed to measure and not something else. Invalid$_2$ experiments are worse than no experiments at all because they encourage misguided belief in the accuracy of their results when, in fact, they altogether fail to provide good reasons for establishing what they purport to establish. In addition to this, a good experiment ought to be **reliable**. A reliable experiment is one which consistently measures what it is designed to measure. A lot of testing consists of the replication (or attempted replication) of results reported by others. Failure to replicate reported results provides grounds for questioning the validity and reliability of the experimental method used in first reporting these results, and thus ultimately in the truth of the results itself.

Humans are liable to succumb to what is called the **demand effect** if they think they know the purpose of the experiment. They are likely to inaccurately report the existence of effects because they believe that this is what the experimenter really wants to see. Don't confuse the demand effect with deliberate lying.

Experimental subjects aren't lying when they report these illusionary results; rather, they are falling prey to their own mind-set. **Placebos** provide a good illustration of this problem. A placebo is an inert substance which none-the-less produces some effect in the experimental subjects because they believe that they ought to be experiencing that effect and therefore do in fact "experience" the effect. The proverbial sugar pill given to the hypochondriac which succeeds in alleviating the hypochondriac's symptoms is a common illustration of this phenomenon in practice.

In order to guard against the demand effect, human subjects should be **blind** to the purpose of the experiment. To say that an experimental subject is blind to the purpose of the experiment is to say that the subject has no knowledge of what the experimenter is interested in testing. Ideally, the subject should not even know that s/he is involved in an experiment in the first place, though there are practical and ethical difficulties involved with this. It is frequently impossible to run an experiment on a human subject without eliciting the cooperation of that subject. In some cases, it is also possible that the person running the experiment may unwittingly help to elicit the demand effect. When this becomes a problem, the experiment is best run **double blind**, which means that neither the experimental subjects nor the person running the experiment knows which experimental subjects are receiving the test object and which are receiving placebos. Researchers place the greatest confidence in results which are the products of double blind experiments.

Whenever any experiment is set up, the experimenters are going to be involved with a number of variables. A well-designed experiment distinguishes carefully between these different variables. One of the most important distinctions between variables is the distinction between **independent variables** and **dependent variables**. Independent variables have their values established or fixed by the experimenter first, and they represent the reputed cause in the experimental situation. Dependent variables are those whose values are controlled by the independent variables, and they are the reputed effects in the experimental situation. Is there, for example, a causal relationship between SAT scores and college grade point average? Ignoring for the purpose of this example the other variables that are involved in this situation, the researcher would first have to determine the independent variable (the SAT scores) and then see whether there was a connection between these scores and college grade point averages (the dependent variable). Before you begin your experiment, you will have to make sure that any variable appearing in your experiment has been defined with sufficient precision so that anyone seeking to replicate your results can be sure that you are both talking about the same thing. This is done by stipulating certain operational definitions (see Chapter II, section II), which will allow anyone to identify and measure precisely the variables in which you are interested.

Suppose you were interested in determining whether there is a relationship between your soccer team playing its games on Mondays and the amount of goals your team scores, i.e., do Monday games cause your team to score greater or fewer goals than games played on other days of the week? Before you run your experiment, you need to give an operational definition of the concept of scoring a goal. Are you going to count in your total goals scored by teams against themselves? Are you going to distinguish between regular goals and goals scored on penalty kicks? And so forth. Presumably the other key term involved here—day of the week—is sufficiently understood so as not to cause any possible confusion.

In this example, the day of the game is the independent variable because its value is established first by the experimenter. The number of goals scored by the team on its different playing days will then become the dependent variable. Having established this, you then look to see if there is any sort of correlation between the day of the week on which the games are played and the number of goals scored. If it turns out that your team scores a significantly different number of goals on certain days of the week, you will have provided some evidence for a causal relationship between the independent and the dependent variables, though you still will have to determine what exactly it is about the day of the week that affects your team's performance in this manner.

In addition to the theoretical problems involved with the design of any research experiment, especially those involving human subjects, there are ethical issues that need to be addressed, too. Let us turn our attention to the following passage, taken from the news.

A French scientist, Dr. Daniel Zagury of Curie University in Paris, has injected himself with a test AIDS vaccine. The French immunologist has emerged as a maverick figure in AIDS research because of his self-experimentation and what colleagues describe as a passionate commitment to speed up the pace of vaccine development. He said he hopes to launch a large-scale clinical trial of this vaccine in Africa and Europe, though he acknowledged he had not yet developed a test suitable for administration to perhaps hundreds of people.

There is no way of knowing yet whether Zagury is actually protected against infection with the virus because he assumes he has never been exposed to it.

Consider some of the theoretical and ethical problems Dr. Zagury's research is caught up in. AIDS has killed millions and it is spreading. Vaccines take time to develop, time in which more people are infected and die. It would be desirable to have an effective vaccine as soon as possible. Dr. Zagury has developed a vaccine, but whether the vaccine is effective remains to be seen. The only way to test this is to administer the vaccine (the independent variable) to a group of people not yet exposed to the virus who are likely to be exposed to the virus and determine whether the vaccine sup-

plies sufficient protection from contracting the virus (the dependent variable). But a proper test of the efficiency of the vaccine entails the existence of a control group which will be administered a placebo. Any possible test results would be worthless unless it was known that some of the subjects in both the research group and the control group actually were exposed to AIDS. Dr. Zagury mentions that he has administered the vaccine to himself, but what does that show unless he then exposes himself to the virus? And what if the vaccine fails to work? Then people (perhaps including Dr. Zagury himself) will die.

How could any test of a possible AIDS vaccine be administered in a way that didn't put peoples' lives on the line? Is it ever right to put peoples' lives on the line? But if peoples' lives are not put at risk, how can any results of the testing of a possible vaccine be valid? Most people believe that it is wrong to play with peoples' lives; this injunction is an instance of a **world view constraint**. World view constraints put limitations on the problem solving parameters which could be adopted were it not the case that their adoption would violate some deeply held belief such as the ethical ones mentioned above. Not all world view constraints are ethical; some are social, political, legal, religious, or economic. It would simply be naive to fail to see the complexities problems such as these can engender.

In each of the following illustrations of the use of the scientific/critical method identify the independent variable and the dependent variable. Are these valid and reliable experiments? Do any of them have problems with demand effect? Are all the important variables given sufficient operational definitions? If not, what is the variable which needs defining? Do any of them have parameters imposed on them by world view constraints?

A. During World War II Nazi concentration camp doctors wished to see how long individuals could be exposed to freezing temperatures in water before they died. They got a group of inmates, dressed them in Luftwaffe flight gear, and immersed them in ice water to see how long it took them to die. Then they got another group of inmates similarly clothed and immersed them until they were nearly dead. Removing the inmates from the ice water, they wrapped them in one, two, or three warm blankets. It was found that the addition of the second or third blanket made no significant difference in the length of time it took the reviving inmates to recover.

B. A study suggests the possibility that depressed men who jog frequently are less likely to die at an early age. The study included 918 men aged 45-59. They were divided in three groups: those who jogged twice or more a week, an intermediate group who jogged twice a month and those who jogged less than monthly. A decade later, researchers found that the death rate among the least active men was twice as high as that of the most active. The death rate in the intermediate group was 1.6 times greater than that for the active group. The death rate for coronary heart disease was 2.2 times greater for the least active compared to the most active. The study also took into account differences in age, social class, smoking and general health.

C. High exposure to second hand smoke nearly doubles a woman's risk of having a heart attack, according to the largest study ever conducted on the issue. The study provides strong new evidence supporting the hotly disputed claim that secondhand smoke poses a major health risk. Researchers asked 32,000 nurses in a large continued study to place themselves in one of three categories: no exposure to secondhand smoke, occasional exposure, and regular exposure. The researchers then monitored the nurses' health during the ten years between 1992 and 2002, and found evidence of chronic heart disease in 152 cases, including 25 fatal heart attacks.

The researchers estimated the relative risk of coronary heart disease for those claiming regular exposure to secondhand smoke at 1.91 times that of women not exposed to tobacco smoke at home or work. Women claiming occasional exposure were 1.85 times more likely to suffer from heart disease than those not exposed. This was estimated as translating into as many as 60,000 deaths each year in the U. S. attributable to secondhand smoke alone. The researchers took pains to eliminate the effect of many of the factors which may have muddied the reliability of past research, including high blood pressure, high cholesterol and other health factors that contribute to heart disease.

D. Researchers have isolated from adult bone marrow a master cell that can be directed to grow bone or cartilage, a laboratory feat that experts call a major step towards learning to make replacement parts for ailing or aged bodies. Stem cells are the body's building blocks. Some, such as the pluripotent stem cells, come only from embryos. Other stem cells, such as mesenchymal cells, are produced in adults. But only the pluripotent stem cells from embryos are thought to be capable of growing into any tissue in the body. The mesenchymal stem cells are the parent line for bone, cartilage, fat, tendon, and muscle.

Laboratory research on animals is underway, and human studies may be possible in three years. While Congress has banned federal financing of research using human embryos, researchers are using private funding for their project. If the technique proves successful, they predict that precursor cells for bone would be used to replace tissue lost to cancer, osteoporosis, injury, or dental disease.

VI. PSEUDO-SCIENCE

It is impossible to finish this discussion without recognition of some of the many zany systems of thought which pass for knowledge, indeed, sometimes even for the "highest" type of knowledge, in this culture. You are probably already familiar with the claims made by those who believe in ESP, astrology, astral projections, UFOs, Dianetics, and other occult "sciences." It is hard to the grocery store in our society without encountering at the check-out counter tabloids which specialize in this sort of silly trash. What a funny state of affairs!

A **pseudo-science** is a system of thought which passes for a well-established science or discipline but cannot pass the tests which any discipline must meet in order to be considered truly scientific. What are these tests? Those presented in Sections I through IV above, especially those having to do with hypothesis testing. Pseudo-sciences are pseudo because, contrary to the claims they make, they fail to offer sensible explanations of what they purport to explain, they fail to make valid predictions, and they fail to offer us any method of controlling the phenomena they are supposed to address. But they may look impressive to the ignorant, and this is mostly the result of the **mere exposure effect**. The mere exposure effect points out that the more you hear something, the more likely you are to believe it. Belief is frequently a byproduct of sheer repetition rather than rational consideration. Advertising and other forms of indoctrination work on this principle, as do propagandists for various causes. Each of us is deluged with claims made on behalf of various pseudo-sciences from the time we are very young, and the claims are frequently sooo dramatic. Elvis was the father of my baby! I was kidnapped by aliens in UFOs! Atlantis found in a mud-puddle! Dramatic new evidence for life after death! Bigfoot found! Loch Ness monster found! Visit the Mother Ship hiding behind the Hale-Bopp comet! Tired of "phony" psychics? Call the "real" psychic hotline! What would these tabloids do without exclamation points?!!!!

While I can hardly hope to divest you of believing in all of the stuff and nonsense you've grown up with, I will single out for consideration just one current example of this type of thought, and I will show you what is wrong with it by applying the scientific/critical methods discussed above, concentrating on the problems pseudo-science has with the rules for hypothesis testing.[xv] Among the wide variety of material from which I could choose, I will select only the "prophet" Nostradamus and one of his famous predictions.

Michael Nostradamus was a sixteenth century "mystic" whose book, *The Prognostication for 1559*,[xvi] is believed by many to be filled with startlingly accurate predictions about events of this century. Recently, various individuals claimed that Nostradamus's book predicted that California (where else?) would suffer a major earthquake and be totally destroyed, fall into the sea, or vote Democratic (choose your favorite disaster!). The destruction was "set" to occur during the week of May 22nd through May 28th. It's a pretty impressive prediction for a sixteenth century monk who had never even heard of California, which of course did not yet exist. Well, various weeks of May 22nd through May 28th have come and gone and still no disaster of the "predicted" sort has occurred. It seems that unlike Einstein, Nostradamus' crucial experiment flopped. But did it (Cue the heavy organ music here)?

Lesson number one: The true pseudo-scientist is never deterred by such minor inconveniences as having his or her predictions repeatedly fail to come true. Pseudo-science does not accept the validity of the rule of falsifiability in hypothesis testing. Nothing could ever count against the "truth" of the predictions of the Master. Right up there with God, the "Master" is infallible, so when things go apparently wrong, there is always some *ad hoc* hypothesis which can be used to explain the failure away. But should any of these "predictions" ever turn out by chance to be correct, the true believer will latch on to it and exclaim to the high heavens "I told you so!" The true pseudo-scientist is a master at practicing confirmation bias. In order to protect yourself from this sort of trash, ask the pseudo-scientist what s/he would count as falsifying his or her position. If nothing could ever falsify it, nothing could ever verify it either. And that's why it's pseudo-science.

How do Nostradamus's predictions fare when measured against the other rules of hypothesis testing? Not so well. In the first place, Nostradamus' predictions have no relevance for our knowledge of future events; they have no intellectual basis whatsoever. Reasonable predictions must be anchored in various disciplines, the laws and theories$_2$ of which make possible the reasonable formulation of testable predictions. Because Nostradamus' claims are not anchored in any theory ($_2$ or $_3$), they cannot possibly make any kind of real predictions, let alone testable ones. If they are anchored in a theory, his proponents owe us an explanation of what that theory is. Merely calling him "Master" (or some such thing) is a dodge to avoid the issue. Secondly, these so-called predictions are completely incompatible with all accepted knowledge. As far as the disciplines of geology and physics could tell, there was no reason to say that California was going to have this sort of earthquake on the week in question—quite the opposite. Thirdly, though Nostradamus's claims certainly appear to be real predictions, they are couched in such vague and obscure language they are compatible with any and all states of affairs; that is, they make no real predictions, only apparent predictions. And finally, Ockham's razor can be used to slice through Nostradamus' false "wisdom" quite neatly; a far simpler explanation of California earthquakes is given by the recognized disciplines of physics and geology. Nostradamus' utterances can be dispensed with easily, and we will know just as much as we already know.

If you think that I am being too hard on Nostradamus, you are in danger of missing my point. The real pseudo-scientist here is not Nostradamus, but the person who uses (or misuses) his sayings to attempt to understand the future in a truly misguided way. Nostradamus' sayings mean what the pseudo-scientist wants them to mean. The pseudo-scientist wants an easy answer to difficult and complex questions, and listening to the sayings of The Master sure beats working for a living. In reality, these sayings become like a verbal Rorschach test, telling us more about what is going on in the mind of the interpreter than the mind of Nostradamus. Pseudo-science is a fraud. It seeks to provide simple and swift answers to what cannot be understood in this fashion. Avoid this seduction, for it poisons rationality.

Using the scientific/critical method explain what is wrong with the following pseudo-scientific claims.

A. If we don't win the big game, the sun will not rise tomorrow.

B. Ralph can influence the role of dice by telekinesis.

C. According to Persian astrology your character is determined by the position of the stars at your birth. According to Chinese astrology it is determined by the year of your birth.

D. The world was created in 4004 BCE.

E. The movie *Independence Day* claims that the government knows that UFOs are spying on the Earth and that some flying saucers have already been captured, complete with aliens, but it's hiding the evidence.

F. According to Master Ray Ruble, God always answers your prayers. The answer is "No."

CONCEPTS

You should be able to define the following concepts, explain their meanings to others not familiar with them, invent your own examples that correctly illustrate the concepts, and apply them correctly to novel applications.

- *Ad hoc* hypothesis
- Algorithm
- Anomalies
- Argument from ignorance
- Background conditions
- Blind
- Compatibility
- Confirmation bias
- Controls
- Crucial experiment
- Deductive nomological model
- Demand effect
- Dependent variables
- Double blind
- Explanation
- Falsifiability

- Heuristic device
- Hypothesis
- Ill-defined problem
- Independent variable
- Law of nature
- Magic
- Mere exposure effect
- Ockham's razor
- Performance factor
- Placebo
- Prediction
- Problem space
- Proving a negative
- Pseudo-science
- Regress argument
- Relevance
- Reliable

- Science
- Serendipity
- Simplicity
- Solution
- Starting point
- Test worthiness
- Theoretical entity
- Theory$_1$
- Theory$_2$
- Theory$_3$
- Understanding gap
- Validity$_2$
- Verifiability
- Well-defined problem
- World view constraints

Foundational concepts: *Ad hoc* hypothesis, confirmation bias, explanation, falsifiability, hypothesis, ill-defined problem, law of nature, pseudo-science, reliable, science, test worthiness, theory$_1$, theory$_2$, theory$_3$, validity$_2$, verifiability, well-defined problem, world view constraints

NOTES

i. See his *Nicomachean Ethics*, Chapters II, V, and VII.

ii. For a well-written popular account of the nature of science, see Garvin McCain and Erwin M. Segal, *The Game of Science*, 4th ed., (Monterey, CA: Brooks/Cole Pub. Co., 1982). The notion that science is largely a puzzle-solving methodology is discussed by Thomas S. Kuhn, *The Structure of Scientific Revolutions*, 2nd ed., (Chicago: The University of Chicago Press, 1970). See especially chapters III and IV. It is not true that all thinking can be reduced to the rules established by the scientific/critical method. Disciplines like art, philosophy, and religion, for example, are not obviously subject to the scientific/critical paradigm. Real trouble arises when the truths established by the scientific/critical method seem to conflict with doctrines accepted by these other disciplines. When this happens, rational means must be established to handle these types of conflicts. A discussion of these issues goes beyond the scope of this text. For an illustration of some of these issues, see Ian G. Barbour, *Issues in Science and Religion* (New York: Harper & Row, 1966).

iii. The four aspects of understanding-as, understanding-that, theory-ladenness, and mind-set apply not simply to what is narrowly understood to be scientific knowledge, but to all cases of knowing. In this text, however, I intend simply to develop my rather broad-based understanding of scientific/critical knowledge. The same type of analysis can be given for types of knowledge which are not normally understood as scientific, such as religious, artistic, or philosophical knowledge.

iv. See J. R. Partington, *A History of Chemistry*, vol. 4, (London: Macmillan, 1972), 537 for Kekulé's discovery. The Smith/Roentgen story is found in *The Making of the Atomic Bomb* (New York: Simon & Schuster, 1986), 38-41.

v. The deductive nomological model of explanation is the one most commonly advanced and discussed by philosophers of science. It is not without its severe critics, but the complications to which this model of explanation gives rise are beyond the scope of this text. I am going to assume its adequacy for the purposes of your understanding of the scientific/critical method. For a standard presentation of this theory, see John Hospers, *An Introduction to Philosophical Analysis*, 3rd ed., (Englewood Cliffs, NJ: Prentice Hall, 1988). For a critique of the deductive nomological model see Jennifer Trusted, *Inquiry and Understanding* (Atlantic Highlands, NJ: Humanities Press International, 1987).

vi. The philosopher who is probably most closely associated with the concept of verifiability is A. J. Ayer, whose book, *Language, Truth and Logic* (New York: Dover, 1935) took the philosophical world by storm when it was first published.

vii. Ironically, fifty years later some scientists claimed that the equipment which was actually used to verify Einstein's prediction was really too primitive to measure the actual change which occurs when light waves are bent by passing close to the sun. Such a change in position is quite small and difficult to determine. Quirks such as this make the history of science interesting to read about. See *The Making of the Atomic Bomb*, 168ff for further details.

viii. The philosopher whose name is virtually synonymous with the issue of falsification is Karl Popper, whose book *The Logic of Scientific Discovery* (New York: Science Editions, Inc., 1961) did much to counterbalance the influence Ayer had on the course of the development of the philosophy of science in the twentieth century.

ix. Thomas Kuhn has done much to advance our understanding of the role revolutions have played in the development of science. See *The Structure of Scientific Revolutions*.

x. William of Ockham—or Occam—(1285-1349) was a British monk whose works were highly influential in the fourteenth and fifteenth centuries. His famous dictum was used frequently in the philosophical and religious controversies of his day. See *Ockham's Philosophical Writings*, edited by Philotheus Boehner, (Edinburgh: Edinburgh University Press, 1957).

xi. For more about the nature of explanation in science and its relationship to law see John Hospers, "What is Explanation?" *Essays in Conceptual Analysis*, edited by Anthony Flew, (London: Macmillan Publishing Co., 1956).

xii. See Jeremy Rifkin, *Entropy: A New World View* (New York: Bantam Books, 1981). Rifkin is hardly alone in his fear of modern technology. Thinkers have been worried about the effects of technological development for thousands of years.

xiii. See *The Making of the Atomic Bomb, loc. cit.*

xiv. *The Theban Plays*, translated by E. F. Watling, (New York: Penguin Books, 1947). Sophocles (496-406 B.C.E.) was one of the greatest Greek playwrights.

xv. For more on pseudo-science busting, see *Philosophy of Science and the Occult*, edited by Patrick Grim, (Albany, NY: State University of New York Press, 1982). Also see any issue of *The Skeptical Inquirer* and many of the books published by Prometheus Press. Both of these outfits specialize in exposing pseudo-science for the trash that it is.

xvi. *English Experience Series No. 186*, edited by Walter J. Johnson.

Lulu the weather-predicting goat is dead. The 10-year-old goat died from injuries suffered when dogs entered a barn in Snow Camp and attacked her. Lulu came to the public spotlight when it was learned that she predicted snowfall, and Dr. Joe Sinclair, superintendent of Burlington City Schools, consulted her owner before deciding about closing schools when snow was forecast. On nine occasions, Lulu's actions predicted snow. On all nine occasions, snow fell.

—News item

CHAPTER SIX

Causation

INTRODUCTION

Many of the issues with which you are confronted involve assessing causal claims. Consider the following:

1. The Columbia blew up because it lost its heat tiles.
2. Ralph's drinking drove Edith crazy.
3. The astronomical foreign debt caused the October, 1987 collapse of the stock market.
4. Effort leads to success.
5. Eating spoiled food can make you sick.
6. Antibodies fight foreign material in the blood stream.

Each of these examples illustrates the concept of **causation**, though, as you can see, only one of them actually uses the word "cause." Though the relationship of causation is indispensable for productive thinking, you probably never have considered what factors are involved in the notion of causation and how

good causal claims may be distinguished from poor ones. In this chapter, I will consider both of these issues.

I. THE NATURE OF CAUSATION

What does it mean to say that one thing causes another thing? This is a question which has occupied philosophers for thousands of years. While the earliest systematic explanation of causation was given by Aristotle,[i] a more contemporary formulation of the concept was produced by David Hume in the eighteenth century.[ii] Hume's analysis of causation has been so influential that the discussion of causation by philosophers begins with it still to this day. Briefly put, Hume's analysis of causation maintains that to say that something (C) causes the existence of some effect (E) is to say that:

1. C and E are spatially contiguous
2. C occurs before E in time
3. all C's are constantly conjoined with E's, and

4. the existence of C necessitates the existence of E.

Consider the causal claim, "The window broke because a rock hit it." According to Hume, this causal claim amounts to the following set of assertions: (1) The rock hit the window. (2) The contact of the rock with the window preceded the breaking of the window. (3) Whenever rocks like this rock hit windows like this window with a force like that force, the window breaks. (4) The window had to break when it was hit by the rock.

In the twentieth century, philosophers have discussed Hume's account of causality intensely, and this discussion has shown that Hume's analysis holds up remarkably well to criticism. In refining this analysis some philosophers have found it helpful to distinguish necessary versus sufficient conditions for the occurrence of a given event E. The **necessary conditions** for E are those in the absence of which E cannot take place. Conditions for E are said to be **sufficient** if, *should* they occur, E must happen. To say that C caused E in this analysis would be to say that C was a necessary and/or sufficient condition for E. It should be noted that a given condition for E might be sufficient but not necessary to bring about E. Though this rock did break this window (it was a sufficient condition), the window could have been broken by something else (the rock was not a necessary condition). Likewise, a given condition may be necessary but not sufficient for the occurrence of E. That the window is fragile is a necessary condition for its being broken, but not a sufficient condition, since the window won't break simply because it is fragile (i.e., something must hit it).[iii] Again, a condition is necessary to a given effect if that effect *cannot occur* without it, and a condition is sufficient for a given effect if that effect *must occur* when the condition happens to be present.

How would Hume's analysis of causation apply to each of the following causal claims?

A. The Challenger blew up because its O-rings were defective.

B. The failure to militarily intervene when Hitler illegally re-occupied the Rhineland in 1936 led directly to Hitler's next conquest—the Austrian *Anschluss.*

C. If I drink coffee after dinner, I can't sleep at night.

D. If you study hard, you'll pass your critical thinking course.

E. Sticks and stones will break my bones, but names will never hurt me.

II. SOME PHILOSOPHICAL PROBLEMS

Hume's analysis of causality has raised and/or called philosophers' attention to some interesting and important philosophical issues. The easiest way to see this is to look at each of the four aspects of causality in turn.

The first element in Hume's analysis of causation is *spatial contiguity*. Hume believed that a cause must produce its effect by somehow touching the object it affects. The rock broke the window because it hit the window. This certainly seems obvious in a case such as this. But is this true for all causes; must they all work literally through touch alone? Even prior to Hume, this question raised problems for philosophers. Isaac Newton, for example, formulated his famous laws of motion which include the notion of "action at a distance" (that is, causal activity that does not occur through the medium of touch). Gravity seems to account for unsupported bodies falling to the earth without "touching" anything in the normal sense of that term. Certainly modern physics does not assume that all causal agents must touch the objects they affect in order to produce various effects.

The second condition, *temporal priority*, has produced its own share of discussion concerning two issues related to the claim that the cause has to exist prior to the effect. First, why can't a cause and its effects exist simultaneously? Using an illustration made popular by Immanuel Kant, doesn't the hot stove (the cause) exist at the same time as the warm room (the effect)? Secondly, and perhaps surprisingly, can there be cases in which the effect actually occurs temporally before the cause? If such a thing could never happen, why couldn't it happen?[iv]

The third aspect of causality, *constant conjunction*, has brought about a great deal of discussion among philosophers. According to Hume the claim that this rock broke this window commits you to the claim that there is nothing singular about this particular rock, this particular window, and the particular causal relationship between them. This is called the **regularity view of causation** by philosophers, because it involves the notion that *any individual causal instance must be understood as only a subset of the category comprised of all relevantly similar situations.* But this raises some perplexities. The claim "This rock broke this window" is a particular claim about only this rock and this window. Given that you know that this particular claim is true, how do you know that the corresponding universal claim "All rocks like this one which hit windows like this one with the same amount of force will cause the windows to break" is true? In what sense can the truth of this specific episode be related to the truth of the corresponding universal claim about the whole class of these sorts of episodes? You cannot validly[1] deduce a true universal claim from a true claim about a particular subset of the greater set; to do so would be to commit a formal fallacy. All experience can show you, as Hume insisted, is the fact that this rock broke this window. Even if you have seen other rocks break other windows, how do you know that they all can? For that matter, why should you have to know that they *all* can in order to know that *this one* did? This problem forms one aspect of the **problem of induction** (as it is called by philosophers), and Hume was the first to recognize it.

There is another closely related issue here. Why assume that the causal claim "This rock broke this window" is bound up in some way with any kind of universal proposition in the first place? Why do we assume that this rock breaking this window is connected with all rocks breaking all windows or with everything being breakable? The reason for this is that, in science, individual events are seen as substitution instances of universal laws. As we saw in Chapter Five, there are various complicated ways in which particular events are subsumed under scientific laws, but regardless of the way an individual event is related to a universal law, the scientific explanation of that event at some point must involve an appeal to some universal law or other.

Further problems arise when the idea of constant conjunction is coupled with the fourth element of causation, *necessary connection.* Hume's analysis maintains that an individual causal incident is bound up both with claims about constant conjunction and claims about necessary connections. According to his analysis, to say that this rock broke this window commits you to saying that the window *had* to break, given that the rock hit it. Generalizing, this means that any rock of this sort which hits a window of this sort this hard has to break the window. This understanding of causal relationships is called **determinism** by philosophers. According to determinism, the cause (C) of an event (E) can give rise to E alone, and not any other outcome. The concept of determinism still is frequently presupposed in the assessment of causal claims, and as a theory about the way the universe operates, determinism has been around a long time.[v] There are, however, three noteworthy issues tangled up with it.

The first issue concerns **chaos theory**, which supplies an alternative analysis of causation to that of classical determinism. Chaos theory (sometimes called the butterfly effect) maintains that tiny, seemingly insignificant changes early in a causal sequence can have drastic effects at the end of the longer causal chain. The flapping of a butterfly's wings, for example, may be sufficient in the long run to initiate a causal sequence which leads to a hurricane that otherwise would never have formed. Classical determinism, it may be argued, fails to take into account the potential of so-called insignificant events.

The second issue is a problem in assessing responsibility for actions performed by human beings. If determinism is true, then it seems that all human actions are equally well determined. And if that is true, what sense does it make to hold you responsible for what you do? If your actions are the causal products of antecedent states of affairs, then it would seem that you had no choice in any given situation but to do what you did in the same way that the window had to break when the rock hit it. In contrast to this, you are likely to believe that you possess some sort of ability to initiate actions that are not determined by antecedent states of affairs immediately preceding your choice and that your actions are sometimes the consequences of your own free choices. Philosophers speak of this last position as affirming the reality of **free will**. It is generally believed that free will and determinism are incompatible.[vi]

Consider the following examples. Do you think that the person's action in each case resulted from the person's free choice or was the action determined for the person by some other antecedent causal state of affairs? If you think the latter, what states of affairs could have caused the action?

A. In 1981 John Hinkley shot President Reagan because Hinkley wanted to impress Jody Foster.

B. "I can stop playing video games any time I want, I just don't want to."

C. "I can stop smoking tobacco any time I want, I just don't want to."

D. "I can stop using heroin any time I want, I just don't want to."

E. After Ralph surprised his girlfriend while she was on a date with the entire defensive secondary of the Green Bay Packers, he killed all of them in a fit of rage. In court Ralph pleaded justifiable homicide, stating, "Hey, I'm a Carolina Panther fan."

The third major philosophical issue bound up with determinism concerns the question of how one could know whether determinism is in fact true. Granted, if you knew that rocks like these had to break windows like that when they hit them with such and such a force, etc., you would know that determinism is in fact true. But all this way of putting the question does is reword it; it doesn't solve the issue. Hume himself saw that there is no way to prove determinism. He thought that the most one could say is that determinism is something the mind cannot help believing, but this is a far cry from saying that you can know that determinism is true because of your observations of the world.[vii]

Whether or not you can know that determinism is true, if it *is* true then you can be sure of one thing—everything you could ever come into contact with (or even think about, for that matter) *must have a cause*. To say that something happened without a cause could never be correct, but suppose no one could in fact ever actually discover the cause of some particular event or other. Would that show that determinism is false? No, it wouldn't, remember the fallacy of the argument from ignorance discussed in Chapter Five. The possibility always would remain that the failure to find the cause of this particular event was due to stupidity or ignorance on our part, and that in fact a sufficiently keen mind would find the cause if the examination was carried far enough.

But hold the phone. In the early part of the twentieth century certain developments in physics led some scientists and philosophers to question the truth of determinism itself. These developments had to do with the discovery of sub-atomic particles (chiefly electrons) and radioactive decay. It is believed, for example, that the change of energy levels of electrons and the decay of radioactive particles into non-radioactive particles is completely spontaneous, uncaused, and unpredictable for any given electron or particle, but statistically predictable for a large enough mass of electrons or particles. The same type of analysis now typically is given for many phenomena involving sets of large numbers of similar things that vary in a number of standard ways. Insurance actuary tables are one obvious example of this sort of causal analysis. While insurance companies cannot tell when any particular individual will die, they can determine very accurately for a large group over a period of time how many may be expected to die during any given year. This is why insurance companies refuse to insure persons who are found to be HIV positive and why the car insurance rates for young drivers are higher than for those who are older. This is **statistical determinism**. In this **statistical analysis of causation**, *determinism is only thought to work at the level of the group as a whole.* For any individual in the group, it is only possible to give a probability estimate concerning the statistical probability of something happening to that individual in a given period of time. Sociology, psychology, medicine, and political science are some of the disciplines that are deeply involved in this sort of statistical analysis of causal claims.

Finally, there is the **regress problem**. Suppose we know that C causes E. But what causes C, some unknown D? If so, then what causes D? And so forth. The regress problem raises the concern that no satisfactory explanation of the existence of something (E) can itself contain something (C) which is just as much in need of an explanation (D) as what it supposedly explained. And if this is true for any (C), where does the regress of causes stop? Think of the little kid asking "Why?" to every response to a long stream of previous why questions, and you will get some idea of how problematic (and annoying) this problem is to any critical thinker.

One interesting analysis of the regress problem points out that the regress of causal explanation never stops in principle, but it must stop in practice. There are two complementary principles at work here: (1) Start the regress by asking for the cause (C) of the effect (E), and (2) Stop the regress at any point which is convenient. These principles are pragmatically consistent and perfectly commonplace. For example, you don't have to know

whom your grandparents were in order to know who your parents were, although it is certainly true that your parents had parents, too.

III. POST HOC ARGUMENTS

The development of statistical models in the twentieth century has led to an important adjustment in Hume's analysis of causality. His analysis is understood now to read in this way: To say that C causes E is to say that (1) C is spatially contiguous to E, (2) C is temporally prior to E; (3a) All C's are constantly conjoined with E's *or* (3b) A certain percentage of C's are conjoined with a certain percentage of E's, and (4a) The existence of any C necessitates the existence of an E *or* (4b) The existence of C necessitates the existence of E only a certain percentage of the time.

Now consider the following problem: In the long and complex debate over the elimination of nuclear weapons, numerous individuals both inside and outside of the government have made the claim that nuclear weapons have prevented a major war between the powers that possess them. "Nuclear weapons," it is said, "have kept the peace." How good is this causal claim? Claims of this kind are called *post hoc* **arguments** by philosophers. This label comes from the Latin phrase used to indicate the kind of issue I am now discussing. The full Latin phrase is *post hoc, ergo propter hoc*, which means "after it, therefore because of it." As you have seen, causal arguments have a temporal component; causes occur before their effects. However, *it is not true that any event X that occurs before another event Y is in fact a cause of that event.* To say that X and Y are temporally related (post hoc) does not necessarily, or even generally, require that X and Y are causally correlated (propter hoc). Mere temporal correlation does not by itself guarantee causality. Compare the statement "Before I hit the winning basket I shot the ball," with "Before I hit the winning basket I thought about where I had parked my car." Though all cases of causality are also cases of temporal correlation, not all cases of temporal correlation are cases of causality. To say otherwise incorrectly treats a necessary condition of causation (temporal priority) as a sufficient condition of causation (see section I of this chapter).

There is a problem that all of this is leading to. It is usually easy to discover cases of temporal correlation. Experience shows us many of these. But not all cases of mere temporal correlation are cases of genuine causal connections. In general, how are we to distinguish mere temporal correlation from real causal relations? In particular, does the fact that there have been no major wars between the nuclear powers since 1945 (*post hoc*) provide good reasons for saying that it is the presence of nuclear weapons which has prevented these possible wars (*propter hoc*)?

Moving too quickly from the fact of mere temporal correlation to the belief in an actual causal relation frequently produces obviously poor arguments. Consider the following: "Everyone who is addicted to heroin started out first by smoking pot. Therefore, smoking pot is a cause of heroin addiction" and, "Everyone who is addicted to heroin started out first by drinking milk. Therefore, drinking milk is a cause of heroin addiction." Both of these arguments are *post hoc* arguments, but the second one is obviously a lousy causal argument. What of the first one?

Because of obvious counter examples like the one just mentioned, philosophers have generally treated *post hoc* arguments as fallacies.[viii] I prefer to say, however, that while all causal arguments are *post hoc* arguments, not all *post hoc* arguments are fallacies (in just the same way that all squares are rectangles, but not all rectangles are squares). Some *post hoc* arguments are good causal arguments; the problem, of course, is determining which ones.

So how good is the nuclear weapon argument presented earlier? It is undeniable that since the advent of nuclear weapons in 1945 there have been no major wars between the nuclear powers. But is the peace that has existed between the powers a result of the nuclear balance of terror or is it the result of other unmen-tioned factors? What about the Cuban missile crisis of 1963, during which the U.S. and Russia almost went to war over the presence of nuclear missiles in Cuba—does that count as counter evidence to the claim? It is difficult to determine whether the presence of nuclear weapons has kept the peace between nuclear powers; indeed, it may have done just the opposite.

Evaluate each of the following *post hoc* arguments. Which ones are good causal arguments? Which ones are fallacies?

A. Chocolate gives me migraine headaches. Every time I eat it I get one.

B. My dog is a genius! Last night I asked him if he wanted a steak bone and, he barked "yes!"

C. Every time coach wears his lucky socks we win. I see that he's got them on again tonight, so the game is in the bag.

D. In 1980, conservatives were spitting mad over U.S. humiliation at the hands of Iran—and the loss of 12 countries to communism in the decade of the '70s. President Reagan's could proudly boast to the party reformed in his image that "in the 2,765 days of our administration, not one inch of ground has fallen to the communists."
   —News item

E. A Canadian psychiatrist has speculated that it is abortion, not unwanted birth, which is associated with child abuse. Philip Ney, chief of psychiatry in a Vancouver hospital, noticed that an increase in child deaths from social causes in Canada coincided with the introduction of elective abortion; that provinces with high and low abortion rates rank similarly in child abuse; and that individual women who abused their children were reported to have higher abortion rates.   —News item

F. "I felt like when impact began, that we were all dead. I think God saved us from death." Larry Davis, captain of the Delta Air Lines jet that crashed at the Dallas-Fort Worth airport Aug. 31,1988. Fourteen people died and 94 survived.   —News item

There is a commonly encountered form of *post hoc* argument that deserves special mention, the **slippery slope argument**. Slippery slope arguments maintain that a proposed action which appears innocent enough on the surface ought to be rejected none-the-less because that action would initiate a causal sequence the culmination of which would be disastrous. Because the proposed initial action (it is said) would set into motion a chain of events leading to an unfortunate conclusion, the wise thing to do would be to not take the first step down the slippery slope in the first place. This argument is also called the **domino theory**. Since knocking over the first domino would lead to destruction of the whole row of dominoes, don't knock over the first domino if you don't want the whole row to fall. Watch one episode of *Survivor* and you'll watch another; pretty soon that's all you'll be doing. Another life lost to the heartbreak of the sweaty, gross, and no longer so pretty. So don't even get started watching that stuff in the first place.

How good are slippery slope arguments? That depends on three things: (a) the claim that the first step would initiate a causal sequence, (b) the claim that this causal sequence cannot be halted once started, and (c) the claim that the final effect of the causal sequence would be a disaster. If all three of these claims can be validated, the resulting slippery slope argument may be very strong indeed. Frequently, however, at least one of these three claims will turn out to be untrue. Philosophers have paid special attention to the claim that, once started, the causal sequence cannot be stopped.[ix] This claim commonly is found to be untrue. Consider this famous example from the 60s: We've got to continue fighting in Vietnam, because if we allow the commies to win there, they'll be in Laos and Cambodia next. After that they'll take over India and the Philippines, and then they'll be in Hawaii and San Francisco. So if you want to keep the Reds out of California, stop them now in Vietnam.

In reality, the fall of Vietnam did not prove to have all of the consequences specified above. The slope wasn't that slippery, but it could have been if a host of other factors had been true, too. *Slippery slope arguments are theory-laden; they claim validity based upon a whole network (or theory) of causal and factual claims being true.* If this network of other claims breaks down, the slippery slope argument enmeshed in it will, too. Whether that network will in fact break down depends upon the particular issue in question, therefore it is unwise to simply dismiss a slippery slope argument as a fallacy. Any given slippery slope argument should be examined on its own merit. Like *post hoc* arguments in general, some slippery slope arguments are good; others are not.

Evaluate the strength of the following slippery slope arguments. If a particular example is not a good causal argument, what would have to be true to make it a good causal argument?

A. Edith: "Ralph, I don't think you ought to choose Sudden Death for your first time on skis. Sudden Death is the most difficult run on the whole mountain."

 Ralph: "No sweat, Edith. I'll go down nice and slowly."

 Edith: "Can I have the car keys before you go?"

B. Ralph: "Mom, can we keep him? He followed me home. I'll take care of him. I promise. I will; I will; I will."

 Mom: "Good God, Ralph, that's a baby mountain lion. If you feed him once you'll never get rid of him."

C. Don't ever smoke tobacco. One puff and you're addicted for life.

D. Lay's Potato Chips. No one can eat just one!

E. "What are you going to say," Susie Anderson, 19, demanded, "when your kids crawl up on your lap and say, 'Grampa, what were you doing when Russia took over America?'" Plano, a Dallas suburb, might seem an improbable setting for a Red Scare. But the issue that provoked it was equally incongruous—a proposal that Plano adopt a Soviet "sister city." A standing room only crowd of Plano residents was warned by a procession of speakers that the town of 126,000 could become "a foothold" for a Russian conquest of America. And the first step, said opponents could be the sister city program. Plano would have been the 32nd American city to embrace a Soviet sister since Seattle adopted Tashkent in 1972.

—News item

Before I leave this section, I wish to call your attention to one other problem that may be embedded in some *post hoc* arguments—the **proximity problem**. Proximity is another word for one of the hallmarks of causality in the standard Humean analysis, namely that cause and effect work by physical contact or touch. Granting for purposes of the argument that this is true, it still does not follow that all cases of touch are causal. Which cases of touch involve causation, and which ones are merely accidental? Here we have a problem exactly parallel to standard *post hoc* arguments, and as is true with *post hoc* arguments, there is no a priori answer to this issue. The problem is theory-laden, and any given discipline must determine, as its own standard, which contact instances "count" and which do not. It is important for the critical thinker to realize that all contact isn't causal, only some of it is.

Evaluate the following proximity arguments. In each of them, what is spatially associated with what? What other spatial relationships can be found that might affect the conclusions drawn from the data presented?

A. Ralph was the last person seen in the room before the camera was stolen, therefore, Ralph must have taken it.

B. Coach lost the game for us again. This time he forgot his lucky socks!

C. Researchers believe they have found a key enzyme that activates Alzheimer's disease. Alzheimer's patients are known to have toxic plaques, or build-ups, of amyloid beta proteins in their brains. Drugs designed to block the enzyme could enter clinical trials soon. Research evidence suggests that a previously known brain substance called presenilin is the enzyme that controls production of amyloid beta proteins.

D. Large numbers of mysterious frog-leg deformities that have caused scientists to fear the impact of an undetermined chemical pollutant may in fact be the result of a simple parasite found in nature, two new studies conclude. Mysterious frog deformities first received widespread attention in 1995 when Minnesota pupils on a field trip discovered that many northern leopard frogs had extra or missing limbs. More malformed frogs were later found in other Midwestern and Northeastern states, the South and on the West coast. Frogs' permeable skin makes them more sensitive to environmental changes than other animals, a fact that makes frogs a good early indicator of certain problems. Many experts have warned that deformities in frogs could be an early warning of much more widespread malformations to come in other species, wrought by some unknown environmental threat. But new research suggests that many multi-limb or missing-limb deformities are caused instead by a tiny parasitic worm that bores into tadpoles, disturbing the cells responsible for leg growth.

IV. CONTROL

Why is it so difficult to evaluate a causal argument like the one involving the nuclear weapons claim? One obvious reason is the lack of information about such things as the history of the development and use of weapons as instruments of national policies in the last forty years, or the Cold War and the fall of the Soviet Union, or the rise of terrorism, and so forth. But even if a sufficient amount of this kind of information were available, it still would be difficult to evaluate this sort of causal argument. The problem here lies in the sheer number of variables that have to be dealt with to assess this kind of claim. Remember (from Chapter Four), a variable is some quantified characteristic that may possess any of a number of values. Daily temperature is a variable, as is the amount of sleep you require, the price of bananas (whether in Portugal or Poland), the batting average of your favorite baseball player, and on. The amount that a given variable may vary is called its range. The range of most variables is generally limited. Daily temperature on earth ranges from about minus 60 degrees Fahrenheit to about 120 degrees Fahrenheit. You probably need between six and nine hours of sleep a night, etc.

The number and power of nuclear weapons also vary. Right now there are about 20,000 nuclear devices in existence, ranging in power from several kilotons to twenty megatons of TNT. To say, "Nuclear weapons have kept the peace," raises the question, "How many nuclear weapons of what power have kept the peace?" and this question has no easy answer at all. In order to have any hope of answering it, an experiment has to be done in which the possible variables of weapon numbers and sizes have to be controlled. Unless **controls** are established, there is no way to determine whether the result of the experiment is due to the variable being tested or some other extraneous variable. *If a control group cannot be established, there is no way to be sure about the reliability of the experimental findings.* A **control group** will be a group exactly like the experimental group except for the variable being tested (which the control group *does not* involve the variable being tested). Using control groups, the experimenter is able to remove the possibility that some extraneous variable was the real cause of the experimental results. Control groups, then, allow the experimenter to distinguish good post hoc arguments from fallacious post hoc arguments; good proximity arguments from bad proximity arguments. The failure to establish a reliable control group has destroyed the value of countless experiments.

But how could you establish a control group to evaluate the nuclear weapons claim? There are so many possible variables here it is difficult to isolate just one. Suppose a single variable could be isolated (say, the number of nuclear devices); it still would be impossible to run an experiment comparing the peace-keeping power of one hundred nuclear weapons to that of one thousand without raising the possibility that a given number of weapons may be too small to keep the peace, which would be an incredible disaster. The practical problems of analysis are formidable, but if knowledge claims about causal issues are to be evaluated meaningfully, adequate steps must be taken to fix the values of the variables involved.

What kind of control group would you devise to test the validity of the following causal claims?

A. Smoking causes cancer.

B. Chocolate gives me a migraine headache.

C. If you believe hard enough, you can make your wishes come true.

D. If you work hard enough, you can make your wishes come true

E. Insects cannot transmit the AIDS virus.

F. The voting on *American Idol* is rigged.

V. MILL'S METHODS

In the nineteenth century, the British philosopher John Stuart Mill formulated five methods for the evaluation of causal arguments. An understanding of these methods will help increase your ability to distinguish good causal arguments from poor ones. Mill's Methods are the Method of Agreement, the Method of Difference, the Joint Method, the Method of Residues, and the Method of Concomitant Variation. I shall discuss each of them in turn.

1. **The Method of Agreement**. This is probably the most frequently used method of assessing causal claims, and it *allows us to confirm a sufficient cause for a given effect.* It works simply by looking for the correlation between the

presence of two kinds of phenomena, one of which (C) is suspected to be the cause of another phenomenon (E). If experience shows that whenever C appears E also appears, then there is a good reason for saying that C is a sufficient condition of E. If my forgetting to remove my CD's from my car on very hot days is correlated with my CD's assuming the shape of salad bowls, I have a good reason for saying that the presence of a lot of heat in my car warps my CD's.

2. **The Method of Difference**. The Method of Difference works by looking for cases in which the absence of the suspected effect E is correlated with the absence of the suspected cause *C*. If my CD's do not warp into salad bowls when they are not exposed to heat, I am justified in concluding that the absence of heat is responsible for the failure of the CD's to warp; conversely, I also can conclude that the presence of heat is a necessary condition for the warping of the CD's. *The Method of Difference allows you to discover necessary conditions for the presence of whatever it is you are trying to investigate.*

3. **The Joint Method**. The Joint Method of Agreement and Difference works simply by combining the first two methods. When it can be applied, *the Joint Method is probably the best method for evaluating causal claims because it allows you to establish the existence of both necessary and sufficient conditions for the effect.* The Method of Agreement allows you to establish the claim "If C, then E," and the Method of Difference allows you to establish the claim "E only if C." The Joint Method allows you to establish the claim "E if and only if C." My CD's turn into the shape of salad bowls if and only if I leave them exposed to a great deal of heat.

4. **The Method of Residues**. In the example I have been using to illustrate these methods, I have maintained that it is the presence of heat (C), and nothing else, which is responsible for the warping of the compact disks (E). How do I know that E is not due to some other possible variable? Notice that even in this simple case there are several variables: CD's, cars, heat, and the owner of the CD's are the most obvious. Any of these variables could theoretically be the cause of E.

The Method of Residues is designed to clear up problems like this. Sometimes, an effect may arise from a number of possible causes. Consider wealth, for example. You may become wealthy in a number of possible ways. You may earn it, steal it, inherit it, win it, and so forth. In a similar fashion, there could be a number of possible reasons for the warping of my CD's. In order to rule out these possibilities, I apply the Method of Residues, and in order to apply this method, two conditions must be met. First, there must be a known and limited number of possible variables. *The method works by systematically eliminating all the possible causes of E except for one*—very much like the detective narrowing down the list of suspects one by one until only the guilty party is left—consider the game *Clue*. Secondly, *the method works only if you can eliminate the false causes from the list of possibilities*, and to do this you typically have to use the first three methods. Therefore, the Method of Residues cannot be used alone to ascertain a given cause of something, but only as a special application of the previous methods. If you cannot use the other methods to eliminate the extraneous variables, you cannot use the Method of Residues.

Applying the Method of Residues to my warped CDs example, I must be able to eliminate all other possible causes (variables) other than heat. To do this I might use the Method of Difference to conduct a series of simple experiments in which one at a time each of the possible variables remains constant except for the one being tested. Should I be able to eliminate all the possible variables but one in this fashion without at the same time eliminating the effect, I will have established that the effect is in fact caused by the remaining variable.

5. **The Method of Concomitant Variation**. Often it is the case that you are not content to say simply that C causes E. Because the variables represented by C and E may range over a number of possibilities, you may be even more interested in knowing how much C causes how much E. To determine this you need to apply the Method of Concomitant Variation. To say that two variables vary concomitantly is to say either the greater the one (C), the greater the other (E)—a **positive correlation**, or the greater C, the less E—a **negative correlation**. How much heat exactly does it take to warp my CD's—a little or a lot? To determine this, I might run an experiment in which I subject my CD's to various amounts of heat for various amounts of time and record the results. By recording and analyzing the results, I may be in a good position to know exactly how long it is safe to leave my CD's in my car under given temperature conditions.

Notice that the Method of Concomitant Variation is itself a version either of the Method of Agreement, the Method of Difference, or the Joint Method. *In order to apply the Method of Concomitant Variation, you have to already know or at least suspect that C in fact causes E.* Concomitant Variation simply allows you to refine this claim.

Using Mill's Methods evaluate the following arguments. Which method(s) work best for each argument? Which one(s) works the poorest?

A. Your car engine will run better if you use Super Unleaded than if you use Regular Unleaded.

B. Two British psychologists have discovered evidence that the brain has at least two separate memory systems, one storing information that can be recalled only upon seeing a given object, the other able to retrieve its data only when hearing the name of the object. The discovery came in experiments with a 63-year-old man who had an unusual form of brain damage of unknown cause. The damage, confined to a small region of his left temporal lobe rendered him unable to remember the meaning of names of objects spoken to him. When he is shown a picture of the same object, however, his memory is normal. Tests indicate his memory is especially weak when the spoken word is the name of a living thing. The researchers say this hints at a specialized memory system devoted to information about animals and plants.   —News item

C. Richard Perle, Assistant Defense Secretary in the Reagan administration acknowledged that an atomic war would cause a "nuclear winter" that might wipe out all life on Earth. The nuclear winter concept holds that even a small-scale nuclear war would cause such tremendous fire storms and clouds of dust and debris to be thrown into the atmosphere that light and warmth from the sun would be blocked and all life would end.   —News item

D. A month before Rod Matthews bludgeoned a 14-year old classmate to death, he watched a videotape docu-drama that portrays brutal killings. At Matthews' murder trial earlier this year, a psychiatrist testified that the *Faces of Death* video may have inspired the 15-year old Canton, Mass., youth to "see what it was like to kill someone." Although there is little data on how films like these affect the way children view violence research on young adults allows psychologists to make some educated guesses about the impact on younger viewers. In the mid-1980s Daniel Linz, a psychologist at the University of California, Santa Barbara, did studies on college-age men exposed to graphic violence in films like *The Texas Chainsaw Massacre*, and *Friday the 13th*. The researchers also had their subjects watch a video of an actual rape trial and then questioned them about their attitudes toward violence and women after they had been exposed to a steady diet of slasher films. They found the same results: The men who had seen the sexually violent films were more accepting of the violence they saw and more callous about the injuries to the rape victim. —News item

E. Canada is considering a total ban on tobacco advertising, but that won't work. Many Canadians can pick up U.S. stations, which will continue to advertise tobacco. Besides, ads are ineffective anyway. Young people start to smoke because of peer pressure; if you want to cut down on the use of tobacco you ought to ban youth.

F. The Suzuki Samurai is an unsafe vehicle. The Consumer Products Testing Corporation tests show that it tends to turn over easily when turned sharply at even moderate speeds. Its center of gravity is simply too high. Since it's been on the market, over 600 people have been killed in turn-overs in the last three years alone. —News item

G. Duke University animal studies show nicotine plays a big role in attacking a fetus's brain, possibly causing learning disabilities and changes in behavior. Nicotine constricts a woman's blood vessels, reducing the flow of blood and oxygen to the fetus. The unborn child is unable to grow at a normal rate and is often born underweight. Nicotine also attacks the central nervous system, putting neurons into overdrive. The fetus is unable to prevent nicotine from interfering with the brain's biochemical processes and neurological circuits. Brain cells that did form were often "wired" incorrectly and the biochemical processes that let cells communicate were harmed. The brain damage is irreversible. — News item

VI. CONCLUSION

I hope that you can see from the material presented above just how much there is to say about causal arguments. Were it not for the fact that so many of the things with which we are required to deal involve assessing claims about causation, life would surely be a lot simpler. But life in any but the most remotely conceivable of circumstances isn't simple. It is vir-

tually impossible to avoid the many complications of existence. The critical thinker will recognize this and attempt to do his or her best as a consumer of information claims. Maybe nuclear weapons have kept the peace for the last forty years, as so many people rather smugly believe. However, it is also possible that the peace may better be kept by their abolition. Until it can be ascertained that the nuclear weapon argument is in fact a legitimate *ad hoc* argument, it is wiser to retain a degree of skepticism regarding its validity.

In evaluating arguments like the nuclear weapon argument, you have to combine knowledge of a great many factual claims with the ability to apply the steps of analysis given in this chapter. Fortunately, many causal claims are much simpler than those as complicated as the nuclear weapons or movie violence arguments presented above. But even in the easy cases, the same methods of evaluation ought to be used. Since you will be confronted with these arguments in the future, it is best to practice their assessment until the techniques presented in this chapter can be applied with ease, even when you are not in a position to determine some of the important information relevant to the example on which you are working. Do not forget that a good causal argument is good because it contains claims that are empirically verifiable or falsifiable and it properly accords with the principles of experimental design. Even when you cannot verify or falsify its empirical claims, you can still determine whether any given argument meets with rules for generating a strong causal argument. Failure to comply with the rules means that the reasons advanced for supporting the conclusion either fail to do so entirely or do so only rather weakly. *Even when the conclusion of a badly constructed causal argument is true, the failure to adhere strictly to the rules of experimental design means that this particular argument provides poor reasons for accepting the truth of its conclusion.* Critical thinking requires the arguer to be right for the right reasons, and not by accident.

Foundational concepts: Causation, Mill's Methods, necessary condition, *post hoc* argument, the problem of induction, proximity argument, slippery slope argument, sufficient condition

NOTES

i. See Aristotle's *Physics,* Book II, Ch. 7, and his *Metaphysics,* Book I.

ii. See *A Treatise of Human Nature,* Book I, Part III (London: 1739), and *An Enquiry Concerning Human Understanding,* Section VII (London: 1748).

iii. For a further discussion of the concepts of necessary and sufficient conditions and causality see *Cause and Effect,* edited by Daniel Lerner, (New York: The Free Press, 1965).

iv. On the first issue see Immanuel Kant, *Critique of Pure Reason,* 1781. On the second see Antony Flew, "Can an Effect Precede Its Cause," *Proceedings of the Aristotelian Society,* Sup. Vol. 28, 1954.

v. A version of determinism first was explicitly recognized by Aristotle in his *Posterior Analytics,* Book I, chapters 6,8, and 13.

vi. The conflict between free will and determinism has existed since the time of Boethius (480-524). See his *The Consolation of Philosophy* for a classical discussion of these issues. On the other hand, Kant (1724-1804) saw no real conflict between these two positions. See his *Critique of Pure Reason,* "The Antinomy of Pure Reason." For a highly readable contemporary account of these issues see Clifford Williams, *Free Will and Determinism* (Indianapolis: Hackett Publishing Co., 1980).

vii. Kant believed that he proved the truth of determinism. See his *Critique of Pure Reason,* "Analogies of Experience." Most philosophers, however, reject Kant's argument.

viii. See for example Perry Weddle, *Argument: A Guide to Critical Thinking* (New York: McGraw-Hill, 1978), Chapter 7.

ix. For more on slippery slope arguments see Trudy Govier, "What's Wrong With Slippery Slope Arguments?" *Canadian Journal of Philosophy,* (vol. 12, June 1982): 303-16.

*"Truths are illusions which we have forgotten are illusions....
Morally, it is the duty to lie according to socially fixed conventions."*

—Friedrich Nietzsche, in *On Truth and Lies in a Nonmoral Sense*

CHAPTER SEVEN

Analogy and Metaphor

INTRODUCTION

You probably were first exposed to analogies and metaphors as literary devices that are hallmarks of good writing. While they certainly serve literary functions, analogies and metaphors are also important thinking tools, which are utilized not simply by so-called great thinkers and writers, they are also used by the rest of us in a wide range of contexts. Because I expect that you have already had some exposure to analogy and metaphor as literary tools, I shall not treat this aspect of their use here. Analogies and metaphors share one common factor—in both cases a certain set of ideas is applied to a situation to which it does not usually apply, producing a new set of ideas and a new set of relationships between these ideas. This chapter will examine some of the ways in which this usually occurs, the advantages of using analogies and metaphors for critical thinking, and some of the limitations that surround these practices.[i]

ANALOGY

I. THE LOGIC OF ANALOGY

All **analogies** are comparisons between two subjects that are claimed to already resemble each other in some important respects. The first subject of the comparison is that which is to be explained by the analogy; I will call this the **original subject** or field. The original field is what the analogy is trying to make sense of. The second subject of the comparison is designed to explain or illuminate the original field; this I will call the **analogue**. The success of an analogy depends upon a correct presupposition that the intended audience is more familiar with the analogue than with the original, and that features true of the analogue can correctly or meaningfully be applied to explain or illuminate the field of the original. The features that make up the analogy are called the **logic of the analogy**. There are two aspects of this logic that must be distinguished, the material and the structural. The **material** part of the analogy consists of all the objects, parts, or pieces which make up the field of the analogy. The **structural** part of the analogy consists in the rules that govern the relationship between the material parts of the analogy as well as those rules that determine how the material parts interact with objects beyond the field of the analogy. An educational organization like a high school and a military group like an engineer battalion might actually be composed of the same people (the material part of the analogy) if the engineers work in the high school in the civilian part of their lives. They might even have similar jobs (principles / CO; teachers / officers; etc.), or, just as likely, their civilian and military duties will both overlap and diverge on a case by case basis. But in all situations, an analogy works by claiming that there is an important similarity between either the material of the analogue and the original field, the structure of the analogue and the original field, or similarities between both aspects of each field.

To help you understand what is going on in the interminable war in Palestine, for example, I might compare events in it to a game of chess. The original field is the Palestinian-Israeli conflict over the occupied territories, and the analogue is the game of chess. If you know little or nothing about the game of chess then the analogue is not familiar to you; in this case the analogy will not only fail to improve your understanding, but will hinder it because you will be trying to figure out the game of chess itself. If you understand at least something about chess, then you know that it is a rule-governed activity in which various pieces are moved around a board, the goal of which is the capture of the opponent's king (called checkmate). The particular analogy of my example is claiming that essentially similar materials or structures constitute the logic of the Palestine-Israeli conflict as constitute the game of chess. I might, for example, compare the Prime Minister of Israel (or the President of the United States, for that matter) and the leader of Palestine to the kings in the game of chess and the members of the various militia or the Palestinian armies to the pawns. I might also compare the events taking place in the occupied territories to some typical moves in a chess game. The original invasion of the West Bank and the Gaza Strip by the Israeli army during the Yom Kippur war of 1967 compares to moving a pawn into a certain space on the board at the start of the game. The assassina-tion of Rabin or of various Hamas leaders compares to removing a knight or a bishop from the game, and so forth. If this analogy is successful, you will come to see the conflict as a vast, complex game of chess. Seeing the conflict in this way can be very illuminating. Now you may come to understand the logic of the events occurring over there, which prior to the introduction of the analogy failed to make much sense.

A good analogy can be extended indefinitely. More and more participants in the conflict can be compared to pieces in the game of chess. What motivates the actions of these pieces can become clear by further comparing these actions to moves in the game. As is the case with all analogies, however, some aspects of the analogue will not have a clear application to the original. What would constitute a checkmate in the Palestinian-Israeli conflict? Who represents the Queen?

All the various uses and examples of analogies are derived from variations of a common root which I shall call **simple analogies**. Simple analogies all have the form X:Y :: A:B ("X is to Y as A is to B"), where the letters X, Y, A, and B stand for simple place holders (or variables). Simple analogies are simple because they purport to pick out only one way in which X and Y, and A and B are related. Ultimately, all analogies are constructed from simple analogies by recognizing more and more ways in which the related items are related. You are already familiar with countless examples of these sorts of analogies, though you may have to think a bit to realize this. In mathematics, these analogies are called **proportions** and you have already had a lot of practice working problems such as: 6:8 as 10: X, solve for X. Simple analogies also crop up on many tests with which you are familiar, such as the SAT or the ACT.

Solving a verbal analogy problem consists of deciding what the relationship is between two given words, and then finding among the possible answers a pair of words related to each other in the same way.

THE THEORY AND PRACTICE OF CRITICAL THINKING

BOAT : SHIP	SWORD : SCABBARD
A. book : volume	A. saber : machete
B. canoe : paddle	B. knife : sheath
C. oar : water	C. carbine : holster
D. aft : stern	D. pin : cushion
E. land : sea	E. letter : envelope[ii]

While verbal analogy problems such as these are commonplace, they are not necessarily easy to solve. To say that problems like these are built on simple analogies is not to say that the analogies contained within them are simple to understand; indeed, they can be quite tricky and/or misleading. Rather, to say that these problems illustrate simple analogies is to say that they are supposedly constructed from the smallest possible comparison between two things. All analogies are comparisons. Simple analogies try to compare two things in only one way. Herein lies the rub! It is very difficult to specify only one comparison when a pair of terms is mentioned. Once specified, simple comparisons have a habit of becoming compound.

It is generally easier to specify a simple analogy as a formula in mathematics than verbally. In the example "6:8 :: 10:X," X only has one possible correct substitution, but in "SWORD is to SCABBARD as..." there are multiple substitution instances because there are various ways swords can be related to scabbards. The trick for the test taker is to figure out which of the possible comparisons is intended. To further complicate matters, the test makers know this and deliberately include examples of "incorrect" answers in the choices given to the test takers. The defense of this seemingly sadistic practice is that there is only one "unique" or "best" answer included in the answer column. Of course, all test answers are unique in some way or other; too bad for you if you didn't figure out the "unique" unique one.

The problem here is that analogies, like perceptions, are relative to theory and mind-set. There are unique or best answers to most verbal analogy problems, but only according to the theory and mind-set from which the analogy originally is created. In solving the analogy problem, the application of the appropriate theory depends not simply on the test takers' theoretical and factual information, but also on what the test makers' and the test takers' mind-sets encourage them to expect to see. Constructing verbal analogy tests free from ambiguous theoretical considerations is every bit as difficult for test makers as taking these tests is for test takers.

II. THE USES OF ANALOGY

Analogies have been used in discussions and arguments for thousands of years. In philosophy some of the greatest and most influential analogies can be found in the works of the early Greek philosophers Plato and Aristotle.[iii] Contemporary philosophers are currently debating the proper function analogy has in thinking, especially in scientific thinking.[iv] Three main uses are claimed for analogy: 1) as a rhetorical device, 2) as a heuristic, and 3) as a method of proof or as part of an argument. I shall say a few words about each of these uses in turn.

A. **Rhetorical devices**. Analogies are frequently used as rhetorical devices. The function of **rhetoric** is to persuade some particular audience of the truth or value of the topic at issue. As such, the object of the rhetorician is to convince an audience of the validity of some viewpoint by directing the audience's attention to an analogue, the logic of which is well understood by the audience, and claiming that in some important way the original field possesses the same logic. Given the validity of the analogy, certain truths will then be said to follow for the original subject. Used as rhetorical devices, analogies can be strikingly effective. When they are, it is because the listener or the reader is hit with a feeling akin to a revelation. "How appropriate," or "How accurate," the reader or hearer thinks when s/he sees the analogy. This is sometimes called the "aha!" experience. It stems from the listener's or hearer's belief that the logic of the analogue suddenly reveals the logic of the original so as to expose vital features previously hidden from view—rather like when the villain is unmasked in a detective story.[v]

B. **Heuristics**. The second use of analogies is as **heuristic devices**. As we have already seen, a heuristic is a rule-of-thumb devised for its possible usefulness in suggesting new ideas for research and development. There is a general consensus among philosophers that analogies can be extremely useful heuristic devices. Thinkers who specialize in some branch of learning, like everyone else in everyday life, frequently find themselves stuck on some particular problem in their field. At these times analogies may serve as useful tools for getting their thought processes rolling again. The analogy then becomes a hypothetical device that says: "Think of your original field as if it were analogous to analogue X. What are the material elements of X? What is the structure of X? How may your original field be compared in its elements or structure to the logic of the analogue?" Sometimes only a fraction of the analogue's field may be found to be useful, but that is permissible because the intent of the analogue is merely to provide new ideas to unblock the thought process. No claim is made here that the analogue is actually true or that it really illuminates the logic of the original. The analogue is only being used here as a tool. When its task is accomplished, the analogue can be dispensed with cheerfully, as thinking about the original field has been renewed.[vi]

C. **Methods of argument**. The third general use of analogy is its use in arguments as a means of proving a conclusion. As we have already seen, there are two kinds of arguments, deductive and inductive. A deductive argument is one claiming that the conclusion follows necessarily from the premises, and an inductive argument claims that the conclusion follows from the premises with only some degree of probability.

Analogies rarely are used in deductive arguments. This is because a deductive argument that uses an analogy would have to be one in which the structure of the analogue is exactly **isomorphic** with the structure of the original, that is, the analogue and original would both have to possess exactly the same structure. Because isomorphic structures may be difficult to find and establish and because any difference between the structure of the original and the structure of the analogue would invalidate the argument, deductive analogies have limited application—chiefly at this time in mathematics and computer science. If, however, the structure of the analogue is exactly the same as the structure of the original, then that analogue may correctly be used as a premise in a deductive argument about the original. Since these types of arguments will not be ordinarily encountered, I will say no more about them.[vii]

Almost all arguments using analogies are inductive arguments. These arguments simply seek to offer some evidence for the truth of their conclusions. An inductive argument from analogy seeks to establish the probability of the truth of its conclusion about the original field by offering as evidence truths about some possible analogue. The most frequently used analogues are examples that closely parallel the original in material or structure. Because these types of inductive arguments are used so frequently in science, philosophers of science have paid close attention to them and have devised rules for evaluating them. To see the point of these rules, you must first be familiar with the general format of an argument from analogy as it is used in science. As used in the scientific/critical, method analogies have the following structure:

1. Original O has some set of properties X, Y, Z.
2. Analogue A has the same set of properties X, Y, Z.
3. Analogue A also has property P.
4. Therefore O probably has property P too.

THE THEORY AND PRACTICE OF CRITICAL THINKING

Consider the following argument from analogy:

In the winter of 2004, NASA succeeded in landing two unmanned vehicles (Spirit and Opportunity) on Mars. Their mission was to seek evidence for the historical presence of liquid water on Mars, a planet that apparently has had no standing water for many millions of years. Such evidence was indeed found.[viii] Mars and Earth are alike in many ways. We know that on Earth liquid water is teeming with life, so was there also life on Mars? Might such life still continue to exist even in the absence of liquid water?

Thus we have the argument that since Mars once shared many properties in common with Earth (unspecified properties X, Y, Z, etc.) and since Earth has both liquid water and life (property P), and Mars had liquid water, then Mars may have had life, too.

How strong is this sort of argument? Philosophers have formulated six criteria used to evaluate the strength of analogical arguments:

1. **The number of things in the comparison**. The greater the number of objects [Earth, Mars] within the kind [heavenly body which may support life] between which the analogy holds, the stronger the argument.

2. **The range of the comparison**. The more different kinds of objects share property P [the presence of liquid water and life], the stronger the argument.

3. **The depth of the comparison**. The more characteristics [X, Y, Z, etc.] the original and the analogue share, the stronger the argument.

4. **How much support does the evidence give to the conclusion**? The weaker the conclusion that is claimed to follow from the presented evidence of the premises, the stronger the argument for that conclusion.

5. **The relevance of the evidence**. The greater the relevance of X, Y, Z to the possession of P, the stronger the argument. Do X, Y, Z, etc., supply necessary or sufficient evidence for P?

6. **The disanalogy problem**. The fewer the differences between the original and the analogue, the stronger the argument.

Briefly put, these criteria claim that the more the original, the analogue and other sorts of things share similarities and fail to share differences, the greater the number of things that possess property P, and the weaker the conclusion being supported by the evidence, the stronger the analogical argument.

A further word about criterion number four is called for, as it may lead to confusion. Criterion four basically states that an inductive argument in which the premises claim to support the conclusion with a high degree of probability is more subject to counter-examples and is therefore less likely to establish the conclusion than a similar argument with the same premises (and evidence) claiming to establish the same conclusion with a lower degree of probability. The argument claiming the lower degree of probability for the truth of its conclusion is thus more likely to be a stronger argument for its weaker claim because it makes a weaker claim. Suppose that in the example above, NASA claimed that the evidence sent back by the Martian rovers almost certainly shows that (a) there was once liquid water on Mars and (b) if there was once liquid water on Mars, then there was life there, too. The evidence presented by NASA to defend this claim would have to be a lot more solid than if NASA merely claimed that the Martian rover evidence showed only that Mars might have contained life at some time.

One should be careful with arguments from analogy. Given sufficient ingenuity it is possible to find several parities between any two things. If everything is analogous to everything else in some way or another, then the use of any given analogy says nothing special about anything. But analogies are important because it is believed that the logic of the analogue relates something special and important about the logic of the original. The logic of the analogue uniquely illuminates the logic of the original, and this uniqueness is one of the things at which the six criteria aim. Unless the logic of the analogue allows the thinker to see something uniquely important about the logic of the original, the analogy becomes a basically trivial relationship best serving some rhetorical or heuristic function. The logic of the analogue must also pick out properties in the original that are directly relevant to the possession of the new property P. If it fails to do so, the analogy is again rendered trivial. Much of the debate about the adequacy of any analogy therefore concerns itself with the questions concerning the relevance of the cited properties for the possession of the new property and the differences between the original and the analogue. Granted that there is a similarity between the logic of the analogue and the logic of the original, are the properties specified (Z, Y, Z) the important properties which are necessary or sufficient conditions for the possession of property P?

Sometimes an analogy makes it big in science. When this happens, the analogue may be treated as a **model**. A model is an analogy that is so successful it has become tied to a theory$_3$ about a whole range of phenomena and has been successfully used to explain particular phenomena and predict the existence of other phenomena. These predictions then become the subjects for further research. By a theory$_3$, remember, I do not mean a mere hypothesis or guess about something, but a systematic way of understanding a wide range of material. A good example of this is the atomic theory used in physics and chemistry. Modern physics and chemistry are so dependent upon the atomic theory that they could not survive its abandonment.[ix] One of the models once used extensively in the atomic theory, but which has since been abandoned because it no longer successfully fulfills a model's functions of prediction and explanation, is the billiard-ball model of the atom. This model pictured the atom as a bunch of tiny billiard-balls (protons and neutrons) surrounded by a bunch of other even tinier billiard-balls (electrons). This model was so successful as a means of grasping the atomic theory that even though this primitive version has long been abandoned, beginning physics and chemistry students continue to use variations of it to aid their understanding of the nature of atoms and molecules. It still may be helpful for certain purposes to picture the nature of the atom the way the billiard-ball model suggests, but analogies can become hindrances too. They do so when the logic of the analogue fails to say something unique, true, and interesting about the logic of the original. Thus, much discussion in science concerns itself with the adequacy of a given model as a method of understanding a certain theory.[x]

Some further observations: No attempt has been made here to quantify the probability with which the conclusion is said to follow the premises in an inductive argument using an analogy. Whether a given analogy is "weak" or "strong" is a judgment formed in the mind of the thinker who examines the analogy, and it is trivially true that different thinkers looking at the same analogy may well disagree concerning the argument's relative strength. There are no algorithms for deciding this issue. In these cases, there is no substitute for knowledge about the field in question; a person with little knowledge of a given field is more likely to be a poorer judge of the strength of an analogy in that field. The rhetorical use of analogies is likely to dominate its other uses. Training in a discipline is designed to impart the information, the special techniques of judgment, and the paradigms needed to correctly evaluate arguments in that discipline. There is no substitute for this training. All philosophers can add to this training is the list of rules presented above for evaluating the strength of analogies, and that list is, of course, too abstract to be of much use independently of the special knowledge acquired by the individual conversant with a given subject.

Evaluate the following analogies using the rules presented above.

A. The legalization of abortion shows that as a society we expect less of women than we do of men. In times of war society has traditionally asked men to risk their own lives. But we are unwilling to ask women to "risk" a few months of their lives in order to give life. Why is it that we expect men to be able to risk their lives while we do not ask a woman to do the same?

B. "You say that not every prophecy is fulfilled. But in the same way not every sick person is cured. Are we then to say there is no art of medicine? The truth is that the gods send us portends of things to come, and any mistakes which may be made in their interpretation arise from human speculation and not from the nature of the gods."

—Cicero, *The Nature of the Gods.*

C. NASA plans to send a space probe to Titan, the solar system's biggest moon and the only one with an atmosphere (much like primordial Earth's) known to have a thick, organic-rich nitrogen atmosphere. While the surface temperature is about minus 354 degrees, scientists believe the chemical processes in Titan's atmosphere may resemble those at work on the primitive Earth before life began.

D. In 1987 the legislature of North Carolina ordered public schools to teach students about AIDS. By this sort of logic, the legislature should also order schools to teach students how to avoid pregnancy because AIDS and pregnancy are similar in many respects.

E. "Just as a flute-player, a sculptor, or any artist, and in general for all things that have a function or activity, the good and the "well" is thought to reside in the function, so would it seem to be for man. Have the carpenter and the tanner certain functions or activities while man has none? Is he born without a function? Or isn't it rather the case that like the eye, hand, foot, or any other part of the body it can be maintained that man too has a function apart from these?"

—Aristotle, *Nicomachean Ethics.*

F. Let the soul be compared to the union of powers in a team of winged steeds and their winged charioteer. With humans it is a pair of steeds that the charioteer controls; one of them is noble and good, while the other has the opposite character. Hence the task of the human charioteer is difficult and troublesome. The steed that is the more honorable one is upright and clean-limbed, in color it is white with black eyes; a lover of glory, but with temperance and modesty; one that consorts with genuine renown and needs no whip, being driven by the word of command alone. The other is crooked of frame, a massive jumble of a creature, with a thick short neck, a snub nose, black skin, and gray eyes; hot-blooded, consorting with wantonness, and vainglory; shaggy of ear, deaf, and hard to control with whip and goad.

—Plato, *Phaedrus.*

G. "Truly we shall learn how to employ our mental intuition from comparing it with the way in which we employ our eyes."

—Rene Descartes,
Rules for the Direction of the Mind.

III. CRITIQUE USING ANALOGY

If the logic of the analogue is relevantly similar to the logic of the original in some important way, then analogies play a vital role in the advancement of understanding. However, analogies are not only used to support or establish some claim to knowledge. Analogies can also be useful in testing knowledge claims in two other ways—**refutation by logical analogy** (*reductio ad absurdum*) and **extending the analogy**. Consider the following the refutation by logical analogy:

To say that a president should be "above politics" when making cabinet choices and other appointments makes as much sense as saying that the Pope should be "above religion" when choosing Bishops.

Suppose that I suspect that there was something wrong with the claim that a president in his or her appointments should be above politics and choose the "best" person for the job.

After all, this claim does seem reasonable, even noble. To show what is really wrong with it, my first task is to reconstruct the original argument, which has as its conclusion the claim that certain political appointees should be made independently of partisan politics. The premises for the argument would run something like this:

1. Certain political offices are too important to prevent the president from choosing the most qualified person for that job.
2. The appointment in question is just such an appointment.
3. Ralph, who is not a member of the president's political party, is the most qualified person for the job.
4. Therefore Ralph should get the job.

To refute this argument by the technique of logical analogy, I must be able to devise another argument that has the same logic as the first one, but its conclusion must be obviously silly or absurd. The argument would therefore have to run something like this:

1. Certain religious offices are too important to prevent the Pope from choosing the most qualified person for that job.
2. The office in question is just such an office.
3. Satan, who is not Catholic, is the most qualified person for the job.
4. Therefore Satan should get the job.[xi]

My final claim is that, since the analogue has an absurd conclusion following from the same logic as that of the original argument about politics, there must be something wrong with the logic of the original argument. Often the whole refutation is compressed into one brief comparison. "You might as well let the fox guard the hen house," illustrates this sort of comment nicely.

In order for this technique to work, the analogue in fact must possesses the same logic as that of the original, and the conclusion of the analogue must in fact be untrue, wrong, or absurd. Should either of these conditions fail to be satisfied, the refutation has no logical force, (though it still may be psychologically persuasive). The proponent of the original analogy can always reply that the attempted refutation is in fact a perfectly good argument. Since the attempted refutation has the same logic as the original analogy, its conclusion in fact must not really be absurd! It follows that in examining the "punch" of a supposed refutation by logical analogy two questions must be asked: "Is the conclusion of the analogue in fact absurd?" and "Is the logic of the analogue in fact the same as the logic of the original?"

Another way of critiquing an argument from analogy consists in extending the analogy until it breaks down. An important point needs to be made here. Any and all arguments from analogy can be extended until they become absurd. Analogies are like rubber bands. They all can be stretched to a point, but they all eventually will snap if stretched too far. *Analogies do not make identity claims.* The original field and the analogue are not the same thing; there are always differences between them. Does that mean that arguments from analogy are without any power whatsoever? Are they all mistakes? No. It is always possible to argue that the extensions of the argument producing the absurdities are irrelevant to the point of the analogy. An analogy is a tool. When it has done its job, quit using it, or you will destroy what you are building. Once you have driven a nail with a hammer, quit pounding the nail or you will wreck the wood into which you are pounding the nail. It is impossible to derive rules which will automatically tell when an analogy is being used properly and when it is being misused other than the ones already listed. In assessing the question of proper use, there is again no substitute for knowledge of the subject matter in question, and even experts in a given field sometimes disagree. The ability to use analogies correctly, like the ability to use a carpenter's tools, is an art which requires plenty of practice to do well, and it is a vital part of critical thinking.

Evaluate the following refutations by logical analogy.

A. "I think a good vice president goes through what a good wife goes through."

—Barbara Bush

"You might as well say: 'Not tonight, honey, I have a headache.'" —Dick Cheney

B. We feel compelled to protest against the squandering of human lives in warfare. Unfortunately, too many respond: "Personally, I'm against it, but I don't want to impose my morality on others." But that's like saying: "Personally, I'm against cheating, but I don't want to impose my morality on others." We would instantly object, and rightly so.

C. "You say that there is nothing in nature superior to the universe itself and that this superiority is a manifestation of its makers, the gods. Well, I say that there is nothing on earth superior to the city of Rome. Must I therefore imagine that the many laborers who made the city of Rome think and reason like the gods?"

—Cicero, *The Nature of the Gods.*

D. You say that we ought not to allow the patenting of new animal life forms because it will lead to the patenting of new human life forms, but I say that your position is silly. No one believes that keeping animals as personal pets would lead to keeping people as personal pets. I believe that allowing the patenting and ownership of new animal life forms as property would not lead to a situation which would allow people to keep other people as person property. Why should it then lead to the patenting and ownership of possible new human life forms?

E. The current administration refuses to use federal tax dollars to buy clean needles for addicts, even though it said needle exchanges fight AIDS. "Why not simply provide heroin itself, free of charge, courtesy of the American taxpayer?" —John Ashcroft

METAPHOR

IV. DEFINITION

The term "metaphor" derives from Latin and means "transfer." A **metaphor** is a figure of speech in which a phrase, name, or term is transferred from its own context to some object entirely different from its own proper application. I shall call the term used as a metaphor the metaphorical meaning or field and the object to which it is applied the original object or field. In the statement "Jake La Motta fought like a raging bull," "fought like a raging bull" is the metaphorical phrase and Jake La Motta is the original object. Metaphors such as the one above that use the terms "like" or "as" to make comparisons are known as **similes**, though many metaphors are not similes. Clearly metaphors and analogies are closely related. However, while metaphors and analogies share the property of transferring the logic associated with one idea onto that of another, analogies typically assume that there is a great deal of affinity between the analogue and the original, while metaphors simply reorient the logic of the original object to the radically different logic of the metaphorical field.[xii]

Metaphors are frequently viewed as mere literary devices which chiefly function in poetic contexts and which are therefore of interest only to English teachers and poets. This way of viewing metaphor is simply another illustration of the "that's what I was always taught" phenomena. Undoubtedly, metaphor is of interest to English teachers and poets, but the metaphor's field of application far transcends these uses. Metaphors are extremely powerful devices for the creation and communication of new meaning. When I say, "Jake La Motta fought like a raging bull," I am suggesting that the reader or listener take one object of thought—Jake La Motta (the world middle weight boxing champion in the 1940s and 1950s)—with all the ideas normally appropriate to that notion and meld it into the logic appropriate to another concept—that of a raging bull. If you have ever had a close encounter with a raging bull, this new blend of ideas—Jake La Motta, the raging bull—can convey to you a graphic understanding otherwise unavailable to you. Would you then be willing to fight this guy? Only if you are completely crazy, or if you have a gruesome death wish, or if you are a matador.[xiii] The strength of this metaphor is that the reader or listener can get an incredibly detailed set of ideas for the price of a few words.

But was La Motta really a raging bull? Of course not, to say that he was would be to take the metaphor literally. To treat the metaphor literally is to make the mistake of thinking that the metaphorical field is in fact identical to the original field. When this happens on a large enough scale, the metaphor is dead as a metaphor. It is the fate of many metaphors to die in this fashion, an ironic ending indeed. Many ideas that are treated now as unquestionably and literally true started their careers as metaphors.

The marvelous thing about living metaphor is that the transfer of meaning seems to completely defy the laws of logic. Jake La Motta is, but he isn't a raging bull, and the reader or listener knows that both things are true at the same time. But how can this be? How can anything be both true and false at the same time? It is metaphor that makes this seemingly impossible situation possible. One way to get rid of the apparent contradiction here is to adopt the position called **reductionism**. (In religious contexts this is also known as **literalism**.) Reductionism maintains that the truth of the metaphor can always be reduced to a list of properties that the original is said to possess. In the La Motta example this would amount to the claims that La Motta fights very hard, he is impervious to pain, the more he gets hit, the madder he gets, and so forth, until the point the metaphor makes is exhausted. The obvious advantage of this approach is that it seems to save what was in danger—the laws of logic. The obvious disadvantage is that it kills the metaphor as metaphor. For the metaphor to exist as a metaphor, both the logic of the metaphorical field and the logic of the original field have to be applied concurrently to the original. If either one of these logics is annulled, the metaphor ceases to exist as metaphor.

Disputes can arise when one party treats a phrase metaphorically and the other literally. But which is it really? It is neither and it is both, depending upon the intentions of the speaker or the writer as well as the context of the culture in which the phrase was produced. It is up to the reader or listener to bear in mind that a particular phrase may or may not be intended as a metaphor; failure to acknowledge this is likely to lead to confused communication and verbal disputes. Serious consequences can result when the subject at issue is very important to those involved in the discussion, as is the case, for example, with many disputes involving religious or political issues. In any event, whatever the subject matter of the dispute, it must be kept in mind that metaphor has a unique kind of meaning that allows for its own special type of understanding. Metaphor is indispensable for conveying ideas of a certain sort, namely when the speaker or writer wishes to refer to a situation where seemingly incompatible claims are being proclaimed simultaneously without thereby canceling each other out.

How would the dispute over literalism lead to different analyses of the following examples?

A. "How many army divisions does the Pope have?" —Joseph Stalin, Soviet Union dictator during World War II.

B. "Might makes right." —Thrasymachus, Greek sophist.

C. "Right makes might." —Abraham Lincoln.

D. "I saw none of the other apostles there except James, the Lord's brother." —in Paul's letter to the *Galatians*, 1: 19

V. KINDS OF METAPHOR

Though anything may be compared metaphorically to anything else, there are four types of metaphor that are so commonly used that instances of them are frequently not seen as instances of metaphors. These four kinds of metaphors are **spatial** and **temporal**, **ontological**, **mechanical**, and **personal**.

Spatial and temporal metaphors locate something in time or space.

1. Joe is really in the doghouse now.
2. War is hell.
3. Judy was about at the end of her rope.
4. Let's go; it's late in the game.
5. Fred is behind the eight ball.
6. The seventh cavalry arrived in the nick of time.

Ontological metaphors allow the placement of boundaries or limitations on what is otherwise vague in scope or extent.

1. Your room looks like a garbage dump.
2. The regiment was put through a real meat grinder.
3. The President's news conference should put that rumor to rest.
4. Special effects in films are way over the top now-a-days.

Mechanical metaphors allow non-mechanical things to be treated like machines.

1. The tornado hit the trailer park like a freight train.
2. The human brain is the most complex computer ever invented.
3. He doesn't have all of his oars in the water.
4. My brain isn't firing on all cylinders today.

Personal metaphors treat non-human things as if they were human or acted like human beings.

1. Mother Nature pulled a fast one on us last night.
2. The sea redoubled its efforts against the dike.
3. Ralph is a real party animal.
4. The federal budget deficit is out of control.
5. To get this car to start you have to know how to talk to it.[xiv]

Metaphors like these and many others are so pervasive our language would be poverty-stricken without them. If the literalists or reductionists have their way, the meaning of these metaphors will be reduced to one specific domain in which it could be said that they were literally true. Different literalists or reductionists could differ because they could choose different domains into which to reduce given metaphorical phrases. Thus one reductionist might say that the truth of a certain range of metaphors could always be captured by some mechanical or material explanation, another by some explanation in terms of personhood, and so forth. Which categories are ultimately real or true regarding a specific example is, of course, a very important philosophical and practical issue. Suffice it to say that most of us hop from one kind of category to another depending upon the pattern of reduction we are familiar with. We also find it difficult to conceive of alternatives to the reductionist categories that we are used to, another illustration of the "that's what we've always been taught" phenomena. This is one reason why so many philosophical disputes like the ethics of cloning human beings or the ethics of gay marriages are so difficult to settle. There is no general agreement about what constitutes reality in these cases, therefore there is no way of determining whether any given phrase is or ought to be treated as literally true or metaphorically true. Again, in these cases there is no substitute for knowledge of the speaker's intentions.

However, merely determining whether a speaker or writer is using a particular phrase metaphorically is hardly sufficient by itself to settle the validity of the use of the phrase. Solving this more important question necessarily takes those involved in the dispute into the core of factual and philosophical material central to the issue at hand, and this can get very complicated very quickly. Many people find these complications tedious and call them hair splitting, logic chopping, and so on. For these reasons, participants in a dispute find it much more convenient to simply start with the root metaphor while simultaneously ignoring the fact that it is a metaphor ("Cloning is playing god" or "Cloning simply is another step in reproductive technology."). They incorrectly assume that all the important questions are now already answered, but they are not. This strategy simply begs the questions at issue. The root metaphors need to be recognized and analyzed. What are their consequences? Why choose this metaphor to begin with instead of another? Most simple answers to complicated questions such as cloning are simple all right; they are simply wrong. To think otherwise is to be seduced by the power of metaphors that usually are unrecognized as metaphors; they are taken as the literal truth about the subject. We need a new road sign along the highways of thought: "Caution. Metaphors working."[xv]

Evaluate the following metaphors. How do they redefine the original field?

A. "It is easier to teach a whale to play the tambourine than to stop smoking."

B. "Toto, we're not in Kansas any more."
    —Dorothy, *The Wizard of Oz.*

C. "The lights are going out all over Europe and I fear that we shall not see them lighted again in our lifetime."
    —Lord Grey, British Foreign Secretary, upon the British declaration of war on Germany in World War I.

D. "Power tends to corrupt and absolute power tends to corrupt absolutely."
    —Lord Acton

E. "An army travels on its stomach."
    —Napoleon

F. "Revenge is a dish best served cold."
    —Supposed Sicilian proverb

G. "Victory has a thousand parents; defeat is an orphan."   —A common saying

H. Plato characterizes society as a "ship of state" and government as the ship's captain.

I. Unethical scholars behave like crusading district attorneys who take shortcuts with evidence in order to ensure a conviction for someone they are convinced is guilty; they cheat for truth.

VI. MYTH, ARCHETYPE, SYMBOL, AND RITUAL

A **sign** is an object that has symbolic importance. Think of the stop sign, for example, an easily recognized object with a great deal more meaning than a mere tool for controlling traffic. A **symbol** is a device that functions metaphorically to call attention to an original field far more complicated and rich than the symbol itself.[xvi] A symbol, as the good metaphor that it is, reorients the original field. The symbol BMW stands, for example, not just for an automobile, but for the whole Yuppie life style that goes with it. Other well-known product labels, like the Golden Arches, function in the same way. These signs have become certain symbolic landmarks around which our daily lives turn. Some symbols play an extremely important role in life by calling attention to original fields that are of ultimate political or religious interest to various individuals. The flag of a country doesn't just label something as made in Japan or born in the USA, but invokes a complex set of emotional responses in those that identify with them. This is why buying American products and burning the American flag are seen as such touchy issues. Burning the flag doesn't just destroy a piece of cloth, it casts disrespect upon the whole country for which the flag is a symbol. The cross in Christianity isn't simply two pieces of wood nailed together to form a certain pattern; it symbolizes part and parcel of the whole religion of Christianity.

Around symbols **myths₁** tend to grow. The term "**myth₂**" means a commonly believed (but really false) story, as when it is said that the claim that Christopher Columbus was the first to discover America is a myth₂. This is not the meaning of the word "myth₁," to which I wish to call your attention. Rather, myths₁ are the **stories** that make sense out of symbols. Thus, the story of the death and resurrection of Christ is a myth₁ (story) which is central to the meaning of Christianity. Retelling these stories gives renewed life to the symbols which lie at their core. These myths₁ are celebrated by the

THE THEORY AND PRACTICE OF CRITICAL THINKING

repetition of **rituals**, which are performances that are repeated on a regular basis and serve to reaffirm the participants' commitment to the goals and values contained in the myth. Church services are obvious examples of rituals. Rituals are often easy to recognize because they involve special ceremonies and invoke the performative use of language as the events they commemorate are reenacted. Individuals (consider the baseball player who goes through the same set of contortions before each time at bat) and groups (boy or girl scout meetings, for example) can also have their own rituals without which things just would not be right. After all, I cannot function without my morning coffee![xvii]

Some metaphors are found in many different cultures. These metaphors are so basic to the myths of different cultures that philosophers call them **archetypes**. A good illustration of this is the symbol of the wise old man and father figure. Consider the characters of Yoda in *Star Wars* and Gandalf in the *Lord of the Rings*, or the notion of the founding fathers (a terrific example of a living metaphor—how many "founding mothers" have you ever heard of?), or the prayer which begins "Our Father who art in heaven...." These archetypes are so influential to the ways in which we think that alternatives to them, like founding mothers, are extremely difficult to take seriously. "Our Mother who art in heaven...." is at best a poor joke to the many sexist cultures dominated by the archetype of the wise old father figure.[xviii]

VII. METAPHOR AND SOCIAL POWER

The metaphors which are enshrined by symbols, the rituals they support, and the archetypes which appear in so many cultural contexts all embody ways of looking at the world which are fundamental to each and every thought system, no matter how otherwise diverse these systems may be. The wise old man figure appears not just in religious symbols like the figures of Abraham and Moses, but in atheistic systems like communism in the figures of Marx and Lenin. They have a double purpose.

The first is epistemic; they tell wherein ultimate truth is obtained—in this case, in the words and actions of the founding fathers. These words and actions supply the paradigms in terms of which all contemporary thoughts and deeds are measured. Secondly, and perhaps most importantly, these metaphors serve to ground systems of values and social control. Societies dominated by males are bound to have wise old men myths at their cores. If these same societies were to become dominated by females, their myths would have to be replaced by wise old women myths and "founding mothers" would no longer seem weird—consider Mother Nature or Mother Earth. Certain metaphors are readily accepted and transmitted by those in power because they serve as means for the maintenance of that power. They encourage the mind-set of the members of the culture to see this distribution of power as natural and necessary when in fact it is neither.

Power may be understood in many senses—political, economic, military, athletic, artistic, educational, psychological, and physical, to name some of its common manifestations. But in all cases, those who possess power in a society are those whose metaphors are accepted, naively, as the literal truth, especially by those who most benefit from their existence. No social system exists without its defining metaphors, which are located within the system of symbols, myths, and rituals that support the fabric of that society's life. Because there are many different power groups in our complex world, there are many different sets of metaphors accepted by members of diverse cultures or even within cultures as complex as those of America, Russia, or China. The acceptance of these metaphors supplies and supports the identity of the members of the groups who reaffirm their commitment to them through the repetition of rituals. Trans-group understanding, therefore, is contingent upon knowing the metaphors, symbols, and rituals of groups to which you do not belong. The alternative is misunderstanding in thought and conduct, all too frequent occurrences.

Analyze how the following metaphors serve to substantiate their power base.

A. "America, love it or leave it."
— Vietnam War bumper sticker

B. "Deutschland, Deutschland Über Alles."
— German national anthem
during Word War II

C. "...one nation, *under God*,..."
— Phrase added to the
Pledge of Allegiance in 1954

D. "Socialized medicine is Un-American."
— Comment made during the debate
over Medicare reform

E. "We hold these truths to be self-evident:
that all men are created equal..."
— Declaration of Independence.

III. THE EVALUATION OF ANALOGY AND METAPHOR

I hope that I have shown you how complicated and rich the fields of analogy and metaphor are. The systems with which we think are replete with them, as well they should be. Metaphors and analogies are indispensable thinking tools; indeed, it would be vain to suggest that we do without them. They present ways of dealing with material rich in content, but how are they to be evaluated? There are certain things that must be kept in mind when considering them. First of all, recognize that they exist. This seems innocuous enough, but things can get rather sticky when social disputes arise in which different groups' metaphors collide. Secondly, recognize that they are indispensable for thought. The logic of the analogical or metaphorical field makes possible the communication of ideas otherwise unthinkable about the original field. However, it does not follow from this that any analogy or metaphor is as good as any other. Consider thirdly the purpose the speaker or writer has in advancing any particular analogy or metaphor. What does the analogy or metaphor maintain about the original object? What is its logic? What does it implicitly deny about its original object? Answering these questions may require a great deal of knowledge about the field of the analogy or metaphor and the field of the original object. There should be nothing surprising about this. After considering such questions, the issue changes. Given what is known or believed about the original object, how does the analogy or metaphor change or advance that understanding? There is no way, of course, that this question can be answered in the abstract independently of the particular example under question, and yet it is the key to the critique of the analogy or metaphor.

Finally, realize that any analogy or metaphor can be pushed past the point of absurdity by continuing relentlessly to unroll its own logic. Sooner or later, the logic of the analogical or metaphorical field must deviate too far from the logic of the original, or else they would have been the same field. This eventual deviation does not mean that the analogy or metaphor is a failure, but only that demands should not be made on them that they never pretended to fulfill. When has an analogy or a metaphor been pushed too far? This is another question in which there are no a priori rules that will suffice to give a definitive answer. This must always remain a subject for critical discussion and debate, the continuation of which is the life of the mind.

Explain how the following metaphors attempt to maintain a specific distribution of social power.

A. God made Adam and Eve, not Adam and Steve.

B. America, love it or leave it!

C. All men are created equal.

D. God bless America.

E. Torture is Un-American.

F. A woman's place is in the home.

You should be able to define the following concepts, explain their meanings to others not familiar with them, invent your own examples that correctly illustrate the concepts, and apply them correctly to novel applications.

- Analogue
- Analogy
- Archetype
- Extending the analogy
- Isomorphic
- Literalism
- Logic of the analogy
- Material of the analogy
- Mechanical metaphor
- Metaphor

- Model
- Myth₁
- Myth₂
- Ontological metaphor
- Original subject
- Personal metaphor
- Proportions
- Reductionism
- Refutation by logical analogy (*reductio ad absurdum*)

- Rhetoric
- Ritual
- Sign
- Simile
- Simple analogies
- Spatial or temporal metaphor
- Story
- Structural analogy
- Symbol

Foundational concepts: Analogy, isomorphic, metaphor, model, myth₁, myth₂, refutation by logical analogy, symbol

NOTES

i. See Max Black, *Models and Metaphors* (Ithaca, NY: Cornell University Press, 1962), for the classical discussion of the nature of analogies and metaphors and the role they play in science.

ii. Taken from *ARCO's Preparation for the SAT*, 5th edition, edited by Edward J. Deptula, (New York: Simon & Schuster, 1984), 239, 241.

iii. See, for example, Plato's *Republic* and Aristotle's *Rhetoric*. Aristotle was more concerned with discussing the theory of analogy, Plato with using them to explain philosophical points.

iv. See Black, *op. cit.*, and Mary Hesse, *Models and Analogies in Science* (London: 1963), and R. B. Braithwaite, *Scientific Explanation* (Cambridge, MA: Harvard University Press, 1953), for a representative sample.

v. See Perelman & Olbrechts-Tyteca, *The New Rhetoric: A Treatise on Argumentation*, trans. by J. Wilkenson and P. Weaver, (South Bend, IN: The University of Notre Dame Press, 1969), for a good discussion of the rhetorical use of analogy.

vi. Philosophers have debated whether this is the only legitimate use of analogy in scientific explanations. See Pierre Duhem, *The Aim and Structure of Physical Theory*, trans. by P. Wiener, (Princeton, N.J: Princeton University Press, 1954), for a classical discussion of this issue.

vii. For more about the use of analogies in deductive arguments see Julian Weitzenfeld, "Valid Reasoning by Analogy," *Philosophy of Science*, (vol. 51, 1984): 137-149.

viii. See NASA's web page for updates on this issue.

xi. Different theories have been used in the past in physics and chemistry. The currently accepted version of the atomic theory is called quantum mechanics. For a detailed account of the development of the modern atomic theory in the Twentieth Century see Richard Rhodes, *The Making of the Atomic Bomb* (New York: Simon & Schuster, 1986).

x. See *The Concept and Role of the Model in Mathematics and Natural and Social Sciences*, edited by H. Freudenthal, (Dordrecht, Netherlands: 1961).

xi. See the book of *Job* in the Bible for just such an example.

xii. For a general discussion of the nature, role, and use of metaphor the classical text is Colin Murray Turbayne, *The Myth of Metaphor* (New Haven, CT: Yale University Press, 1963). See also Phillip Wheelwright, *Metaphor and Reality*, Bloomington, IN: The University of Indiana Press, 1962).

xiii. On April 11, 1989, Sugar Ray Robinson, Jake La Motta's nemesis, died. Robinson fought La Motta six times in his career, winning five of the encounters.

"He developed the skills that put some reason into calling boxing the Sweet Science. He became the matador, eluding the horns but loving their menace, a rational man among savages. His victories were our victories. He was what we would all like to be—indomitable." Herman Helms, *The Charlotte Observer*, April 13, 1989.

xiv. For an excellent discussion of these and other forms of metaphor see George Lakoff and Mark Johnson, *Metaphors We Live By*, (Chicago: The University of Chicago Press, 1980).

xv. For a discussion of the important role metaphor plays in philosophical disputes see Douglas Berggren, "The Use and Abuse of Metaphor," *Review of Metaphysics*, (vol. 16, 1962-63): 237-258, 450-472.

xvi. For a general discussion of the role symbols play in thought see Susanne Langer, *Philosophy in a New Key* (New York: Penguin Books, 1948).

xvii. For a general discussion of the importance symbols, myths, and rituals have for religion see Paul Tillich, "The Religious Symbol," *Journal of Liberal Religion*, (vol. 2, 1940): 13-33 and "Theology and Symbolism," in *Religious Symbolism*, edited by F. E. Johnson, (New York: 1955), 107-116.

xviii. For a general discussion of the role archetypes play in our thinking see Carl Jung, *The Portable Jung*, edited by Joseph Campbell, trans. by R. F. C. Hull, (New York: The Viking Press, 1973). For a feminist critique of the domination of culture by masculine symbols see *Sexist Language*, edited by Mary Vetterling-Braggin, (New York: Littlefield, Adams, & Co., 1981).

"Have you no sense of decency, sir?"

**Joseph Welsh's question put to Joseph McCarthy during the
1954 Army McCarthy hearings in which Senator McCarthy branded everyone
who disagreed with him (including President Eisenhower) as a communist**

CHAPTER EIGHT

Authority

INTRODUCTION

We constantly are placed in situations that require judgments on our part concerning issues about which we have little or no expertise. Is that "funny" sound coming out of my car engine anything to worry about? Should I spend some of my money on a new game system now when its replacement may come out soon? Is this DVD player a better value than that one? These topics all have one thing in common; given your own ignorance of the issue and given that you do not have the time or ability to overcome that ignorance yourself, the wise and rational thing to do would be to consult and rely upon the informed judgment of experts or authorities. Experts, after all, are supposed to know about these things. If you have car problems, you should ask a mechanic; with money problems it could be helpful to talk to your parents; before buying electronic equipment check out *Consumer Reports*. But even experts can be wrong, and it is equally likely that experts will disagree. What are the rules that should guide us when consulting expert opinion? How can we distinguish between the rational use of expert opinion and its misuse?

In answering questions such as these, it will be helpful to distinguish questions of **knowledge** from questions of **credibility**. The possibility of transmission of AIDS by insects is a question about the facts involving possibly true or false claims to knowledge. Questions about knowledge include questions about the verifiability of the content of what is being reported as well as questions about the grounds or reasons used to justify these reports. But an expert's claim to know facts which are unknown to the layperson and difficult to verify also involves a decision on the layperson's part concerning the expert's credibility, that is, the expert's right to be believed regarding claims that s/he makes. Questions about credibility are questions about the reliability of the person making the report as a bearer of the truth. These two issues are commonly interconnected in that a credible witness is credible because the truth of what s/he reports can generally be verified. Thus in evaluating arguments from authority, there are two separate questions that need to be considered: "Is the testimony of the authority credible [Does s/he have the right to be believed?]," and "How can the authority's claim to special knowledge be verified? [Is s/he in fact correct?]"[i]

I. ARGUMENTS FROM PRIVILEGED POSITION

The appeal to experience is in fact broader than the foregoing may suggest. A lot of things we believe to be true we accept on the basis of the testimony of others. Historical accounts are obvious examples of this. We believe certain things about the execution of Mary, Queen of Scots, because we accept the truth of certain eye-witness testimony passed down to us by letters written by those at the trial and execution and from other accounts written by those contemporaneous to the events. We like to hear granddaddy tell stories about the big war. We trust the accuracy of the material about Paris we read in the travel section of the newspaper when preparing for our first visit there. All of these claims presuppose that certain individuals were in a **privileged position** to know the truth of what they reported. Being in a privileged position to know about something is to possess unique information due to the fact that you happened to be present when an event occurred and others were not, or you are the first person to think of an idea and you have not communicated it to someone else. We only have the time and resources to check out a handful of reports made by others, so we generally accept these reports as true, except when these reports make claims contrary to what we already know or believe. When this happens, we remain skeptical. And this is certainly a rational procedure. It makes good sense for me to accept your claims about your toothache. After all, I cannot feel it; only you can. But if you are known to me to be a hypochondriac, it may be reasonable for me to be skeptical about the truth of what you say.

Ultimately, the claim of privileged position is a claim that some individual is in a unique position to know the truth of something that you could know firsthand, too, if you had the relevant data, but you do not, in fact, have the relevant data. You do not have the toothache, or you have not been to Paris, and certainly you were not at Mary, Queen of Scots' trial and execution. But if you had the relevant data, you would then see too that certain things are true. So goes the argument.

Arguments from privileged position are not above challenge. Maybe the fellow with the toothache is just trying to win sympathy. Maybe the travel writer has an unduly romantic conception of Paris. Maybe the witnesses to the trial and execution of Mary, Queen of Scots, hated Catholics. In these cases, it would be rational to shift the evaluation of what they report to take into account the factors which motivated their reports; that is, it would be relevant to what they say to consider the question of the credibility of their testimony. Indeed, not to do so would be to run the risk of falling victim to the biased opinions of others. Communication situations presuppose trust in the truthfulness of the reporter. Because of this presupposition of trust, the reports of others generally are accepted at face value, and usually they should be, but there are circumstances that rightfully call for the suspension of that trust. Among these circumstances are questions concerning the accuracy of what is reported and questions about the competency or reliability of the reporter. If someone claimed that his Uncle Herbie once had a car that got 184 miles to the gallon of gas, it would be foolish to accept the truth of what was said because it goes against all common experience about gas mileage.

Claims made from privileged position can always be challenged. We can even challenge our own claims. Did I really see what I thought I saw? Am I dreaming? Am I mistaken in my interpretation? Answers to these challenges frequently shift the issue from questions of credibility to questions that routinely involve recourse to standard methods of gathering and assessing data, and these methods are subject matter relevant. To check out the accuracy of the travel report, you have to read up on Paris and consult other travel reports, your own travel agent, and other visitors to Paris. If you are still in doubt, you have to go there yourself. Indeed, it must ultimately be possible to put others (including yourself) in the position of the one who is claiming the privileged position, if the accuracy of the claims is ultimately to be verified to your own satisfaction. If that is not possible, then the accuracy of the claim cannot be established objectively, and those not sharing the privileged position will never know whether the claims are true.

Discuss the following claims from privileged position.

A. "When I was your age, we had to walk nine miles through snow to school."
  —Grandpa Abe Simpson, *The Simpsons.*

B. The Holocaust never happened.

C. "She turned me into a newt! I got better."
  —from *Monty Python and the Search for the Holy Grail*

D. I have the flu.

E. Elvis is still alive. I saw him last night in the produce section of the grocery store.

F. Rasputin was poisoned, strangled, shot, stabbed, and thrown in the Neva river by a bunch of incompetent Russian nobles, but he survived all of this.

G. My dog can stand on its front legs alone.

II. EXPERT OPINION

Some claims we are asked to accept or reject present us with special problems because their subject matter is well beyond the range of competence of the average person but is within the range of competence of someone with special training and knowledge in a relevant field—the **expert**. An expert is a person with a high degree of competence in a given subject area who knows many facts about the subject area unknown to the average person as well as the theoretical basis of the subject matter. The expert not only knows the truth about things in his or her field, s/he also knows why these things are true and other things are not true about the subject. Expert opinion has always been of vital importance to society. This is even more so in a technologically sophisticated society such as ours. Could you repair your own car, computer, or watch if they broke, or heal your body when it becomes sick or injured? Can you even fix the drip in your bathroom sink? For the vast majority of us who cannot do any of these things, the only possible answer is to call in the expert—the mechanic, the electronic expert, the jeweler, the doctor, or the plumber. If the mechanic says my car needs a new fuel pump, then s/he is most likely right; after all, s/he's the expert.

But appeals to expert opinion are not all equally reasonable. Experts, after all, are fallible and some people who claim to be experts are not really experts. What distinguishes good or reasonable appeals to experts from bad or unreasonable ones? Philosophers have developed seven criteria that must be used in answering this question.

1. **Subject matter competence.** An expert E in some area S really must have special competence in that area; s/he cannot simply claim to be an expert. More importantly, evidence of this competence must be demonstrable. Expertise in most fields is certified by recognized procedures. What is E's formal training? Doctors and lawyers, for example, post their degrees on office walls as external signs of their training. In addition to this, the expert usually has successfully practiced in the field of his or her expertise. S/he usually is recognized by fellow practitioners in the field as an expert. The greater the depth and range of training and practice E has, the better established E's claims to expertise in S are. The better E's expertise is, the more reasonable it is for the layperson to accept E's claims and the more credible E's claims about S are.

  It is a mistake to assume that someone is an authority simply because s/he has said some things about a certain topic which happen to turn out to be true; there is such a thing as being right by accident. To be right by accident is to have a true belief about something, but, as we have seen, true belief is not the same thing as knowledge.

The fact that someone happens to be good at guessing the winners of next Saturday's college football games does not qualify that person as an expert on football; s/he may merely be lucky. To be an expert s/he must know the theory of the game, s/he must know why his or her predictions are good or reasonable, and when asked to defend them s/he must be able to cite the logic of the subject matter that provides the basis for making reasonable predictions.

2. **Evidence**. It should be possible in principle to give direct evidence to verify the claims made by an expert. What E claims to be true about S must be verifiable in principle by an appeal to the evidence that leads E to make the claims s/he is making. E is not right just because E says so, but because E knows certain things. In principle, anyone could know the same thing if s/he were given the proper training. E is right about S, and therefore is a competent trustworthy authority on S, because E possesses the special knowledge of S that validates E's claims about S, not because E just happens to luck out with his or her guesses.

There is one apparent exception to this rule. Many subject areas are so complex that not every judgment made by an expert can always be verified immediately. In subject matter S, the theoretical principles which govern S can extend to a huge, if not infinite, amount of things. These rules frequently cannot be applied in a mechanical fashion. They must be applied in accordance with insight and practical experience. Sometimes these insights may be so tacit or ill-defined they are termed "gut feelings" or "intuitions." When a detective, for example, rejects an apparently plausible explanation for a crime as being "too pat," it may not be for any reason that the detective can put his or her finger on immediately. "It seemed fishy." "It didn't smell right." These kinds of claims made by the detective are signs that some thought mechanism is operating in the detective's mind which at least tem-

porarily defies explanation, and yet it may very well be wise for the layperson to trust the detective's intuition. However, when the case is finally solved, it should be possible in practice for the detective to lay out the method of reasoning for what was previously inexplicable. If s/he cannot do this, s/he is best described as having made a lucky guess. While lucky guesses turn out to be true by definition, the point of being an expert is to take the guesswork out of the problem in the first place. This point leads to the next rule.

3. **Field of competence**. In order for E to be an expert on S, there must be a discipline S. If S is not a discipline, no one can be an expert in it. If S qualifies as a discipline, subject matter S must have rules that govern the operation of events in S. Physics is a discipline because there are physical laws and theories that explain the behavior of matter. Albert Einstein was an expert in physics because he knew these laws and theories very well and he knew how to discover and apply them. But not all topics for discussion have disciplines that govern them. Xenopsychology is not a discipline because (as of yet) we know of no extra-terrestrials to psychoanalyze, except, of course, in science fiction stories. Since there are no known extra-terrestrials, there is no discipline of Xenopsychology, and therefore there are no experts in Xenopsychology (supermarket tabloids and countless Hollywood movies not withstanding). Is there a discipline that encompasses psychic predictions? No; though many people foolishly believe that there is ("Tired of phony psychics? Dial the Real Psychic Hotline!"). Because there is no discipline of psychic predictions, there are no experts in this field, and claims to expertise are simply bogus. The credibility of anyone making these kinds of claims should be suspect.

But at some time in the future, there could be a discipline of psychic predictions and then there could be experts in this field. The existence, or lack thereof, of a given discipline is not set in stone. At one time there was no discipline of psychology and no experts in psychology, but now both exist; at one time there was a discipline of alchemy, but it has since been abandoned. Assume for purposes of argument that someone successfully produces precise psychic predictions, many of which turn out to be true. Could it be proper to call this person a psychic expert? Not unless and until this person (or someone else) can explain the theoretical basis for these predictions. That is, not unless a discipline can be developed on the basis of which any of its practitioners can duplicate the performance record of our hypothetical psychic expert. This could be the case, though as of yet it is not; until a discipline is structured to govern the making of psychic predictions, there can be, at best, people who are good at producing psychic predictions.

Notice that there are two separate conditions used to test the authenticity of an appeal to an authority—pragmatic and theoretical. Pragmatically an authority is an authority because s/he is usually right in his or her predictions. But mere accuracy is not sufficient to make someone an authority, because accuracy may be based on luck [being right] or mere true belief [being right for the wrong reasons]. *To be a proper sign of authority the predictions also have to be based on knowledge [being right for the right reasons], which presupposes an understanding of the theoretical factors inherent in the discipline.* If a discipline can be developed to give a theoretical basis to claims, these claims can then, and only then, be said to possess a high degree of credibility, for they will then be right about the future for the right reason—knowledge—and not for the wrong reason—luck.

4. **Staying within the field of competence**. Authorities are authorities only within their discipline. Claims made by experts speaking on subjects outside of their field of competence deserve no more respect than claims made by any other layperson. Just because a

person is an authority in one field, it does not follow that s/he is an absolute authority in all fields; authority is nontransferable. However, it is reasonable for the layperson to prefer the opinions of an authority in one field X about another field Y if X and Y both share some relevant similarities and a real expert in field Y is currently unavailable. If, for example, your car engine quits and two people stop to look at it, one of whom is an expert diesel mechanic and the other a mere layperson like yourself, then, even though your car engine is fueled by gasoline, it would certainly be rational to take the advice of the diesel mechanic over that of the layperson. In cases like this, the diesel mechanic may be said to be a **limited authority** on questions concerning your gasoline engine. Limited authorities are experts in one field who make pronouncements on fields that are relevantly similar to their own. Which fields are relevantly similar to which others is itself a possible matter of debate. Veterinarians are relevantly similar to doctors, but not very similar to car mechanics and hardly at all like baseball players. There will be cases in which it may be difficult to decide whether an expert is speaking outside of his or her field of competence. These cases can only be settled by laying down the data and theory of both fields and seeing where they overlap and where they differ. If the question at issue occurs in the area of overlap, then an authority in one field may be said to have a limited authority in the overlapping field.

5. **Experts can disagree**. Arguments utilizing appeals to authority can become ensnared by conflicting claims made by different authorities. It is naive to expect all experts to agree on everything in their discipline. All disciplines involve many issues that are completely unexplored or under-explored. There are also bound to be many issues in which exploration has produced conflicting results. Therefore, it is reasonable to expect experts to disagree at times. A good argument from

authority will note (when it is appropriate) that experts disagree about the issue at hand. Philosophers are working on methodologies for settling disagreements among experts.[ii] Frequently the problem in these cases is that there is too much conflicting data, some of which must then be rejected; the question then becomes which data to reject. At other times the disagreement involves more complicated theoretical disputes within a discipline concerning the basic rules and principles of the discipline itself. In some disciplines, such as physics or biology, there is in fact a far greater consensus than there is in other, frequently younger, disciplines such as psychology or economics. Most disciplines have a core of accepted facts and theories surrounded by increasingly complex or under-explored areas in which expert disagreement is much more likely to occur. An appeal by a layperson to an authority is more reasonable if the appeal is to the area where there is consensus in the discipline, and less reasonable if it is an appeal to an area that is still subject to much debate within the discipline.

6. **Correctly understanding the claims made by the authority**. By definition, an appeal to authority involves a layperson's attempt to prove a point by referring to opinions held by experts in areas in which the layperson has little or no competence. The layperson must be on guard to insure as much as possible that s/he understands what the authority to whom s/he is appealing to is really saying. In practice this can be very difficult. Experts are experts because they possess a great deal of theoretical knowledge. Laypersons do not have this knowledge. Laypersons may therefore easily misunderstand the claims the experts are making and thus falsely believe that an authority is claiming something the authority is not in fact claiming. See the Appendix at the end of this chapter for some of the complexities involved here.

7. **Conflict of interest**. An authority is someone with knowledge of the data and theory connected with a particular discipline. But authorities are people too, and, like all people, experts have jobs to do, families to care for, desires for successful careers, and so forth. These other factors may come into conflict with their role as experts. When this happens it is wise for the layperson to be concerned with the possibility of conflict of interests. A conflict of interest may give an expert a motive other than providing objective information for stating his or her claim, so his or her reliability and credibility as an authority may rightfully be questioned. An authority in this case may have a vested interest in defending a position not endorsed by the discipline itself. When disputing claims made by independent doctors that smoking tobacco is bad for your health, tobacco companies bring out their own "experts" who argue that the health risks of smoking have not yet been proven or have been overstated. Laypersons can then use the claims of tobacco company experts to defend their own decisions to smoke. Realistically, an expert hired by a tobacco company to support the tobacco company's own position would not, in fact, dispute that position and agree with the doctors, at least not if s/he wanted to keep his or her job for long. The possibility of a conflict of interest raises credibility questions about whether the claims made by experts are motivated by some hidden agenda rather than by the evidence itself. In cases such as this, it is appropriate that appeals to authority are suspect.

One of the most common and systematic misuses of appeals to authority is found in **advertising**. Advertising has several purposes: to acquaint an audience with the existence and the nature of a product, to explain the purposes and uses of the product, to tell where the product may be obtained, and to sell the product. There are many reasonable and legitimate ways of meeting these goals, but wrongfully using arguments from authority is not one of them. Authority figures frequently appear in ads. When these ads meet the qualifications discussed above for valid appeals to authority, they are perfectly legitimate; when they do not, they are not. There are two main ways that advertisers can slip in the use of authority—by using authorities outside of their proper fields of competence and by violating the conflict of interest requirement. Taking the latter first, an authority figure may be presumed to be paid for his or her endorsement of a product. Because the advertisement works by associating the reputation of the authority figure with the product being marketed, it may be legitimate to question whether the authority figure is sincere in his or her endorsement. Is s/he saying this simply because of the money s/he is being paid to say it? Would s/he just as soon say the opposite of what s/he said if s/he were paid to say that? Questioning the sincerity of a speaker's motives here is perfectly legitimate and necessary. If s/he is only saying what s/he says because s/he is being paid to say it, why trust the truth of what s/he says? Why trust his or her credibility? This complaint is compounded if the authority figure is also speaking outside of the field of his or her competence. Nothing qualifies the claims of an athlete or movie star, for example, to know anything about the virtues of motor oil.

When an authority speaks outside of his or her field, it is perfectly reasonable to question the truth of what s/he is saying because in areas beyond their fields of expertise authorities know no more than laypersons do. This type of question becomes trickier to answer when an authority is speaking about a related field. Assume, for instance, that an expert racecar driver endorses a certain brand of motor oil. Driving a car well and servicing a car engine so that it runs well are two separate things, which may or may not be related. The racecar driver may also know motor oils as part of his or her greater job as a driver, but s/he may not. Questions like these become impossible to answer without further information. Coupling this with the problem of a possible conflict of interest makes it legitimate for the layperson to exercise a certain degree of skepticism concerning the reasonableness of what is being maintained. Yes, the oil may be a great oil, but it is unclear whether ace driver's endorsement is a good reason for the layperson to believe that this is so.

To summarize, appeals to authority involve the following seven considerations: subject matter competence, evidence, the existence of a discipline, staying within the discipline, disagreement among experts, correct interpretation of experts' claims, and questions about conflict of interest. Strong appeals to authority must successfully satisfy all seven of these criteria. If any one of the conditions set by them is violated, the appeal to authority loses the reasonableness that it would otherwise have. Weaken enough of these conditions, and this appeal can even become a fallacy, a poor argument that unfairly convinces an audience because of the aura of respect surrounding the authority itself.

Assess the following arguments from expert opinion in accordance with the criteria presented above.

A. Einstein claimed that the speed of light is a constant that is the absolute speed limit of everything. He ought to know, since he invented the whole theory of relativity.

B. NASA scientists claim that the space shuttle Columbia blew up because it lost some of its protective heat tiles. They ought to know; after all, they built the shuttle.

C. The pet psychic said that my dog was depressed because it wanted its own pet. She must be right because she's the pet psychic.

D. My doctor said that my illnesses were all imaginary because he couldn't find any physical causes for them. He even called me a hypochondriac! Maybe he's right. Maybe it's all in my head.

E. "If (a) student wants to say the world is flat, the teacher doesn't have the right to try to prove otherwise. The schools don't have any business telling people what to believe."

—Jim Cooper, educational lobbyist for Arizona Gov. Evan Mecham, testifying on a state bill that would require schools to teach evolution as a theory, not a fact

III. *AD HOMINEM* ARGUMENTS

Ad hominem **arguments** are arguments directed, according to the literal translation of the Latin, "against the man." They are commonly used in a variety of contexts, most visibly, perhaps, in issues of public policy debates. By definition, they all consist in ignoring the position your opponent has advanced in a discussion and attacking the personhood of your opponent instead. Thus *ad hominem* arguments work by labeling your opponent as a kind of **negative expert**, a person the position of whom ought to be rejected out of hand because of some negative personal characteristic possessed by your opponent. Because *ad hominem* arguments work by shifting the focus of the debate from the context of the argument advanced by your opponent to the character of your opponent, they generally have been treated as fallacies by philosophers who have examined them.[iii] Even the most corrupt opponent, the argument against *ad hominem* argument runs, may speak the truth, because the truth of what is said by anyone is a separate issue from the character of the one who has spoken. This last point is surely correct. Authorities can be mistaken, and morally disreputable people can speak the truth; but the situation is somewhat more complex than this.

Philosophers have distinguished between two types of *ad hominem* arguments: the **abusive** and the **circumstantial**. An abusive *ad hominem* argument works by heaping abuse on your opponent. The circumstantial *ad hominem* argument claims that there is something about your opponent's special circumstances that undercuts his or her credibility as a witness to the truth of what s/he is saying. I shall look at the logic of each of these forms of arguments in turn.

To commit an abusive ad hominem *argument you have to ignore the content of your opponent's position and attack his or her character instead.* When you call your opponent a communist or a liar or an idiot, it can be a very effective way of undermining the credibility of your oppo-

nent in the eyes of some audience. What constitutes abuse, of course, depends upon the values of the audience to whom you are speaking. A convention of Rabbis is unlikely to be impressed by your characterization of your opponent as a "dirty Jew;" rather, you would be undermining your own position while building up that of your opponent.

What is at stake here is a question of credibility. Personal abuse of your opponent effectively halts the debate about the truth of the original subject matter and shifts the audience's attention to the character of both speakers, the opponent under attack and the one who launches the attacks in the first place. As a rhetorical device the shifting of the focus of the debate may or may not be warranted, depending upon the circumstances. Is a discussion of the character of your opponent more important than a discussion of the original issue at hand? If it is, then shifting the topic of the discussion may be perfectly appropriate, as when an attorney attacks a witness's truthfulness in past dealings. "Because Ralph has been shown to be a notorious liar, we ought not to believe Ralph now." Maybe. Maybe not. Here the audience (the jury in this case) must make an important decision based upon limited evidence.

Care must also be taken not to succumb to a **straw man argument**. A straw man argument is one in which an arguer does not attack an opponent's real position, but one which may at best bear a superficial resemblance to it, but is utterly inane. Hence the title of this fallacy—a straw man. [Notice there are no straw women!] Decisions in situations like this can be made reasonably only when enough relevant data have been gathered and evaluated. How much data is enough to fairly weigh the character of the witness is a question that is impossible to answer in the abstract.

The fore-piece at the beginning of this chapter cites a classic case of the use of the straw man argument during American political history. During the 1950s Senator Joseph McCarthy of Wisconsin engaged in a political witch hunt, labeling anyone who disagreed with his politics a communist, and destroying many reputations, as well as some lives, in the process. Because McCarthy (ironically) chose to attack the "character" of his opponents rather than the truth of the opponents' original position itself, the question of McCarthy's own character was also called into question by the attack. The audience is left to decide whether the attack is warranted and what the attack unveils about the character of the attacker. Thus abusive *ad hominem* arguments may well rebound in the face of those who use them if the audience feels that the abuse is unwarranted or that it has been pulled grossly off track from the original argument. This is what ultimately led to McCarthy's downfall.

Circumstantial *ad hominem* arguments may be more sophisticated than the abusive variety. They also may be difficult to distinguish from the abusive. You commit a circumstantial *ad hominem* when you argue that something about the circumstances of your opponent renders what s/he has said dubious, though what s/he said might otherwise pass as a good point if made by someone not in these circumstances. In the example cited above, if I argue that we ought not to believe what a particular scientist says about the health risks associated with smoking because the scientist is employed by a tobacco company, I claim that because of the identity of his or her employer, the scientist's special circumstances render his or her claims untrustworthy. In short, I am worried about the problem of a hidden agenda in the scientist's position. Could s/he keep his or her job if s/he said anything else?

It is the question of a **hidden agenda** that renders circumstantial *ad hominem* arguments appropriate or not. Hidden agendas may so poison a speaker's credibility that it is appropriate to doubt his or her words because they may spring from the hidden agenda and not from the facts of the case. When questions like this arise, it is appropriate to bring into view the circumstances which motivate the testimony of the speaker. You must distinguish raising this question from winning your argument.

Even one who speaks from a hidden agenda may be telling the truth. *Again, questions of credibility must be distinguished from questions of knowledge.* But when no means of obtaining knowledge is directly or indirectly available to a particular audience which cannot postpone making a decision about a particular case, assessing a speaker's credibility is the only rational option the audience has. In this type of case, the circumstantial *ad hominem*, which seeks to move the debate from a question of knowledge to a question of the credibility of the speaker, may be the most legitimate move to make when attempting to evaluate a particular argument.

A common variety of circumstantial *ad hominem* argument charges that your opponent should not be believed because there is a contradiction between what the opponent has said and the way s/he acts. If someone preaches the gospel of poverty, for example, and appears to also amass a large personal fortune, it seems appropriate to point out this apparent contradiction. But to what extent does this apparent problem provide good reasons for rejecting the gospel of poverty? It doesn't, though it may very well raise the question of hypocrisy. Is this person serious about what s/he is saying? Does s/he really believe it? Here the answer may be either yes or no. Not enough of the facts of the case as of yet have been given to make an intelligent judgment. Maybe the preacher has found that the gospel of poverty is a great way to make a buck; paradoxically enough, it sells. Maybe this preacher needs this money, however, not for personal wealth, but to further spread the gospel of poverty or other good deeds. There need be no contradiction here, but it equally well may be the preacher preaches the gospel of poverty but has insufficient willpower to stick to it in his or her own life. Weak wills are common enough. "Do what I say, not what I do," is a common saying and perfectly reasonable advice, even if I do not have enough will power to take my own advice. Thus Shrek may be correct about the health problems of obesity but unable to control his own weight. The apparent contradiction between what he preaches and what he does is not necessarily an indictment against what he preaches, but it certainly raises a question that demands a legitimate answer; if his doctrine is so great, why can't he follow it himself? This question may have a reasonable answer in some cases, though equally well it may not. Therefore, the appropriateness of the circumstantial *ad hominem* in any given case can only be addressed by further information concerning the circumstances of the one charged.

Equally important, it is possible to consider the circumstances of the one who is making the attack. What was the speaker's intent in using an *ad hominem* argument against his or her opponent in the first place? If it was to challenge the validity of the opponent's case by raising legitimate concerns about the credibility of the opponent's character or position, that may be all well and good. However, if it was to cover up the weakness of the attacker's own case by distracting the audience into an irrelevant topic, that is quite another thing. Worries about cases such as this last possibility motivate philosophers to suspect any use of *ad hominem* arguments. They are legitimate concerns, but they can be appeased by showing that the former condition is met by any given example.

Questions about the validity of the use of *ad hominem* arguments, therefore, necessarily raise two distinct but related issues—questions of knowledge and questions of credibility. Regarding questions of knowledge, it is correct to say that *ad hominem* charges are one and all irrelevant. To attack your opponent and not his or her argument is to raise an irrelevant issue if the sole concern is the question of the truth of your opponent's position. No matter how corrupt or incompetent s/he may be, anyone may speak the truth on any given occasion. Questions about what is the truth are best evaluated by the usual methods presented in this book and by the procedures established by the special disciplines. When, however, you are not in a position to ascertain the correctness of someone's position, and/or you do not have the time to delay making a decision on the issue you are facing, and the credibility of your opponent becomes the basis for the reasonableness of accepting his or her argument, then questions about your opponent's credibility are highly legitimate. In these cases, questions of credibility can be answered by considering the conditions mentioned above.

Evaluate the following *ad hominem* arguments.

A. Dan Quayle [running for vice-president] ignited a bonfire when he repeated his campaign boast that he'd had as much experience as John F. Kennedy did before JFK ran for president.

   "Senator, I served with Jack Kennedy, I knew Jack Kennedy, Jack Kennedy was a friend of mine," his opponent, Senator Lloyd Bentsen, said levelly. Then he unloaded the biting punch line: "Senator, you're no Jack Kennedy."

B. Cassandra, upon observing the birth of her brother Paris: "Dad, get rid of him now; he'll be the death of all of us." King Priam: "Cassie, I've heard of sibling rivalry, but you're *such* a wet blanket!"

C. Dear Ann Landers: I am male, 70, and want to speak my piece. I have never seen a pregnant man nor have I ever heard of a man who became a mother. Therefore it seems to me that men should keep their mouths shut when the subject of abortion is raised. The woman is the one who has to carry the baby nine months and give birth. Her voice is the only voice that should be heard on this. When medical science can arrange it so a male can become pregnant and give birth, then men should have something to say about abortion. Until this time, shut up.
   —Texan

D. William J. Bennett, President Bush's drug czar, had a noisy gift for hip-shooting, ruckuses, and headlines. "How," a reporter asked him, "can you be a drug czar when you're addicted to nicotine?"

The two-pack-a-day czar admitted contritely that he was hooked on the weed. "I've been scolded about it," said Bennett. "I'll quit."

Reporters, some of them tobacco-stained degenerates, hooted and demanded, "When?"

"Well, it's hard," said Bennett. "But I guarantee you that you won't have a Director of National Drug Control Policy who smokes."

E. After being convicted of the brutal murder of his parents, Ralph argued against his own death penalty by claiming that "It would be wrong to execute an orphan."

IV. TRADITIONAL WISDOM

There are special kinds of appeals to authority which merit separate consideration—appeals to the authority of **traditional wisdom**, **popularity**, and **social indoctrination**. Though these are separate concerns in theory, in practice they may closely interrelate and reinforce each other.

To appeal to the authority of tradition is to argue that good reasons for believing something or doing something can be found by considering the traditional mores of society. Believe this or do that because that's the way society (or some subset within society) has always done it. Do (don't) believe this or do (don't do) that because that is (that's not) the way it's always been done around here. Philosophers have usually treated this kind of appeal to authority with contempt, dismissing it out of hand.[iv] Traditional wisdom, the rejection runs, may provide a reason for doing or believing something, but it can hardly provide a *good* reason for doing or believing that thing. While there is merit in this repudiation of arguments from traditional wisdom, the real case is a bit more complicated than that. Applying the rules for evaluating arguments from authority cited above will help clarify this situation.

If the authority of tradition is to present a good reason for accepting the truth of some claim or the value of some practice, there must

be some set of experts on these traditions. This does not seem to present any special problem. Though there are no methods of accrediting experts on traditional wisdom *per se* (as there are in biology or mathematics), people who study these areas such as cultural anthropologists, sociologists, folklorists, historians, and philosophers could certainly qualify as experts about a given society's way of life. It is also true that the average well-informed member of society could count here as an expert. But for the authority of tradition to function correctly in an argument, there must be some discipline that experts on traditional wisdom are experts about. What is this discipline? Here is where the problems begin. It is fairly easy to say what is not or ought not to be considered in this discipline, namely those many topics treated by the special disciplines in the arts and sciences such as chemistry or history. It would simply be silly to evoke an argument from the authority of tradition to establish the truth of some claim in astronomy or mathematics. To say that we know that the moon is 237,000 miles from the earth because tradition has always had it that way is to invoke a kind of argument which causes philosophers to pull out their hair and contemptuously dismiss any argument from traditional wisdom.

However, traditional wisdom does have a discipline, which for lack of an official name, I shall call the **way of life**. Traditional wisdom properly concerns itself with issues of social customs, values, and goals. These are important categories that serve to define a society and shape its continuity over time and distance. Americans, for example, share a more-or-less common way of life. This way of life unavoidably touches on all the other disciplines, as all disciplines occur within society. Though social traditions are not relevant means of determining truth in the other disciplines, and society ends up both looking silly and injuring itself when it attempts to manipulate claims belonging properly to other disciplines, when it comes to a discussion of social issues reflecting alternative possible ways of life, previous or current social traditions about these issues contain relevant concerns. Knowing what our form of life has been and what it presently is can be highly relevant in considering how to attempt to adjust it to meet present and future challenges.

Arguments from traditional wisdom are especially subject to the problem of dispute between experts. This should not be surprising. Ways of life are not homogeneous in theory or in practice. Modern societies want many things, some of which are inconsistent. Promoting one value may frequently only be done at the cost of diminishing others, but the diminished value is still a value with its proponents, too. Until the world becomes a great deal simpler than it is now, arguments from traditional wisdom will always be vulnerable to counter-arguments from a different aspect of the same society's tradition. It is one of the jobs of philosophy to clarify and minimize these disputes within value systems, but even philosophers cannot resolve the conflicts between values, each of which is held to be equally legitimate. Ironically, the problem with arguments from traditional wisdom is not that they have no force, but that there are too many of them that conflict with roughly the same degree of force.

There is another problem here. Arguments from traditional wisdom for certain ways of life have an additional agenda that frequently is not perceived. Social traditions embody positions about the desirability of some social structure or other. Any social system distributes power and awards in some ways and not in others. People speaking from traditional wisdom are, consciously or not, attempting to perpetuate or enact some possible division of power. While these divisions of power may be irrational because they are based on mistaken beliefs about the world and the capacities of various peoples in the world, they are still divisions of power. Social change inherently threatens to rearrange these power divisions, and this is one of the reasons all societies have a difficult time dealing with it. Arguments from the authority of tradition,

therefore, are always subject to the question of whose power they are trying to perpetuate. They all, therefore, tread closely to conflict of interest questions. Of course, this holds true for all sides in the debate about ways of life. Conservatives want to continue an existing division of power; reformers want to substitute a new division, but a division none-the-less.

What does traditional wisdom have to say about the desirability of the following:

A. Women in combat

B. Prayer in public schools

C. The invasion of Iraq

D. Requiring individuals to take drug tests as a condition for employment or for playing on a school athletic team

E. Prohibiting the smoking of tobacco

F. Teaching sex education in public schools

Another similar form of argument from authority frequently seen is an argument *ad populum* or **argument from popularity**. To argue from popularity is to argue that something is true or false, good or bad, because many people believe it or value it. Advertisement, for example, frequently attempts to sell products by proclaiming the product's popularity. Buy a Ford pick-up truck, the largest selling vehicle of its kind in America. How good is this type of argument?

Again, philosophers have typically stressed the problems with this type of argument. Popularity, it is said, only indicates how well something sells, not how good it is. How well something sells can be the mark of a good salesperson, not the mark of a good product. How widely something is believed can be a mark of gullibility, not truth itself. Both of these points are well made, and they should be taken seriously.

Certainly many things have been purchased in the past because of successful salesmanship having nothing to so with the intrinsic properties of the marketed product; and certainly many things have been accepted as true in the past which have proven to be untrue. Mere popularity does not necessitate truth or value. But popularity frequently is a sign of truth or value. Many things are popularly believed because they are in fact true and are recognized to be true. Many things are popularly valued because they are in fact valuable and are recognized to be valuable. Popularity provides prima facie evidence for the truth or value of its object, but popular belief about truth or value can be overridden by the presentation of the evidence upon which the truth or value of the object is properly based. It is this evidence which provides the real reason for the truth of a claim or the value of a product and thus for the object's proper popularity.

Popularity, then, is a sign that there is a good reason for believing or valuing something. If circumstances prohibit the examination of the underlying basis for something's popularity, the mere fact of its popularity provides some basis for evaluating an object in the popular fashion. It provides a case such that the burden of proof is on the one rejecting the value of the product or the truth of the claim. In this manner, arguments from popularity resemble arguments from traditional wisdom—they both provide some reason for accepting some claims, though these reasons can be overridden or substantiated by testing the claim or product itself.

Assess the following arguments from popularity:

A. McDonald's, over 100 billion sold.

B. 75% of Americans favor legalized abortion.

C. 63% of Americans disagree with the right of homosexuals to marry.

D. Nine out of ten Americans profess a belief in God.

E. 51% of Americans go to church on a weekly basis.

Traditional wisdom and popularity are important forms of **social indoctrination**, especially when these common forms of authority become enshrined within the formal educational system in a given society. All societies have developed systems of formal education, the function of which is the indoctrination of individuals new to that society's form of life. To indoctrinate someone is to get that individual to believe something, frequently without questioning it. If a society could not do this it could not survive, because its survival depends upon replicating itself through its new members. Indoctrination is a necessary condition of social life. Problems arise, however, because social and educational indoctrination systems are too effective. Persons subjected to them become so deeply conditioned that they find it virtually impossible to break out of the molds they have been poured into, or even show much awareness that they have been poured into a mold in the first place.[v]

Social indoctrination and education serve to inhibit thought just as much as they facilitate it. If you are indoctrinated with a given set of beliefs, for example, not only will you believe what you have been taught, you will disbelieve what you perceive to be inconsistent with or simply different from what you have been taught. Time and time again, I have observed that when discussing some issue or other, my philosophy students will respond to a particular problem with, "Well, I have always been taught..." or "I believe..." as if these observations are all that can be said about the issue. When I respond with attempts to get students to further reflect on the issue, my response is invariably greeted with puzzlement because they do not see that I am trying to get them to think past the spot where they normally stop thinking about the issue in question. The reason students cannot think past their normal stopping places lies in the hold previous indoctrination has on their minds. The best way to break the hold is to point out that such a hold exists and that it is the function of philosophy to uncover these indoctrinated stopping places in thinking and subject them to a critical examination. But this is difficult for students to accept and perform because they have had no practice in doing it. It is also perceived as threatening by the student, which is why philosophy is frequently seen as a subversive and dangerous activity.

Philosophy is subversive! Critical thinking is subversive! They attempt to get students to examine whether the reasons they have for holding a particular belief are good reasons and to examine whether the indoctrinated beliefs are really true. Many beliefs, in fact, cannot survive examination, but equally well many of them can. Philosophy takes as its motto the Socratic saying, "The unexamined life is not worth living."[vi] This examination of opinions by philosophers is not confined to any particular social, political, economic, or religious group, but to everyone alike. Each of us is a product of social and educational indoctrination. But that is not all that we are. We are also creatures who are capable of being rational and thus capable of subjecting our beliefs to critical assessment.[vii]

CONCEPTS

You should be able to define the following concepts, explain their meanings to others not familiar with them, invent your own examples that correctly illustrate the concepts, and apply them correctly to novel applications.

- *Ad hominem* argument (abusive or circumstantial)
- *Ad populum* argument (argument from popularity)
- Advertising

- Argument from expert opinion
- Credibility
- Expert
- Hidden agenda
- Limited authority

- Negative expert
- Privileged position
- Straw man argument
- Traditional wisdom
- Way of life

Foundational concepts: *Ad hominem* argument, *ad populum* argument, argument from expert opinion, credibility, expert, privileged position, traditional wisdom

APPENDIX

"England and America. Two countries separated by a common language."

—Oscar Wilde

WHAT'S THAT SUPPOSED TO MEAN? UNDERSTANDING CLAIMS MADE BY OTHERS

Students frequently are unaware of some of the many problems that can arise concerning discussions and/or disagreements about the ideas presented in the material they come into contact with, regardless of whether or not this material is presented by experts. Here is a list of some of the issues that might cause misunderstandings between the speaker/writer and the audience.

I. INTENTION PROBLEMS

The main problem here is the distinction between what the speaker/writer means to say and what you see the speaker or writer as actually saying. There may be a big difference between the two.

1. Did the speaker/writer intend that *you* receive the material in question? If not, how did you get a hold of it?

2. Did the speaker/writer intend to actually say what s/he said, or did s/he intend to say something else instead? You have to distinguish between what s/he meant to say and what the language used actually says. Has s/he misspoken?

3. Is the speaker/writer lying to you? If so, is s/he lying to you by stating what s/he knows to be untrue or merely by failing to disclose the whole truth (sometimes called a "sin of omission")?

II. LANGUAGE PROBLEMS

The main concern here is with the actual words chosen in the message.

1. Does the language contained in the message mean the same thing to you and the speaker/writer?

2. Is the speaker/writer still available to answer questions about the message in the event that the language of the message is unclear?

3. If the speaker/writer is available, will (or can) s/he answer questions about the message? Is s/he both willing and able to clarify any possible confusion about the content of the message?

4. If the speaker/writer is unavailable, can anyone else correctly answer questions about the contents of the message? If so, who is this other person, and what are his or her credentials to speak with authority about this issue? How are you to know whether this other person has presented an accurate account of the original material and not, in fact, some garbled or self-serving version of it?

5. If the original message was originally written or spoken in a foreign language, what is that language, and do you understand it sufficiently well to understand the original message?

6. If you do not know the foreign language well enough to understand the original message, who translated that message for you? What are the translator's credentials

such that the translation of the original material can be trusted to actually mean what its author originally meant by it rather than what the translator made it to mean?

III. THEORY PROBLEMS

Because knowledge is theory laden and communication is intended to supply information, all the factors discussed in Chapter One concerning direct firsthand knowledge by acquaintance also appear in these cases of secondhand knowledge by description.

1. Do you and the original speaker/writer adopt the same theoretical stance towards the issues covered by the material in question? Do you accept the same crucial data?

2. What problems are contained in the theoretical stance of this material that may be relevant to the author's understanding of this material? To your understanding of the material?

3. Are these theoretical stance issues recognized by both you and the original author? Only by you? Only by the original speaker/writer? By neither you nor the original speaker/writer?

4. If you and the speaker/writer have different theoretical stances on this material, how do they differ? How do they make reasonable different conclusions about this material?

Discuss how the concerns presented above may shape the understanding of the following examples.

A. The Declaration of Independence says that "...all men are created equal," but it doesn't say anything about women.

B. Words feared most by parents during Christmas: "Some adult assembly acquired."

C. "In the beginning was the *logos*, and the *logos* was with God, and the *logos* was God."

                      —*John* 1.1

D. "Obey my authority!"

                    —Cartman, *South Park*

E. Gym teacher: "OK, class, line up in a row and count off by 2's." Class: "2's. 2's. 2's. 2's...."

F. "Dreams are messages from the Id."

                    —Freud

G. "But I saw none of the other apostles except James the Lord's brother (*adelphon*)."

        —from Paul's *Letter to the Galatians*, 1.19

NOTES

i. Philosophers and teachers of rhetoric have got them-selves nicely tangled in knots over this issue. Typically, philosophers severely limit the legitimacy of appeals to authority because they claim (rightfully, I might add) that the claims made in reports are true or false independently of the nature and character of the reporter. On the other hand, rhetoricians allow for a wide-ranging use of appeals to authority because they claim (rightfully, I might add) that almost all of our knowledge depends on the acceptability of appeals to authority. In fact, philosophers and rhetoricians are both correct. They simply are talking about different issues. Philosophers are worried about issues of verifi-cation; rhetoricians are worried about issues of credi-bility. Human knowledge is inextricably tied to both credibility and verification.

The apparent conflict between philosophy and rhetoric goes back a long way. Plato was the first to address the issue in his *Gorgias* and *Protagoras*, circa 380 BCE. For a modern discussion of these issues see Walter Minot, "A Rhetorical View of Fallacies: *ad Hominem* and *ad Populum*," *Rhetoric Society Quarterly*, (vol. 11, 1981): 225-235. From the philosophy side see John Woods and Douglas Walton, "*Argumentum ad Verecundiam*," *Philosophy and Rhetoric*, (vol 7, 1974): 135-153.

ii. See Nicolas Rescher, *Plausible Reasoning* (Assen/ Amsterdam: Van Gorcum Press, 1976), and Keith Lehrer, "Social Information," *Monist*, (no.60, 1977): 473-487, for a complex account of these issues.

iii. The best, and most exhaustive, examination of *ad hominem* arguments from the philosopher's point of view is found in Douglas Walton's *Arguer's Position* (Westport, CT: Greenwood Press, 1985).

iv. See, for example, Irving Copi, *Introduction to Logic*, 11th edition, (New York: MacMillan, 2002), and Howard Kahane, *Logic and Contemporary Rhetoric*, 4th edition, (Belmont, CA: Wadsworth, 1984). Rhetoricians, again, are typically much more liberal regarding the validity of appeals to traditional wisdom. See, for example, Lloyd Bitzer, "Rhetoric and Public Knowledge," in *Rhetoric, Philosophy, and Literature*, edited by Don Burkes, (West Lafayette, IN: Purdue University Press, 1978).

v. When this happens, we call the social conditioning process brainwashing. Edward Wilson, a Harvard biologist, maintains that, "Human beings are absurd-ly easy to condition." See *The Sociobiology Debate*, edit-ed by Arthur Caplan, (New York: Harper and Row, 1978). Sociobiology is a new discipline founded by Wilson, the purpose of which is the determination of the biological causes of social behavior in humans and animals. See his *Sociobiology: The New Synthesis*, (Cambridge: Harvard University Press, 1975).

vi. See Plato's *Apology* for a further presentation of what Socrates and philosophy are all about.

vii. Richard Paul calls this task of philosophy critical thinking in the strong sense because it attempts to establish our beliefs on rational and defensible foun-dations, as opposed to critical thinking in the weak sense, which is merely a set of tools individuals can use to chew up other peoples' opinions. See "Teaching Critical Thinking in the 'Strong Sense,'" *Informal Logic Newsletter*, (vol 4, no. 2, May 1982): 2-7.

CHAPTER NINE
Law, Religion, and Morality

INTRODUCTION

There are three areas of practices that are present in every society—the legal, the moral, and the religious. These areas stretch into all of the fabrics of your lives, and they often stretch into each other as well. As systems of concepts, rules, and paradigms they present to us the frameworks in which we live; they generally are taken for granted until some aspect of their practices intrudes on us. You get a speeding ticket, for example, or are called for jury duty; you don't like the way your friend is treating you. Your parents suddenly announce that they are getting a divorce; you go to a new church of a different denomination. You wonder what could have possessed anyone to fly airplanes into the World Trade Center or why someone would blow up the federal office building in Oklahoma City because they were mad at the federal government for Waco. The list goes on and on.

How should these issues be evaluated? When we evaluate them, we tend not to do so very wisely because we are not aware of the many complexities—legal, religious, and moral—which they may involve, and because we commonly take different positions concern-

ing the many factors that may be involved. In this chapter, we will look at some of these complexities.

I. LAW

"The Constitution distinguishes between those issues which are subject to the democratic process and those which lie permanently outside of this process. It is the job of the Supreme Court to apply this distinction to the issue at hand."

—William Rehnquist,
Chief Justice of the Supreme Court.

The complications of social life have given rise to one important social institution specifically established to deal with these complications on a formal basis—the legal system. Legal reasoning is based on arguments from authority, the authority of the legislature in making the laws, the executive branch of government in enforcing the law, and the judicial branch of government in interpreting the law. I shall say something about the use of authority in each of these areas. Each branch of government appeals to the traditions and authority that are peculiar to its own function in organizing our social lives and in settling our legal disputes. In general, legal authorities are those who possess the socially endowed power to make or enforce certain forms of rules for society coupled with the legal right to use this power.

A. Legislative legal authority. The function of the legislative branch of government is the enactment of the laws and programs that govern society and the funding of the bills that pay for these programs. All forms of government, be they democratic, socialist, fascist, or monarchical, perform these functions, though it is not true that each of these forms of government uses a separate assembly to accomplish these jobs. Legislatures are somewhat like the rules committees that govern organized sports. Their job is to define the rules (laws) which will govern the playing of the sport (social activity). Members of rules committees may be wise or stupid, silly or profound, experienced or inexperienced, but they (and they alone) can determine what the rules shall be. In turn their deliberations can range from sophisticated and knowledgeable concerning the issues to be discussed, through moderate knowledge of the issues, down to the utterly capricious, whimsical, or dogmatic. Silly or profound, dogmatic or rational, they alone have the legal authority to make the rules. The laws and programs they fund may be valuable or wastes of money (they may not even be adequately funded, or funded at all), but this division of government is the only one empowered to do these jobs. The authority to do these things is based on the form of life the society has chosen to live. Society's will may be specifically affirmed as a written document like the American Constitution or it may be far less formal like Great Britain's common law, but there must be known and somewhat fixed legislative procedures or chaos would result.

In many countries, there are subdivisions within that country (e.g., states) and subdivisions within these subdivisions (counties) and further subdivisions (cities, which actually may overlap with county or state borders). These produce multiple layers of legislatures in the form of state legislatures, county commission-

ers, and city council members, any of which can claim legal rights within their own domain against any other domain in accordance with traditional, court approved, federally, or state approved manners. As you can see, it can get quite complicated just to determine which rules, laws, or ordinances actually govern what areas. There is generally no clear formula which says that federal law always trumps state law (though it usually does), which trumps county law, which trumps city law. Be it so simple!

Historically in Western culture, since the time of the Romans, legislative (or civil) law has been considered to be an intentional refinement of natural law and common law. **Natural law** is a label used to stand for what is considered to be the unalterable and perfect moral/physical laws of nature laid down for man by God. It was believed by thinkers who followed this tradition that these laws could be discerned by reason alone unaided by revelation.[i] Natural law legislation greatly influenced Roman legal traditions and has found its way into our practices chiefly in this format.

Contemporary Western legislatures (especially those influenced by English traditions) also take guidance from common law. **Common law** labels those traditional mores and procedures that are so ingrained in Western traditions that they represent the status quo from which the burden of proof has to be wrestled. Common law, therefore, is generally not the result of conscious legislative decision making, but more of a matter of recognizing the strength of custom.[ii]

Discuss what common law and natural law could say about the following examples:

A. The age at which a person should be considered an adult—does the sex of the person in question affect this issue?

B. Genetic alterations of food

C. Sex change operations

D. The use of performance enhancing drugs by athletes

E. Cloning animals or humans

Within legislatures there usually are found **political parties**. A political party is a group of individuals united around a common political philosophy. Political parties are inherently at odds with rival political parties, with which, by definition, they do not share the same political philosophy. Different political parties inevitably have their own list of qualified persons (**party leadership**) and preferences (**party platform**) which they seek to get elected, accepted or enacted. While not all countries recognize or allow political parties, those that do fall into two camps, those like the U. S., which historically has been dominated by a two-party system, and those like Italy, which has historically been a multiparty system.

Political parties or factions blend into other issues concerning the making of laws or the funding of programs and the problems associated with majority rule. In democracies, it is an axiom that majority votes rule on decisions, but this is not always so. At times a minority in a legislature (or even one single member of the legislature) may succeed in thwarting the will of the majority simply by employing political clout and knowing the rules of legislative debate. This is known as the problem of the **tyranny of the minority**, which often results in a bill or funding program being twisted to accommodate the will of the minority or the lone individual. On the other side of this coin is the problem of the **tyranny of the majority**. This occurs when the power of numbers allows the majority to consistently out-vote the will of the minority. Members of minority parties or factions may find this quite frustrating, but there is no single remedy.

To further complicate matters there is the **paradox of democracy**. In a democratic system, leaders and policy are commonly determined by elections. This is all well and good when the candidate or policy you favor wins, but what happens when it loses? Then you are bound by your commitment to the democratic process to support the person or the policy you have just voted against! This seems crazy, but without this "crazy" switch, the system could not func-tion. If losing teams refused to play the game again simply because they lost, the democratic system could not function in practice. These problems are prime examples of the wrinkles of politics. They require political phronesis so as not to make the political process a poor problem solving and leadership system.

Discuss whether the following examples should properly be viewed as instances of tyranny of the minority or of the majority.

A. The 2000 presidential election results in Florida.

B. In the 2000 presidential election, George W. Bush won the majority of Electoral College votes (and thus the presidency) even though he lost the majority of the popular votes.

C. A filibuster is a legal strategy by which a member of a legislature opposed to some bill may hog the time allotted to the discussion of the bill, thus preventing the bill from ever coming to a vote. Does this strategy amount to an abuse of power?

D. Mother watching her son go by in the marching band: "Oooh, everyone's out of step but my son, Billy."

E. In the fall of 2004 the Ukrainian Presidential election outcome was apparently rigged by the incumbent Viktor Yanukovych to "defeat" the challenger, Viktor Yushchenko. When hundreds of thousands of Ukrainians protested this, Yanukovych's supporters tried to poison Yushchenko with Dioxin. Yushchenko survived the poisoning, and in a new and honest election received 52 % of the vote.　　—News item

Finally, within many legislative systems are found **lobbyists**. Lobbyists are persons who have no legal legislative power, but who commonly may possess significant practical ability to persuade the legislature to adopt a specific position on some view of importance to their employer. Thus lobbyists are people who seek changes in the law or special funding by the legislature for special interests that are generally unique to a distinct sub-set of society (e.g., peanut farmers). These interests can oppose the interests of the majority or even the rest of the society but still become legislatively sanctioned.

B. Executive legal authority. Executive authority is the legal right and power of enforcing the law.[iii] It is embodied in a leader who may happen to be a democratically elected president, prime minister, governor, mayor, or city council chief, but who may equally well be a hereditary monarch, a dictator, a tyrant, a revolutionary leader, or even a ruling committee or cabinet. There are always three issues involved with executive authority: Who holds it, (one or many?), how s/he got it (by standard social processes like elections or by violence or usurpation?), and which laws and programs is it being used to enforce (those of the legislature, those of the "people," or those of the leader's own choosing?). Executive legal authority often provides the most socially visible form of power. It is normally what you think of when you think of power—the right to lead and police society.

This form of social right and power spawns continual disputes when all members of society are not content with the direction leadership takes in making decisions and policing society, which is about all the time in most societies. In modern, complex societies there are many conflicting ideas and goals which citizens have which concern the enforcement of leadership. In reality, not all rules are enforced equally. They never have been, and they never will be. Society wants strong leadership so that problems can be attacked and dealt with as they arise, but it doesn't want its leadership to be too strong such that others' opinions and concerns are simply ignored. Social life is a continual grappling with questions of leadership and rule enforcement. The term for this is politics. Political questions are always on the agenda of individuals and groups within society. There is no way to avoid this that doesn't also turn persons into assembly line production robots.

In any system other than a dictatorship, political leadership is structured by the legislature and the courts. Through laws and by means of social programs and funding, the legislature provides a grid within which executive power operates. The courts, in turn, function to determine whether the executive has exceeded its legitimate authority. This presents a good illustration of the **system of checks and balances** as it operates within government.[iv] No branch or division of the government can operate independently of the control of the others. This also means, however, that political issues are never settled once and for all. As long as any sort of society exists, even one undergoing a revolution, political issues are always on the agenda. Unlike the sporting metaphor used above, the clock never runs out on these concerns.

C. The judicial system. The function of legal judicial power is to judge the legality of what is brought before it. These areas of judgment include laws, social programs, funding, executive actions, the actions of private citizens, or even the decisions or processes of other judges within the judicial system itself. In examining the judicial system only as it works in America (because that's complicated enough) the process of argument from authority is easy to see in action. To win in a court of law you have to establish the legality of your position. From the point of view of the formal legal system this is done in two closely related ways, either by an appeal to the relevant state or federal codified rules of law or to the concept of **precedent**, or both. Precedent is established by citing previous court decisions that support your position or by citing the English common law tradition from which our formal legal system originated. If the position you wish to defend has no exact legal precedent, the next logical move is to cite some previous case and argue that your case is relevantly similar to what was previously decided. If you cannot do either or both of these things, you will probably lose your case. This is one of the reasons **lawyers** are so vital.

Lawyers are professional players of the legal game. They claim special expertise in knowing how to present positions for their clients in ways that work within the rules of the legal game. Their goal is to benefit the client, regardless of the merits of the client or the client's case. If you or your lawyer cannot anchor your claim in the legal tradition of the society as exemplified by its common law, current statue books, or previous court decisions, you have no legal way of establishing your position. Lawyers commonly take a great deal of heat in this society as purveyors of injustice when the clients they represent who are clearly guilty are released on some sort of legal technicality or other. Lawyers are then seen as supporters of rotten and unworthy causes. These charges, however, are unfair. The role of lawyers is that put to them by the legal system—to represent their clients to the best of their abilities. It is not to do the morally right thing, to see that moral justice is done, or to establish the kingdom of God on this earth or in the courtroom. Because our legal system is based on competition, it is built into the philosophy of our system that truth and justice are best served if there are at least two competing sides to legal issues who seek to win by defeating the opposing side. There are obvious drawbacks associated with this sort of **zero sum game**. A zero sum game is one in which for every winner there must be a loser (win/lose). Win/win and lose/lose are ruled out from the start. In life outside of the legal system, however, win/win and lose/lose are all too real as possibilities. In this sense, the judicial system is an artificial problem solving system with built in limitations. But this is not the lawyer's fault. They are stuck with playing by the rules mandated and permitted by society at large.

Among the rules that have evolved within the judicial system are the various **federal and state rules of evidence**. The rules of evidence determine what material may be presented in trials and what material may be excluded. Evidence that is seized illegally is typically excluded from admission. Hearsay evidence, that is, evidence derived from sources having no firsthand experience of the events at issue, is generally excluded. Yet expert testimony is included in trials, even though expert witnesses no more witnessed the actual events than did those persons who make up the jury. Expert witnesses lend their expertise regarding the application of theory to the data presented by the evidence in the hope that the jury will be able to combine the two to form a sound judgment. Finally, juries are the absolute arbitrators of fact in the American legal system. Their verdict regarding the facts of the case, especially concerning the guilt of the defendant, cannot ordinarily be appealed. Though jury members take an oath to judge the case before them only in accordance with the evidence presented in the court and the relevant laws, juries can go so far as to practice **jury nullification,** in which the application of the law to the evidence is ignored in favor of some other non-legal or extra-legal standard such as fairness or prejudice. When this is done by a judge in a trial situation, it is called **judicial nullification**.

Discuss the application of the rules of evidence to the following situations:

A. If you are stopped under the suspicion of drinking and driving and refuse to take a Breathalyzer test, your driver's license will be suspended for a year right on the spot.

B. "You have a right to remain silent: what you say can be used against you in a court of law; you have a right to counsel; if you cannot afford an attorney, one will be appointed for you. Do you understanding these rights?" —The *Miranda* rule

C. "I decline to answer that question based on my 5th Amendment right against self-incrimination."

D. In a criminal case the burden of proof is on the state. A defendant is presumed to be innocent until shown otherwise beyond a reasonable doubt."

—Judge's charge to the jury before deliberation

Legal issues, then, are decided in courts of law always by an appeal to the authority of social/political tradition. The important question then is whether you have appealed to legal tradition in the right kind of way. But, again, this appeal is also conditioned by the abilities and quirks of the judges, jurors, and lawyers who are the players of this game. If you can answer this question in the affirmative, then you have offered a good legal reason for your position, though you may still lose your case because no one was listening to your brilliant argument. Nonetheless, these arguments must be made within the context of a particular legal tradition. Legal issues frequently get mixed up with ethical issues, but the two are separate, though related, disciplines. People frequently make the mistake of going into a court of law thinking that they will win their case because they are morally in the right, only to find (much to their dismay) that being morally in the right has little to do with the law.[v] This sort of confusion is encountered and encouraged, for example, by the popular presentations of the legal system found in TV and movies. These popular presentations make hash out of the actual legal system because they aim for entertainment, not enlightenment, and the actual workings of courts of law are seldom entertaining. A similar situation occurs when we attempt to evaluate the sometimes downright bizarre actions of the legislatures. So-called blue laws are but a mild manifestation of this. In judging cases such as these, it is good to remember that, from the legal point of view, whatever the legislature decides about the law is the law until corrected by the legal process, no matter how strange the law may look from a non-legal point of view.

Because legal authority is so important to society, there are almost never any problems in determining those who rightfully possesses it. Society formulates easy and efficient methods of recognizing the holders of executive, legislative, and judicial authority together with the methods of selecting and removing said office holders. No one other than the duly authorized office holder has the legal right to use the power contained in the office. But it should be noted that the form of authority conveyed by the legal system is more akin to the sort of authority found in traditional wisdom. It is the sort of authority that determines (legally) correct goals and actions, not the sort of authority which determines the truth of claims about the world as it exists independently of social convention. Legal authority cannot determine mathematical or scientific truth, for example, but it can (and does) determine the direction society chooses to follow. Do not confuse the authority to determine social goals (which is based upon convention) with the authority to determine the truth about nature (which is not based upon convention). Highway speed limits are not immutable laws of nature. When truths about social goals become entwined (as they usually do) with, for example, claims about scientific or mathematical truths, the critical thinker must carefully disentangle these separate issues. To the extent that social directions and goals are built upon an incorrect understanding of the way the world works independently of the desired directions society may wish to travel, these social directions are doomed from birth, no matter how disappointing this may be to their proponents.[vi]

Discuss the following decisions of the American judicial system:

A. In *Roe v Wade*, 1973, the Supreme Court legalized abortion.

B. In *Brown v the Board of Education*, 1956, the Supreme Court ruled that "separate, but equal" was not a Constitutionally valid principle which could be used to justify the segregation of public schools.

C. In *Cruzan v. Missouri Department of Health*, 1990, the Supreme Court ruled that an adult has the right to refuse (life saving) medical treatment.

D. In December of 2000 the Supreme Court ruled that Katherine Harris could certify the presidential election results in Florida even though many suits were filed alleging voter fraud and miscount.

II. ETHICS

Ethics is one of the oldest branches of philosophy. There are two main divisions within ethics—that which deals with issues concerning what is of value and that which deals with issues concerning what is right or wrong. Over the past 2500 years, Western civilization has amassed a host of answers to the many questions which have arisen in both of these areas, and these answers frequently conflict with each other. The result of this is that there are many conflicting claims about any ethical issue that can be defended, and each of these possible claims may be defended by arguments that seem to offer good reasons in support of them. From the point of view of rationality, this hardly seems a desirable state of affairs, though in reality it is the actual state of affairs with which we are stuck. No wonder we are so often at odds with each other on matters of ethical importance. But to make matters worse, we are at odds within our own selves because each of us will use conflicting theories when it fits our purposes to do so, even regarding the same ethical issue. If we were seeking a single, all-inclusive, supremely right, absolute moral theory (so dear to the hearts of so many classical philosophers), we would be incapable of making any reasonable decision on concrete moral issues here and now because no such absolute moral position has, as of yet, been discovered or proven to everyone's satisfaction.

We could, of course, simply choose to ignore the swamp of ethical theories and dogmatically attach ourselves to any given theory and take it with us to the grave. The problem with this approach, however, is that in reality, no one ever really does it, although they might think that they are doing it. Other principles and perspectives creep in as soon as any attempt is made to articulate what any given judgment means in practice and how that judgment and only that judgment makes sense in a given situation. Therefore, we must look at moral theories as tools that have different functions. Each one does certain tasks well, while no one does every task equally well. Ethical theories are heuristics, not algorithms. Let's look at the major ones (certainly not in any sort of ranking of importance or popularity), and let's see how they might apply to an issue which is floating around your school—using the Internet to download papers while pretending that you have composed the downloaded material yourself.[vii]

A. Ethical relativism. All ethical relativists claim that judgments of right and wrong are dependent upon (or relative to) the identity of the person(s) making the judgment. Various versions of ethical relativism that may be defended range from the **individual relativists** (who maintain that morality is relative to the individual making the judgment) to the **group relativist** (who maintain that morality is relative to some sort of sub-cultural unit such as the family, the clan, or the ethnic group) to the **cultural relativists** (who maintain that morality is relative to the whole society making the judgment). All forms of relativism state that there is no absolute right or wrong, and that what is right for someone (or any group) may be wrong for another person or group.[viii]

The theory of personal ethical relativism should not be confused with **ethical egoism**, though the two are related. The ethical egoist maintains that what makes an act right is that it succeeds in its aim, which is always to benefit the agent. The ethical egoist may act so as to benefit someone else, but only if it is believed that this action would also benefit the agent and would have been done anyway even if the good of others didn't happen to be involved. The ethical egoist may not be an ethical relativist because s/he might maintain that there are common goods for every agent because all agents share a common nature. Ethical relativists frequently use their doctrine to distinguish their own goods from the goods of others. Ethical egoists need not do this at all. But they could, which is why it may be difficult at times to determine which theory a person is using in any given case.[ix]

To the untrained eye, egoist and relativist are also hard to distinguish from ethical **exis-**

tentialists. Ethical existentialists maintain that there is no intrinsic right or wrong in actions, but rather actions are made right or wrong in being chosen by those who perform them. These many choices made by individuals simply add up to their own ways of life, which, of course, differ for each individual. For the existentialist, the important thing is simply to choose. Do it. Whatever "it" is, "it" will be right simply because "it" was chosen. Other choices would have been equally right if they had been chosen too.[x] In this manner existential ethics overlaps with command theories of ethics.

Let's see how these versions of relativism apply to downloading material off the Internet while pretending that this material is your own original work. Individual relativists maintain that the morality of this practice is relative to the person making the judgment. If any person thinks that it is right (or wrong) then it is right (or wrong) for that person only. The morality of downloading, like the taste for pepperoni pizza, lies in the judgement of the individual (who, in cases of moral deliberation and action is sometimes called the "moral agent"). I like it; you don't. I might do it; I might not. It depends on my judgment at the time, and I might even change my mind. The existentialist could agree with this position, except s/he would say "Do it or don't. It's all the same. Just get on with it." The egoist would decide the issue depending on what is to his or her advantage (though this may also be to others advantage, too). The cultural relativist would decide the issue by seeing what his or her family, clan, social/ethnic class, or culture says about this issue and following their lead. Troubles would arise, however, should the position of the family, clan, or social/ethnic class not agree with that of the culture or with each other (which is common). When they disagree, which unit is to be followed?

It should be noted that, except for cultural relativism, these theories make each judge a moral expert, but only for his or her own self or group, not for anyone else or for any other group. This fact has led most philosophers to

reject this theory as simply another name for moral anarchy. It also raises the following concern: Why should the judgment of any individual or any group not itself be judged? The problem with the pizza metaphor is the Jeffrey Dahmer cookbook. The problem with the family metaphor is the Charles Manson family, and so forth. It looks as if any judgment is just as morally infallible as any other, and this just seems to allow or approve of too much. Surely there are cases when we would reject a sincere moral judgment made by the individual or the group as wrong nonetheless, and all the variants of relativism discussed above don't seem to be able to supply a satisfactory answer to this problem.

Discuss how various forms of relativism would analyze the following examples:

A. Dad: "No son of mine will ever take a home economics class in high school. Those classes are strictly for girls."

B. Disgruntled sports fan watching a player show off on TV: "NBA and NFL players think only of themselves nowadays. When I was a kid, they played the game for its own sake."

C. Oregon now accepts physician-assisted suicide. If this keeps up, Dr. Kevorkian will be out of a job.

D. My kids want to go to Europe or the Bahamas for high school graduation. I went to a bowling alley.

E. When in Rome, do as the Romans do.

B. Command theories of morality. Command theories of morality maintain that only certain people (or groups) have the right to determine what is morally right or wrong, namely those who possess the power to create morality by issuing certain commands. Morality is equal to what has been commanded. Until something has been commanded, nothing is inherently right or wrong, morality simply doesn't yet exist. Accordingly, no matter what is commanded, that becomes right or wrong simply by being commanded. In this sense, commands are like the basic rules of a game. By themselves they are neither right nor wrong. Right and wrong come into existence only with the formulation of the game and the game doesn't even exist until after the rules are formulated. Game and rules are interdependent. Once formulated, of course, the rules can always be changed, even in the middle of the game, but only by the appropriate rule committee (commander).

Versions of this theory vary according to the identity of the party in command. One common version is the **divine command theory**, according to which only God has the real power to *create* morality. What God has commanded is moral, and only because God has commanded it. What God prohibits is immoral, and only because God has prohibited it.[xi] Another common version of this theory is called **positive law morality**. The leaders of the state are those who possess the power of command in the form of the various edicts and laws passed by these leaders. Positive law morality collapses the distinction between legal and moral right. Yet another version of this theory could be called the **parental command** theory of ethics. In this theory, actions are right or wrong because they are commanded by one's parents. "Because I said so!" is the rallying cry of this theory.

According to command theories of ethics, it seems to be easy in principle to determine what is right or wrong—simply determine what has been commanded in a given situation. Problems arise, however, when (1) nothing specific has, in fact, been commanded for a certain situation, and the commander is out of reach at the moment. Should this be the case, then nothing would be either right or wrong (yet) in this situation. In order to get around this problem, all versions of command ethics fall back on standard operating procedures or blanket commands, which are issued to cover a range of cases. But no blanket command or standard operating procedure can cover all possible contingencies. When the unforeseen occurs the agent is on his or her own. Similarly, (2) what is it that is commanded? Is it a specific action in a specific case or is it a general principle? If it is a

specific action, to what extent does that case provide precedent or a paradigm for any other case? If it is a general principle, how is the principle to be interpreted when it is applied to a new case, all the circumstances of which are not identical to the given case? (3) In cases where the proper authorities have issued inconsistent commands, the same action would be both right and wrong. Any child knows how to milk this one. If one parent says no and the other says yes, the child will "obey" the parent who lets him or her do what s/he wanted to do in the first place. Followers of the divine command theory frequently pick and choose verses out of the Bible or the Koran, for example, that allow them to "justify" what they wanted in the first place while ignoring other verses which seemingly prohibit what they want. Another problem (4) is raised when one doesn't know whether the command is still in effect. Maybe the command was changed. Laws do. The commands of the state are subject to manipulation by its citizens. Parents change their minds, especially if they're nagged enough. Could God's laws change too? Why not? Who are humans to tell God that He can't change His mind? Therefore, even in command ethics the agent has to make his or her own decision regarding the application of the theory to the issue at hand. But that, after all, is what it is to be an agent.

Command theories of ethics can readily be applied to the question of copying material off the Internet. The morality of copying depends simply upon whether it has been commanded or prohibited by the proper authority. The determination of this issue requires that the individual making the decision in a particular case consult the appropriate commander and the appropriate command of that commander and act according to the dictates of the command. If no command actually exists which applies to copying, then copying isn't either right or wrong. If the authority's commands are inconsistent or incomplete, then copying is both right and wrong. Because there are so many potential commanders in this theory and so many interpretations of these so-called commands, it may be best to see command theories in practice as other versions of relativity theories. The apparent unity of any version of this theory certainly seems to fragment when pressed for details. In practice, all versions of the command theory permit some copying of Internet material, but no version permits unrestricted copying.

Apply command theories of ethics to the following examples:

A. There's the right way, the wrong way, and the Army's way.

B. "Then the Lord said, "Because the outcry against Sodom and Gomorrah is great and their sin is very grave, I will go see about it...." But Abraham stood before the Lord and said, "Will thou indeed destroy the righteous with the wicked? Suppose there are fifty righteous within the city?" And the Lord said, "If I find at Sodom fifty righteous, I will spare the whole place..." Abraham answered: "Forty five righteous...? Forty...? Thirty...? Twenty...? Ten...?" The Lord answered, "For the sake of the ten I will not destroy it."   —*Genesis* 18.20-32

C. "Strike three! You're out!"
                         —Home plate umpire to batter

D. "Three strikes! You're in!"
                         —Judge to defendant

C. Utilitarian theories of ethics. There are two versions of utilitarian ethical theories that need to be distinguished—**act utilitarianism** and **rule utilitarianism**. Act utilitarian theories of ethics maintain that actions are right or wrong depending on the consequences of the action in question. If the consequences of some action are good, the action is right, if they are bad the action is wrong. Act utilitarians see ethics on an empirical model involving variables that cannot be known with certainty. Ethical actions are based on predictions of the likely outcomes of various projections. Whose good should count in the equation? The common answer to this is that everyone counts in

the equation. How long should one wait for these good consequences to surface? What happens when short-term good (or evil) is followed by long term evil (or good)? Various versions of act utilitarianism can also be distinguished in terms of the different accounts that can be given about what is good or valuable. One of the most common accounts identifies goodness with pleasure. This theory is known as **hedonism**. Other accounts maintain that things like justice, truth, and beauty are inherently good in addition to pleasure.

Rule utilitarianism maintains that right actions are those which are ordained by the right rules, and that the right rules are those which would produce the most good for everybody if they were enacted. Rule utilitarianism differs from act utilitarianism in the role it assigns to rules in determining the morality of a given action. Act utilitarianism uses rules only as rules-of-thumb, that is, shorthand summaries of the likely results of certain kinds of actions useful for helping to predict the probable outcome of a certain set of choices. Rule utilitarians tend to treat rules as absolute moral principles, which should be followed in all situations, including those cases where following the rule will actually produce less good than breaking the rule. Yes, for example, it is arguable that there are cases in which more good will be done by breaking the rule (breaking the speed limit by rushing the injured person to the hospital), but the rules are still the rules, so don't speed.[xii]

There are some major problems with each form of utilitarianism. Act utilitarianism (1) leaves the agent with the problem of calculating probable utilities of different courses of action. But this, in addition to being time-consuming and difficult, may require wildly implausible guesses about how certain choices may, in fact, work out. Few of us would be happy with this sort of ethical uncertainty. Again, (2) this theory gives us no reason to select long term goods over short term goods except the hope that the long term goods may turn out to be "better." What becomes of hope and self-sacrifice? Further, (3) how are these goods to be distributed? Traditional act utilitarianism seems far more concerned with producing more goods and far less concerned with distributing them fairly or justly. And finally, (4) this theory would have us do some very nasty things to others (e. g., murder or torture) if we believed that doing so would produce more good for others in the long run. But wouldn't these actions still be wrong anyway? Does the end justify the means?

Rule utilitarianism is not without its own problems. (1) How many rules are there and how do they relate to each other? Are some sub-sets of others? Are they all equally important? In effect, (2) this means that it seems implausible to affirm that any rule is always equal to another or always "trumps" another. Morality seems more complex than that. But, (3) why follow a rule when doing so in a given case is obviously immoral or would produce disastrous consequences? Rule utilitarians seem to love rules for the sake of the rules themselves. This lets the tail wag the dog.

Regarding the question of the morality of copying material off the Internet, the act utilitarian would argue that its proper moral assessment depends upon the consequences it will have for all those who would be directly affected by the act in question. In order to determine this question, the following issues would have to be addressed: What constitutes good consequences? They are good consequences for whom, the student, the teacher, the student's parents, or the entire student body (think of End of Grade / No Child Left Behind pressures)? Different answers to these questions will produce different positions for act utilitarians regarding the morality of any particular case of copying off the Internet. And how long are we to wait for these consequences to show up? Every time another case involving copying arises, the act utilitarian would have to repeat the same process because the morally correct decision in one case would not be the same in another unless the circumstances of both cases were fundamentally similar.

The rule utilitarian would also have to answer all of the questions posed above in order to determine whether permitting or prohibiting Internet copying was the correct moral rule to adopt. Once these questions have been properly answered, however, rule utilitarianism has no need to reexamine them again in order to determine the morality of any other instance of copying. Actual cases are judged simply by appealing to the established moral rules. But there are at least two conflicting rules here: (1) don't cheat; and (2) anyone has the duty to do well on standardized tests. But of course the two collide! Now what?

Apply act and rule utilitarianism to the following examples:

A. The end justifies the means.
B. Mom: "I'm so happy you got Mr. Smith for your honors biology class. He's hard, but he's supposed to be an excellent teacher." Son: "Yuck to Mr. Smith. He's awful. Do you realize how hard it is to get an "A" from Mr. Smith? An "A" in the class is all that matters."
C. "Try it; you'll like it."
D. "Turn on; tune in; drop out."
    —Timothy Leary, the Harvard psychologist/guru who was one of the hippie's spokespersons of the 1960s
E. If it feels good, do it.
F. "He who sets out to fight monsters should see to it that he in turn does not become one."   —Nietzsche

D. Deontological theories of ethics. Some theories of ethics maintain that there is no need to consider the consequences of actions or rules when determining the morality of whatever issue concerns you. These theories say that there are certain actions that are inherently right or wrong independently of their actual consequences. These theories appeal to the nature (or *ontos*—hence the fancy name) of the activity in question. An individual act is right (or wrong) if it is an instance of a type of action that is inherently right (or wrong). Since the eighteenth century, it has become fashionable to recognize the value of certain forms of existence by referring to them as **rights**. Rights are claims either to be given certain things (**positive rights**) or to be free from interference from others in certain ways (**negative rights**). Rights are characteristics said to belong to persons (or things) because of the very nature of the kind of thing to which the rights are said to adhere.[xiii] The concepts of rights have always had both a legal and an ethical face, and they seem to be both at the same time. Putting this in another way, we move from one arena to another without seeming to notice that anything has happened. Currently, claims involving rights are ubiquitous; everybody's got them and is quick to scream when they (in the opinion of the so-called rights holder) are violated.

Two other values which have been defended on deontological grounds, though not on these grounds alone, are **autonomy** and **paternalism**. Autonomy means that a moral agent has the right and power to decide a variety of issues concerning what things are important to him or her. It amounts to the claim that the agent is self-legislating on these matters and should be protected from outside interference. When for whatever reason an agent cannot exercise his or her autonomy, the legal system may appoint someone with the power of attorney to do so. Here the point is that the legal guardian acts as the disabled person's advocate. On the opposite note, paternalism claims that someone other than the agent has the right and power to decide what is in the (real) interest of the agent, even if the agent disagrees with the choice being made on his or her behalf. This may occur if the agent is a young child, for example. Autonomy and paternalism frequently collide, but both values are important components of moral deliberation.

Apply the concepts of autonomy and paternalism to the following examples.

A. Teenager: "Mom! Can I get a tattoo? Can I have some of my body parts pierced?" Mom: "Gwauck...!"

A. Being a lastborn child is much better than being a firstborn. By the time the lastborn gets to the age of the firstborn, mom and dad are too exhausted from dealing with the traumas of the firstborn to care about what happens to the lastborn.

A. "Freedom!"
—William Wallace's final word as he is being ripped limb from limb. *Brave Heart.*

A. "Dad, can I get a puppy? I promise I'll take care of him."

A. Ralphie: "For Christmas I want a Red Rider BB gun." Mom, his fourth grade teacher, and Santa (all together now): "You'll shoot your eye out!" Dad later buys him the gun.
—from *A Christmas Story.*

There are some complex problems associated with any deontological theory. (1) Which things are inherently right or wrong? A little knowledge of history and sociology shows that many societies haven't recognized what others have taken to be inherently right (or wrong) to be such, or even to be ethical issues at all. Are they just blind, or are societies which "see" these truths simply seeing things? These sorts of claims are easy to make, but how are we to verify their validity? (2) A related issue concerns what to do when seemingly inherent truths or rights collide. Can they? Or are all of them nicely consistent? If they can and do collide, which one gives way and when do they give way? Do the same ones always give way? Further, (3) is the list of rights finite and known, or can new, as yet undreamed of rights be discovered? And, by the way (4) are they discovered or simply invented in the first place? If they are invented, this is starting to sound like the command theory of ethics under a new name. Is it?

Applying the concept of rights to the question of downloading material off the Internet has generated a debate. On one side of the debate are those who argue for the rights of the student to access knowledge, which usually comes down to the right to information necessary to make decisions. This is the goal of education, after all (of course, gathering information from online sources is a very different thing from copying an online paper and claiming it is your own, but that's another topic altogether). On the other side are those who wish to defend the original author's copyright. The material in question was not produced magically form thin air, after all. Doesn't the person who created it own it? Unfortunately, both of these values collide. It's not as if one side defends autonomy and the other side paternalism. Autonomy and paternalism are at work on both sides of this debate. It's easy to see the conflicting claims involving rights, autonomy, and paternalism in this case.

Apply deontological ethics to the following examples:

A. "Crito, we owe a cock to Asclepias. See that it is paid."
  —Plato, *Phaedo*. The reported last words of Socrates, spoken before he drank hemlock, his death sentence from the Athenian government in response to charges that he was a corrupter of Athenian youths. Asclepias is the Greek god of healing.

B. The Abu Ghraib prisoner/Iraqi prisoner abuse scandal consisted in the sexual abuse of male Iraqi POWs by U.S. service personnel following at least the tacit permission of their American military superiors in the effort to break the will of the prisoners. Its exposé led to international condemnation.

C. It is wrong to kill, so capital punishment can never be permissible.

D. No one has the right to shout "Fire!" in a crowded theater.

E. Virtue ethics. Virtue ethics is the product of classical Greek and Roman civilization.[xiv] These cultures were in turn absorbed by Christianity and Islam through which they continue to exert a major influence on western social values through such concepts as sportsmanship, chivalry, and *noblesse oblige*. Virtue ethics is not an ethics of rules or of acts per se; rather it is an ethics of character. For virtue ethics, the key

question is not how one calculates utility or counts up rights or flexes one's ego, but how one displays responsibility. Do one's actions show a good and noble character or not? The key in virtue ethics is to produce good people and, this is what is achieved through phronesis.[xv]

The problem with virtue ethics is that it sounds a bit too noble minded. Noble character and noble actions are fine, but they must occur in a context of social rules and guidelines that predefine the rules of the game, so to speak. Cheating is wrong and the noble person would never cheat, but cheating means violating the rules, and you can't do that until the rules exist. So at best, virtue ethics can only come into play after some other theory has already established the rules that govern the game itself. Then, the virtuous person can play the game with refinement. This, however, would not settle disputes between two or more noble persons. Noble actions may be broad or ambiguous enough to still leave room for disagreements within the ranks of the virtuous. But, presumably, virtuous persons could virtuously settle disputes among themselves.

The implication for virtue theory in ethics is hard to assess because the ground rule theory regarding the copied material off the Internet is hardly under dispute. Copying such material while pretending that it is your own is simply cheating, and it is hard to see how this could ever be done in a noble or virtuous manner. This is pretty much of a slam-dunk.

Apply virtue ethics to the following situations:

A. Grandma W: "I hope that Grandson M does not take the Christmas money I gave him and waste it on video games."

B. Older brother thinking to himself: "Breaking both of my younger brother's arms would be excessive for what he did to me. On the other hand, not breaking any of them would be too lenient. I'll only break one of them." To younger brother: "Yo, bro, I've got a surprise for you. Close your eyes and stick out a hand."

C. Sister: "What happened to my bag of potato chips?" Brother: "The commercial says no one can eat just one. I ate one, so I had to finish all of the rest. Burp."

The theoretical and practical complexities that arise in discussing concrete examples of ethical issues have led some to believe that there are no valid appeals to authority in ethics, either because there is no discipline of ethics in which to be an authority or because there are no ways of recognizing real authorities in ethics if it were a discipline. Real disciplines, they say, don't contain such fragmentation. But these claims are false. There is a discipline of ethics, and it is possible for someone to be a recognized expert in that discipline. The real problem (as I have stated above) is that there is so little agreement about the theoretical underpinnings of the discipline of ethics, and this is because ethical traditions are simply too rich to be successfully captured by any single theory. In this respect, ethics is like the discipline of psychology, where one psychologist may be a Freudian, another a behaviorist, and so forth. A person who applies one of the theories of psychology (or ethics) to a given situation need not apply another theory to that situation, though s/he must know that there are different theoretical approaches and different ways of practicing within each approach. As with psychology, an ethical practitioner may specialize, so to speak, in one theory of right and wrong, but s/he must know that there are other theories and that different practitioners are likely to disagree about a given issue because of their different theoretical orientations. In these cases, good appeals to ethical theory made by practitioners should note the possibility of alternative claims made by other practitioners whose theoretical orientation differs from those being cited. Once this is acknowledged, arguments from different ethical theories may proceed just like those in other fields.

Most people tend to consistently misuse ethics by glibly appealing to the authority of their upbringing. Ethical issues seem to bring out the "that's what I was always taught" argu-ment at its worst. Each of us receives an ethical indoctrination from the particular circumstances that happen to characterize our socialization. No two persons are socialized identically. Socialization, unfortunately, leaves each of us merely with a long list of things we value. Few attempts are ever made to examine our values to see whether they are consistent or defensible. They are simply accepted as a given; this amounts to moral immaturity. Critical thinking demands that we recognize that our values need to be ordered and defended, and not simply announced as if they are unquestionably true. Rationally ordering and defending values demands an awareness of the theories in which these values are anchored. Ethics needs epistemology.[xvi]

III. RELIGION

The last field of arguments I wish to consider in this chapter is one which is, perhaps, the most controversial—**religion** and **religious arguments**. A religion is a way of recognizing and reacting to the experience of the supernatural or divine. Religions are made by humans in response to their perceptions of divinity. They are not, as is mistakenly believed, products of God's workshop handed newly minted to us for our consumption. They are living things that are always in the process of change; they grow, die, and transmogrify. Religion's ever-changing nature results in growing pains and friction, and friction gives rise to arguments. Arguments in religion are frequently lively, if not downright contentious, and it is commonplace that one person's orthodoxy is another person's heresy. In fact, religious conflicts are rivaled only by political/ideological conflicts in the amount of harm they can do. Equally true, they are rivaled only by political/ideological conflicts in the amount of good they can do. In any event, neither sort of disagreement is likely to go away soon.

Mere disagreement is an insufficient reason to abandon all arguments about religion, however; the situation is no different from that found in the areas of ethics, law, and social tradition. Believers in a certain system are unlikely to credit believers of a different system as having correct opinions, though, as always, diversity of opinion should be acknowledged. Diversity is a fact of life. It is an equally common mistake, however, to assume that the system which one uses to defend a particular religious doctrine has an unlimited unquestionable application to all possible persons, times, and places. If this last procedure were valid, then some reason must be given as to why any particular so-called authority is the only real or proper authority and some other possible authority (say, from a different religious tradition) is not. Commonly, those who assume that their favorite religious authorities have universal application never consider this problem in the first place, which makes their claims questionable appeals to authority when considered on a universal basis, though still, perhaps, credible within a particular religious tradition.

In what follows, I will take a middle ground between the dogmatist who recognizes only the existence or validity of his or her own tradition and the relativist who would treat any and all religious claims and traditions as equally vital and valid. The dogmatist leaves too much out of the equation; the relativist allows too much in. Instead, I propose to consider certain components common to most religions and see what sort of a picture this gives us. The components are system, natural religion, revelation, tradition, social/clerical structure, cult practices, and text. Though I shall deal with these ideas separately in principle, it is impossible in practice to disentangle them. Every religion interlocks its cult practices with its clerical structure, texts, and revelations.

A. Systems. There are several possible sorts of systems one could have with regard to the **divine**. The divine is commonly understood to be the supernatural source of the natural world. The divine is the object of religious attention or worship. Different religious systems have different understandings of the divine. Some are **monotheistic** (believing in

only one God); others are **polytheistic** (believing in many gods). Some are **henotheistic,** believing in many gods, of which one (supreme) god is the chief one to be worshiped. Manichaein dualism is a variant of henotheism in that it believes in two equally powerful but ethically opposed gods who are forever at war with each other, using the cosmos as their battleground. Other systems believe in no substance like any of the gods of the previous sorts mentioned, but perhaps a god in the form of a force or even in no formal god-like thing at all.[xvii]

Every religious system has a **theology**. A theology is a system of interconnected ideas designed to make sense out of the many attributes and stories which are attributed to the gods (God) and the relationship between the gods (God) and the natural world. Theologies are to religion what theories$_3$ are to science. Many theologies, such as those in Judaism, Christianity, and Islam, distinguish between the natural created world and God the creator. Some theologies, such as **pantheism** (which identifies God with nature) don't make this distinction. In many polytheistic systems (such as those of Classical Greece and Rome), some of the gods are identical to parts of the material world (e. g., earth, sea, thunder) while others are not.

All theological systems reject **atheism**, which claims that there is no divinity at all. Sometimes, the label of "atheist" is used as a malphemism to describe theologies that characterize gods in "undesirable" ways. **Deism** is sometimes subject to this sort of treatment. Deism is the claim that God is not a person, but an impersonal force. In contrast to deism, **theism** claims that God can only be correctly seen as a personal being, not an impersonal force. To further complicate matters, **agnostics** claim that no one can know whether any sort of God exists or not, be it deistic or theistic. Agnosticism is a form of skepticism.[xviii]

Discuss the theology contained in the following:

A. "You're either on God's side or the devil's side."   —Bumper sticker

B. "There is no God but God, and Allah is his name."   —Muslim prayer

C. God tested Abraham, and said to him, "Abraham.... Take your son, your only son Isaac, whom you love, and go to the land of Moriah, and offer him there as a burnt offering upon one of the mountains of which I shall tell you."   —*Genesis* 22.1-2

D. "In God we trust."   —Motto on U.S. coins.

E. "In God we trust; all others pay cash."
          —Sign over a cash register.

F. "'God is dead.'   —Nietzsche.
    'Nietzsche is dead.'   —God."
          —Bathroom graffiti

B. Natural religion. Natural religion is the attempt to derive religious truths from the study of the natural world. It has its origins in classical Greek philosophy,[xix] but it received its best formulation in the seventeenth and eighteenth centuries.[xx] Natural religion assumes that reason has a valid place in religion, thus natural religion does not see itself as opposing faith, but as complimenting it. Natural religion has sought to establish primarily two things—the existence and nature of God (the gods) and the existence, nature, and immortality of the human soul.

Natural religion offers two main arguments to establish God's existence, the **cosmological** and the **teleological**. All versions of the cosmological argument have two essential premises: (a) an existential claim which affirms the existence of some thing other than God (the gods) [e. g. the world, or motion, or a causal sequence] and (b) a causal claim that only God (the gods) could bring about or sustain the existence of the subject mentioned in the existential claim. The teleological argument is really a subset of the cosmological argument. Its existential claim, however, is thought to be very special, namely, the order that is perceived in the natural world. This order gives the teleological argument its common name—the **argument from design**. From the design seen in the natural world, natural religion seeks to develop a full-blown theology:

Follow nature, for our nature is what God intends for us.

Problems arise when nature doesn't seem to work to our benefit. This is called the **problem of evil**. If the world is a product of a perfectly good, all knowing, all-powerful divinity (or set of divinities), then how could there be any natural evil in it? Why do plagues, hurricanes, and droughts exist? This is the **problem of natural evil**. But to make matters worse, if humans are the creations of God (the gods), why do we ever sin? This is the **problem of moral evil**. Attempts made to rationally solve these issues are called **theodicies**. Every theodicy seeks to resolve these problems without abandoning claims to God's (the gods') perfection.[xxi]

Discuss the following as aspects of the problem of evil:

A. "Zeus, whose will has marked for man the sole way were wisdom lies;
Ordained one eternal plan: Man must suffer to be wise."   —Aeschylus, *Agamemnon*

B. "We grow too soon old and too late smart."
          —Old saying

C. In December of 2004, a gigantic earthquake and tsunami struck Banda Aceh, Indonesia, and the surrounding area, killing more than 220,000 people. When this happened many of the survivors asked, "Where was God?"

D. During the Second World War, the Nazis killed over 6,000,000 Jews. How could the God of Abraham, Isaac, and Jacob allow this to happen?

E. God has given man free will. Don't blame God when man misuses it by doing evil.

F. "Whatever is, is Right."
          —Alexander Pope, *Essay on Man*

G. "Intrigue is the work of Satan, who thereby seeks to annoy the faithful. Yet he can harm them not at all, except by the will of Allah."
          —*Koran*, "She Who Pleaded," 58:9

Secondly, natural religion has attempted to prove the **existence and immortality of the**

human soul. Arguments for the existence of the soul as a substance distinct from the body (or more specifically, the brain) center on the distinctive nature of consciousness, which, it is claimed, cannot be the product of a physical thing because it possesses no physical attribute like mass or size. Arguments for immortality of the soul add to this by claiming that there is something about the soul that makes it incapable of being destroyed by any means, or at least in the normal manner in which things are destroyed.[xxii]

Natural religion is the locus of the intersection of science and religion. If the two perspectives are ever to overlap, it will be here. Can the two ever contradict each other? Yes, to the extent that a given religious tradition includes claims concerning the natural world (e.g., the history of the world, evolution, the age and size of the cosmos), these claims would be subject to the same sort of scrutiny as any other empirical claim. Historically, religious traditions have embodied the commonly accepted empirical claims made by its believers into the newly developing religion as a simple matter of course. Some claims, however, like that of the existence and immortality of the soul, are not obviously empirical claims. As such, they may not be subject to the scrutiny of the scientific/critical method after all. This whole area is a running debate in recent epistemology and philosophy of religion.[xxiii]

C. Revelation. Revelation as a source of religion is quite different from natural religion. Revelation does not rely on a subject's ability to reason, but treats the recipient as a passive subject of experience. Something is given (revealed) directly to him or her. Ordinarily, it is thought that God is the direct source of the experience, but the recipient could as well say in certain cases that s/he was experiencing only the will of God indirectly via a messenger and not actually God. Some individuals may thus be "called" to witness certain religious truths directly by God (the gods). In certain traditions, this experience may be so overwhelming it overrides all other experience or reasoning process-

es. This sort of experience is commonly called **mystical**. It should be noted that mystical experiences might be terrifying as well as joyful. In either event, they are certainly not normal and recognized not to be normal by the recipient.[xxiv]

Discuss the following examples of religious revelation:

A. Jocasta: "No man possesses the secret of divination. And I have proof. Apollo gave an oracle to Laius that he should die by the hands of his own child. His child and mine. Ha!" —Sophocles, *Oedipus Tyrannus*

B. The angel Gabriel was sent by God to Mary. "Hail, O favored one, the Lord is with you!" But she was greatly troubled at this and considered in her mind what sort of greeting that might be. —Luke, 1.26-29

C. The ancient Romans practiced *extispicium,* a form of divination in which the color, shape, and disposition of the internal organs of animals was a sign from the gods. Those who were skilled in this practice were called *haruspices.*

D. Today's horoscope for Libra reads: "You will meet a tall, dark, handsome stranger. He will have a waggle tail and a cold nose."

D. Traditions. There are many traditions within the field of religion. The major ones (in terms of numbers of adherents) range from Confucianism, Hinduism, Taoism, and Buddhism in the East to Christianity, Islam, and Judaism in the West. All of these religions are sub-divided in turn into many different segments or denominations. Thus, the first problem to be recognized is the identification of the religious affiliation of the person or text being utilized. Christians, for example, are not going to recognize the authority of Muslims when it comes to understanding Christianity, and so forth. This is hardly surprising. But Christians, for example, may refuse to see any Muslim as an authority within the Muslim community because the Muslim community is not seen as possessing any real validity. The Christian might not even see members of other Christian denominations as "real Christians." Then things get very sticky. What we have here is a mind-set issue. Until a concerted effort is made by its practitioners to reconcile divergent religious traditions (or divergence within religious traditions) legitimate appeals to the authority of religious traditions will only take place within some possible religious subdivision.

Religious authorities are only authorities within the context of their actual religious traditions, though there is nothing that prevents anyone from being an authority in more than one (or even very many) tradition(s). As of yet, there has not been developed a tradition-neutral way of settling disagreements that crosses the boundaries dividing the traditions. Each subdivision has its own methods of determining who or what counts as authoritative. Christian subdivisions like Protestants have established their own denominational seminaries, for example, the graduation from which constitutes a recognition of expertise within the denomination, but certainly no Buddhist would be swayed by that. The situation resembles that of sports. There are many of them—football, soccer, baseball, gymnastics, etc., each with its own fans. Every sport is defined by its own rules and traditions. These rules and traditions don't apply across sports. Baseball umpires can't call balls and strikes at a hockey match. But all of the sports do possess certain goals and conditions in common—winning and playing by the rules, for example. The problem becomes one of finding the common goals and conditions for members of different religious communities to acknowledge the existence and practices of other "sports" and other "teams."[xxv]

Discuss the following religious traditions. Which values are ruled in; which ruled out?

A. Once in a lifetime each Muslim is obligated to make the Hajj to Mina, Saudi Arabia. During the Feast of Sacrifice (Eid al-Adha) each pilgrim throws a pebble at stone pillars, symbolically stoning the devil in an act of purification.

B. In Christian, Muslim, or Jewish areas, it is traditional for couples to be married by clergy.

C. Some Christian denominations baptize children, some only adults.

D. Followers of Hari Krishna wear orange robes and shave their heads.

E. Judaism celebrates Hanukkah commemorating a military victory over the Syrians in the second century BCE.

E. Social/clerical structure. All religions have social structures in which they are embedded. Seldom are things as simple as going one-on-one with God (the gods). Religion is a social institution because its practitioners are social beings. We live in communities, and faith communities are *communities* after all. What shape a particular community takes shapes the individual's encounter with the sacred. Some communities have elaborate hierarchies. Others have more simple ones. But they all have structure of some sort. "All clergy may be created equal, but some are more equal than others," to paraphrase Orwell. Catholicism has, on the whole, tended to be rather restrictive in determining who or what is to be counted as a valid authority from the top down, recognizing the teaching power of the Church hierarchy as found in Popes, Bishops, and priests as well as the traditions of the Church as the chief means of determining authority over ordinary laypersons. Protestant churches have responded to this by tending to adopt a model that carries authority from the bottom up, from church members to the pastors, bishops, etc.[xxvi] Some religious denominations, such as the Quakers, have no formal clergy whatsoever.

F. Cult practices. All religions engage in **worship**. Worship is the proper interaction between the human and divine when this interaction is seen from the human side of the equation. Worship takes many forms—prayer, meditation, good works, and so forth. Some of these interactions are formal, such as church services, and this is what is meant by cult practices.[xxvii] They include ritual behavior that exists to define correct religious practices. Church services wouldn't be church services unless they were done in the correct manner. Of course, what constitutes the correct manner differs between religious communities and even within religious communities as well as across time. Many cult practices—such as Christian communion—have very long traditions behind them, traditions, in fact, which predate Christianity. Frequently, traditions from other religions are absorbed into religions. Consider, again, the Christmas tree or the Easter bunny. These are pagan symbols and practices taken from ancient religions. I bet you've never thought of those chocolate Easter eggs brought by the Easter bunny as implements of pagan cult practices!

Discuss the following religious practices:

A. Christianity celebrates the birth of Christ in the Latin West on one day (December 25) and on another (January 6) in the Orthodox East. Yet both the Latin West and the Orthodox East celebrate Christ's death an resurrection on the same day of the year, but that day occurs within a six week period in March and April determined by the date of the first Sunday following the first full moon after the Spring equinox.

B. All forms of Judaism celebrate a boy's bar mitzvah when he has his 13th birthday. Reform and Conservative Judaism celebrate a girl's bat mitzvah when she has her 13th birthday, but Orthodox Judaism does not.

C. Ancient Greek pagans celebrated *Choes*, the day when a child turned three years old and was weaned. The child was given his first choes (drinking cup) to signify the occasion. Very young children who died were often cremated and had their ashes interred in their choes.

D. Ancient Egyptians embalmed their dead, believing that the preservation of the body was necessary for an afterlife.

G. Texts. Many religious traditions have **sacred texts**. A sacred text is a religious document which the religious community believes contains the direct word of God (or the gods) or the sayings of the master who founded the religious tradition. While not all religious traditions have such texts (native American tribes generally don't), the presence of such documents changes the religious scene greatly. Now a practitioner of the religion can go to the text to get the proper understanding of a particular religious issue. For example, most Protestant traditions allow many of their members to appeal directly to their own understanding of the sacred scriptures.

This practice makes for all kinds of interesting activities and issues. 1) Which text is being appealed to (e.g., Bible, Koran, etc?) Within that text, which part of it is being utilized? Which chapters and verses? Which chapters and verses are not being utilized? Why aren't they? The problem here is that of picking and choosing from texts to prove what the practitioner wants to prove, and not necessarily what the document itself says. 2) Has the practitioner got good reasons to believe that s/he understands what the chosen text is really saying, and not what s/he wants the text to say? That is, has the practitioner begged the very question at issue? In appeals to the authority of texts, even within any given tradition, only casual attention often is paid to assure that the pronouncements of the religious texts have been correctly understood. 3) Are the teachings of the text consistent, relevant, and applicable to the issue at hand? In reality, the practitioner may make the text speak about an issue about which it says nothing. 4) What happens when the teachings of the text appear to be in conflict with God's (the gods') revelation to a given individual or to the religious tradition or the church hierarchy, etc.? Which component is to take the lead in this sort of case? There is no systematic ranking of religion components to tell us what to do when parts of them collide.

The list of concerns affecting the understanding of the communication claims made by others which is presented in the Appendix to the previous chapter is never more relevant than now. Many devoutly religious persons wrongly assume that they can pick up the Bible, Koran, or Torah, for example, and read its "message" plainly and simply without any idea of the cultural/historical components that went into the production of the text they hold in their hands. Unfortunately, they all too often also assume that being aware of these sorts of complexities undermines or attacks the religion they are trying to defend. This is simply a childlike naivete which hardly makes one a better religious person. In ancient Greek society, the sayings of the Oracle of Delphi were frequently appealed to as authoritative. But it was also recognized that these sayings often were difficult to understand and sometimes even downright misleading until subsequent experience revealed their "real" meaning. Many modern people who use the same kind of technique as the ancient Greeks (though substituting other sacred texts for the Delphic Oracle) are much more glib about the problem of understanding the real meaning of the authority cited. *Given that so little attention is paid to the problem of ascertaining the real meaning of passages from these sacred texts, appeals from authority based on them are highly suspect until a reasonable effort has been made to determine what the sacred texts actually say about the issue in question.* To paraphrase Mark Twain, "I don't have a problem with people who are ignorant about a particular matter, what bothers me is people who darn well know what ain't so." Sadly, many religious people are terribly ignorant about their own self-professed religious traditions.

Questions of time and complexity prevent the further pursuit of these matters here. Suffice it to say that within any given religious tradition, valid reasoning can only occur within the boundaries set by the system, religion, social context, history, revelation and text in question. Until such time as compelling reasons can be advanced for preferring one particular religious tradition to another, the most that arguments based upon religious traditions can do is to establish authority for those who adhere to that given tradition. There are, as of yet, no valid appeals to some kind of generic religious authority lying outside of all particular religious traditions, though there is certainly no lack of individuals who would mistakenly seek to credit their own particular religious tradition with absolute and universal validity.

I trust that you can see from the above that there are certainly a lot of issues bound up with the use of arguments in ethics, religion, and law. Just remember that in order for any uses of these areas to be valid₂ the conditions governing the legitimate use of any argument within these areas must be satisfied. I think that you will find that the appropriate use of arguments in these areas is quite a bit more restrictive than mere frequency would have you believe.

Consider some of the issues involved in the passages from the following sacred texts:

A. The unbelievers say: "The *Koran* is a forgery of [Mohammed's] own invention." Unjust is what they say and false. And they say: "Fables of the ancient he has written." Say: "It is revealed by Him who knows the secrets of the heaven and earth."

—*Koran*, "Al-Furqan," 25:5

B. "Do you know of the leisurely philosopher who has gone beyond learning and is not exerting himself in anything? He neither endeavors to avoid idle thoughts nor seeks after the Truth. [For he knows that] ignorance in reality is the Buddha-nature, [and that] this empty visionary body is no less than the Dharma-body."

—Yoka Daishi, *Song of Enlightenment*

C. "Whether you are a god or a goddess to whom this grove of trees is sacred, it is proper to sacrifice to you a pig as a propitiatory offering for the disturbance of this sacred place."

—Cato the Elder, *On Agriculture*

B. "Thou rise, thou rises brilliantly; Thou art victorious over thy enemies. Thou causes the day-boat to sail past and repel the dragons of the storm at night."

—Egyptian hymn to Amon Re

You should be able to define the following concepts, explain their meanings to others not familiar with them, invent your own examples that correctly illustrate the concepts, and apply them correctly to novel applications.

- Act utilitarianism
- Agnosticism
- Argument from design
- Atheism
- Checks and balances
- Clerical hierarchy
- Command theory of ethics
- Common law
- Cosmological argument for the existence of God
- Deism
- Deontological ethics
- Divine command ethics
- Ethical authority
- Ethical egoism
- Ethical relativism (cultural, sub-cultural, and individual)
- Ethics
- Executive legal authority
- Existentialism
- Free will defense
- Hedonism
- Henotheism
- Judicial system
- Judicial nullification/ jury nullification

- Law₂
- Lawyers
- Legal reasoning
- Legislative legal authority
- Lobbyist
- Manichaein dualism
- Monotheism
- Mystical religious experience
- Natural law
- Natural religion
- Pantheism
- Paradox of democracy
- Paternalism
- Personal religious experiences
- Political leadership
- Political parties
- Political platform
- Political philosophy
- Polytheism
- Positive law morality
- Precedent
- Problem of moral evil
- Problem of natural evil
- Psychological egoism
- Religion

- Religious arguments
- Religious authority
- Religious cult practices
- Religious revelation
- Religious structure (social and clerical)
- Religious system/ denomination
- Religious texts
- Religious traditions
- Rights
- Rules of evidence (federal and state)
- Rule utilitarianism
- Soul
- Teleological argument
- Theism
- Theodicy
- Theology
- Tyranny of the majority (or minority)
- Value (intrinsic and extrinsic)
- Virtue ethics
- Worship
- Zero sum game

Foundational concepts: Act and rule utilitarianism, atheism, autonomy, command ethics, deontological ethics, ethical relativism, executive legal authority, judicial system, law₂, legislative legal authority, monotheism, paternalism, political philosophy, problem of evil, religion, religious authority, religious structure, religious texts, rights, theism, theology, tyranny, virtue ethics

NOTES

i.   Natural law philosophy is the product of Stoic philosophy as it became enshrined in Roman legal practices. For information on Stoic philosophy, see A. A. Long and D. N. Sedley, *The Hellenistic Philosophers*, vol. I, (New York: Cambridge University Press, 1987). Cicero's (106-43 B.C.) *De Legibus* and *On the Commonwealth* present a good example of Roman law as understood by one of the greatest minds Rome ever produced. Natural law becomes incorporated into Christianity by such Catholic church fathers as St. Augustine (354-430) in his *City of God*; St. Thomas Aquinas (1224-1274) in his *Summa Theologiae*; Hobbes (1588-1679) in his *Leviathan*; and Locke (1632-1704) in his *Second Treatise on Government*. Locke's ideas were to serve as the basis of our Declaration of Independence and our Constitution.

ii. Because common law had its origin in English customs there are no common law texts or law books per se. What one does find, however, are the explicit formalization of these customs in things like the Magna Carte. Common law, nonetheless, maintains a powerful presence, although it may not be easy to recognize because it so surrounds us.

iii. The relationship between rights and power is a complicated one, the details of which need not concern us.

Certainly, however, one may have some sort of right and not have the power to express or defend it, and one may have some sort of power and not have the right to express or defend it. Hobbes, Montesquieu, Locke, and Marx have all contributed to the debate on this issue, which remains a contention in current political philosophy. See Morton E. Winston, *The Philosophy of Human Rights* (Belmont, CA: Wadsworth Publishing Co., 1989) and *Applied Social and Political Philosophy*, edited by Elizabeth Smith and H. Gene Blocker, (Englewood Cliffs, N J: Prentice Hall, 1994) for collections of articles on these issues.

iv.   The governmental system of checks and balances was formulated by the French philosopher Montesquieu (1989-1755), who especially influenced the American founding fathers. See his *Spirit of the Laws*, translated by Thomas Nugent, (New York: Oxford University Press, 1949).

v.   In philosophy of law the tradition that maintains that what is moral is moral solely because it is legal is called the *positive law position* or legal positivism. See H. L. A. Hart, *The Concept of Law* (New York: Oxford University Press, 1961), for a classical discussion of this position.

vi.   For a detailed discussion of these and other issues discussed in the philosophy of law see *Law, Language, and Ethics*, edited by William R. Bishin and Christopher D. Stone, (Mineola, NY: The Foundation Press, Inc., 1972).

vii.   A related issue that you may find more interesting is the practice of copying music off the Internet. Similar issues apply.

viii.   For a good general presentation of the ethical theories in this section, see John Hospers, *Human Conduct*, shorter edition, (New York: Harcourt Brace Jovanovich, Inc., 1972). For a good discussion of the various versions of ethical relativism, see Edvard Westermark, *Ethical Relativity* (New York: Harcourt, Brace, 1932). For a classical defense of cultural relativism, see Ruth Benedict, *Patterns of Culture* (New York: Penguin, 1996). John Ladd, *Ethical Relativism* (Belmont, CA: Wadsworth Publishing Co., 1973), contains a useful anthology of articles examining various versions of ethical relativism. Walter Stace, *Ethical Relativity* (New York: Random House, 1936), provides an excellent critique of all forms of ethical relativism.

ix.   The classical case for ethical egoism is presented by Thomas Hobbes. See his *Leviathan*, Bk. I. Friedrich Nietzsche (1844-1900) presents a form of ethical egoism in many of his works. See, for example *Beyond Good and Evil*, translated by Walter Kaufmann, (New York: Random House, 1966), and *The Will To Power*, translated by Walter Kaufmann and R. J. Hollingdale, (New York: Vintage Books, 1968). For a critique of egoism see Brian Medlin, "Ultimate Principles and Ethical Egoism," *Australasian Journal of Philosophy*, (35, 1957): 111-118.

x.   Existential ethics finds its classical expression in the works of Jean-Paul Sartre (1905-1982). See *The Philosophy of Existentialism*, (New York: The Philosophy Library, 1965).

xi.   The divine command theory of morality is a mainstay in Christianity, Judaism, and Islam. See Augustine, *The City of God* and Aquinas, *Summa Theologica* for the classical Christian presentations of this theory. The classical analysis of a divine command theory of ethics is still the one presented by Plato in his *Euthyphro*. See also *Moral Issues, Philosophical and Religious Perspectives*, edited by Gabriel Palmer-Fernandez, (Upper Saddle River, NJ: Prentice Hall, 1996) for a current bibliography on this issue. For a defense of legal positivism see Endnote 5 above.

xii.   The classical presentation of utilitarianism is found in John Stuart Mill, *Utilitarianism*, originally published in London, 1863, and reprinted in numerous editions and anthologies. Mill himself failed to distinguish act from rule utilitarianism. This is a twentieth century distinction. For more about this distinction see *Contemporary Utilitarianism*, edited by Michael Bayles, (Garden City, NY: Doubleday & Co., 1868).

xiii.   While there are many philosophers who defend deontological ethical theories, probably the most famous of them is Immanuel Kant. See his *Lectures on Ethics*, translated by Louis Infield, (London: Methuen & Co., 1930) and *Critique of Practical Reason*, translated by Lewis White Beck, (New York: Bobbs-Merrill Co., 1956). Kant does not make use of the notion of rights. For a general discussion of rights see A. I. Melden, *Rights and Right Conduct* (Oxford: Oxford University Press, 1959), and Morton E. Winston, *The Philosophy of Human Rights* (Belmont, CA: Wadsworth Publishing Co., 1989).

xiv.   Socrates and Plato are major philosophers who are influential in this tradition, but neither is as influential as Aristotle. See his *Nicomachean Ethics*. The Stoics also played a major role in virtue ethics. See the works of Marcus Aurelius (121-180), especially his *Meditations*.

xv.   Aristotle puts this position beautifully: "...but to feel these emotions of desire, anger, pity, fear, and the pleasant and the painful at the right time and on the right occasion and towards the right people and for the right motives and in the right manner is a middle course and the best course; and this is the mark of goodness.... The agent must be in a certain condition when he does them; in the first place he must have knowledge, secondly he must choose the acts, and choose them for their own sake, and thirdly his actions must proceed from a firm and unchangeable character." *Nicomachean Ethics*, Bk. II, Chs. 4 & 6.

xvi.   For more about the relationship between ethics and epistemology, see *Moral Knowledge? New Readings in Moral Epistemology*, edited by Walter Sinnott-Armstrong and Mark Timmons, (New York: Oxford University Press, 1966).

xvii. This, of course, raises the question of whether God (the gods) exists in the first place. Philosophers have discussed arguments for the existence of God (the gods) for thousands of years. See, for example, *Issues in Religion*, 2nd edition, edited by Allie Frazier, (New York: D. Van Nostrand Co., 1975), for a sampling of such arguments. The lack of a substance like God in a religious system would not make that system atheistic unless theism is defined as necessitating a substance like God or gods. Buddhism, for example, does not have a substance like divinity. Western religions such as Judaism, Christianity, and Islam have adopted substance theories of the divine because they have been so heavily influenced by Greek philosophical works such as Plato's *Timaeus* and Aristotle's *Metaphysics*. For more on a Buddhist view of God see Christmas Humphreys, *Buddhism* (New York: Penguin Books, 1951).

xviii. David Hume's *Dialogues Concerning Natural Religion* contains a charming debate between its characters on the virtues of atheism, agnosticism, deism, and theism.

xix. Anaxagoras of Clazomenae (500-428 B. C.) is an outstanding representative of this tradition. Interestingly, this sort of theory and mind-set was first viewed as highly dangerous to religion. To this day the so-called dispute between philosophy (science) and religion continues. For more on the early Greek philosopher/scientist/theologian see John Mansley Robinson, *An Introduction To Early Greek Philosophy* (New York: Houghton Mifflin Co., 1968), and F. M. Cornford, *From Religion To Philosophy*, New York: Harper Torchbook, 1957).

xx. Wilhelm Leibniz (*Theodicy* [1765]), Rene Descartes (*Meditations* [1639])), Francis Bacon (*Novum Organum* [1620]), Isaac Newton (*Principia* [1693]), Samuel Clarke (*The Leibniz-Clarke Correspondence* [1715-1716]) and William Paley (*Natural Theology* [1802]) are great representatives of this position. It is well critiqued by Voltaire (*Candide* [1759]), David Hume *(Natural History of Religion* [1750] and *Dialogues Concerning Natural Religion* [1756]), and Immanuel Kant ("On the Failure of all Philosophical Essays in Theodicy"[1799] and *Religion Within the Realm of Reason Alone* [1793]).

xxi. The cosmological and teleological arguments are very old. Something like them first appears among early Greek philosophers like Anaximander (612-545 BCE). They are explicitly attributed to Socrates by Plato (e. g., *Republic, Timaeus* and many other Platonic dialogues) and Xenophon (426-354 BCE) (*Recollections of Socrates* [360 BCE]). The Stoics like both of these arguments. See *The Hellenistic Philosophers, loc. cit.* Thomas Aquinas repeats them in his *Summa Theologica.* Modern philosophers like Descartes, Leibniz, and Locke defend their own versions of them. The arguments get their most thorough critiques from Hume (*Dialogues Concerning Natural Religion*) and Kant (*Critique of Pure Reason* [1781]). Theodicies have been around since the time of Plato. The *Theodicy* of Leibniz is an excellent example of its kind. Theodicies are criticized by both Hume and Kant as beyond explanation.

xxii. Just because one believes in a soul, it does not follow either that the soul must be an immaterial substance or that it is immortal, though Plato and Descartes believed both. The Stoics and the Epicureans believed that the soul was material in nature and mortal. For the Stoic and Epicurean arguments see *The Hellenistic Philosophers, loc. cit.* For Plato's position see his *Phaedo, Phaedrus*, and *Republic*. Descartes's position is presented in his *Meditations*.

xxiii. Plato advances at least five separate arguments for immortality in his *Phaedo, Phaedrus*, and *Republic*. I shall not attempt to present or discuss them here, as they would draw me too far away from my primary purpose. However, I will say that Christianity is not committed to the immortality of the soul, contrary to what most Christians think. Christian theology believes in the resurrection of the body. For more on this see *Immortality*, edited by Paul Edwards, (New York: Macmillan Publishing Co., 1992), and *Immortality*, edited by Terence Penelhum, (Belmont, CA: Wadsworth Pub. Co., 1973). On questions concerning the intersection of religion and science see *Philosophy, Religion and Science*, edited by Charles H. Monson, (New York: Charles Scribner's Sons, 1963), and Ian G. Barbour, *Issues in Science and Religion* (New York: Harper Torchbooks, 1966) for overviews on some of the many aspects of this complex set of issues.

xxiv. For more on mysticism and other forms of religious experiences see William James, *Varieties of Religious Experiences* (New York: The New American Library, 1958). Problems arise for any form of religious experience of the sort mentioned in the Appendix to Chapter Nine. How can one tell what one is really experiencing? How does one know that s/he has correctly understood the message? These are not silly concerns. History is full of people wrestling with just these sorts of issues.

xxv. Ludwig Wittgenstein champions the use of this sort of game metaphor to understand different religious traditions. See his *Lectures & Conversations on Aesthetics, Psychology and Religious Beliefs*, edited by Cyril Barrett, (Berkeley, CA: The University of California Press, 1972), and *Notebooks 1914-1916*, translated by G. E. M. Anscombe (New York: Harper Torchbooks, 1961).

xxvi. In reality neither model works quite as purely as I have put it. There's a continual jockeying among laypersons and clergy for positioning within the church. This is true because religion, as I have said, is the product of human interaction, the parameters of which are continually changing.

xxvii. By "cult" I do not mean the malphemism "evil, dirty, devil worship." Unfortunately, the word "cult" is often used precisely in this manner, which complicates things.

CHAPTER TEN

Problem Solving and Decision-Making

INTRODUCTION

Solving problems and making decisions are necessary facts of life. It is virtually impossible to get through even the simplest day without having to make decisions about a whole host of issues ranging from when to get out of bed in the morning to when to go back to bed at night. Fortunately, most of the decisions we are called upon to make can be done routinely. A **routine** is simply a systematic problem solving procedure designed to minimize or eliminate the need to devote much attention to a particular type of issue. Routines are so efficient at dealing with recurring problems that they are not even recognized for what they are—problem solving techniques. *Only recurring problems can be handled routinely.* Non-recurring problems require far more time and effort because special attention has to be devoted to them in order to handle their unique features. The analysis of their unique features can take such a great deal of time and effort that we tend to assume that problem solving and decision-making are relevant only to those problems and situations that are unique. We tend, that is, to ignore routine problems precisely because they are routine.

Whether you are called upon to make a decision or solve a problem that is unique or merely routine, problem solving and decision-making have certain common features. First, there must be the recognition of the existence of the problem to be solved. If you are unaware of the existence of the problem in the first place, then you cannot possibly solve it (except by accident). You cannot intend to solve a problem the very existence of which you are unaware.[i] Secondly, you must have some sort of preliminary idea as to how you think an adequate solution to the problem might look. This preliminary idea provides the necessary goal, thereby supplying a provisional direction to the activity of problem solving. *All problem solving and decision-making is goal-directed.* The initial statement of the goal, however, may be so revised in the process of solving the problem or making the decision that the final statement of the goal may bear little resemblance to its original formulation. Finally, problem solving and decision-making presuppose that the difference between the initial state and the final state may be overcome (at least in principle if not always in practice) by taking certain specific steps. If no steps could be taken in principle to close the gap between the initial state and the solution state, the problem is said to be insoluble in principle. If the problem in question is soluble in principle but there are practical impediments preventing the actualization of the effective solution (such as the lack of time or money), the problem is said to be insoluble in practice.

In this chapter, I want to review some common problem solving and decision-making procedures and practices. All of you have already been using most of these techniques throughout your lives, without reading a text about them, but you have probably not paid much attention to them. Critical thinking demands that you become aware of the procedures and practices you use when solving problems and making decisions, because the self-conscious use of these procedures and practices is far more likely to be fruitful at producing well-founded decisions than the unconscious (and unquestioned) use of these techniques. It is also true that the use of these techniques is not error or risk free. Problem solving and decision-making techniques are heuristics, not algorithms; there is no guarantee that they will always work, even when used correctly. The use of problem solving techniques can itself lead to problems, and the use of decision-making techniques is prone to certain traps and pitfalls. We will look at some of these potential troubles later in this chapter.

Consider the following examples, which typically are found in problem solving and decision-making texts.

Problem solving:

1. Which set of letters is different from the other 3 sets?
   a. EFGE b. BCDB c. KLML d. OPQO

2. Which pair of words fits best in the blanks? Arm is to wrist as _____ is to _____.
   a. leg: foot b. thigh: ankle
   c. leg: ankle d. leg: knee

3. Select the answer that is most nearly equivalent in meaning to the following statement.

"Show me the man you honor. I know by that symptom, better than any other, what you are yourself."   —Carlyle
a. The works of great scholars should be read and studied.
b. A man can be judged by his works.
c. A man can be judged by those he emulates.
d. Each human being has his own unique worth.[ii]

Decision-making:

1. Your doctors approach your bed. No one is smiling. The results of the biopsy are in. One doctor explains that the cells were irregular in shape; they appear abnormal. It is possible that the tumor was not completely malignant, but not completely normal either. They probably removed the entire tumor, but it's hard to be certain about these things. You have some choices. You could leave the hospital this afternoon and forget about this unpleasant episode, except for semi-annual checkups. There is an above-average chance, however, that some abnormal cells remain and will spread and grow. On the other hand, you could choose to have the entire area surgically removed. While this would be major surgery, it would clearly reduce the risk of cancer. What should you do?[iii]

2. You are a negotiator for the U. S. government trying to conclude a reduction of strategic nuclear weapons with Russia. The Russian negotiator has just proposed a 50% across the board reduction of all nuclear weapons. Should you accept the offer?

A word about terminology before I begin. Writers on these topics tend to write separate texts on either **problem solving** or **decision-making**.[iv] Writers who discuss both topics tend to give separate treatments to problem solving and decision-making, as if the two were easily distinguishable tasks.[v] In fact, it is not easy to distinguish conceptually between problem solving and decision-making. Decisions are judgments made by persons in order to solve problems. From this perspective, decisions can be treated as a sub-class of problem solving situations, problem solving situations can be treated as a sub-class of all decisions, or decisions and problem solving situations can be treated as identical. I do not think that any of these three possible ways of understanding the relationship between making decisions and solving problems is clearly preferable. The major difference between these two classes of thought activity lies in the type of example the different authors have normally used to illustrate each class. Problem solving texts tend to focus on well-defined problems with unique answers. Decision-making texts tend to focus on ill-defined problems or problems which do not have unique answers.

Well-defined problems meet all of the following conditions: the initial state is well-defined or understood; the final state is well-defined or understood; there are a limited number of mutually exclusive or easily distinguishable solution paths, each of which may already be well known. The job of the problem solver is merely to determine which of the solution paths is the correct one. I trust that examples like this are very familiar to you because you have been answering questions like these in school for years. Ill-defined problems are ill-defined because not all of the conditions that make problems well defined are met. Textbook examples ask you to test your decision-making powers on ill-defined problems. Even textbook examples of decision-making situations, however, simplify the ill-defined problems that are presented so that at best the difficulty you are faced with is only that of choosing between conflicting choices, neither of which is clearly correct. Your task is to choose between complex alternatives. Even textbook examples of ill-defined problems do not ask you to consider whether the statement of the problem or the statement of the solution need to be changed or altered in any way. Presumably, problems which are so rude as to be that ill defined need never be asked or answered.[vi]

Whether a problem is well defined or ill defined, or even downright unruly, there are certain techniques that can be brought to bear on them so as to make them more manageable. In the next two sections, I will examine some of these techniques. I will retain the traditional distinction between problem solving and decision-making only because it is a convenient way to handle the vast amount of material to be considered; but be forewarned, because a technique is presented and discussed in one of the sections only does not mean that it doesn't apply equally as well to the other section, too.

I. PROBLEM SOLVING TECHNIQUES

Consider the following simple problem: you're on your way to class for an important test and your car won't start. Should you: a) try and get it started yourself, b) try to get someone else to start it, c) try to get another ride to school, d) call the teacher and whine, or e) throw yourself on your sword immediately?

Problems like the one presented above are common enough. What's the best way to solve them? The short answer is that there is no way to solve such a problem as stated here. Surprised? You shouldn't be. The reason there is no way to solve a problem such as this is that the first sentence in this paragraph is false. No one ever experiences a problem of the sort stated above because the stated problem omits a whole host of relevant background information. Like perceptual knowledge and conceptual knowledge, problem solving and decision-making is theory-laden. You know that, but you chose to ignore this fact in your initial reading of the problem because you took it for granted that this background information was to be assumed as given. But this background information wasn't actually given in the initial statement of the problem and the original problem cannot be solved without some stipulation of this information. This brings me to **Rule #1** of problem solving and decision-making: *fill in all unstated but important pieces of background informa-*

tion. Here is another way of putting this same rule: *before attempting to solve a problem state the problem as completely as possible.* Rule #1 is an application of the requirement for total evidence discussed in Chapter Four. Fulfilling the requirements of Rule #1 requires you to supply a great deal of information unstated by the original presentation of the problem. Should you be unable to supply all of the important background information, you will find yourself dealing with a different problem than that with which you originally thought you were dealing.[vii]

Rule #1 is clearly violated by the first problem solving example in the box at the beginning of this chapter. This example asks you to choose which set of letters is "different from the other three sets." But each set of letters is different from the other three listed sets. Indeed, each set is different from the other three in multiple ways, including set content, pattern, and placement. The question for the problem solver is compounded by having to guess which difference is intended by the person who formulated the question in the first place. The statement of the problem is incomplete. Good luck figuring this out. I hope that you are a mind reader.

There is a good reason, however, why textbook examples of problems are frequently incomplete—simple considerations of space make it inconvenient to present any detailed consideration of the theoretical framework or relevant background information in which real problems are actually embedded. If textbooks presented you with the theoretical framework and all the relevant background information for each of their examples, there would only be room to present a few problems in the text. To avoid this problem, academic texts (including this one) assume that the reader can supply the theoretical context and the missing bits of relevant data needed to flesh out the examples used.

Consider how missing data alone might affect your answer to the car won't start example. Which of the five available options is "correct?" That depends on how the missing data

are filled. Should you try to start the car yourself? What do you know about cars? What do you know about this car? Have you had this kind of problem before? If so, could you fix it quickly then? Do you know anyone else who might fix your car quickly? If so, is this person available when you need him or her? Are there any other rides you can use to get to school? Have you ever had to do this kind of thing before? Can you get in touch with your teacher before the test? Will whining help? Do you own a sword? Could you borrow one if you promised to clean and return it after you were done? And so forth. Information of this sort has to be provided in order to make the statement of the original problem a well-defined problem.[viii]

Apply Rule #1 to the following situations. What other information do you need in order to solve these problems?

A. Your computer froze up in the middle of an essay before you had a chance to save its contents.

B. On an SAT question you determine that none of the listed options correctly answers the question.

C. You can't find the TV remote.

D. Two classes you want to take next semester are both given at the same time.

Once a problem has actually been well defined, there are a variety of problem-solving strategies that can be utilized to solve it. Some of these strategies work better than others in certain kinds of situations, but with all of them it is wise to remember that they are mere heuristics. Heuristics cannot guarantee a solution, even when they are correctly utilized in practice, but they generally are still quite useful. The strategies in question are: a) working forwards, b) trial and error, c) means-end analysis, d) working backwards, e) modeling, and f) detouring. I shall briefly discuss each of these in turn.

A. Working forwards. Many problem-solving techniques are forward looking. This means

THE THEORY AND PRACTICE OF CRITICAL THINKING

that problem solving typically has the thinker start at the beginning with what is called the initial state and proceed with a step by step process steadily towards the solution. For obvious examples of this, consider simple arithmetic operations such as addition and multiplication. When you first learned how to do these kinds of problems, you were taught some basic forward-looking techniques. The techniques worked, and rather efficiently, too. Many forward working techniques are discipline specific; that is, they are techniques which work very well in a given subject matter domain. They may work so well that they become algorithms. Algorithms are problem-solving techniques (frequently called **formulas**) which guarantee success if correctly applied to the domain in question. Even if the forward working problem solving techniques in question fail to achieve the status of algorithms, they become such proficient heuristics that they reduce problem solving in their areas of application to routines. These routines are devised and applied in a specific fashion to recurrent problems within a given subject area, and learning the subject area means, in part, learning the routines practiced by that discipline.

Because there are so many routines which need to be learned in order to understand a given discipline and because these routines are usually discipline specific, I will not attempt to say anything more about them here. To learn them you need to learn the discipline in question. All routines, however, present special problems to the critical thinker. Sometimes they fail to work as promised. When this happens, the problem solver is likely to get stuck very quickly. Since thinking in a discipline is largely defined by the correct use of the routines in question, thinkers can unwittingly become enslaved to the routine. When this happens and the use of the appropriate routine fails to work or works poorly in a given case, the mind-set produced by the habitual use of these routines can make it difficult for the thinker to get out of the rut s/he has gotten into. When this happens, the critical

thinker is well advised to use the other problem solving techniques listed in the sections below.

Devise forward working problem solving techniques for solving these sorts of problems:

A. Balancing your checkbook.

B. Contacting your friends when your party's time has been changed.

C. Cooking a new meal.

D. Christmas shopping for your friends and family.

B. Trial and error. The trial and error strategy is one of the most common problem solving techniques used when standard forward working routines cannot be applied or when their application has gotten the thinker stuck in a rut. Consider the following problem: you have just been hired to mow the lawn in a yard you have never mowed before. What is the most efficient way to mow this lawn? There are a variety of ways you can divide up this task. You are likely to simply start randomly with a way that seems easiest at the time. The next time you mow this lawn, however, you may try a different system to see if it turns out to be more efficient than the old way. You may then repeat the experiment until you are satisfied that one of the ways is clearly the most efficient method. This procedure is a good example of the trial and error method of problem solving in action.

In order to work, the trial and error method presupposes that certain conditions have been met. The first condition is that there must be only a limited number of solution paths. If there are ten thousand possible ways to mow the yard, you will never run through all of the possibilities to determine which is most efficient. Secondly, each of the solution paths must be equally (or nearly equally) plausible. If certain possible solutions appear to require a great deal of extra work, these possibilities will be ruled our a priori from the start. Thirdly, it must be possible to try each of the plausible solutions in isolation from the other possibilities. If the owner of the yard, for example, does not like to watch you mowing in a circle, it will not be possible for you to actually use that possibility (even though it may be the most efficient method). Or you may find that the contours of the terrain rule out what otherwise would be a possible method. Finally, the implementation of one possible solution cannot so alter the problem that other possible solutions can no longer be attempted. If the owner fires you for mowing the lawn in a circle on your first attempt, you'll not get another chance to experiment. Ditto if you break the lawn mower by running it (and yourself) off a cliff.

Examine how trial and error could be used to solve the following problems.

A. "Max, see if that snake is a deadly Wagga-Wagga." —Crocodile Steve
   [Yeah, yeah, Steve, we already know "she's a beauty!"]

B. "Great, seven different cars parked in a row at the Mall parking lot, all of them the same make, model, and color as mine. I wonder which one has the most gas in it?"

C. Molly thinks to herself, "So little time; so many prom dresses to choose from."

D. Max thinks to himself, "So little time; so many prom dresses to choose from."

C. Means-end analysis. A means-end analysis is another commonly used problem solving technique. In order to use it, the problem solver must be able to break the original problem down into a series of sub-goals, the satisfaction of which will equal the solution to the original problem. Suppose, for example, that your baseball team is down by one run in the bottom of the ninth inning. In order to tie the game, you have to score in this inning. In order to score, you have to get a batter from the home plate back to home after having touched the other three bases in turn. One way to do this is to have your batter hit a home run. But that may not be very likely given your selection of possible batters (leaving steroids out of the equation for the minute). Another way is to break down your original problem into a

series of sub-goals. First you have to get a batter to first base; then you have to get the first base runner to second, etc. If you can accomplish each of the sub-goals, you can by that fact alone achieve your major goal.

Means-end analyses work only if the following conditions can all be met. First, the original goal must be capable of being broken down into a series of mutually exclusive but mutually supportive sub-goals. If the sub-goals fail to exclude each other or fail to support each other, it is impossible to use the sub-goal procedure. Secondly, you must be capable of at least roughly foreseeing how the original goal may be broken down into sub-goals. If the original goal cannot be successfully divided into sub-goals, the means-end analysis cannot be used. This does not entail that you have to see each of the actually component sub-goals perfectly before you begin. It certainly may be possible that a refined understanding of the requisite sub-goals may appear as the solution process is implemented.

The more complicated the original goal the more appropriate it is to use sub-goals. If, for example, I wanted to teach you philosophy, I would be forced to break down this vast subject area into a series of divisions and work on each of these divisions separately. I might begin by dividing philosophy into the subdivisions of ethics, metaphysics, and epistemology and spend time with each of these areas. Then, I might break down each of these subdivisions into smaller units. I could, for instance, divide metaphysics into a series of separate issues like proofs for the existence of God, the mind-body problem, the problem of free will and determinism, or questions about the nature of space and time. Going further, I might divide the question of proofs for the existence of God into a consideration of the cosmological argument, the teleological argument, the ontological argument, and so forth. If you wanted to know what analyzing the cosmological argument for the existence of God had to do with doing philosophy, I would reply to you that doing philosophy simply is considering this and a host of other possible arguments and issues in a manner akin to the examples utilized.[ix]

Discuss how means-ends analysis could be applied to the following problems:

A. Assembling a jigsaw puzzle.

B. Saving Social Security.

C. Cleaning up your room.

D. Graduating from high school.

D. Working backwards. Working backwards is a technique that really is a subdivision of the means-end analysis technique. Working backwards occurs when the problem solver already knows what the proposed solution to the problem ought to be but does not know how to get from the initial state to the given solution. As we have already seen, most thinking about issues involves working forwards, that is, most thinking starts from the initial state as given and looks for the next appropriate step to take, finds it, proceeds to the next step, and so forth. For a good illustration of this, consider the alphabet song you learned as a child in order to help you remember the name and the order of all the letters of the alphabet. Obviously, the technique worked because even after all these years you can still sing it, can't you? But can you sing it backwards? I doubt it, at least without actually writing out the alphabet first and merely reading it off backwards.[x] While working forwards is the "correct" way to solve many problems (and, as such, the most commonly taught problem solving technique), this technique breaks down when the problem solver does not know which step to take next. That halts the whole forward working process immediately.

Working backwards is a convenient strategy to adopt when the solution is known and when there are only a few possible steps which could immediately proceed the solution. In effect the problem solver reverses the problem. A new problem is invented which has as its given the solution of the old problem. The new problem now becomes the production of the first step (which is really the next to last step of the old problem). If you have ever worked

through a maze, you have a good illustration of this procedure. Only a person with nothing else to do starts where the picture is labeled "start." Instead of this time consuming strategy, the critical thinker starts where the maze picture is labeled "finish" and works "forwards" to the beginning. Plotting travel routes presents another good example of this practice. You start by assuming that your destination is really your starting point and you work your way back to the point from which you actually are going to start. In this manner, all kinds of possible dead ends and side trips may conveniently be avoided. Other good examples of this can be found in the proofs you are often asked to do in geometry or deductive logic. The key to the whole business is the realization that there is nothing wrong with switching the starting and stopping points. With a little bit of practice, this can become quite easy.

Discuss how the following problems may be solved by using backwards working problem solving techniques:

A. Finding you car in the Mega-Mall parking lot.

B. "Ah, I know the answer to that one. It's right on the tip of my tongue."

C. "OK, so how did the magician switch the lady in the box with the tiger in the cage?"

D. Finding the answer to an even numbered math problem when the answers to the odd numbered problems are in the back of the book.

Some complex problems can be solved only by combining means-end analysis, forward working strategies and backwards working strategies. Each sub-goal is treated as a separate end and a separate beginning in itself. In this fashion, problems that are very complicated can be broken down gradually into mini-problems and a combination of forward and backward looking strategies can be used to connect the mini-problems until the whole problem is solved.[xi]

E. Modeling. Sometimes problems have subject matters which are initially too big or complicated to work with on their own. When this happens, problem solvers may be well advised to construct a scale model of the object in question. Suppose, for example, that you were given the job of constructing the first manned space ship to go to Mars. Clearly the real thing is going to be enormous in size and complexity, and just as clearly the actual ship will resemble existing spaceships. Among the things you would do as a designer is to construct models of the important parts of the craft. These parts would share the important characteristics of the large craft you are interested in testing. The working assumption here is that if the scale model works as planned the actual craft will work, too. And you know that this is true because you have constructed the scale model to be isomorphic to the original in the relevant sense. Modeling also assumes that the size of the object makes no functional difference concerning the properties being tested. When these conditions can be met, experimentation on a scale model can be a very efficient form of problem solving.

Before the Martian explorer Pathfinder and its little robotic vehicle Sojourner were sent to Mars, the people at NASA who designed it put duplicates of these vehicles through extensive testing to see whether their designs would hold up in practice. Before they were launched, the duplicates were run through a simulation of the conditions NASA expected to encounter based on their previous knowledge of Mars. Not only were the test vehicles functionally similar to the actual Mars vehicles, the controls of the vehicles were also determined using the same conditions that determine controlling a robot vehicle from 100 million miles away so as to make the test as isomorphic as possible. The stunning success of the Mars mission was thus no accident, but a result of a great deal of realistic practice under "game conditions." Any important goal, the successful path to which can be improved with practice, can benefit from the use of sim-

ulation, provided that the simulations are constructed as close to the actual playing conditions as possible. As your piano teacher said, "practice, practice, practice."

Frequently, scale models do not actually have to be physically constructed to serve their purposes. Running a computer simulation may be quite adequate. A computer simulation is a (usually graphic) representation of the features you are interested in exploring. As with physical scale models and simulations, care must be taken that the relevant features and relationships are correctly included in the computer model. Incorrectly constructing the model is a sure way of producing misleading conclusions. Correctly constructed computer models can be very handy and inexpensive ways to help form initial conclusions with which to guide further research. Currently this form of problem solving is utilized by researchers, engineers, and designers both in obviously technical fields, such as automotive construction and architecture, as well as fields that are not so obviously technologically oriented, such as medicine and psychology.

Discuss modeling as a problem solving technique in the following cases:

A. "All right, boys and girls, today we're going to see how to follow a suspect without being seen."   —CIA field agent training

B. "Controlling a jet with a dead engine in a spin is tricky. Watch how it is done."
                    —Military flight training

C. "In order to beat this team, we're going to have to do the following..."   —Any coach

D. "To learn how to survive on Mars, we will run a research station in the mountains of Antarctica."   —NASA

F. Detouring. Forward-looking problem solving strategies would have you start at the beginning, go through all of the intermediate steps, and finish at the end. Nice work, if you can get it. Unfortunately, reality isn't always so accommodating, as you well know. What you may not know, or at least pay much attention to, are detour problems. As the name signifies, detours are deviations from the normal way of proceeding. The paradigm case of a detour problem is the highway detour. You have to detour when the normal route is blocked for whatever reason. Detours always require side trips, which at the very least add mileage and time to your travels; they may even require **backtracking**. Backtracking requires you to give up some territory you have already traveled. Because backtracking apparently moves you further away from your destination, backtracking is always looked upon as a setback, a step in the wrong direction. This is why detour problems are so hard to either recognize or deal with. Our mind-set tells us that movement forward is good (after all, it's movement towards the goal) and movement backward is bad (after all, it's movement away from the goal). But these last claims aren't always true. Sometimes it is necessary to travel "backward" in order to proceed "forward."

Detour problems are problems in which it is necessary to go backward in order to go forward. But there is really a conceptual problem here. Motion which is labeled as "backward" isn't really backward since it is motion necessary for the attainment of the desired goal. So-called "forward" motion isn't really forward since it is not motion necessary for the attainment of the desired goal. What is really the case is that detours require the critical thinker to give up some steps that represent apparent progress. But apparent progress in these cases is not real progress. Real progress brings us closer to the goal only when the goal can actually be reached by that route. When the goal cannot actually be reached by the route you are taking, motion along that route cannot be motion in the right direction no matter how seductive the it may be. The critical thinker and problem solver must be intellectually nimble enough to change routes when a change of routes is called for.

Discuss the following detour problems:

A. Soldier to Sargent: "Sarge, we've got to get out of here before we get massacred."

Sarge: "Son, Marines never retreat. OK, men, listen up. About face! Charge!"

B. During the Vietnam War various protesters argued that the U.S. should declare victory and go home. Now that we're in Iraq, some are advising the same strategy.

C. "Great move, nitwit. You had the blueprints upside down."
   —Pharaoh Nobody III to the foreman of his pyramid as it sank out of sight.

D. "No, no, no, put dehorse before Descartes."
   —Mama Descartes to little René.

II. DECISION-MAKING TECHNIQUES

As I have already stated, books on decision-making tend to distinguish decision-making from problem solving by the type of issue confronting the thinker. Problems that are well-defined and have clear-cut answers and a limited number of solution paths tend to be treated under the rubric of problem solving; problems which are ill-defined or have no clear-cut answers or have many possible solution paths tend to be treated under the rubric of decision-making. In reality, both "decision-makers" and "problem solvers" use thinking to reach acceptable answers to issues they are facing. But it is helpful to consider some of the special complexities that arise in cases involving ill-defined problems. Remember, however, that the problem solving techniques discussed above may also apply to the decision-making situations discussed below.

Consider the following situation:

You are a high school student finishing your junior year. You have not yet decided which colleges you will apply to. Your college choices depend in part upon what you will choose as your college major. Your parents want you to major in business so that you can get a good job when you graduate, but the prospects of being a business major and getting a "good" job when you graduate don't turn you on at the moment. You've seen the kinds of jobs your parents call "good," and none of them really interest you. On the other hand, you rather liked the stuff you've studied which touches on anthropology and you think that you would like to try majoring in anthropology in college. But your parents object to this, arguing that all you can do with an anthropology major is study the primitive characteristics of your colleagues in the unemployment line. In addition to this, they point out the unpleasant fact that they are footing the bill for your college education, which at least tacitly suggests that the purse strings may be cut if what you do fails to meet with their approval. What should you do?

All problems like this have certain features in common: a) they present at least two apparently incompatible alternatives between which the decision-maker must choose;[xii] b) each choice has important advantages and disadvantages; c) regardless of the option chosen, the choice will be subject to extensive critique by both the decision-maker and others; d) the decision-maker will not be able to go back and choose the other alternative once a choice has been made, because making the original decision will itself change the situation so that it is impossible to start all over again; and e) the decision-maker will likely never know if the "correct" alternative was chosen.

In situations like this, what can you do as a critical thinker to maximize the possibility of making a good decision? There actually is a procedure you can adopt which will do all that reasonably can be done to insure that you have made a good choice. This procedure involves the following steps:

1. Define the issue. You can't make an intelligent decision until you know what you are deciding about. In order to do that, you must do your best to insure that you really know what is at stake in your situation. This, in turn, makes it possible to distinguish between good and bad choices, because choices are means to the ends involved in the issue. Commonly, there is a range of options available to you within a given

issue. While it is easiest (for purpose of argument) to assume that you are only choosing between two alternatives, it may well be the case that you have more choices than this. Sometimes, further choices can be made possible by combining aspects of the two original (or most obvious) options. It need not always be the case that the original alternatives be mutually exclusive. Often, the number of options with which you are presented may only become clear after you have made an initial run through the whole decision-making process so we will return to this stage again later.

2. Define your goals. In the best of all possible worlds what would you like to see happen? You have no way of making an intelligent choice between alternatives until you know what states of affairs would, in fact, please you. These states of affairs don't simply involve states of the world such as how much money you can actually make in a given profession; they also involve the actualization of certain values that you possess or ought to possess. Choices are always value-laden. What, truly, is really important to you? Just how important, for example, is it to you to make money in the first place? Are there any other values more important to you? Unless you have a clear idea of your goal preferences, it is going to be impossible to determine whether your actual choice was wise, and it is going to be virtually impossible to avoid second guessing whatever choice you actually do make.

Things are even more complicated than this. Even after you have identified the things that are important to you, you still need to consider how much of each you want. Goals come in basically two amounts: enough and never enough. To say we have enough of a given goal is to speak of that goal as being satisfied. Everyone gets out of formal schooling at some stage or other; no one stays in school forever. At some point enough is enough. The alternative is to say there's never enough of goal X. This is to maximize the goal in question. Some people treat the acquisition of money or power or fame in this sort of way; its pursuit never ends for them. Whether one treats a goal as one to be merely satisfied or as one to be maximized is, of course, up to the individual, and even the individual can change his or her mind at any time regarding a particular end to be pursued. In any event, the critical thinker must keep in mind whether a given goal is being viewed as one to be satisfied or as one to be maximized or goal confusion can easily result. Know when to say when.

3. Examine fully each viable option. Some possible choices are ruled out from the start as unthinkable, others are ruled in as good candidates, while still others are marginal possibilities. Assuming, in its simplest format, that there are really only two options available to you, first select one of the options and invent a **scenario** in which you imagine that you have in fact chosen that option.[xiii] A scenario is an imaginary outline for a planned series of events you have good reasons to believe would really unfold as imagined should the option in question actually be chosen. In constructing such a scenario, decision-makers have found certain techniques helpful. Among these techniques are the use of a **decision matrix** and the use of a **cost/benefit analysis**. A decision matrix is a checkerboard type grid where each axis is used to plot important factors in the scenario. One axis is used to list the values that are important to the decision-maker; the other axis is used to plot some of the probable consequences of the decision. See Figure 1 for an example of this procedure.

In a decision matrix, the characteristics of the scenario can be illustrated for simultaneous viewing. The advantage of this is that it helps to overcome the normal thinking procedure of successively (in a linear order) considering various factors, which concentrates attention only on one aspect of the situation at a time and invites you to ignore what you may have already considered but are no longer considering when each of these factors is viewed successively. Viewing factors successively makes it easier to fall victim to problems associated with availability heuristics, especially the mistake of overestimating the importance of a given factor in a decision-making situation merely because your attention is focused upon that factor.

The use of a decision matrix may also be coupled with the use of a cost/benefit analysis. A cost/benefit analysis is one in which each important factor in a decision is weighed in terms of the amount of time, energy, money, etc. which it would take to produce it when compared with the amount and kinds of benefits which would accrue from having produced it. When considering a cost/benefit analysis, many people make the mistake of assuming that all costs and benefits can only be measured by money. Avoid this potential mistake. Monetary costs and benefits are real enough but so are many other types of values. Frequently, decision-makers will rightfully allow non-monetary values to override monetary values. There's more to life than money.

In constructing such scenarios, care must be taken to be as accurate and fair as possible

Figure 1. A hypothetical decision matrix. Ralph's dinner at Lé Spoon Greasá

	Hamburger	Chicken	Veggie Plate	Quiche	Mineral Water
Taste:	questionable	"fowl"	so-so	little	none
Price:	$2.50	$4.00	$3.00	$4.50	$1.05
Time:	20 minutes	40 minutes	10 minutes	30 minutes	10 seconds
Calories:	1200	800	400	600	0
Nutrition:	little	medium	high	mixed	none
Satisfaction:	5 burps	4 burps	3 burps	2 burps	no burps

when predicting the supposed outcome of a given choice. This is part of the requirement for total evidence. Attempting to predict the future is inherently risky; there are many contingencies that may occur in a variety of ways, not all of which may be easy to anticipate. Unforeseen factors may spoil even the most reasonable predictions—look at the invasion of Iraq! But there is a difference between merely failing to foresee a given factor that is difficult to foresee and willfully closing your eyes to avoid what you do not want to see ("Don't confuse me with the facts; my mind is made up!"). Decision-makers run the risk of having their pet ideas overrun by reality. Avoiding reality may tempt you to beg some crucial questions. Critical thinking demands that you be as objective as possible in formulating the possible outcomes of the scenarios utilized in weighing conflicting alternatives no matter how unpalatable certain facts may be.

After you have devised a fair scenario for testing the first option, do the same thing for the other option(s). Remember that the function of inventing these imaginary scenarios is to allow for the intelligent comparison between conflicting alternatives prior to actually having to choose between them. An informed choice is likely to be a better choice than one made by simply guessing or by considering only the ideal situation of your dreams.

4. Compare the results. Now compare the results of each scenario. In order to make such a comparison, you will find that you have to be able to rank, in order, the circumstances you value by weighing your priorities. You also have to rank, in order, your priorities and decide which of them is only to be satisfied and which maximized. One of your priorities may be so important to you that the option which satisfies even some of it may outweigh the option which fails to satisfy any of it at all, even at the cost of sacrificing the greater amounts of other values offered by the rejected option. Situations like this are not commonly the case however. It is generally true that both of your options will satisfy at least some of each of your values.

It should be noted that it is always possible to compare the results of your scenarios by assigning to each of your values and factors to be considered a specific numerical weight and by calculating the probability of each possible occurrence. Such a procedure provides the superficial appearance of objectivity. After all, the argument runs, the results are now determined strictly by the laws of mathematics. Thus you may seek to avoid the interjection of any subjective factors into the equation.[xiv] Such an argument, however, would be fallacious. Subjectivity has already been introduced into the equation by the process of assigning the values and factors specific numerical significance in the first place. Why did you assign a certain factor the specific number you assigned it? Because you, the subject (and therefore the source of subjectivity, as opposed to the objectivity found in objects outside of you), judged it appropriate for that value to have just that weight. There is no way to remove this sort of "subjective" factor from the decision-making situation. However, this is not to say that these decisions are arbitrary. Good reasons need to be given as to why certain factors or values are weighed in the manner they are weighed. Clearly, not all decision-makers will value the same things or place the same amount of weight on the things they value. Decision-makers must be prepared to defend both the values they wish to introduce into their scenarios and the weight they assign to these values.

5. Review the analysis. Having run a scenario for each of the two options you originally proposed in your initial analysis of the decision situation, it is now time to review the process. Have you run each scenario correctly given the inevitable constraints of your knowledge? Did you omit any important factors from either scenario? Did you present each option fairly, including the negative factors as well as the positive factors in each situation? Finally, has your trial run through each of the scenarios suggested by other possible options you had not previously considered? Can you combine various factors in each scenario to form a third possibility significantly different from the first two? In this fashion, it may be possible to have more of your cake and eat more of it, too.

Construct a decision matrix and a cost/benefit analysis for the following issues:

A. Getting a new pet. Cat? Dog? Reptile? Fish? Bird? Werewolf? If any of the above, a young one or an adult? Male or female?

B. Where to go on vacation. The beach? The Mountains? Camp? Grandmother's house? Iraq?

C. Getting a car. Convertible? Pick-up truck? All wheel drive? Sports car? New or used?

D. Getting a summer job. McDonald's? Wendy's? Burger King? Backyard Burger? Red-hot Latin Lovers?

III. PERILS IN PROBLEM SOLVING AND DECISION-MAKING

Thinking that involves problem solving and decision-making is subject to a host of potential problems. In this section, I wish to briefly summarize some of these perils for you. Because many of these pitfalls have been encountered in other sections of the text, I will not attempt to duplicate my previous discussion here. When it is appropriate, I will tie in my previous discussion only to the special wrinkles that problem solving and decision-making present to the critical thinker. In general, there are three types of perils that the critical thinker may run into here: data acquisition problems, theoretical oriented problems, and mind-set problems. I shall discuss each of these in turn.

A. Data acquisition problems. Before you can hope to solve a problem correctly or make an intelligent decision, you must be as certain as possible that you have understood the real problem or decision you are involved with and not some other issue you've confused with the real issue because you "misread" the data. The problem of misreading data can range from the trivial to the most complex. Consider this

sort of trivial problem: Traditional academic textbooks in the languages, in the sciences, and in mathematics, for example, typically present their readers with examples of problems and exercises they are expected to solve. If you understood the data presented by one of these problems as something they were not, then any attempt you may make to work with this mistaken data will doom your efforts from the start. Silly errors made by miscopying problems from the book to a sheet of paper or those made by misreading your own handwriting may not be very sophisticated mistakes, but they surely are common enough. Here your worst enemy is likely to be your own impatience.

At the other extreme, there are data acquisition problems which may be very difficult to overcome because the data are so difficult to obtain. It is extremely difficult and time consuming, for example, to obtain certain data in medicine or subatomic physics.[xv] What would you do if you were skeptical about the validity of the data, run the experiment again? That may be easy to say, but who is going to pay for it, and who is going to do it? And what happens when the repetition of the experiment fails to achieve a similar result from the original? Empirical difficulties may tempt us into simply accepting data as they are "given" and not worry about their validity$_2$. With considerations like this in mind, it is not difficult to see how even the most conscientious problem solver can fall victim to fallacies like those of questionable statistics or unknowable statistics.

Most data acquisition problems fall somewhere between the trivial and the super complex. Data acquisition in this vast midrange is discipline relative, that is, how data are acquired and evaluated is determined by the rules set up within the discipline itself. These rules are designed, in part, to address the question of what constitutes good data. Because these rules are specific to given disciplines, it would be foolish of me to even begin to attempt to discuss them here. For this information, you will need to go to the discipline in question yourself.

What issues may make data acquisition difficult in the following situations:

A. Researching a topic on the Internet.

B. Figuring your take-home pay over the summer for your new job.

C. Deciding which cell-phone plan to go with.

D. Buying a used car.

B. Theory oriented problems. Theory oriented problems are those connected to the theory the knowing mind must apply in order to make sense out of the data in question. Theory literally is what makes sense out of the data. There are no theory-neutral data because data mean just what the theory says they mean. Several consequences follow from this. First, because theory is only theory within some discipline or other, the proper place to understand both the theory and the possible misuses of the theory belongs within the discipline in question. As such, it is just as inappropriate for me to comment on the potential misuses of theory within a given discipline as it is for me to comment on the potential misuse of data within that discipline. Learn the discipline yourself before you decide to critique the application of the theory and/or data by others working within that discipline.

Secondly, even though theoretical errors are discipline-relative, it is also the case that the errors to which practitioners fall prey tend to recur. Neophytes typically make the mistake of assuming that the errors they make in understanding a given subject matter are absolutely unique in the history of the world. They are not. The problems you may be having in understanding the proper use of the rules of grammar in sentence construction, for example, are the same problems that millions have had before you. They just seem absolutely unique to you because you have fallen victim to a wrinkle in availability heuristics in the assumption that the examples with which you are dealing are inherently the most important and difficult examples in the entire galaxy rather than commonplace bumps in the road. Further knowledge about the theory of the field in question should be sufficient to cure you of this sort of naivete. This is what grammar textbooks are all about. The many different forms of grammatical errors they discuss are inherent within the discipline itself.

Thirdly, there are theoretical errors common to many disciplines.[xvi] I have already mentioned the problem of availability heuristics; another example is confirmation bias. For whatever reason, there is a common tendency for problem solvers and decision-makers to beg the question at issue by assuming that they already really know the answer, and the only thing remaining to be done is to demonstrate that what they already "know" is, in fact, the case. Frequently, however, thinkers do not, in fact, know what they so readily think they know. One of the most common and difficult challenges I face as a teacher is getting students to call into question the assumption that they already know the truth about some issue when, in fact, they only have a strong belief. To bring to the students' attention the fact that they have fallen victim to problems associated with confirmation bias, it is helpful to stress the question of falsification. What would it take to get the students to see that their favorite beliefs about a given topic are wrong, or at least questionable? If an examination of the issue in question shows that no amount of negative evidence would sway their opinions, then we are dealing with a dogmatically asserted case of confirmation bias. An honest self-questioning regarding the possibility of falsification of dearly held assumptions is as important as it is difficult to anyone who takes critical thinking seriously. Incidentally, confirmation bias is a problem for anyone involved in a given issue, not just those who are at the early stages of apprenticeship in the discipline in question. The Bush administration was all hot to invade Iraq in 2003 because it was sure that Iraq had weapons of mass destruction and was set to deliver them to al-Qaeda. The administration was sure of the truth of their position, but now we know for sure that they were wrong. Experts can be pig-headed, too.

How might theory oriented issues affect the following decisions:

A. Using embryonic tissue for stem cell research.

B. Manned space flight verses robotic space exploration.

C. Questions concerning the reality of global warming.

D. Issues concerning your academic future.

C. Mind-set problems. The last class of errors that decision-makers and problem solvers typically succumb to are mind-set problems. Mind-set problems are those associated with the thinker's mental expectations about what ought to be the case in a given subject (whether it is the case or not). Begging the question by utilizing confirmation bias can occur on this level of analysis in addition to its involvement with the theoretical end of problem solving and decision-making. There are a host of other common mind-set problems here. Among them is the problem of world view constraints, the limitations imposed upon the thinking process by the broad philosophical, religious, political, or social positions that the thinkers bring with them to the problem solving or decision-making situation. World view constraints prevent thinkers from utilizing solutions or decision-making techniques because they are considered to be a violation of what is proper. Consider, for example, the considerable flap that Indian author Salman Rushdie caused with the publication of his book *The Satanic Verses*. This book has caused an uproar in the Islamic world because it is believed to blaspheme the Prophet Mohammed. In reaction to the publication of the book, Iran's Khomeini ordered Rushdie's death, a move that shocked the non-Islamic Western world. Clearly, believers of Islam and the non-Islamic Westerners have radically different views as to what may permissibly be thought or spoken in this situation. Everyone's thinking processes are affected by world view constraints. When these constraints are violated, those who accept them react with shock.

The more important the constraint, the greater the shock when it is violated.

Consider how mind-set issues might affect thinking about the following:

A. Inter-racial dating.

B. Friendship between persons with very different religious perspectives.

C. Moving into a different region of the country.

D. Accepting marriage between homosexual couples.

Entrapment is another common phenomena which affects the mind-set of a decision-maker or problem solver. Entrapment occurs when the thinker has already implemented a problem solving procedure or made a decision designed to resolve a particular difficulty, but the chosen process hasn't as of yet succeeded in obtaining the desired result. Further time, effort, or money seems to be needed, but there is also no guarantee that this further investment will produce the desired effect. The thinker now seems to be presented with a dilemma—either put more time, effort, or money into the original decision with no guarantee that what is added will produce the desired choice, or put no more time, effort, or money into the situation and run the risk of seeing all of the previous efforts go for naught.

Anyone who has driven an old car is well aware of this sort of problem. Old cars are prone to require frequent repair. How many repairs does it make sense to put up with before it becomes counter-productive? Remember, each repair still leaves you with an old car. When is it cheaper to junk the old one and get another one? Working a problem such as this one may tempt you to commit the fallacy of wishful thinking by assuming that something desirable is more likely to happen simply because it is desirable. You may think that the latest repair will be the last one you will have to do for a great deal of time. You may also be tempted to commit the fallacy of biased discounting by assuming that something undesirable is inherently unlikely merely because it is undesirable. Surely, you may think, you will not need to do any more expensive repairs to your clunker in the near future.

No one likes to be confronted with the admission that his or her beliefs are wrong or inconsistent. When they are and when there is a danger of having to admit this, thinkers are likely to react by changing their minds about the desirability of a course of action in the effort to avoid **cognitive dissonance**. Cognitive dissonance is the unpleasant recognition that some of your beliefs are wrong or inconsistent. You may have originally preferred, for instance, one choice for dinner over another but then found out that your original preference was not available or was too expensive. Rather than admit that your original preference was mistaken you might rewrite history in your own mind, so to speak, so as to devalue your original preference. When challenged on this, you may then conveniently forget your original decision and attempt to belittle the original choice by arguing that it probably wasn't very good anyway. In a case like this, the thinker needs to explain away the dissonance caused by the failure to achieve the original goal and chooses to do so by denying the reality of the original choice.

Finally, there is always the danger of becoming entwined in cognitive dissonance when reviewing a previous decision after it has been implemented. If the consequences of this decision are unfortunate, you may well wonder why you made such a poor choice in the first place. **Hindsight** is the review of a decision that assumes the thinker knew in advance of the decision that the choice made would turn out poorly. Because hindsight is always 20/20, its use always establishes the need to create some sort of scapegoat, which will take the responsibility for the poor choice off of the thinker's shoulders. In reality, the original decision might have been a great deal wiser than hindsight shows. You may sometimes have had good reasons for choosing the wrong option given the evidence available to you at the time. In order to avoid the fallacy of hindsight when reviewing your decision, you should practice **retrospective review**, which is the review of your judgment taking into account only what really was known (or should have been known) to you at the time and not what post decision events later established. Decision-making and problem solving are not infallible techniques. Even judgments which are well founded may later be overturned by subsequent occurrences. If every reasonable effort was made to insure the validity of the information available to you at the time of the original decision, and that information was analyzed in terms of reasonable decision-making procedures, then it is irrational to blame the thinker for effects which no one could have been reasonably expected to anticipate. There is an element of luck in decision-making and some of that luck is, unfortunately, bad.[xvii]

How might entrapment and cognitive dissonance affect your decision in the following situations?

A. "My girlfriend said she couldn't go out with me tonight because she had to wash her hair, but when I called again her brother said she had gone to bed. Is she being honest with me?"

B. Molly: "OK, bro, call it." Max: "Heads." Molly: "It's tails. You lose." Max: "Two out of three?"

C. "It seemed like a good idea at the time."
—Driver after being caught speeding the wrong way down a one way street

D. "My teachers don't like me."
Student expelled for bringing assault weapons to school

E. "Surf's up!"
—Tourist brochure, Phuket, Thailand

IV. STEREOTYPING

ALVY: Y-y-you like New York Jewish Left-Wing Liberal Intellectual Central Park West Brandeis University...uh, the Socialist Summer

Camps and the...the father with the Ben Shahn drawings, right? And you're really, you know, strike-oriented kind of—uh, stop me before I make a complete imbecile of myself.

ALLISON: No, that was wonderful. I love being reduced to a cultural stereotype.

ALVY: Right, I'm a bigot, but for the left.[xviii]

—from Woody Allen's *Annie Hall*

As I have stated repeatedly throughout this book, we are almost always confronted with too much data when we think. Means must be found to eliminate much of this data so that we may focus our minds, whittling down a mass of data to a manageable size. One method of doing this in problem solving and decision-making is to use **stereotypes**.

A stereotype is a fixed or stable notion or convention about some group of individuals. Statements using stereotypes (and arguments embodying these statements) form a subset of the set of generalization statements.[xix] All generalization claims designate some target group containing a characteristic which varies over a range of possibilities, abstract certain members from that range, and stipulate that the abstracted characteristic is typical (or definitive) of the whole group. For some characteristic to qualify as a stereotype, it is necessary that a whole social group (the **in group**) employ the same understanding to the group being stereotyped (the **out group**).

The use of stereotypes is one of the common characteristics employed by group think. In our society, for example it is common to label football players as big, dumb jocks. The qualities "big" and "dumb" are more or less automatically associated in our thinking processes with being a football player. If you are about to meet a person who is a football player, these associations lead you to expect the person you are about to meet to be big and dumb. Imagine your surprise if the person turns out to be small, intelligent, and female.[xx]

There are four dimensions of stereotypes that need to be examined separately in greater detail: the cognitive dimension, the psycholog-ical dimension, the values dimension, and the social dimension. I shall look at each of these elements in order.

A. The cognitive dimension. Stereotypes serve as handy guides to individual and group thinking processes. Walter Lippmann called this process forming "pictures in our heads."[xxi] As we have already seen, all of us bring a great deal of mental baggage with us to our experiences. Among other things, this baggage includes the intellectual knowledge of theories, concepts, and ideas with which we understand what we experience as well as the psychological mind-set that prepares us to perceive and understand what we are about to experience in certain ways. If we didn't have this form of relative a priori knowledge,[xxii] we would have to begin anew with each occasion, and that would make life as we know it impossible. Fortunately for us, the human mind is constituted so that it more or less automatically applies its previously learned theories to the subjects of new experiences to form an integrated understanding of the world. Stereotypes form part of this theoretical problem solving and decision-making baggage. They allow the mind to quickly interpret what is presented to it. They help prepare the mind in advance to form these interpretations. If I invite you over to my house to meet my pet crow Felix, you expect the bird you are about to meet to be black in color, not red, green, or plaid. And you have this expectation because you know prior to actual experience with this particular crow that crows are black. Stereotypes help supply you with this sort of foreknowledge.

Using stereotypes would have no cognitive point and would even be counterproductive unless the stereotypes in question frequently turned out to be true. If you find it surprising that stereotypes frequently turn out to be true it is probably because of your stereotype of stereotypes. Consider Alvy Singer's portrait of Allison Portchnik in *Annie Hall*, presented at the beginning of this section. It is basically accurate; Allison is a Jewish, liberal, left-wing, intellectual New Yorker, and she has done the kind of things attributed to her. Generalizations are useful because they help the mind to eliminate a lot of extraneous data quickly when making judgments about a particular thing. If this process weren't generally accurate, the resulting misjudgments would render the process pointless at best and fatally mistaken at worst.

Stereotyping as a cognitive process would not survive if it weren't so useful, but herein lies the real problem. Stereotyping is sometimes too useful. Because stereotyping is so handy, the convenience it offers to the judging mind becomes an entrapment. What happens when the mind, conditioned as it is to the convenient use of stereotypes as a judgment technique, runs into a valid counter example to the stereotype? Three possible things can occur in such a situation. First, surprise: "Well, I'll be darned," the mind may say, "here's a female football player (or a plaid crow, etc.)." This is innocent enough. Secondly, and not so innocently, the mind may reduce the example in question to the stereotype even when the example may not completely fit the stereotype. Thus the mind may fall prey to the mistake of confirmation bias[xxiii] by reinterpreting the counter example to more exactly fit its previous beliefs. This is akin to what Allison Portchnik accuses Alvy Singer of in the example above. She objects to being reduced to a mere stereotype, regardless of its apparent applicability. Thirdly, the mind may go so far as to completely ignore the example in front of it that would otherwise refute its convenient stereotype. "What counter example?" the mind may tell itself, "all I see is just another ____" (where the ____ is filled in by the convenient stereotype or literally by nothing at all). Strange as it is, a priori assumptions about things can so condition the mind that it rejects the evidence of the senses without hesitation, even when that evidence is "as plain as the nose on your face."

The last two intellectual maneuvers, of reducing a valid counter example to the stereotype in question or simply ignoring the counter example, are excellent illustrations of the problem of cognitive dissonance. All of us would like to believe that our ideas are all perfectly consistent. When they are not consistent and when we would be forced to recognize their unwanted inconsistency by having inconvenient illustrations brought to our attention, our minds rebel by adopting certain convenient defense mechanisms. These little intellectual tricks allow us to deny the inconsistencies in our beliefs while pretending to be perfectly rational.

As a critical thinker, you must be on the lookout for these seductive head games. It is always easier, of course, to see these types of excuses being utilized by others while ignoring your own thinking procedures. Being adept at pointing out to others their attempts at alleviating their own cases of cognitive dissonance while ignoring your own is rank intellectual arrogance, a trait easily succumbed to, especially by those who have made little attempt to recognize their own tendencies here. It takes a great deal of practice at reflective self-criticism to see your own examples of attempts to eliminate cognitive dissonance by appeals to cute intellectual games like confirmation bias.

B. The psychological dimension. The psychological dimension of the use of stereotypes in forming judgments is closely bound up with the cognitive dimension. By the psychological dimension, I mean the set of attitudes, associations, and expectations the mind brings with it when it forms judgments about actual cases. This dimension may be summed up by the term "mind-set." We never enter into a new situation calling for our minds to pronounce judgment on what is or is not the case without some previously formed patterns of judging (forming the cognitive element) and various attitudes, associations, and expectations (forming the psychological dimension)[xxiv] about what to anticipate in this new situation. These attitudes, associations, and expectations embody an emotional component as well as our basic personal traits. Emotions and personality traits set (or channel) the individual's reaction to events in ways that can become easily predictable to anyone who knows the personality of the individual in question. If, for example, I know that you don't like to eat quiche, I can confidently predict in advance that you won't like tonight's dinner, Quiche la Barf, even if it actually tastes exactly like your favorite meal.[xxv]

Stereotyping persons, places, and things has an obvious psychological dimension. The judgments made using stereotypes can be so tempting even when they are clearly factually incorrect because they so nicely accord with the psychological dimension of the mind-set of the person making the judgment. In these cases the important thing to recognize is that the truth or falsity of the judgment is not the issue with which the judge is really concerned. What really interests the user of the stereotype in cases like this is the way the judgment so nicely fits the judge's mind-set. *Judgments utilizing stereotypes may therefore depict much more accurately the attitudes of the judge rather than the truth about the judged object.* Accordingly, pointing out to the user of the stereotype that his or her judgment is factually incorrect is likely to be a waste of time. The user of the stereotype is really attending to the emotional "fit" of the judgment, not its cognitive truth.

C. The values dimension. Though stereotypes are a subset of generalizations, the claims and arguments embodying stereotypes are important to us because stereotypes frequently contain implicit or explicit value judgments. *Stereotypes rarely are mere descriptions of things, they are also evaluations of them.* If I refer to Ralph the football player as a "jock," I suggest that Ralph is big and dumb. "Big" may serve as a marked term,[xxvi] implying a certain evaluation of the persons denoted by it. "Dumb" certainly expresses an evaluation, and a highly negative one at that. Therefore, simply referring to Ralph as a jock labels Ralph with a certain set of values.

There are two important points to note here. First, evaluations are notoriously subject to dispute. It is difficult to find anything that is evaluated equally by everyone. But it doesn't follow from this that all value judgments are equally defensible. Value judgments, like judgments of subjects not involving values, may be

wise or silly, appropriate or inappropriate, solid or silly.[xxvii] The value judgments implicitly or explicitly contained in many stereotypes present terrific opportunities for disputes. It would be a wise thing for the critical thinker to be aware of this potential and to be careful that the glib use of stereotypes doesn't unwittingly suggest unintended evaluations of the stereotyped objects. The very least that can be expected of the critical thinker is that s/he be aware of the actual values conveyed by the stereotypes when they are used as labels for things in general and persons in particular. How something is evaluated is frequently even more important to people than how it is simply described.

Secondly, not all evaluations are negative. The stereotype of stereotypes is that they always embody a negative evaluation of the objects to which they are applied. This is certainly not always the case. Some stereotypes are highly positive in character. Consider the Cadillac motor car. Though the term "Cadillac" originally was simply the name of a luxury automobile, it quickly outgrew its original usage and became synonymous for any superior quality, top of the line item, as indicated by expressions such as "the Cadillac of cell phones" or "the Cadillac of motor oils." Again, in this sort of example the punch the stereotype has when used as a label is really the values that its use suggests, not its mere descriptive qualities. No one thinks that a person is literally phoning with a motor vehicle if s/he uses "the Cadillac of cell phones."

D. The social dimension. Stereotypes are important because the cognitive, psychological, and value dimensions contained in them are usually manifested in society. Humans are assuredly social animals. Stereotypes present social pronouncements. Social pronouncements affect all of us. The stereotypes with which members of society label things can tell the critical thinker a great deal about how things work in the society in question.

Sociologists who have examined the phenomenon of stereotyping distinguish between in groups and out groups. An **in group** is a collection of individuals who form and utilize stereotypes in common so as to characterize persons or things which do not properly belong to the in group. The persons or things that the stereotypes are used to label are called the **out group**. Each of us belongs to many in groups. Our families, school chums, co-workers, fellow church members, and fellow countrymen form some of the many in groups to which we belong. But remember, for every inside there must be a corresponding outside. For every group you are a member of, there is at least one other group you are not a member of (namely, the corresponding out group).

In group labels of out groups are frequently the product of in group **ethnocentrism**. Ethnocentrism is the assumption that the way the in group thinks and the values that the in group shares are the correct (or only) ways to think and things to value. In groups naturally tend to treat their own methods and conclusions as definitive in forming judgments about all groups. Any group failing to reflect the in group's methods and conclusions is thereby deficient.

Discuss the four dimensions of the following stereotypes.

A. The jocks, Goths, nerds, and princesses that make up your high school classmates

B. Islamic terrorists

C. Migrant workers

D. Teenagers and their parents

E. Siblings

But why exactly do in groups produce the exact stereotypes of out groups they produce? Psychologists and sociologists who have studied this problem recognize five rules which in groups employ in generating their stereotypes of out groups:

1. The greater the real differences which exist between the in group and any other group(s) regarding physical appearance, customs, modes of behavior, or material artifacts, the more likely these differences are to appear in the in group's stereotypes of the out group.

2. The differences cited above which are most directly involved in interaction between the in group and the out groups will most likely appear in the in group's stereotypes of the out group.

3. The differences cited above which are most strongly rejected by the in group will be more likely to appear in the in group's stereotypes of the out group.

4. If the differences cited above are sufficient to be noted by the in group, they will tend to be reinforced and amplified by the in group's stereotypes of the out group.

5. There is a tendency for the in group to attribute inherent rather than environmental causes to the differences noted between the in group and the out group.[xxviii]

A bit more discussion is called for concerning the fifth criterion the in groups use to form their stereotypes of out groups. Broadly speaking, there are two different factors recognized when an attempt is made to determine why persons have the characteristics they have, inherent traits and environmental conditioning. People typically are not held accountable for possessing the inherent traits they possess, but they usually are held responsible for possessing the characteristics they have owing to environmental conditioning.[xxix] In group members (IM) who wish to belittle members of an out group (OM) may use this distinction with the following devastating results:

1. Should OM possess a characteristic (C) that the IM value, IM only have to attribute OM's (C) to the luck of the environment of OM.

2. Should the characteristic possessed by OM be rejected by IM (-C), then IM can happily claim that OM's (-C) is innate for OM.

3. Should IM possess (C), then IM can happily claim that (C) is innate to IM.

4. Should IM possess (-C), then IM can excuse this failing by claiming that IM who possess (-C) are unfortunate victims of bad breaks.

By using this line of reasoning IM presents OM with a double-whammy, "Heads I win; tails you lose." Thus in no way is it possible for the in group members to be in the wrong or for the out group members to be in the right no matter which characteristic either group possesses. God is always on the in group's side, never on the side of the out group. For convenience sake, I shall call this intellectual sleight of hand the **double-whammy fallacy**. The use of stereotypes presents the in group members with a wonderful opportunity to use this mind game without even suspecting that they are doing so.

Here's a "fun" assignment: (1) Arbitrarily divide your class into two or more groups and have each group construct a stereotype of the other group(s). (2) Let the fur fly.

V. GROUP THINK

If you are like most of us, you probably tend to assume that problem solving and decision-making are activities performed only by individuals. This notion seems so obvious that it is difficult even to conceive of an alternative possibility. How could thinking be carried on by anything other than an individual? There are, after all, no group minds or organisms composing a "collective conscious," so how could anything other than an individual think?

While it is probably true that there are no group minds outside of the fantasies of various science fiction writers,[xxx] it is not true that each of us has a mind which functions absolutely independently of the social circumstances in which we happen to find ourselves. Traditional texts in philosophy and cognitive psychology (including this one) tend to help foster the illusion that all thinking is done by atomic individuals isolated from the thought processes of the communities to which thinkers just happen to belong. However briefly, I wish to take some time to help dispel this mistaken assumption.

A large percentage of our thinking can correctly be labeled **group think**. "Group think" is a term that describes the role collectives play in shaping both what individuals think and the

way they think. Humans are undeniably political animals. We associate with each other by means of a manifold number of groups such as social clubs, political organizations, family units, peer groups and our own circle of intimate friends. Membership in these groups not only reinforces the individual's belief in certain commonly held ideas, but it also encourages the individual to react in certain ways to the psychological and social factors inherent in intra-group dynamics. The branch of psychology that studies the psychology of group think is called **social psychology**; the branch of sociology (and anthropology) which studies the social factors inherent in group think is called **ethnography**.[xxxi] When discussing the factors contributing to the thought processes displayed by collectives, it is important to distinguish between the **internal** and the **external environment** in which the collective operates. The external environment consists of whatever problem or issue the group happens to be dealing with. You are probably accustomed to thinking of these problems or issues as ones with which any individual could deal easily, because so many of the problems and issues you deal with are ones with which you have to deal yourself. But a moment's reflection should allow you to think of many examples which are best understood as group problems or issues either because the problems affect all the members of the group in common (e.g., political policy issues, problems of domestic and foreign issues on the national scale, fraternity membership policies, team strategy, family finances, and so forth) or because the problems or issues are simply too complicated for any individual, or even small collection of individuals, to handle on their own (e.g., complicated problems in scientific research or time-consuming problems of data collection such as census taking).[xxxii]

What has gone largely unnoticed by many individuals are the many factors that make up the internal environment of group think. Groups are often assigned the task of problem solving because there is strength in numbers.

Because many problems cross traditional disciplinary lines or require expertise not found in any one individual alone, it is certainly helpful in solving these problems to harness the potential of many individuals working together. Teamwork can produce results impossible to the individual. Turning a collection of individuals into a team is not as easy as it sounds, however—there are a host of problems associated with the production and employment of teamship. Leadership is one such problem. Who will become the team leaders? What style of leadership will the team leaders use? Will they lead by consensus or will they adopt an authoritarian style? There are advantages and disadvantages to any style of leadership. It is difficult for leaders who are accustomed to one style of leadership to adjust that style when it proves to be counterproductive.

The personal autonomy of the individuals who compose the group is another factor that presents a potential problem for group think. How much real power will each group member actually retain to influence the activities and deliberations of the group? Groups of saints or gods may still be able to function if decision-making authority is shared equally by all, but for us humans Orwell's quip is much more apropos: "All pigs are created equal but some pigs are more equal than others." What determines "pig equality" in the group in question? Something will, and not always to the advantage of the thinking process.

A third factor affecting the quality of the deliberation and decision-making that goes on within a group is the performance factor. We tend to view thinking and decision-making as events that occur solely within the individual's own mind, in abstraction from the external conditions of the individual's situation. Thinking is what goes on in the privacy of your own head, so to speak, but this is not always the case. Sometimes we have to think in public in front of an audience, and when this happens, thinking becomes a performance. Have you ever been asked to give a speech to a group or to put a math problem on the board? Did your mind go blank? Did you mess up the whole thing? When we are called upon to perform publicly, the mere reality of the audience can be unnerving at best, terrifying at worst. In the theater, this is called stage fright. Stage fright is best overcome through plenty of practice, though there are many veterans who still suffer the same attack of nerves whenever they are called upon to perform. Stage fright can just as surely cause the mind to "choke" in thought as nerves cause the performance of a star athlete to choke, resulting in a missed last second shot to lose the big game.

Sometimes collectives composed of the most rational and intelligent of persons can produce spectacularly stupid decisions with which no member of the group would have agreed for five seconds if s/he was consulted solely as an individual. Consider the 1962 Bay of Pigs invasion or the Susan B. Anthony dollar coin, for example. How can cowflop like this occur? Social psychologist Irving Janis has devoted much of his career to the study of the internal environment of group think [including coining the term].[xxxiii] He lists eight symptoms of the **group think syndrome**.

SYMPTOMS OF THE GROUP THINK SYNDROME

1. An illusion of invulnerability, shared by most or all members, which creates excessive optimism and encourages taking extreme risks

2. Collective efforts to rationalize in order to discount warnings which might lead the members to reconsider their assumptions before they recommit themselves to past policy decisions

3. An unquestioned belief in the in group's inherent morality, inclining the members to ignore the ethical or moral consequences of their decisions

4. Stereotyped views of enemy leaders as too evil to warrant genuine attempts to negotiate, or as too weak and stupid to counter whatever risky attempts are made to defeat their purposes

5. Direct pressure on any member who expresses strong arguments against any of the group's stereotypes, illusions, or commitments, making clear that this type of dissent is contrary to what is expected of all loyal group members

6. Self-censorship of deviation from the apparent group consensus, reflecting each member's inclination to minimize to himself the importance of his doubts and counter arguments

7. A shared illusion of unanimity concerning judgments conforming to the majority view (augmented by the false assumption that silence means consent)

8. The emergence of self-appointed mind guards—members who protect the group from adverse information that might shatter their shared complacency about the effectiveness and morality of their decisions.[xxxiv]

What causes groups of rational people to fall prey to the group think syndrome? There are three factors that govern the internal environment of group think, which either individually or in combination make the group vulnerable to the production of poor decisions: group cohesiveness, (the positive attraction of each group member to the group); group consensus, (the positive feelings generated by group solidarity); and insulation, (the need to maintain cohesiveness and consensus by downplaying or ignoring the virtues of the out group). In short, the internal environmental needs of the collective serve as a hidden agenda that can be allowed to override the factors present in the external environmental agenda.

As a person living in a society that makes great use of group think, you will probably belong to a great number of organizations that require you to serve as a member of a decision-making group. Be aware of the internal environmental factors conditioning the decisions these groups will make. *Critical thinking demands that you do your best to maximize the strengths of group thinking processes and minimize the flaws inherent in it.* A good way to try to minimize these inherent flaws is to appoint some member of the group to play the role of the **devil's advocate**. The person who plays the role of the devil's advocate for the in group is assigned the job of purposely seeking to discover flaws in the decision-making process by pointing out the destructive role that cohesiveness, consensus, and insulation may play in the decision-making process and by making sure that the internal environment doesn't override the external environment. There is, of course, no sure-fire way of accomplishing these important goals, but group think is far more likely to go wrong unless members of the group keep these issues in mind in their deliberations.

How might the group think syndrome affect the following decisions?

A. You and your buddies are out cruising when another group of teens challenges you to a race.

B. You have a great idea for a story for your student newspaper, but others think it's too controversial.

C. Mom to teenager: "I suppose if all of your friends jumped off a bridge, you'd follow them." Teenager: "Well…sure."

D. Shaggy: "Maybe we shouldn't go in that haunted house."
Thelma: "Don't be such a weenie."

CONCEPTS

You should be able to define the following concepts, explain their meanings to others not familiar with them, invent your own examples that correctly illustrate the concepts, and apply them correctly to novel applications.

- Backtracking
- Cognitive dissonance
- Cost/benefit analysis
- Decision-making
- Decision matrix
- Detouring
- Devil's advocate
- Double-whammy fallacy
- Entrapment
- Ethnocentrism
- Ethnography

- External environment
- Group think
- Group think syndrome
- Hindsight
- In group
- Internal environment
- Labeling
- Means-end analysis
- Modeling
- Out group
- Problem solving

- Retrospective review
- Routine
- Rule #1
- Scenario
- Simulation
- Social psychology
- Stereotype
- Trial and error
- Working backwards
- Working forwards

Foundational concepts: Backtracking, cost/benefit analysis, decision-making, entrapment, means-end analysis, modeling, problem solving, Rule #1, stereotype, trial and error, working backwards working forwards

NOTES

i. For more on the issue of defining problems see Chapter Six, Section II. In Chapter Six, I was concerned with a whole methodology of problem solving. In this chapter, I am more concerned with certain common techniques which were not discussed individually in Chapter Six.

ii. Taken from Whimbey & Lochhead, *Problem Solving & Comprehension*, op. cit., 4, 10.

iii. Halpern, *Thought and Knowledge*, 209.

iv. For a discussion of problem solving techniques see, for example, Wayne A. Wickelgren, *How to Solve Problems* (San Francisco: W. H. Freeman and Company, 1974); John D. Bransford and Barry S. Stein, *The Ideal Problem Solver* (New York: W. H. Freeman and Company, 1984); Arthur Whimbey & Jack Lochhead, *Problem Solving & Comprehension*, Fourth edition, (Hillsdale, NJ: Lawrence Erlbaum Associates, 1986); and A. Newell and H. Simon, *Human Problem Solving* (Englewood Cliffs, NJ: Prentice-Hall, 1972).

For a discussion of decision-making techniques, see, for example, R. M. Hogarth, *Judgment and Choice: The Psychology of Decision* (Chichester: Wiley, 1980); Irving Janis and L. Mann, *Decision-making: A Psychological Analysis of Conflict, Choice, and Commitment* (New York: The Free Press, 1977); and *Decision-making: An Interdisciplinary Inquiry*, edited by G. R. Ungson and D. N. Braunstein, (Boston: Kent Publishing Co., 1982).

v. For an example of this kind of approach see Diane F. Halpern, *Thought and Knowledge* (Hillsdale, NJ: Lawrence Erlbaum Associates, 1984).

vi. Certainly many of my philosophy students think it highly rude of me to ask such questions of them. The vast majority of students I teach are more or less well prepared to work on problem solving, poorly prepared to work on traditional text book examples of ill-defined problems, and not at all prepared to work on everyday examples of really ill-defined problems. They wish that such really ill-defined problems did not exist and try to help make this the case by refusing to recognize them.

vii. All of us have experienced this in school. Haven't you taken a test with true/false or multiple choice questions where you confidently answered one thing only to find out that another answer was correct because the person who made up the test was assuming some important piece of background information which you failed to assume? Arguing didn't help, did it?

viii. As a college professor, I find that many of my students do not possess the theoretical knowledge or relevant background information necessary to understand what would otherwise be considered quite humdrum or everyday issues. Since examples of issues with which students are unfamiliar mean little to them, I find that I am continually forced to spend a great deal of classroom time searching for enough common ground to make the techniques and rules of reasoning with which I am concerned seem real to the students.

ix. In fact, my philosophy students do experience just this process and ask this kind of question about the process. They have a hard time seeing the point of the answer I have given here because they don't understand the original goal well enough to recognize the relevance of the constituent sub-goals. The same issue appears in teaching critical thinking. My solution to this is to break the original problem down into the sub-problems contained in each of the chapters of this text.

x. Which of course is cheating. This failure shows that operations even as apparently trivial as reciting the alphabet involve what Piaget calls concrete operations and not formal operations for most of us.

xi. This is exactly how this book got written!

xii. For purposes of convenience, I will generally ignore the fact that there are always more than two alternatives from which to choose in even simple examples like the one used above.

xiii. Philosophers call these kinds of scenarios "thought experiments." Thought experiments are commonly used by philosophers to mentally test the validity of certain assumptions they may wish to make.

xiv. Those who understand cost/benefit analysis solely in terms of money fall prey to this mistake.

xv. See footnote 32 below for an example of just this sort of problem.

xvi. If there weren't, this book wouldn't make any sense.

xvii. Constructing scenarios in advance of decisions is the only way to minimize the element of luck. But no scenario is infallible.

xviii. Woody Allen, *Annie Hall*, in *Four Films of Woody Allen* (New York: Random House, 1982), 20.

xix. For more on generalizations see Chapter Five, Section II.

xx. Did I throw you a curve here? How can females ever be football players?

xxi. Walter Lippmann (1889 - 1974) was an American social philosopher and popular culture analyst. See his *Public Opinion* (New York: Harcourt, Brace and Company, 1922). Lippmann's work pioneered the study of stereotyping and the role stereotyping plays in individual and group thinking.

xxii. The term "a priori knowledge" here means only knowledge which precedes the particular use which is about to be made of it. When philosophers use the term "a priori knowledge" they usually mean knowledge which is obtained or verified independently from all possible experience.

xxiii. For more about confirmation bias see Chapter Six, Section IV.

xxiv. Strictly speaking psychology certainly includes the study of rationality as it is actually utilized by the mind. This division of psychology is called cognitive psychology. Here I have chosen to emphasize the non-rational dimensions of thinking under the rubric of "the psychological dimension." What I have called the cognitive dimension and the psychological dimension of thinking are closely intertwined.

xxv. If you've ever had the experience of trying to get a child to try some food only to meet the stone wall of "I don't like it," you have a perfect example of this sort of mind-set at work.

xxvi. For a discussion of the marked terms see Chapter One, Section III.

xxvii. For more about the evaluation of value judgments see Chapter Nine, Section V.

xxviii. For a more complete discussion of how stereotypes are formed see D. T. Campbell, "Stereotypes and the Perception of Group Differences," *American Psychologist*, (vol. 22, 1967): 817- 829. For an excellent collection of studies of stereotyping ,see *In the Eye of the Beholder*, edited by Arthur G. Miller, (New York: Praeger, 1982).

xxix. For the point I am making here, it makes no difference whether this questionable analysis is correct or fair. My point is simply that this is, in fact, the way we usually think. For an assessment of the philosophical problems inherent in the in this sort of analysis see AlanWolfe, "Defining Repression," *The Seamy Side of Democracy*, edited by Alan Wolfe, (New York: David McKay Company, Inc., 1973).

xxx. For purposes of brevity, I shall ignore concepts found in western psychologists like Carl Jung, which seem to suggest that these psychologists take seriously the notion of a group mind, as well as the Eastern religious perspective of some forms of Hinduism and Buddhism that postulate after-life existence in the form of some kind of group mind. As interesting as these notions may be, they lie far outside of the boundaries of this book. For more about Jung's position see *The Portable Jung*, translated by R.F.C. Hull, (New York: The Viking Press, 1971). For more about Hinduism see A.B. Keith, *The Religion and Philosophy of the Veda and Upanishads* (Cambridge, MA: Harvard University Press, 1925). For more about Buddhism see Edward Conze et al., *Buddhist Texts Through the Ages*, (Oxford: Oxford University Press, 1954).

xxxi. For an overview of all of the areas involved in the in social psychology see Gardner Lindzey, *Handbook of Social Psychology* (Cambridge, MA: Addison-Wesley, 1968). For a general discussion of ethnography, see Clifford Geertz, *Local Knowledge* (New York: Basic Books, 1985), especially Chapter 7 "The Way We Think Now: Toward an Ethnography of Modern Thought."

xxxii. For more on this commonly overlooked issue, see John Hardwig, "Epistemic Dependence," *Journal of Philosophy*, (vol. LXXXII, No. 7, July 1985): 335-349. Hardwig cites an illustration of this issue taken from a recent issue of the *Physics Review Letter* in which some fifty physicists devoted approximately fifty man-years [!] of time to the analysis of 2.5 million pictures of a certain sub-atomic effect. Clearly, knowledge of this sort is far beyond the capacity of any individual other than Lazarus. The sheer complexity of much of contemporary science mandates such cooperation if continual progress is to be made.

xxxiii. See Janis' *Victims of Group think* (Boston: Houghton, Mifflin Company, 1972), and Janis and L. Mann, *Decision-making* (New York: Free Press, 1977), as well as P. E. Tetlock, "Identifying Victims of Group Think from Public Statements of Decision-makers," *Journal of Personal Social Psychology*, (vol. 37, 1979): 1314-24.

xxxiv. *Victims of Group Think*, 197-8.

GLOSSARY

A

Act utilitarianism: An ethical theory which maintains that actions are right or wrong depending on the consequences of the action in question. If the consequences of some action are good, the action is right, if they are bad the action is wrong.

Ad hoc **hypotheses**: A hypothesis advanced by a thinker solely for the purposes of explaining away inconveniently negative evidence. The hypothesis may nevertheless be true.

Ad hominem **argument**: Ignoring the position your opponent has advanced in a discussion and attacking the personhood of your opponent instead. This labels your opponent as a kind of negative expert, as a person whose position ought to be rejected out of hand because of some negative personal characteristic possessed by your opponent. Comes in two varieties—the **abusive** and the **circumstantial**. An abusive *ad hominem* argument works by heaping abuse on your opponent. (Ordinarily this is considered to be a fallacy.) The circumstantial *ad hominem* argument works by arguing that your opponent's special circumstances undercut his or her credibility as a witness to the truth of what s/he is saying. (This may be a strong argument.)

Ad populum **argument**: See argument from popularity.

Advertising: Has several legitimate purposes—to acquaint an audience with the existence and the nature of a product, to explain the purposes and uses of the product, to tell where the product may be obtained, and to sell the product—but can degenerate into mere propaganda when it engages in deceptive practices to sell products which may not possess the values advertisement claims for them. Then advertising is a form of lying.

Affirming the consequent: A formal fallacy of the format: 1) If A, then B. 2) B. 3) Therefore A. An invalid$_1$ deductive argument format.

Agnosticism: An epistemological position that maintains that one cannot know whether God (or gods) exists.

Algorithm: A problem solving technique that is guaranteed to work if it is correctly applied.

Ambiguity: A characteristic of words that have at least two entirely separate meanings. Ambiguous words easily give rise to verbal disputes, which can issue in the fallacy of equivocation.

Analogue: That part of an analogy to which the original is compared.

Analogy: A comparison between two or more things based on some factor that they already have in common. Analogies can be used as rhetorical devices, heuristic devices or methods of argument. Has the following components (where "Original" = the subject to be understood and "Analogue" = what the original is being compared to):

1. Original O has some set of properties X, Y, Z.
2. Analogue A has the same set of properties X, Y, Z.
3. Analogue A also has property P.
4. Therefore Original O probably has property P too.

Analogies are to be evaluated in terms of the following criteria:

1. The greater the number of objects within the kind between which the analogy holds, the stronger the comparison. [The breath of the comparison between objects.]
2. The more characteristics [X, Y, Z, etc.] the original and the analogue share, the stronger the comparison. [The depth of the comparison between objects.]
3. The fewer the differences between the original and the analogue, the stronger the comparison.
4. The more different kinds of objects share property P, the stronger the comparison.
5. The weaker the conclusion is claimed to follow from the premises, the stronger the reasoning for that comparison, but not for another possible comparison.
6. The greater the relevance of X, Y, Z to the possession of P, the stronger the comparison.

Analytical philosophy: An anti-metaphysical approach to philosophy which seeks instead to examine the conditions for thinking and speaking coherently about the world.

Anecdotes: Short and entertaining stories designed to illustrate some point. Also tidbits of data which provide little evidence upon which to base conclusions.

Analytic propositions: Those which can be known to be true simply by knowing the meaning of the terms which are contained in them. Analytic propositions are such that if they are true they cannot ever be false (or if they are false they cannot ever be true). Analytic propositions are true for all possible worlds. They are also known as **necessary truths**.

Anomalies: Phenomena that the existing explanatory schema seemingly cannot explain.

Antecedent: The part of a hypothetical proposition that begins with "if." ("If __, then __.")

Applied epistemology: Concerned with discovering what constitutes good reasons for maintaining and defending any given (controversial) opinion.

Apprenticeship model of learning: A theory of education consisting of three levels. On the first level, the student learns the basic concepts and facts in a subject area. In the second level, the student correctly applies the basic concepts to examples not used to teach the mastery of the first level. On the third level the student teaches others unfamiliar with the basic facts and concepts of the subject area.

A posteriori probability: Probability judgments which do not suppose that any of the three conditions for a priori probability judgments have been, or even can be, met beforehand for a given subject matter. Probability judgments which depend on empirical knowledge of past track records. Also called applied or empirical probability.

A priori probability: Probability judgments which must satisfy three conditions: 1) The range of the variable in question must be known in advance. 2) What constitutes a success must be specified in advance. 3) It must be known that each of the items in the range is equally likely to occur. The actual results are due to the laws of chance alone. Also called theoretical or mathematical probability.

Archetypes: Metaphors which are basic to the myths of many different cultures.

Argument: A series of claims, some of which (called premises) purport to provide evidence for the truth of others (called conclusions).

Argument format: The logical structure of a deductive argument which renders that argument valid₁ or invalid₁.

The argument from design: A cosmological argument for the existence of God which takes as its existential premise the claim that the universe (or some part of it) displays order and that only God could have caused such order.

Arguments from expert opinion: Inductive arguments which are evaluated in terms of seven conditions:

1. **Subject matter competence**. An expert E in some area S really must have special competence in that area. S/he just cannot claim to be an expert. Evidence of this competence must be demonstrable. Expertise in most fields is certified by recognized procedures.

2. **Evidence**. It should be possible in principle to give direct evidence to verify the claims made by an expert. What expert E claims to be true about subject S must be verifiable in principle by an appeal to the evidence that leads E to make these claims about S.

3. **Field of competence**. In order for E to be an expert on S, there must be a discipline S. If S is not a discipline, one cannot be an expert in it. In order to qualify as a discipline, subject matter S must have rules that govern the operation of events in S.

4. **Staying within the field of competence**. Experts are experts only within their discipline. Claims made by experts speaking on subjects outside of their field of competence deserve no more respect than claims made by any layperson. Authority is nontransferable.

5. **Experts can disagree**. Arguments utilizing appeals to authority can become ensnared by conflicting claims that are made by different authorities. It is naive to expect all experts to agree on everything in their discipline. All disciplines involve many issues that are completely unexplored or under explored. There are also bound to be many issues in which exploration has produced conflicting results. Expect experts to disagree at times.

6. **Correctly understanding the claims made by the authority**. By definition an appeal to an authority involves a layperson's attempt to prove a point by referring to opinions held by experts in areas in which the layperson has little or no competence. Experts are experts because they possess a great deal of discipline specific knowledge. Lay persons do not have this knowledge and may therefore easily misunderstand the claims the experts are making and thus falsely believe that an authority is claiming something the authority is not in fact claiming.

7. **Conflict of interest**. A conflict of interest may give experts motives for stating their claims so that their reliability as authorities may rightfully be questioned.

Argument from ignorance: The claim that the absence of evidence for something means that the thing is not true or does not exist. This may be a fallacy, depending on whether an adequate attempt has been made to search for all of the evidence. Absence of evidence may not be evidence of absence.

Argument from popularity (argument *ad populum*): To argue that something is true or false, good or bad because many people believe it or value it. This is a possible fallacy. Mere popularity does not necessitate truth or value, but popularity frequently is a sign of truth or value that can be overridden by the presentation of the evidence upon which the truth or value of the object is based.

The Aristotelian analysis of causation: Contains four factors which explain any change which something undergoes—**material**, **formal**, **efficient**, and **final**. The material cause of any change is that stuff which undergoes the change. The formal cause of any change is the set of properties, the possession of which makes an object the kind of object it is. The efficient cause of any change is that by which the change is brought about. The final cause of anything is that for the sake of which the thing is done, the thing's goal, or the end of the activity.

Assumptions: Presuppositions that make possible the states of affairs which are constructed from them. Extending this building metaphor, assumptions are the foundation upon which any given intellectual edifice is erected.

Atheism: A metaphysical position which claims that no God or gods exist.

Autonomy: The capacity and right that an individual or an organization has to select its own goals and values. This is generally understood to be an important moral or social value.

Availability heuristic: Thinking procedures which over-estimate the importance of particular pieces of data simply because these data make a psychologically strong impression on the mind, commonly because of their current availability.

Average: An ambiguous term which is used by statisticians to distinguish three different kinds of averages—**mean**, **median**, and **mode**. The mean is the arithmetic average. It is determined by adding all of the scores and dividing this total by the number of scores. Determination of the mean is the starting point of most statistical analysis.

B

Background conditions: All of the specific circumstances (e. g., instruments in proper working order) which must be right to assure the validity and reliability of an experiment.

Backtracking: A problem solving procedure which requires one to give up some territory you have already traveled. Also called detour problems because it is necessary to go backward in order to go forward. One must give up apparent progress for real progress. Real progress brings one closer to the goal only when the goal can actually be reached by that route.

Begging the question: (1) the hasty assertion of the truth of some claim which may in fact not be true or (2) the failure to recognize the assumptions upon which an opinion is built.

Betting line: An attempt to predict before hand the actual results of the contest and establish how much you will have to bet to win what reward.

Biased discounting: The underestimating of the actual likelihood of very bad consequences. A form of risk taking.

Biased sample: Samples which may look random to the untrained eye but are not. To make things even worse, samples which look obviously "loaded" may in fact really be random.

Blind: Tests in which the experimental subjects are ignorant of the purpose of the experiment or whether the subject is receiving the experimental drug, for example, or only a placebo.

Broad-based fallacy: Takes a rare event and makes it sound more commonplace by moving from one small group (who really are at risk) to a much broader group who really aren't at risk.

Burden of proof: To set the agenda of the discussion such that one side of the discussion has the obligation to refute the claims made by the opposition or loose the debate. An intellectual version of the child's game, king of the hill.

C

Category mistake: Errors in reasoning which are made when language users misunderstand the proper use (or the category) of language in a given case and misjudge the situation because they use the wrong system of evaluation to analyze the example in question. Category mistakes also refer to cases in which objects are incorrectly typed as belonging to a class to which they could not logically belong.

Causation: A relationship between any two things such that the first thing, the cause C, brings into the existence the second thing, the effect E. More generally, to say that something C causes the existence of some effect E is to say that: (1) C and E are spatially contiguous; (2) C occurs before E in time; (3) all Cs are constantly conjoined with Es; and (4) the existence of C necessitates the existence of E.

Ceremonial language: A use of language on important occasions in which the ritual repetition of certain words is used to embed the audience in some important ritual which traditionally has to be done in a certain manner to be done correctly.

Chaos theory: A metaphysical position which claims that in a long causal sequence, slight changes at an early stage of a complex can cause massive changes down the line. Metaphorically, this theory is sometimes called the butterfly effect.

Checks and balances: A division of governmental power and authority so that no single individual or subdivision of government may gain too much control over the rest. Designed to prevent tyranny.

Clerical hierarchy: The command structure within the priesthood of an organized religion.

Claim: A statement which maintains that something or other is the case. Claims must be either true of false, but not both at the same time.

Cognitive, **expressive**, and **directive language**: Three separate functions of language. Language is being used in its cognitive sense when its main purpose is to convey information. It is used in its expressive sense when its main purpose is to convey or express feelings and emotions. It is used in its directive sense when its main purpose is to convey commands, orders, or instructions. Confusion between these functions is a chief cause of category mistakes.

Cognitive dissonance: The unpleasant recognition that some of your beliefs are wrong or inconsistent.

Cognitive starter: A goal of critical thinking which seeks to help us through our psychological smugness that we already know "the truth, the whole truth, and nothing but the truth" about a particular subject matter by encouraging continual thought about the topic in question.

Cognitive stopper: Any limitation on the range of topics to which critical thinking may be applied.

Cognitively closed: The psychologically incapacity of understanding an issue owing to ignorance of that subject, lack of intelligence, inexperience, or the unwillingness of someone to attempt to grasp what it would even be like for the subject matter in question to be the case.

Cognitively open: The psychological willingness to attempt to understand a particular idea or viewpoint, regardless of how adept your understanding is in that area. The opposite of cognitively closed.

Coherence theory of truth: The claim that a proposition is true only because it fits into a wider body of other propositions, not because it corresponds to the facts.

Command theories of morality: Theories of morality which maintain that only certain people (or groups) have the authority to determine what is morally right or wrong, namely those who possess the power to create morality by issuing certain commands. Morality is equal to what has been commanded.

Common law: Traditional mores and procedures that are so ingrained in Western history that they represent the status quo from which the burden of proof has to be wrestled.

Common sense: Supposedly what allows you to see the truth of certain propositions which seem to be silly or downright stupid to deny. Can also be invoked to defend false beliefs from inspection.

Compatibilism: The metaphysical claim that free will and determinism are not mutually exclusive. Usually maintained be restricting the domain of one or the other.

Compatibility: A good hypothesis must be consistent with previously affirmed knowledge. Whatever truth is, all the things which are true are consistent with each other.

Compound argument: When a given set of claims contains an argument with more than one conclusion.

Compound claims: Propositions which are composed of two (or more) simple claims connected by a claim conjunction.

Compound probabilities estimate: A probability equation when there is more than one possible successful outcome. The opposite of a simple probability estimate.

Conceiving of: The subject or object of an idea or a concept. A synonym for understanding as.

Conceiving that: Conceiving that fulfills two functions. Conceiving that signifies that any conception can be expressed by asserting a proposition which is either true or false—true if the conception is correct, false if it is not. Conceiving that also signifies that any given conceptual claim is tied to a host of other possible claims both by the laws of logic and the theory in which the subject matter of the judgment is embedded. A synonym for understanding that.

Concepts: Ideas which form the basic material which enable you to think about and act within a subject area.

Conceptual knowledge: Knowledge based upon the understanding of the meaning of the concepts contained in the claims.

Conceptual truths: Claims which transcend empirical methods of analysis. Some of these claims may be true simply because of the way language is used in them, others purport to offer deeper insights about the logic of their subject matters.

Conclusion: What purports to be proven by the premises of an argument.

Conclusion indicators: Terms such as "it follows" and "therefore" which indicated that the statements they introduce are to be taken as conclusions of arguments.

Confidence fallacy: The belief that being confident amounts to being correct. There is in fact no correlation between how confident you are about being right about what you claim and how correct you really are.

Confirmation bias: Stemming from the thinker's mind set, this cognitive closer consists in the desire only to look for the evidence which will verify the thinker's pet theory and willfully neglecting to seek evidence which will falsify it. Should such unsought negative evidence nonetheless turn up, confirmation bias encourages the investigator to simply ignore it, or what is even worse, to treat it as funny evidence which really supports the theory in question.

Connotation: A set of rules used to establish a word's denotation.

Consequent: The part of a hypothetical proposition which begins with "then." ("If __, then __.")

Contingent truths: Claims which may be true at one time or place and false in another. The opposite of necessary truths.

Controls: Guidelines on an experimental situation which allow for the manipulation of only the variable in question and not the other variables which would otherwise impact the outcome of the experiment.

Conversation starter: The attempt by critical thinking to continue the dialogue and not stop short of full understanding about the subject in question.

Conversation stoppers: Devices to get those with whom we disagree to stop bugging us because what we think we know is undeniably true. "It's a fact—so why are you so dumb so as not to see this too?" or "That's just your opinion," are attempts at disarming and trivializing any possible objections to a position.

Correlation: A relationship found between two or more variables. If this relationship is positive, when one variable went up the other one did, too. If it is negative, when one variable went up the other one went down. Correlation should not be equated with causal relationship, the establishment of which requires further information.

Correspondence theory of truth: A theory of truth which maintains that a true statement is true because it "corresponds" (or points) to some state of affairs in the world.

Cosmological argument for the existence of God: All versions have two essential premises: (a) an existential claim which affirms the existence of some thing other than God (the gods) [e. g. the world, or motion, or a causal sequence] and (b) a causal claim that only God (the gods) could bring about or sustain the existence of the subject mentioned in the existential claim.

Cosmology: The branch of philosophy which deals with fundamental questions about the nature of the universe, such as did it have a beginning in time and is it limited in space.

Cost/benefit analysis: A decision method which lists expenses verses expected pay-offs in choosing between decision options.

Credibility: Questions about the reliability of the person making a report as a bearer of the truth. Does this person's have the right to be heard?

Critical thinking: A meta-discipline which seeks to determine whether the processes or results of ordinary thinking are valuable, sound, or valid. The giving of correct theoretical explanations for crucial material.

Crucial data: Irreplaceable evidence around which any proper understanding of what is being experienced is built.

Crucial experiments: A test believed by the scientific community to be so significant for establishing the truth of some controversial issue that the community, in fact, is willing to count the results of the test as definitive.

Crucial material: Ideas which are basic for any correct understanding of the subject in question. Alternative accounts can then be evaluated or rejected because of their inability to correctly account for the crucial material.

Cultural relativists: An ethical theory which maintains that morality is relative to the whole society making the moral judgment.

Cynic: A person who belittles someone else's beliefs about something by declaring that the other person's beliefs are really self-serving rationalizations designed to disguise the real (in the cynic's opinion) self-interested reasons for holding the doctrine in question.

D

Data: Evidence, generally provided by the senses. One of the essential components of empirical knowledge claims.

Decision making: Unlike problem solving, in which there are right or wrong answers, decision making deals only with better or worse choices, bearing in mind that all choices have positive and negative aspects.

Decision matrix: A grid which lists each choice cross indexed with all important positive and negative outcomes. Designed to overcome the limitations of availability heuristics.

Deductive argument: An argument is deductive if the premises purport to establish the conclusions with necessity.

Deductive nomological model: A model of explanation and hypothesis testing procedure in which a deductive argument is formulated using as its premises the laws and theories which form the backbone of any given discipline, the relevant background conditions, the hypothesis to be tested, and the appropriate initial states in order to derive a prediction regarding some new data. Should the prediction be verified, inductive weight would then affirm the probability of the hypotheses in question.

Definitions, **labels**, **characterizations**, or **descriptions**: Synonyms which refer to linguistic devices which attempt to establish exactly the meaning of a word or a phrase or attempt to pin down the objects to which the word can correctly point. Definitions serve five primary functions: a) eliminate vagueness, b) eliminate ambiguity, c) increase vocabulary, d) explain theoretical ideas, and e) influence beliefs or attitudes.

Deism: A theology which understands God to have created a world which now governs itself in terms of the natural laws instilled in it at creation. Personal communication with God is pointless in this theology.

Demand effect: Results research subjects are prone to report because they believe that this is what the experimenter really wants to see.

Denotation: A set made up of all the things a word may be correctly used to point or refer to.

Denying the antecedent: A formal fallacy of the format: 1) If A, then B. 2) Not A. 3) Therefore not B. An invalid$_1$ deductive argument format.

Deontological ethics: Maintains that there are certain actions which are inherently right or wrong independently of their actual consequences. These theories appeal to the nature (or ontos—hence the fancy name) of the activity in question. An individual act is right (or wrong) if it is an instance of a type of action which is inherently right (or wrong).

Dependent variables: Those experimental variables whose values are controlled by the independent variables. Dependent variables are the reputed effects in the experimental situation.

Determinism: A metaphysical position which holds that the cause C of an event E can only give rise to E and not any other outcome.

Detouring: Deviations from the normal forward working problem solving strategies when the normal route is blocked for any reason. Difficult to recognize at times and frustrating to deal with, they require at the very least backtracking and added effort.

Devil's advocate: A person assigned the job of purposely seeking to discover flaws in the decision making process of a group by pointing out the destructive role that cohesiveness, consensus, and insulation may play in the decision making process and by making sure that the internal environment doesn't override the external environment.

Dialectical thinking: Any reasoning which seeks to discover the rules which underlie a given linguistic term, game, social role, or intellectual discipline and subject these rules to a rigorous appraisal. This is often practiced in the form of a dialogue or conversation between two or more people.

Dilemma: A choice between only two options, each of which is bad. More generally, a choice between a limited number of options, each of which may or may not be bad.

The directive function of language: See the cognitive function of language.

Disjunctive syllogism: The valid$_1$ format—1) Either A or B. 2) Not A. 3) Therefore B.

Divine command ethics: Maintains that only God has the real power to create morality. What God commands (prohibits) is moral (immoral) and only because He commanded (forbids) it.

Dogmatism: The belief in or the assertion of a doctrine as true beyond question. This is one of the most common form of errors in reasoning. Because the truth of any opinion rests upon some set of assumptions or other, dogmatism commits the mistake of begging the question.

Domino theory: See slippery slope argument.

Double blind: Experimental situations in which neither the experimental subjects nor the persons running the experiment know which experimental subjects are receiving the test object and which are receiving placebos.

Double-whammy fallacy: "Heads I win; tails you lose." Thus in no way is it possible for the in group members to be in the wrong or for the out group members to be in the right no matter which characteristic a member of either group possesses.

Dualism: Any system of classification which divides a class into two separate and incompatible halves. More specifically, the metaphysical claim that humans are made up of two separate substances, minds (or souls) and bodies.

E

Education: The indoctrination of individuals new to an area into an accepted understanding of that area.

Egocentrism: The belief that the individual is the sole arbitrator of truth and value for himself.

Empirical truths: Claims which can be verified or falsified by experience, usually through the data presented by the senses.

Empiricism: A doctrine in epistemology which attempts to evaluate the question of what counts as a good reason for believing something. The empiricist claims that all knowledge about the world is somehow obtained through experience (chiefly sense experience) and certainly verified through experience.

Enthymeme: An argument any part of which is not explicitly stated.

Entrapment: A mind set which occurs when the thinker has already implemented a problem solving procedure or made a decision designed to resolve a particular difficulty but the chosen process hasn't as of yet succeeded in obtaining the desired result. Further time, effort, or money seems to be needed but there is also no guarantee that this further investment will produce the desired effect. The thinker now seems to be presented with a dilemma—either put more time, effort, or money into the original decision with no guarantee that what is added will produce the desired choice or put no more time, effort, or money into the situation and run the risk of seeing all of the previous efforts go for nought.

Epistemology: "Epistemology" is derived from the two Greek words "episteme" and "logos" and is translated in English as the theory of knowledge. This division of philosophy is concerned with the issues of what we know and how we know it. Epistemology is concerned with the question, How do we know that? (where "that" means any particular thing which we think we know). This question can be understood in two different senses. First, it may mean: How did we discover that or find out about that? Where did you read it, hear it, see it? Who told you? Secondly, the question, "How do we know that?" may also mean something more complicated: How should we go about verifying whether that is really true or not? The question is not simply whether these claims are true or false, but how beliefs about them could be confirmed or verified by anyone. What would or could count as good reasons for saying that we know these things, or anything at all?

Equivocation: A mistake in reasoning in which an argument employs a term with two entirely different meanings without recognizing the ambiguity contained therein.

Essence: The essence of something is the list of characteristics, each of which must be present to make that thing the kind of thing it is.

Ethical authority: One who possesses the right by virtue of his or her wisdom or power to make valid ethical judgments.

Ethical egoism: A theory of morality which maintains that what makes an act right is that it succeeds in its aim, which is always to benefit the agent.

Ethical relativism: Theories of morality which claim that judgments of right and wrong are dependent upon (or relative to) the identity of the person(s) making the judgment. Comes in the form of personal, group or cultural relativists. Each form allows for multiply correct moral claims.

Ethics: One of the oldest branches of philosophy. There are two main divisions within ethics—that branch which deals with issues concerning what is of intrinsic value and that branch which deals with issues concerning right or wrong conduct.

Ethnocentrism: The assumption that the way the in group thinks and the values that the in group shares are the correct (or only) ways to think and things to value.

Ethnography: A division of anthropology which deals with the origins, divisions, and characteristics of humans.

Euphemisms: Emotionally neutral expressions which are used to describe emotionally negative things or activities so as to make what is inherently questionable more respectable. The opposite of malphemisms.

Evidence: Commonly discovered through experience. One of the key components in the construction of knowledge in that in the absence of evidence a person is not going to perceive anything. Also called data and sense data.

Executive legal authority: The legal right and power to enforce the law. The head of the state or government.

Existentialism: A theory of morality which maintains that there is no intrinsic right or wrong in actions, but rather actions are made right or wrong by being chosen by those who perform them.

Exit polling: A sampling technique in which voters who have just finished voting are questioned about their opinions. Generalizations regarding the outcome of elections, for example, are then made from these samples.

Expert: A person with a high degree of competence in a given subject area who knows many facts about the subject area unknown to the average person and who also knows the theoretical basis of the subject matter.

Explanation: A) Something is explained when it (or its occurrence) no longer is felt as surprising. Explanation seeks to transform the surprising into the ordinary, the unfamiliar into the familiar. B) Regarding classes of events involving things like activities or actions, explanations take the form of reasons.

They purport to offer the reasons why, for example, someone did something or refrained from doing anything in a certain situation. C) A sense of explanation which frequently overlaps with the one just mentioned involves the reference to purpose. Someone has a purpose for doing what s/he did if s/he had some sort of goal in mind. Objects may have purposes, too. They may be designed to perform certain functions. D) Another sense of explanation involves the inclusion of that which is to be explained into a class of events. When the item to be explained is itself already a class, explaining it consists in showing that the original class is a subset of a greater class.

The expressive function of language: See the cognitive function of language.

Extending the analogy: Stretching the comparison between two or more things until the comparison becomes absurd. Can be done with any analogy.

External environment: The external environment consists of whatever problem or issue with which the group happens to be dealing.

Extrinsic value: That which is valuable or desirable for the sake of what it produces. The opposite of intrinsic value.

F

Facts and **opinions**: Facts are usually understood to be those matters about which everyone agrees, or which are undeniably true, or about which an already established method (e. g., looking) could easily determine. Opinion is a label for the correlative of "fact," namely, for those issues about which either there is no agreement, which are not undeniably true (or even true at all), which are expressions of preferences, or about which there is no ready method which could be used to easily determine their truth. Facts are things which we know (or could know); "opinions" are things which we may only properly believe. Facts must be true. Opinions may be false.

Failure to accept the logical task: An error in reasoning which consists in the substitution for the assigned task—which is the determination of the validity of a deductive argument—with another possible task—which may be the determination of the truth value of the given premises (or conclusion) of the argument or of different premises (or conclusion) than the ones actually given because the thinker didn't like the actual premises (or conclusion).

Fair: Probability situations in which each possible outcome in the range has an equal chance of occurring. A component of *a priori* probability. The opposite of skewed.

Faith: Believing in something or in someone; accepting the truth of what s/he says or the reality and value which s/he stands for when that truth, reality, or value presently (or permanently) exceeds the possibility of verification. Because the objects of faith go beyond the possibility of knowledge, it is wrong to call faith a form of knowledge. Faith exists in the absence of knowledge, not as a form of knowledge. It is also perfectly possible to have a mistaken faith in something or someone. In this sense, faith resembles belief, not knowledge.

Fallacy: An incorrect way of reasoning; a poor reason for believing in the truth of something, even if that thing is, in fact, true.

Fallacy of the suppressed correlative: Correlatives are terms which are defined as the negation of each other (e.g., hot/cold; up/down) and rightfully applied only to one end of a spectrum of objects. When one of the terms is improperly used to define the whole spectrum, the fallacy has been committed. Similar to the problem of marked terms.

False dilemma: The incorrect belief that all option choices are bad or that there are only a limited number of options in a given situation.

False memory syndrome: The psychologically persuasive, but mistaken belief that one remembers something when one is merely imagining that s/he remembers that thing.

False negatives: Analysis of test results or data which fails to find correlation or causal relationships which do, in fact, exist.

False positive: Analysis of test results or data which seem to indicate a correlation or a causal relationship when none, in fact, exists.

Falsifiability: The flip side of verification. A good scientific hypothesis is highly falsifiable but not falsified.

Formal fallacy: Any logically invalid deductive argument whose mistake lies in its incorrect structure. There are many varieties of formal fallacies.

Formula: See algorithm.

Free will (free choice): A metaphysical position which holds that persons have the power to make completely different decisions and choices or do entirely different things even when all the states of affairs which immediately precede these decisions, choices, or actions remain completely the same. It is generally believed that free will and determinism are incompatible.

The free will defense: An attempt to solve the problem of moral evil by claiming that God gave humans free will from which evil springs contrary to the wishes of God.

Frequency: How often a particular situation occurs, usually expressed as a statistic. It refers to the numerator of the probability fraction when probability is expressed by a fraction.

Frequency curve: A graph, the function of which is to provide a pictorial presentation of statistical information. Graphs are presented with two axes. The horizontal axis represents the range of the variable being considered, the vertical axis the frequency of appearance of items in the range. If the resulting picture comes close to being symmetrical, it is called a normal distribution curve. This is the well known bell shape curve.

G

Gambler's fallacy: The mistaken assumption that in a game of chance past results actually effect the odds of future results. They don't.

Generalization: Inductive arguments which: 1) Refer to classes of things which share at least one—and usually many—possible variable(s). 2) Pick out a few examples (the sample population) from the main class (the whole population). 3) Attribute certain characteristics to these samples. 4) Draw conclusions about the whole population based upon the evidence presented by the sample.

Good reasons: The analysis of whether the motives or principles involved in as issue can withstand critical inspection, the ultimate goal of which is being right for the right reasons.

Group relativist: A moral theory which maintains that morality is relative to some sort of sub-cultural unit such as the family, the clan, or the ethnic group.

Group think: A term which describes the role which collectives play in shaping what individuals think as well as the way they think. This is studied by a branch of psychology called social psychology and a branch of sociology and anthropology called ethnography, which distinguish between the internal and the external environment in which the collective operates.

Group think syndrome: The possibility that a group of otherwise intelligent persons will make a terribly decision because of group cohesiveness, (the positive attraction of each group member to the group), consensus, (the positive feelings generated by group solidarity), and insulation, (the need to maintain the cohesiveness and consensus in the in group by downplaying or ignoring the virtues of the out group).

H

Hallucination: A "perceptual" mistake which occurs when the perceiver seems to be experiencing something, but there is no objective reality which corresponds to what the perceiver seems to be experiencing. For example, "hearing" voices.

Hasty generalization: A fallacy in which a general conclusion is drawn about a whole class of objects based solely upon evidence taken from only a few members of that class when it is not known whether the sample is sufficiently similar to the whole population and when the sample, in fact, may not be sufficiently similar to the whole population.

Hedonism: Identifies intrinsic goodness with pleasure.

Henotheism: A religious system which believing in many gods, of which one [supreme] god is the chief one to be worshiped.

Heuristic device: A practical rule of thumb which shows some promise as a means for the accomplishment of some desired goal, in many cases the problem being working on.

Hidden agenda: To bring into question the motives or intentions behind a position as distinct from the surface intentions of its defender.

Hindsight: The review of a decision which assumes that the thinker already knew in advance of the decision that the choice made would turn out poorly.

Hume's analysis of causation: Maintains that to say that something C causes the existence of some effect E is to say that: 1) C and E are spatially contiguous; 2) C occurs before E in time; 3) all Cs are constantly conjoined with Es; and 4) the existence of C necessitates the existence of E.

Hypothesis: An educated guess designed to bridge the gap between the initial state and the solution of a problem. Hypotheses are heuristic devices.

Hypothetical statement: Any statement that has the logical form: If A, then B, where A and B stand for specific claims.

I

Ideology: A systematic body of beliefs held by an individual or a class of individuals in terms of which judgments of reality and value are made.

Ill-defined problem: One in which the starting point, ending point, or solution pathways are not or cannot be understood.

Imagination: A fundamental component of thinking. More than the ability to form "pictures in our heads" which are "copies" of original experiences or ideas or which are constructed from bits and pieces of ideas, the imagination is the mental ability to supply missing data. Imagined things may or may not be real or have happened, nor are all images "picture copies" of their originals.

Immortality of the soul: The claim—sometimes offered in the form of a proof—that the soul is incapable of being destroyed.

Independent variables: Those experimental variables, the values of which are established or fixed by the experimenter first. They represent the reputed cause in the experimental situation.

Indoctrination: To get that individual to believe something, frequently (though not necessarily) without questioning it. A basic component of education.

Inductive argument: Arguments which claim only that the premises make the conclusion likely or probable, not necessary. A good inductive argument is a strong one; a poor inductive argument is a weak one. It always makes sense to say with any inductive argument that the addition of further evidence will strengthen (or weaken) the probability that the conclusion does, in fact, follow from the argument's premises.

Infinite regress argument: A fallacy in which the issue to be explained in the conclusion of an argument reappears in the premises of the argument repeatedly, no matter how many layers of premises are added to the original argument.

Informal fallacy: The sort of logical error made by poor inductive arguments in that they fail to provide strong evidence or reasons to establish their conclusions, though their conclusions may still be true.

In groups: A collection of individuals who form and utilize stereotypes in order to characterize persons or things (the out group) which do not properly belong to the in group.

Internal environment: The dynamics which occur within a society or a group and influence that group's ability to solve problems (the external environment).

Intrinsic value: That which is valuable or desirable for its own sake. The opposite of extrinsic value.

Intuition: A cognitive ability which enables the mind to recognize the truth of certain basic ideas directly independently of any ability to explain how this is done.

Isomorphic: When two or more things possess exactly the same structure or materials.

J

Jargon: Language identified with certain professions or trades (as in the jargon of the philosopher) designed to indicate distinctions that the dominant culture sees no need to make.

The judicial system: The governments power to judge the legality of what is brought before it, whether it concerns a law, a social program, funding, an executive action, actions of private citizens, or even the decisions or processes of other judges or judicial systems itself.

Jury nullification: When the application of the law to the evidence is ignored by the jury in favor of some other non-legal or extra legal standard such as fairness or prejudice. When this is done by the judge in a trial situation, it is called **judicial nullification**.

K

Knowledge: Commonly defined by philosophers as justified, true belief obtained or defended in the right manner. To believe something is to have an opinion about that topic, to think that something is the case. But beliefs can be either true or false, while there is no such thing as false knowledge. For any belief to qualify as knowledge it must be true. But it cannot be accepted as true by the thinker for the wrong reasons. For a belief to qualify as knowledge it must be justified, which means that the thinker must believe it for the right kinds of reasons, for example, it was obtained in a reliable manner.

Knowledge by acquaintance: (Commonly) direct or immediate knowledge of the data of the senses, memories, and the introspective awareness of our own self and our thoughts, feelings, and desires.

Knowledge by description: Indirect or mediated knowledge derived by applying general principles to what is known directly through acquaintance.

L

Labeling: The identification of an object's essence with certain characteristics which it might only possess accidentally.

Law$_1$: Any statement is a law (or a law of nature) if it is an empirical proposition which refers universally and necessarily to all of the members of some class of phenomena.

Law$_2$: Any rule of conduct passed by a duly authorized legislature. Laws may first have to survive court challenges or executive overrides to be valid.

Law of (Non)Contradiction: A basic axiom of logic which states that all claims must be either true of false, but not both at the same time.

Law of Excluded Middle: A basic axiom of logic which says that all claims are either true or false and there is no other possibility between being true and being false.

Law of small numbers: The mistaken belief that a few—or even one—instance of a negative (positive) report is believed over what is already known to be many instances of positive (negative) reports. The belief that the exceptional are more important or telling than the common.

The laws of chance: Situations in which the appearance of each instance of a variable is equally likely.

Lawyers: Legal professionals with expertise in knowing how to present positions for their clients in ways which work within the rule of the legal, judicial game to the benefit of the client, regardless of the non-legal merits of the client.

Legal reasoning: This is based on arguments from authority, the authority of the legislature in making the laws, the executive branch of government in enforcing the law, and the judicial branch of government in interpreting the law. This is used to decide civil right.

Legislative legal authority: That branch of government which enacts the laws and programs which are to govern society and funds the bills which are to pay for these programs.

Lexical definition: Designed to either clear up cases of ambiguity or to settle vocabulary questions. Found in dictionaries, which list each of the ordinary meanings of a word as it is used by a population in order of the frequency of its use.

Limited authority: Experts in one field who make pronouncements on fields which are relevantly similar to their own.

Literalism: A theory of interpretation which maintains that the truth or meaning of a metaphor can always be reduced to a list of properties that the original really possesses.

Lobbyists: Persons with no formal legal legislative power, but who commonly possess significant practical ability to persuade the legislature to adopt a specific position on some view of importance to their employer.

Logic: The branch of philosophy which studies the concepts, rules, and paradigms which govern the correct use of reasoning.

The logic of an analogy: The principles of reasoning which connect together the specific component ideas of an analogy. What the analogy is all about.

M

Magic: The attempt to force the compliance of some part of the environment by the mere use of the right words or formula. This can be confused with science when the observer is ignorant of the theory or technology behind the solution.

Malphemisms: Emotionally negative expressions which are substituted for emotionally neutral things or activities so as to raise questions about what is not inherently questionable. The opposite of a euphemism.

Manichaein dualism: A theological system which believes in two equally powerful but ethically opposed gods which are eternally at war with each other using the cosmos as their battleground.

Margin of error: Refers to the possibility of error regarding the representativeness of the data sampling. Most researchers accept the .05 level as having established good statistical evidence that a causal relationship does indeed exist here within the stated margin of error.

Marked term: A situation in which one of a pair of terms which are used to describe opposite characteristics is used neutrally to describe the whole range of items in question. A term that can be used indifferently to designate either the whole range of items or only one end of the range of items. To refer to a term as "marked" is not simply to theoretically characterize it. Marked terms are also essentially evaluative.

The material of an analogy: A comparison between two or more things based on the similarity of their contents.

Materialism: A metaphysical position which maintains that all reality is composed of physical substances and their properties. More narrowly, the claim that there are no nonmaterial substances (e. g., souls) and that what are commonly called immaterial substances are really composed of bodies.

Mean: The mean is the arithmetic average. It is determined by adding all of the scores and dividing this total by the number of scores. Determination of the mean is the starting point of most statistical analysis.

Means-end analysis: A problem solving technique which presupposes that the original goal can be broken down into a series of mutually exclusive but mutually supportive sub goals.

Mechanical metaphor: A device which treats persons as if they were machines.

Median: The score which lies in the exact middle of a range of scores when the scores are rank ordered from lowest to highest. If there is an even number of scores the mean of the middle two scores forms the median.

Memory: The capacity of the mind to recall past experiences, commonly through the use of images. This capacity can be divided into factual memory and performance memory. Some factual "memories" may only be apparent, not real.

Mere exposure effect: The psychological fact that the more often a person hears something, the more likely they are to believe it. Repetition encourages belief, even when what is repeated is incorrect. This is a problem for empiricism.

Meta-discipline: Any subject area which examines the validity of the presuppositions of another subject area. Philosophy is a meta-discipline.

Metaphor: A comparison between two things which are not generally thought to have anything in common.

Metaphysics: The branch of philosophy which deals with the ultimate nature of reality. Traditionally divided into cosmology and ontology.

Mill's Methods: Methods used to determine causal relationships.

1. **The Method of Agreement**: This seeks correlation between the presence of two kinds of phenomena, one of which (C) is suspected to be the cause of another phenomenon (E). If experience shows that whenever C appears E also appears, then you have a good reason for saying that C is a sufficient condition of E.

2. **The Method of Difference**: This seeks the absence of the suspected effect E is correlated with the absence of the suspected cause C. This discovers necessary conditions for the presence of whatever it is you are trying to investigate.

3. **The Joint Method**: This combines the method of agreement and the method of difference and allows the establishment of E if and only if C.

4. **The Method of Residues**: This systematically eliminates all the possible causes of E except for one. First, there must be a known and limited number of possible variables. Secondly, the method works only if it is possible to eliminate the false causes from the list. Eliminating all the possible variables but one in this fashion without at the same time eliminating the effect establishes that the effect was in fact caused by the remaining variable.

5. **The Method of Concomitant Variation**: This addresses the question of how much C causes how much E for how long. The greater the one (C), the greater the other (E) if it is a positive correlation; or the greater C, the less E if it is a negative correlation.

Mind-set: The psychologically conditioned patterns of expectations and responses which the knower brings to the knowledge situation which encourages the knower to see things in certain ways and not in others.

Mode: The score in a group of scores which appears the most often. There may be more than one mode in any given group.

Model: A whole range of interlocking ideas which have successfully been used to explain particular phenomena and predict the existence of other phenomena. A model must be isomorphic to its original in important ways to be accurate.

Modeling: A problem solving technique which assumes that if a scale model or practice works as planned, the actual craft or event will work, too. This presupposes that the modeling behavior is isomorphic to the original.

Modus ponens: A valid$_1$ deductive argument format which has the form: 1) If A, then B. 2) A. 3) Therefore B, where A and B stand for any simple claim.

Modus tollens: A valid$_1$ deductive argument format which has the form: 1) If A, then B. 2) Not B. 3) Therefore not A, where A and B stand for any simple claim.

Monotheism: A religious system which believes in only one God.

Mystical religious experience: Knowledge of God through direct first-hand experience. Commonly described as ineffable by those who experience it.

Myth$_1$: Stories which make sense out of symbols.

Myth$_2$: False stories which may still be believed.

N

Naive realism: An epistemology which holds that the things which we perceive really do exist just like we perceive them to be and that the process of perception accurately transmits knowledge of these things to the mind of the perceiver.

Natural law: A metaphysical label used to stand for what is considered to be the unalterable and perfect moral/physical laws of nature laid down for man by God.

Natural religion: The attempt to derive religious truths from the study of the natural world through the use of reason alone. This perspective does not utilize revelation.

Necessary conditions: Conditions for event E in the absence of which E cannot take place.

Necessary truths: See analytic propositions.

Negative correlation: The greater the amount of one variable, the less of another.

Negative expert: The opposite of a real expert. *Ad hominem* arguments work by labeling their subjects as persons whose position ought to be rejected out of hand because of some negative personal characteristic or circumstance possessed by them.

Negative skew: A variation from a normal distribution curve such that more items exist above the 50th percentile than would be expected given a normal distribution of the variable in question.

Neologism: Using an old word to mean something new or inventing an entirely new word. A living language is inherently dynamic. Language users frequently find that no existing word adequately captures what needs to be said. Neologisms are invented to fill these gaps.

Newspeak: A neologism coined by George Orwell in *1984*. It refers to the government's attempts to remove lexical meanings of terms from the dictionary so as to diminish the range of thought. An application of the Sapir-Worf hypothesis of linguistic relativity.

Non sequitur: An invalid₁ argument whose conclusion does not follow from its premises.

Normal distribution curve: The spread of data in the well-known bell shape curve, the mid point of which represents the mean, median, and mode for that data.

Null hypothesis (H₀): The hypothesis to be tested by statistical analysis (H₁) claims that there is a statistically significant relationship between the variables in question. The null hypothesis means that there is no causal relationship between the variables specified by the hypothesis and changes in variables are due to the operation of chance alone. The purpose of applying a statistical analysis to the data is to rule out the null hypothesis.

O

Objective probability estimates: A priori or a posteriori probability. Rational probability judgments. The opposite of subjective probability estimates.

Ockham's razor: Named after the fourteenth century monk who first formulated it. "Plurality is not to be assumed without necessity." An hypothesis which will explain all of the evidence is preferable to a more complicated hypothesis which assumes the truth of things unwarranted by existing evidence.

Ontological argument: An argument for the existence of God which claims that because God's nature includes perfection and existence is a part of perfection, God must exist.

Ontological metaphor: A comparison between two or more things based solely on the claim that they are of similar types.

Ontology: That part of metaphysics which deals with the basic divisions of reality.

Operational definitions: Definitions which attempt to nail down the precise meaning of the variables involved in the experiment so that those who seek to replicate the experiment may start from the same beginning point regarding the variables in question.

Opinion: See fact.

Optical illusion: A perceptual mistake which occurs when it appears to the perceiver that something is happening in the world when what is actually happening does not resemble what appears to be happening.

Ordinary thinking: The capacity to correctly follow the basic rules of a subject matter. Found in the first and second level of the apprenticeship model of learning.

Orientational metaphor: A re-categorizing of something based on the claim that the original should be seen in a fundamentally new way.

Original subject: The subject of an analogy or a metaphor.

Ostensive definitions: A definition which attempts to define a term by supplying a paradigm example of it for the viewer's inspection. Typically used in science to give the reader of a report a more precise understanding of the value of a variable.

Out groups: Persons or things which stereotypes label. See in groups.

Outlier: An instance of a variable which lies at the extreme end of the range of data used in a statistical analysis. Outliers are usually dropped from the analysis immediately because their inclusion would deform the mean for that sample.

P

Pantheism: The identification of God (the gods) with nature.

Paradigms: Examples of materials and procedures that are so important to the proper understanding of a given subject matter they define the discipline by example. Paradigms are best understood as definitive illustrations. Paradigm examples don't simply tell you what is the case, they tell you what is importantly the case.

Paradox: Statements which seem to be both true and false at the same time.

The paradox of democracy: The problem that one who loses an election is none-the-less bound to accept the governance of a leader that s/he thinks is incompetent and/or a party platform which s/he thinks is incorrect.

Paternalism: The claim that someone else has the power, right and duty to make decisions on behalf of another person when doing so is in the best interest of that other person.

Percentile equivalencies: The percentile equivalency tells what percentage of the total sample lies within each standard deviation. O standard deviation equals the 50th percentile.

Perceptual knowledge: Knowledge claims applied to the world of sense experience for its subject matter and its data, but also dependent upon conceptual knowledge in that there are no data without a theory, and there is no theory without data.

The performance factor: Problem solving or decision making situations in which the right or best choice is known, but cannot be acted upon due to the incapacity of the agent(s) situation or abilities.

Performative language: A use of language in which the actual expression of the terms in question brings about the state of affairs to which the words refer.

Personal metaphor: A device which labels or treats an impersonal object as if it were a person. Also called anthropomorphism and personification.

Personal relativists: An ethical doctrine which maintains that morality is relative to the individual making the judgment.

Personal religious experiences: The claim that an individual's own direct, immediate experience of God or God's will has ultimate religious authority.

Persuasive definition: Definitions which attempt to influence attitudes and beliefs. They are commonly used to set the agenda for the audience when reasoning about a particular topic.

Philosophy: The pursuit or love of wisdom. Wisdom is generally understood to have two components, theoretical (sophia, how to know well) and practical (phronesis, how to do well).

Phronesis: Practical wisdom; knowing how to act or choose well in a given situation.

Placebos: Inert substance which none the less produces some effect in the experimental subjects because of the subject's believe that s/he ought to be experiencing that effect, and therefore s/he does "experience" the demand effect.

.05 level (Point zero five level): This means that only 5 times out of 100 samples would this statistical relationship result from chance alone as a result of sampling error.

.001 level (Point zero zero one level): Sometimes researchers want even greater precision than the .005 level and they will apply an analysis which is significant at the .001 level. This means that there is only 1 chance in 1,000 that the sample data results were due to chance alone.

Political leadership: Those who possess the actual political power within a state or a political party.

Political parties: A group of individuals united around a common political philosophy. Different political parties inevitably have their own list of qualified persons (**party leadership**) and laws and programs (**party platform**) which they seek to get elected, accepted or enacted.

Political philosophy: A set of ideas and ideals used by a political party to form its platform.

Polytheism: A religious system which believes in many gods.

Positive correlation: The more of one variable the more of another.

Positive law morality: A moral theory which holds that the leaders of the state are those who possess the rightful power of command in the form of the various edicts and laws passed by these leaders. This theory collapses the distinction between legal and moral right.

Positive skew: A variation of the normal distribution curve such that more items are found below the 50th percentile than would be allowed by a normal distribution of the variable in question.

Possible world: An imaginary construct by philosophers designed to serve as a thought experiment to examine the validity of some particular belief.

***Post hoc* arguments**: Latin for *post hoc, ergo propter hoc*, which means "after it, therefore because of it." A possible fallacy. To say that X and Y are temporally correlated (*post hoc*) does not necessarily entail that X and Y are causally related (*propter hoc*).

Precedent: The legal practice of citing previous court decisions which support a position or by citing the (English) common law tradition from which our formal legal system originated.

Precising definition: A definition designed to narrow the possible applications of a vague term.

Prediction: Empirical consequences believed to follow logically from the conjunction of the theories and laws of the discipline and the given hypothesis in question.

Prejudice: A (questionable) prejudgment which the knower brings to the knowledge situation on the basis of which the situation is seen as a certain sort of situation.

Premise: A claim in an argument which purports to provide the evidence for the argument's conclusion.

Premise indicators: Words like "If," "given that," and "since" which function in statements to indicate that the statement is to be taken as a premise in an argument.

Primer: A textbook for beginners.

Privileged position: To, in fact, possess unique information about a subject owing to the accident of circumstances which anyone else could have had, but didn't.

Probability: Informally, the odds or chances of something happening. More formally, the relationship formed by dividing the frequency of an object's occurrence by the range of all possible instances of that object.

The problem of evil: A problem for natural religion. If the world is a product of a perfectly good, all knowing, all-powerful divinity (or set of divinities), how could there be any natural or moral evil in it? Contains two subdivisions: **The problem of moral evil**: If humans are the creations of God (the gods), why do we ever sin? And **the problem of natural evil**: If the world is a product of a perfectly good, all knowing, all-powerful divinity (or set of divinities), how can there exist such natural disasters as plagues, hurricanes, or droughts?

The problem of induction: Since a true universal claim cannot be validly deduced from a true claim about a particular subset of the greater set, what reasons can be given for saying that all members of a given set have a certain property merely because some of them do? What reasons can be given for saying that any as yet unexamined case is like any examined case? A challenge to empiricist epistemology. See generalization arguments above.

Problem solving: Issues in which there are correct and incorrect choices and the agent is required to choose between them.

Problem space: The gap between the statement of the initial conditions of a problem and its solution. This space may consist of a knowledge gap or a performance gap.

Proof₁: In logic, a synonym for a sound deductive argument, or for that arguments' conclusion.

Proof₂: In science, the successful application of the deductive nomological methodology to a problem. Not to be confused with Proof₁. Any scientific claim is always subject to revision pending further evidence.

Propaganda: The use of language and ideas designed to persuade the audience about the truth, justice, or rightness of its subject matter. In propaganda, persuasion becomes more important than truth. Propaganda makes frequent use of euphemisms and malphemisms.

Proportion: A comparison between only specific components of a complex system.

Proposition: A synonym for claim or statement.

Proving a negative: The attempt to establish the claim that "There are no Xs," where "X" = some matter of fact. Absence of evidence is not necessarily evidence of absence. This attempt may be especially difficult because of practical empirical limitations or availability heuristics.

Proximity argument: The spacial analogue of the temporal *post hoc* argument. This argument moves from the fact that cause and effect work by physical contact or touch to the claim that any physical association is not merely accidental, but causal. This may be a fallacy.

Pseudo-science: A system of thought which passes for a well established science or discipline but cannot pass the tests which any discipline has to meet in order to really be considered scientific. Pseudo-scientific beliefs are generally false and/or silly.

Psychological egoism: A metaphysical theory that claims that agents always act in their own perceived self-interest.

Q

Questionable statistics: Statistical claims which one may be inclined to accept at first glance, but they may prove to be dubious upon further inspection. They need to be checked.

R

Racial/ethnic language: Language which either (a) identifies the race or ethnic character of the person to whom it refers when to do so is inappropriate to the context of the discussion, (b) treats all racial or ethnic groups as if they are really all members of one racial or ethnic class (in English speaking cultures, usually white, Northern Europeans are assumed to be the dominant class), or (c) treats all racial or ethnic groups as if they were inherently inferior to the paradigm class.

Random sampling: A data gathering technique in which ideally each member of the subject class has an equal chance of being chosen.

Range: The possible spread of a variable.

Rational risk assessment: This takes into account three factors: (a) the objective probability of harmful or good consequences, (b) the severity or extent of the harmful or good consequences, and (c) the reversibility of the harmful or the good effects.

Rationalism: An epistemology which maintains that there is at least some knowledge about the world which can be obtained independently of (sense) experience.

Reasons: The principles or motives, be they right or wrong, which underlie an issue or a person's position on that issue.

Reductio ad absurdum: Reduction to absurdity. A shorthand version of a refutation by logical analogy in which only the conclusion of an apparently dumb argument is presented to show the silliness of another argument or position.

Reductionism: The metaphysical claim that a particular level of being or reality can be correctly understood to be another, different, underlying level.

Refutation by logical analogy: The construction of an argument which is logical parallel to a given argument, but whose conclusion is absurd to show the absurdity of the conclusion of the original argument. See *reductio ad absurdum* above.

Regress argument: An argument in which the supposed explanation of some situation is itself just as much in need of an explanation as the original issue. An "explanation" which really explains nothing.

Regression towards the mean: Scores which lie at the extreme end of a distribution scale tend not to be duplicated during retests. They tend to appear closer to the mean.

Regularity view of causation: The notion that any individual causal instance must be understood as a subset of a larger set consisting of all relevantly similar situations.

Relative frequency: The comparison of the numerators of the numbers being compared by probability fractions when the denominators of the probability fractions being compared remain unchanged. Relative frequency and frequency are interchangeable only when the denominators are the same.

Comparisons between frequencies otherwise are fallacies. See frequency above.

Relativity theory of truth: The position that a true claim is true relative only to some person's or peoples' beliefs. In this theory many otherwise apparently contradictory claims can be true if they are held to be true by different persons or peoples.

Relevance: An hypothesis is relevant to a problem when some fact which you are trying to explain is logically deducible from the background theories which govern the subject area of the experiment together with the proposed hypothesis, which is not deducible merely from the background theories alone. A relevant hypothesis adds something to the explanation of the problem which cannot be determined without the hypothesis.

Relevant similarity argument: An inductive argument format which claims that its variables bear enough likeness to establish further likeness to other variables, properties or objects.

Reliable: An experiment which consistently measures what it is designed to measure and not something else.

Reliabilism: A knowledge heuristic which usually works but is not infallible.

Religion: A human construct which embodies and attempts to understand or relate to the divine. It contains some or all of the following components—sacred texts, cult worship practices, social/clerical structure, traditions, revelation, systems, and natural reasoning. It may also include claims about the being and nature of God (the gods), the problem of evil, and the nature of man and the immortality of the soul.

Religious arguments: Any reasoning format designed to establish the truth of some religious claim. These must be supported by the methods appropriate within a religious tradition. No agreed upon system exists for evaluating these arguments across religious traditions.

Religious authority: One who has the right, duty, and power to decide religious questions. Who is an authority on these matters can ordinarily be settled within a religious tradition, but across traditions no consensus has been reached for legitimate appeals to authority.

Religious cult practices: All religions engage in activities some of which are formalized in terms of worship, which include ritual behavior which exists to define correct religious practices.

Religious revelation: A source of knowledge which treats the recipient as a passive subject of experience of the divine. Usually contrasted to reason.

Religious social/clerical structure: The bureaucratic side of religion occasioned by the social needs of the institutions and communities in which its practitioners live.

Religious systems: Invoke the divine as the supernatural source or essence of the natural world which, as such, is the proper subject of religious attention or worship. In western culture this is chiefly manifested in polytheistic, henotheistic, or monotheistic form.

Religious texts: Written documents or collections of oral sayings attributed to God or the founder of a religious tradition.

Religious traditions: The historical record of a religious system. Often recognized by its duration and the number of its followers, e. g., Christianity, Islam, Buddhism. Religious cult practices, texts, social structures, etc. apply only within a given tradition, not across traditions, though sometimes different traditions have similar practices, etc..

Requirement of total evidence: 1) The thinker must make every reasonable effort to assure the accuracy of the data being considered. 2) The thinker must not fail through inattention or sloth to consider whether key issues are being ignored in the argument being analyzed. 3) The thinker must consider whether the premises of the argument are relevant to the conclusion being advanced.

Retrospective review: The review of your judgment taking into account only what was in fact known (or should have been known) at the time and not what post decision events later established.

Rhetoric: The function of rhetoric is to persuade some particular audience of the truth or value of the topic at issue.

Rights: Legitimate moral or legal claims either to be given certain things (positive rights) or to be free from interference from others in certain ways (negative rights).

Risk aversion: A problem solving strategy which stresses the desire to save what one already has.

Risk taking: A problem solving strategy which stresses the desire to obtain what one doesn't already have.

Rituals: Performances which are repeated on a regular basis which serve to reaffirm the participants' commitment to the goals and values exemplified in the myths contained in them.

Routine: A systematic problem solving procedure designed to minimize or eliminate the need to devote much attention to a particular type of issue.

Rule # 1: Fill in all unstated but important pieces of background information. Applies to problem solving and decision making.

Rules: Directive language which tell the user how to correctly combine the concepts inherent within the subject. Explicit rules such as those in formal games have clear formulations, often in the form of rule books or math theorems. Tacit rules are not explicitly stated, but are expected to be "understood" by the players, as in reading between the lines.

Rule of addition: A compound probability estimate in which more than one end state is defined as a success for each try. This rule is used whenever the word "or" appears in the initial statement of the problem.

Rules of evidence: Principles of evidence used by the federal and state government to determine what material may be presented in trials and what material must be excluded.

Rule of multiplication: A compound probability estimate which occurs when calculating the odds of a success two or more times in a row. This rule is used when the word "and" appears in the initial statement of the problem.

Rule utilitarianism: An ethical theory which maintains that right actions are those which are enjoined by the right rules and that the right rules are those which would produce the most good for everybody if they were enacted.

S

Sacred religious texts: A religious document which the religious community believes contains the direct word of God (or the gods) or the authentic sayings of the master who founded the religious tradition.

Sample: A subset of a population. Commonly used as a component of a statistical analysis.

The Sapir-Whorf hypothesis of linguistic relativity: A theory about the relationship between thought and language which maintains that all thought occurs only using language and that the words you use in thinking about any given subject, the language in which you think (English, Spanish, Russian, etc), and even the dialect you speak of that language (big city ghetto, rural Southern, California yuppie, etc.) determines how you think as well as what you think. This is the strong version of the hypothesis. The weak version maintains merely that language influences thought, not that language totally determines thought.

Scenario: An imaginary outline for a planned series of events or a series of conditions which one believes would really unfold as imagined should the preconditions of the option in question actually occur. Also called a thought experiment.

Science: A public, repeatable problem solving format the primary purpose of which is the explanation, prediction, and control of the phenomena to which our attention has been directed.

Seeing as: To observe something is to see it as some particular thing or other, even if that observation is mistaken.

Seeing that: A mental operation which gives our present perceptions their other temporal dimensions and allows us to extend our perceptual knowledge claims to what lies beyond the immediate range of our senses.

Self-contradiction: The simultaneous assertion of two incompatible truths. Self-contradictions must be false.

Self-evident: A truth which is knowable immediately simply by knowing the meanings of the ideas contained in it or by understanding what it is claiming.

Semantics: The study of the origin and meaning of words.

Sense data. See data.

Serendipity: The discovery of an important hypotheses when a thinker was not immediately engaged in thinking about the problem. A lucky thought.

Setting the agenda: 1) To establish what you are going to talk about. 2) To attempt to establish certain value-laden positions about the items under discussion. A person who seeks to set the agenda in a discussion may well be more interested in attempting to persuade the listeners or readers to adopt a certain attitude and/or set of beliefs about the values interwoven into the discussion. If this is successful, s/he will have established the burden of proof on his or her opponent to refute the values established by the agenda in question.

Sexist/racist language: Language which either (a) identifies the sex/race of the person(s) it to which it refers when to do so is inappropriate to the context of the discussion, or (b) treats the sexes/races as if they are really only of one sex/race (almost always male/white), or (c) treats one sex/race (almost always females/nonwhite) as if it/they were inherently inferior to the other sex/race (usually males/whites).

Sign: The physical embodiment of what has symbolic meaning.

Simile: An analogical or metaphorical comparison between two things using the terms "like" or "as."

Simple analogy: A comparison between two or more things based on the claim that they have only one thing in common.

Simple claims: Propositions which are composed of a single subject (which may be a class of things) connected to a single predicate.

Simple probability estimate: The determination of the odds of a single event occurring. In all simple probability estimates if you add together the chances of success and the chances of failure, you will always get the number 1. The opposite of a compound probability estimate.

Simplicity (Ockham's razor): An hypothesis is simple when it proposes no more than is needed to explain the phenomena in question. "Plurality is not to be assumed without necessity."

Simulation: Realistic practice under game conditions. A common component of modeling.

Skepticism: A doctrine which doubts that (1) a person knows (or could know) a certain thing, or (2) another particular person or group knows (or could know) a certain thing, or (3) a certain thing can really be known by anyone at all.

Skewed: Probability situations in which each possible outcome does not have an equal chance of occurring. Skewed probability indicates that an additional causal factor is at work. The opposite of fair.

Slang: Highly informal language usually found outside of normal or conventional usage which is used to point at, characterize, and evaluate that to which it refers. Most uses of slang are inherently evaluative. The function of slang is not simply to pick out and neutrally describe that to which it refers, but rather to pass judgment on the object in question.

Slippery slope argument: Maintain that a proposed action which seems innocent enough on the surface ought to be rejected none-the-less because that action would initiate a causal sequence the culmination of which would be disastrous. Because the proposed initial action (it is said) would set into motion a chain of events which would have an unfortunate conclusion, the wise thing to do would be to not take the first step down the slippery slope in the first place. These arguments are properly evaluated in terms of the reality and objectivity probability of the causal sequence in question as well as whether the consequences would be as disastrous as claimed. This is also called the domino theory.

Small sample: A fallacious inductive argument in which the size of the sample drawn does not give a large enough basis to know whether the sample can correctly be applied to the general population.

Social psychology: A division of psychology which examines the social basis for psychological phenomena.

Sociobiology: The study of the biological basis for social phenomena in humans and other animals.

Solution: The correct answer to a problem.

Sophia: Intuitive insight into the truth or value of some situation. Opposed to logic/rationality, which imply discursive reasoning.

Soul: The metaphysical position that there exists a substance which is the seat of consciousness distinct from the body (brain) and possessing no physical attribute like mass or size.

Sound argument: In deductive logic, a valid argument which has only true premises and a true conclusion.

Spatial/temporal metaphors: Comparisons between two or more things based solely on the fact that they should be seen as possessing common spatial or temporal characteristics.

Standard deviation: The measure of the average degree with which items in a given range differ from the mean for that range. By convention, the mean of a given frequency range is established at 0, which is located at the exact center of the normal curve's range. Standard deviation is a measurement of the average amount by which items in the range differ from 0, and is signified by the Greek letter K.

Starting point: The information given which logically should form the beginning of a problem solving situation. This information may in fact be missing.

Statements: Linguistic expressions which purport to tell the audience what is, in fact, the case. Statements are either true or false. In logic, a synonym for claim or proposition.

Statement form: The logical structures embedded within the body of actual statements.

The statistical analysis of causation: The position that causation between groups of variables can only

be correctly analyzed using statistics. Used to generate the figures for statistical determinism.

Statistical argument: One which employs quantified data.

Statistical determinism: An analysis in which determinism is only thought to work on the level of the group. For any individual in the group it is only possible to give a probability estimate concerning the possibility of something happening to that individual in a given period of time.

Statistically significant: The point of a statistical analysis is to determine whether the differences between sets of data are important or only trivial. A one & difference is usually taken to be the bench mark of statistical significance.

Statistics: Quantified, as opposed to qualified, data claims.

Stereotype: A fixed and stable notion or convention about some group of individuals. Has four components: A cognitive component which purports to provide reliable information about the subject of the stereotype and allows the mind to quickly interpret what is presented to it. A psychological component which predisposes the mind of the judge to expect members of the stereotyped group to possess the cognitive characteristics mentioned above. A values component which recognizes that stereotypes often don't just describe things, they also evaluate them. And a social component because stereotypes present social pronouncements, not mere individual judgments.

Stipulative definition: Stipulative definitions are usually used by their authors to set the agenda for their topic by presenting to their audience the sense of a term to which they are referring when the term has more than one sense or to introduce an entirely new term to their audience.

Story: See myth₁ above.

Strawman argument: A fallacy in which one attributes a really dumb position to one's opponent instead of the position which s/he actually holds and then proceeds to demolish this pseudo position, claiming to have refuted one's opponent.

Strength: Used to evaluate inductive arguments. A good inductive argument is a strong one; a poor inductive argument is a weak one. Very weak inductive arguments are called informal fallacies.

Strength of conviction: The mistaken assumption that correct beliefs are correct because they are believed very firmly. There is no correlation between being right and firmly believing that you are right.

Structural analogies: Comparisons between two or more things based on the claim that they have similar shapes, designs, blueprints, functions, etc.

Subjective probability estimates: Probability which is determined by using any methods other than objective probability methods. These are irrational probability judgments.

Successful result: One you are interested in obtaining. A result about which you want to determine its odds of occurring.

Sufficient condition: A component of causal claims. Conditions for event E are said to be sufficient such that should these conditions occur E must happen.

Symbol: A device which functions metaphorically to call attention to and participate in an original field far more complicated and rich than the sign which displays the symbol itself.

Symbolic logic: The translation of ordinary English into a symbolic notation. This notation allows one to assess the validity of an argument presented in ordinary language by considering its form alone.

Syntax (grammar): The study of the proper arrangement of words.

Synthetic propositions: Those which cannot be known to be true simply by knowing the meaning of the terms which constitute them. Synthetic propositions are such that even if they are true they still could have been false (or if they are false they still could have been true). Additional (usually empirical) information must be added to determine whether any synthetic proposition is true. Synthetic propositions are also called contingent truths because they may be true in one possible world and false in another.

The system of checks and balances: A system of government in which no branch or division of the government can operate independently of the control of the others.

T

Teleological argument for the existence of God: A version of the cosmological argument with an existential claim about the order that is perceived in the natural world. This is also called the argument from design.

Test worthiness: The test worthiness of a hypothesis is determined by six conditions: relevance, verifiability, falsifiability, compatibility, predictiveness, and simplicity.

Theism: A theological position which holds that God has a person like existence and that humans can have a personal relationship to God.

Theodicy: An attempt to resolve the problem of evil without abandoning claims to God's (the gods') perfection.

Theology: A system of interconnected ideas designed to make sense out of the many attributes and stories attributed to the gods (God) and the relationship between the gods (God) and the natural world.

Theoretical definitions: Definitions designed to explain the real meaning of some term in the context of what purports to be its proper explanatory theory. When disagreements about the nature of reality arise, these sorts of definitions are commonly employed. They purport to tell what the subject of a term really is, where the term "real" refers to what is the case independently of whatever the language community happens to think about the issue in question.

Theoretical entities: Things which have not yet been directly observed but are predicted to exist as components of the deductive nomological model of explanation.

Theory₁: A hypothesis which may be either true or false.

Theory₂: A research program. A problem solving methodology coupled with a core of accepted material which can then be used to suggest new problems and augment the core with newly proven findings.

Theory₃: A whole system of ideas devised to explain a large range of phenomena. Evolutionary theory and atomic theory are two examples of this. A good theory must include three elements: statements which present the definitions of the key terms contained in the theory, statements which explain the relationship between these key terms, and statements which relate these key terms to actual or possible phenomena the theory is designed to explain. Theories form the backbone of any given discipline.

Theory-laden: Theories are instruction sheets. They tell you how to go about assembling conceptual or perceptual data to form ideas or observations. Knowledge is theory laden.

Thought experiment: See **scenario** above.

Traditional wisdom: A form of authority which argues that good reasons for believing something or doing something can be found by considering the traditional mores of society. Concerns itself with social customs, values, and goals which make up a society's way of life. They are vulnerable to counterarguments from a different aspect of the same society's tradition as well as values not found in that society.

Trial and error: A problem solving technique which presupposes only a limited number of solution paths, each of which is equally (or nearly equally) plausible. It must be possible to try each of the plausible solutions in isolation from the other possibilities. The implementation of one possible solution cannot so alter the problem that other possible solutions can no longer be attempted.

Type 1 error (False positives): A mistake committed when the researcher wrongly accepts H_1 and rejects H_0 on the basis of the statistical analysis. The probability of committing this is equal to the significance level adopted.

Type 2 error (False negatives): Statistical or causal analyses which fail to find correlations or causal relationships which do indeed exist. The higher the significance level (or margin of error) the greater the chance of committing a type 2 error.

Tyranny of the majority: When the will of the majority runs roughshod over the will of the minority.

Tyranny of the minority: When the will of minority (or even one person) runs roughshod over the will of the majority.

U

Understanding: See conceiving of and conceiving that.

Understanding gap: The inability to solve a problem because of the lack of knowledge of what the problem is all about. A form of cognitive closure.

Unknowable statistics: Statistical claims such that no one could know whether they were true or not. They are impossible to verify or falsify.

Unrepresentative sample: A fallacious inductive argument in which the variable being considered does not apply to the whole population class because all members of the class are not relevantly similar with respect to this variable.

Utilitarian theories of ethics: Any theory of ethics which maintains that consequences determine morality. See act utilitarianism and rule utilitarianism.

V

Vague language: Terms which may properly be applied to a range of possible applications.

Validity₁: A deductive argument is valid if and only if it is impossible for all of its premises to be true and its conclusion false at the same time.

Validity₂: An experiment is valid if and only if it tests what it is designed to test and not something else.

Value: Anything worthwhile having or pursuing. See intrinsic value and extrinsic value.

Variables: Factors which may manifest themselves in a number of possible ways. The extent to which a variable may possibly vary is called its range.

Verbal dispute: Disagreements which occur when each party in the dispute is concentrating on a different sense that the disputed word legitimately possesses. Can lead to the fallacy of equivocation.

Verifiability: A verifiable hypothesis is one which when used with the deductive nomological method provides predictions about future observations which turn out to be true when experiment designed to test the hypothesis are run.

Virtue ethics: Not an ethics of rules or of acts per se, but an ethics of character. For virtue ethics the key question is how one displays responsibility.

W

Way of life: Social customs, values, and goals which are the subjects of traditional wisdom arguments because these values define a society and shape its continuity over time and distance.

Weighted sample: A data gathering technique which recognizes that there are distinct subsets within the data and randomly samples appropriate amounts from each of the subsets.

Well defined problem: One in which the starting point, ending point, and solution strategy are clearly known or knowable.

Wisdom: Generally understood to have two components, theoretical (sophia) and practical (phronesis)—knowing well and doing well. Wisdom implies that what is known is important or valuable, not simply mundane or trivial.

Wishful thinking: The overestimating of the actual probability of some very good consequences happening. A form of risk taking.

Working backwards: A problem solving technique in which the problem solver already knows the proposed solution to the problem but does not know how to get from the initial state to the solution state.

Working forwards: A problem solving strategy which requires that the thinker start at the beginning of a problem (with what is called the initial state) and proceed with a step by step process steadily towards the solution state.

World view constraint: Limitations on problem solving methods which could be adopted were it not the case that their adoption would violate some deeply held ethical, religious, social, or financial belief.

Worship: Concerns the proper interaction between the human and divine when seen from the human side of the equation. This may take many forms, such as prayer, meditation, or good works.

X, Y, Z

Zero sum game: A contest in which for every winner there must be a loser (win/lose). Win/win and lose/lose are ruled out from the start.